REVIEWS OF UNITED KINGDOM
STATISTICAL SOURCES

VOLUME XXI

FINANCE

Financial Data of Banks and Other Institutions. Life Assurance and Pension Funds

REVIEWS OF UNITED KINGDOM STATISTICAL SOURCES

Editor: W. F. Maunder

Assistant Editor: M. C. Fleming

Volume I	*Personal Social Services,* B. P. Davies *Voluntary Organizations in the Personal Social Service Field,* G. J. Murray
Volume II	*General Government Routine Health Statistics,* Michael Alderson *Social Security Statistics,* Frank Whitehead
Volume III	*Housing in Great Britain,* Stuart Farthing *Housing in Northern Ireland,* Michael Fleming
Volume IV	*Leisure,* F. M. M. Lewes and S. R. Parker *Tourism,* L. J. Lickorish
Volume V	*General Sources of Statistics,* G. F. Lock
Volume VI	*Wealth,* A. B. Atkinson and A. J. Harrison *Personal Incomes,* T. Stark
Volume VII	*Road Passenger Transport,* D. L. Munby *Road Goods Transport,* A. H. Watson
Volume VIII	*Land Use,* J. T. Coppock *Town and Country Planning,* L. F. Gebbett
Volume IX	*Health Surveys and Related Studies,* M. Alderson and R. Dowie
Volume X	*Ports and Inland Waterways,* R. E. Baxter *Civil Aviation,* Celia M. Phillips
Volume XI	*Coal,* D. J. Harris *Gas,* H. Nabb *Electricity Industries,* D. Nuttall
Volume XII	*Construction and the Related Professions,* M. C. Fleming
Volume XIII	*Wages and Earnings,* Andrew Dean
Volume XIV	*Rail Transport,* D. H. Aldcroft *Sea Transport,* Derrick Mort
Volume XV	*Crime,* Monica A. Walker
Volume XVI	*Iron and Steel,* David W. Heal *Shipbuilding,* Anthony Slaven
Volume XVII	*Weather,* B. W. Atkinson *Water,* E. C. Penning-Rowsell and D. J. Parker
Volume XVIII	*Posts and Telecommunications,* S. Wall and P. Nicholson
Volume XIX	*Intellectual Property Rights,* D. L. Bosworth
Volume XX	*Religion,* L. M. Barley, C. D. Field, B. A. Kosmin and J. S. Nielsen

REVIEWS OF UNITED KINGDOM STATISTICAL SOURCES
Edited by W. F. Maunder
Professor Emeritus of Economic and Social Statistics, University of Exeter
Assisted by M. C. Fleming
Professor of Economics, Loughborough University
VOLUME XXI

FINANCE

Financial Data of Banks and Other Institutions

by

KATE PHYLAKTIS
CENTRE FOR BANKING AND INTERNATIONAL FINANCE,
THE CITY UNIVERSITY BUSINESS SCHOOL

Life Assurance and Pension Funds

by

GERALDINE KAYE
THE CITY UNIVERSITY

Published for
The Royal Statistical Society and
Economic and Social Research Council
by
PERGAMON PRESS
OXFORD · NEW YORK · BEIJING · FRANKFURT
SÃO PAULO · SYDNEY · TOKYO · TORONTO

U.K.	Pergamon Press, Headington Hill Hall, Oxford OX3 0BW, England
U.S.A.	Pergamon Press, Maxwell House, Fairview Park, Elmsford, New York 10523, U.S.A.
PEOPLE'S REPUBLIC OF CHINA	Pergamon Press, Room 4037, Qianmen Hotel, Beijing, People's Republic of China
FEDERAL REPUBLIC OF GERMANY	Pergamon Press, Hammerweg 6, D-6242 Kronberg, Federal Republic of Germany
BRAZIL	Pergamon Editora, Rua Eça de Queiros, 346, CEP 04011, Paraiso, São Paulo, Brazil
AUSTRALIA	Pergamon Press Australia, P.O. Box 544, Potts Point, N.S.W. 2011, Australia
JAPAN	Pergamon Press, 8th Floor, Matsuoka Central Building, 1-7-1 Nishishinjuku, Shinjuku-ku, Tokyo 160, Japan
CANADA	Pergamon Press Canada, Suite No. 271, 253 College Street, Toronto, Ontario, Canada M5T 1R5

First edition 1987

Library of Congress Cataloging in Publication Data

Finance.
(Reviews of United Kingdom statistical sources; v. 21)
Includes indexes.
Contents: Financial data of banks and other institutions / by Kate Phylaktis — Life assurance and pension funds / by Geraldine Kaye.
1. Finance — Great Britain — Statistical services
I. Phylaktis, Kate II. Kaye, Geraldine III. Royal Statistical Society (Great Britain) IV. Economic and Social Research Council (Great Britain) V. Series
HG186.G7F53 1987 332'.0941 87–7247

British Library Cataloguing in Publication Data

Finance. — (Reviews of United Kingdom statistical sources; v. 21).
1. Finance — Great Britain — Statistical services
I. Phylaktis, Kate II. Kaye, Geraldine
III. Royal Statistical Society IV. Economic and Social Research Council V. Series
332'.0941'021 HG186.G7

ISBN 0–08–034780–0

Printed in Great Britain by Richard Clay Ltd, Bungay, Suffolk

VOLUME CONTENTS

FOREWORD

The Sources and Nature of the Statistics of the United Kingdom, produced under the auspices of the Royal Statistical Society and edited by Maurice Kendall, filled a notable gap on the library shelves when it made its appearance in the early post-war years.Through a series of critical reviews by many of the foremost national experts, it constituted a valuable contemporary guide to statisticians working in many fields as well as a bench-mark to which historians of the development of Statistics in this country are likely to return again and again. The Social Science Research Council* and the Society were both delighted when Professor Maunder came forward with the proposal that a revised version should be produced, indicating as well his willingness to take on the onerous task of editor. The two bodies were more than happy to act as co-sponsors of the project and to help in its planning through a joint steering committee. The result, we are confident, will be judged a worthy successor to the previous volumes by the very much larger "statistics public' that has come into being in the intervening years.

Mrs SUZANNE REEVE
Secretary
Economic and Social Research Council

January 1987

Mrs E.J.SNELL
Honorary Secretary
Royal Statistical Society

January 1987

* SSRC is now the Economic and Social Research Council (ESRC).

MEMBERSHIP OF JOINT STEERING COMMITTEE

(November 1986)

Chairman: Miss S. V. Cunliffe

Representing the Royal Statistical Society:

Mr M. C. Fessey

Dr S. Rosenbaum

Mrs E. J. Snell

Representing the Economic and Social Research Council:

Professor J. P. Burman

Mr I. Maclean

Miss J. Morris

Secretary Mr D. E. Allen

INTRODUCTION TO VOLUME XXI

The termination of ESRC support for the series leaves individual projects in a variety of different states and its effect on the coverage of financial statistics is that this volume represents only a part of the field with which it was intended to deal when originally planned. The first review herein describes the financial data of banks and building societies while the second is devoted to life assurance and pension fund data. Doubtless this constitutes a sensible and useful collection of statistical sources at which to look but it is also clearly a restricted sub-set of all those coming within the financial sector in general. In particular, public finance, the stock exchanges and general insurance are some of the more important topics on which a second volume was planned. This illustrates the fact that the ending of ESRC support does not signify the exhaustion of the potential of the series.

Unless some other sponsorship is found quickly, the series must end with the publication of work already completed. Although reviews delivered or about to be delivered amount to another half-dozen volumes,it means inevitably that the project will have failed to achieve the aim with which it started of providing a complete coverage of sources in the whole economic and social field. Apart from the example provided by this volume, there are many topics in other areas which have not yet been commissioned at all while several already published now require updating. The project has accummulated a wealth of experience in its task and while it is a going concern it would need only a relatively modest grant to keep it in business but to start *de novo* could entail the need for a major injection of resources which are unlikely to be found in the forseeable future.

The primary aim of this series is to act as a work of reference to the sources of statistical material of all kinds, both official and unofficial. It seeks to enable the user to discover what data are available on the subject in which he is interested, from where they may be obtained, and what the limitations are to their use. Data are regarded as available not only if published in the normal printed format but also if they are likely to be released to a *bona fide* enquirer in any other form, such as duplicated documents, computer print-out or even magnetic tape. On the other hand, no reference is made to material which, even if it is known to exist, is not accessible to the general run of potential users. The distinction, of course, is not clear-cut and mention of a source is not to be regarded as a guarantee that data will be released; in particular cases it may very well be a matter for negotiation. The latter caution applies with particular force to the question of obtaining computer print-outs of custom specified tabulations. Where original records are held on magnetic media it might appear that there should be no insuperable problem, apart from confidentiality, in obtaining any feasible analysis at a cost; in practice, it may well turn out that there are capacity restraints which override any simple cost calculation. Thus, what is requested might make demands on computer and programming resources to such an extent that the routine work of the agency concerned would be intolerably affected.

The intention is that the source for each topic should be reviewed in detail, and the brief supplied to authors has called for comprehensive coverage at the level of 'national interest'. This term does not denote any necessary restriction to statistics collected on a national basis (still less, of course, to national aggregates) but it means that sources of a purely local character, without wider interest in either content or methodology, are excluded. Indeed, the mere task of identifying all material of this latter kind is an impossibility. The interpretation of the brief has obviously involved discretion and it is up to the users of these reviews to say what unreasonable gaps become apparent to them. They are cordially invited to do so by communicating with me.

To facilitate the use of the series as a work of reference, certain features have been incorporated which warrant a word or two of explanation. First, the text of each review is designed, in so far as varying subject matter permits, to follow a standard form of arrangement so that users may expect a similar pattern to be followed throughout the series. The starting point is a brief summary of the activity concerned and its organisation, in order to give a clear background understanding of how data are collected, what is being measured, the stage at which measurements are made, what the reporting units are, the channels through which returns are routed and where they are processed. As a further part of this introductory material, there is a discussion of the specific problems of definition and measurement to which the topic gives rise. The core sections on available sources which follow are arranged at the author's discretion – by origin, by subject subdivision, or by type of data; there is too much heterogeneity between topics to permit any imposition of complete uniformity on all authors. The final section is devoted to a discussion of general shortcomings and possibly desirable improvements. In case a contrary expectation should be aroused, it should be said that authors have not been asked to produce a comprehensive plan for the reform of statistical reporting in the whole of their field. However, a review of existing sources is a natural opportunity to make some suggestions for future policy on the collection and publication of statistics within the scope concerned and authors have been encouraged to take full advantage of it.

Secondly, detailed factual information about statistical series and other data is given in a Quick Reference List (QRL). The exact nature of the entries is best seen by glancing at the list and accordingly they are not described here. Again, the ordering is not prescribed except that entries are not classified by publication source since it is presumed that it is this which is unknown to the reader. In general, the routine type of information which is given in the QRL is not repeated verbally in the text; the former, however, serves as a search route to the latter in that a reference (by section number) is shown against a QRL entry when there is a related discussion in the text.

Third, a subject index to each review acts as a more or less conventional line of enquiry on textual references; it is a computerised system and, for an individual review, the only advantage is the possibility of easily permuting entries. The object at this level is merely to facilitate search by giving as many variants as possible. In addition, however, it also makes possible selective searches by keyword over any combination of reviews and a printout of the entries found may then be prepared.

Fourth, each review contains two listings of publications. The QRL Key gives full details of the publications shown as sources and text references to them are made in the form [QRL serial number]; this list is confined essentially to data publications. The other listing is a general bibliography of works discussing wider aspects; text references in this case are made in the form [B serial number].

Finally, an attempt is made to reproduce the more important returns or forms used in data collection so that it may be seen what tabulations it is possible to make as well as helping to clarify the basis of those actually available. Unfortunately, there are severe practical limitations on the number of such forms that it is possible to append to a review and authors perforce have to be highly selective.

As editor, I must express my very grateful thanks to all the members of the Joint Steering Committee of the Royal Statistical Society and the Economic and Social Research Council. It would be unfair to saddle them with any responsibility for shortcomings in execution but they have directed the overall strategy with as admirable a mixture of guidance and forbearance as any editor of such a series could desire. Especial thanks are due to the Secretary of the Committee who has been involved with the project almost as long and almost as closely as the editor himself.The authors joins me in thanking all those who gave up their time to attend the seminar held to discuss the first draft of the reviews and which contributed materially to improving the final versions.

We are most grateful to Pergamon Press Ltd. for their continued support and in particular to Grace Belfiore, the Behavioral Sciences section head, and to the Production Department who put all the pieces together. The subject index entries have been compiled by Mrs. Marian Guest who has also acted as editorial assistant throughout. Special thanks are due to Mr.Ray Burnley who again has masterminded our use of the Lasercomp System at Oxford University Computer Service and to the latter for the use of this facility. Finally, we also wish to record our appreciation of the permission granted us to reproduce certain copyright material by the Controller of Her Majesty's Stationery Office and by the Bank of England.

W.F. Maunder

University of Exeter

January 1987

37: FINANCIAL DATA OF BANKS AND OTHER INSTITUTIONS

KATE PHYLAKTIS

Centre for Banking and International Finance

The City University Business School

REFERENCE DATE OF SOURCES REVIEWED

This review is believed to represent the situation as it obtained in March 1986, with amendments being made, where appropriate, up to the proof stage of September 1986.

LIST OF ABBREVIATIONS

APACS	Association for Payment Clearing Services
ATMs	Automated Teller Machines
BACs	Bankers Automatic Clearing Services
BBA	British Bankers' Association
BSA	Building Societies Association
CSO	Central Statistical Office
CLCB	Committee of London Clearing Bankers
CLSB	Committee of London and Scottish Bankers
DCE	Domestic Credit Expansion
ECGD	Export Credit Guarantee Department
FHA	Finance Houses Association
LDTs	Licensed Deposit Taking Institutions
LDMA	London Discount Market Association
NI	Northern Ireland
OFIs	Other Financial Institutions
PSL1	Private Sector Liquidity 1
PSL2	Private Sector Liquidity 2
PSBR	Public Sector Borrowing Requirement
TSBs	Trustee Savings Banks
W	Wales

ACKNOWLEDGEMENTS

I am grateful for the very valuable help that I have received in preparing this volume from colleagues at the Centre for Banking and International Finance, The City University, Mr. C.D. Lang of CLSB, Mr. A. Coles of BSA, Ms J.K. Marson of the Department of Trade and Industry, Mr. Kentfield and Mr. Pennington of the Bank of England and the series editor, Professor W.F. Maunder. I am also grateful to all the participants at the seminar held in October 1984 to discuss an early draft of this volume. I would like to thank my secretary Mrs. Gladys Parish who typed and retyped successive drafts of this volume with great efficiency and good humour.

Some of the material on the official statistics is taken from official descriptions published in the *Bank of England Quarterly Bulletin* and the *Financial Statistics*. The use of this material is gratefully acknowledged.

CONTENTS OF REVIEW 37

CHAPTER 1

INTRODUCTION

1.1 Importance of Statistics on Financial Institutions

Statistics on financial institutions have been given a lot of attention by both the monetary authorities and the institutions themselves. The authorities need statistical information from financial institutions for various purposes. Firstly, individual institutions' figures are required for the carrying out of prudential supervision. Prudential constraints ensure the institutions' ability to meet their obligations to depositors at all times. That implies that the institutions should maintain liquidity and capital adequacy. Secondly, aggregated information is needed to assist the monetary authorities in their execution of monetary policy and in the assembly of statistics for economic analysis.

The banks themselves use such statistical information to monitor their own performance and adjust their marketing strategies. In addition, there is a variety of private users, ranging from stockbrokers and economic journalists to academic research workers. Furthermore, there are many users outside this country, including in particular international organisations.

The recent emphasis on financial statistics started with the publication of the Radcliffe *Report* [B.51] in 1959 on the Working of the Monetary System. The report laid stress on the need to increase the range of available information released to the public; and called for these statistics to be published in a more convenient and consistent form. Following from these recommendations, the Bank of England introduced the *Bank of England Quarterly Bulletin* [QRL.5] in 1960; and the Central Statistical Office (CSO) the monthly publication *Financial Statistics* [QRL.24] in 1962. To this day, these are the two main official sources of data.

The Radcliffe *Report* [B.51] also called for statistics which would measure the effects of monetary pressure on demand. In 1966, figures of money stock and the factors influencing money supply, were first published. Since then, there have been many changes and new developments in the collection and presentation of statistics on financial institutions. Some of the changes have resulted from changes in the system of monetary control, others reflect developments in banking supervision and the need for improved reporting of international financial business, while others have been stimulated by the growth of new areas of the institutions' business. This rate of development is likely to continue in the future.

1.2 Changes in the System of Monetary Control, Banking Supervision and the Structure of Financial Institutions

The changes in banking supervision and in the system of monetary control have been a response to the changes in the structure of British banking. The banking system has changed tremendously in the last 30 years with respect to the range of facilities offered and the way in which they are provided.

The development of the system was shaped by the financial innovations and the competitive environment. In the mid-1950s, the British banking system was dominated by a cartelised oligopoly, consisting of the London Clearing Banks and their associates in Scotland and Northern Ireland. They had 85 per cent of all commercial banking business in sterling, domestic and foreign.

Entry into the oligopoly was difficult while entry into competition with it was relatively simple. The majority of institutions outside the established banking system were not required to have a licence or face other supervisory requirements in order to take deposits from the public. Thus, the system was open to profitable competition and innovation outside the oligopolistic sector.

Several institutions took advantage of profitable opportunities created by official regulations. The instalment credit finance houses, which were engaged in the rapidly growing market of consumer credit, began in the mid-1950s to bid competitively for wholesale deposits (i.e. deposits that involved large amounts of money) because official regulations did not permit them to obtain adequate additional finance either from the banks or from the capital market. The local authorities were encouraged by the government of the day to borrow directly from market sources rather than from the central government. The merchant banks and the foreign banks then established in London were encouraged by the suspension of direct controls in 1958 to expand their domestic sterling business in direct competition with the clearing banks. As a result, the wholesale deposit market was developed and the inter-bank market emerged.

Despite the above developments, the monetary authorities did not change banking supervision. They extended, however, the scope of direct credit controls to cover deposit-taking finance houses and non-clearing banks.

The changes in the structure of the banking system that took place during the late 1960s and the 1970s were even more striking. The number of the clearing banks was substantially reduced by mergers. All the banks extended their representation overseas in order to meet modern requirements.

At home the clearing banks expanded by taking over subsidiaries and by developing merchant banking services and medium-term lending. For details see the *London Clearing Banks* [B.49].

These structural developments were further boosted by the abolition of direct credit controls in September 1971. The monetary authorities abolished controls over bank lending in order to improve the competitive environment within the banking system and to allocate credit more by price and less by rationing, while ensuring the authorities control over the amount of money and credit in the economy as a whole for the purposes of monetary policy. Accordingly, new reserve asset ratios were introduced and applied uniformly to all banks; quantitative ceilings were abolished; and it was confirmed that the Bank of England's mode of operation in the gilt-edged market would permit sharper fluctuations in interest rates. For details of the Competition and Credit Control see [B.12]. For their part, the London Clearing Banks dismantled their interest rate cartel. (See chapter 16 of the *London Clearing Banks* [B.49]).

Although direct credit controls like the Supplementary Special Deposit Scheme were re-imposed at intervals during 1974-80 the banking system developed the innovations first introduced during the 1950s and 1960s. Credit cards, cheque cards and cash dispenser or automatic-teller machine cards became more readily available. There was a widespread introduction of medium-term lending by the banks at variable rates linked to inter-bank rates. Finally, the growth of industrial leasing by the banks, an innovation of the 1960s was similarly stimulated.

At the same time, Building Societies experienced an extraordinary growth. Their assets rose from 5.6 billion in 1965 to 24.4 billion in 1975. This growth was due to a number of factors. Building Societies were open on Saturdays; they could offer better interest rates and easy withdrawal facilities from interest-bearing accounts. Furthermore, they were engaged in meeting a strong upward trend in the demand for mortgage credit.

The pace of competition and innovation had rendered central features of the prudential arrangements obsolete. Following the secondary banking crisis in 1973/74, and a growing public concern with consumer protection, a new supervisory framework was established with the 1979 Banking Act. The Act gives statutory force to the Bank of England's regulatory responsibilities and provides, for the first time, comprehensive legislation on the authorisation and supervision of banking institutions in the UK which take deposits from the public. Since deposit taking is such an essential part of banking, the Act can reasonably be regarded as effectively controlling the entire business of banking. The ultimate purpose of the Act however, is the protection of depositors against loss.

The two main provisions of the Act are the general prohibition on the acceptance of deposits without specific authorization from the Bank of England; and the establishment of a Deposit Protection Fund to be administered by the Deposit Protection Board, to which both recognised banks and licensed institutions are required to contribute according to the size of their deposit base, subject to a minimum level of contribution. The trend is in general designed to protect the smaller depositor against loss in the event of a failure of a contributory institution. The Act brought supervision of banks and deposit-taking institutions in line with the requirements of the first European Community directive on credit institutions established in 1977.

Since then there has been another wave of deregulation involving both the banks and the Building Societies. The government suspended foreign exchange controls in October 1979, supplementary special deposits in June 1980 and restrictions on consumer instalment credit in July 1982. The suspension of the Supplementary Special Deposit Scheme was one of many changes in monetary control which took place at that time. The changes in monetary control were brought about following the issuance of various background papers by HM Treasury and the Bank of England [B.50], [B.21] and [B.22].

The new monetary control provisions which are given in [B.23] took effect on 20 August 1981. They comprised a redefinition of the banking sector, the abolition of the minimum lending rate, the change of rules regarding what the Bank of England will recognise as an 'acceptable name' on a Bill of Exchange, the extension of the list of eligible banks, and the abolition of the cash ratio. These developments have further encouraged competition. On the retail side, the London Clearing Banks have come under competition from the Trustee Savings Banks, the Girobank and the Building Societies. On the wholesale deposit side, the American and the non-clearing banks have become more aggressive. At the same time the Building Societies have been faced with increased competition from the clearing banks in the residential mortgage market. On the borrowing side, the government has been aggressive in selling non-marketable savings bonds.

This competitive environment, together with technological innovations, will encourage rationalisation and concentration of the banking system which will have supervisory as well as monetory policy implications in the future.

1.3 Definition of the Field

This review of statistical sources consists of two volumes. In the first volume deposit-taking financial institutions will be covered. This includes the financial institutions in the monetary sector (i.e. the UK offices of institutions, either recognised as banks or licensed to take deposits under the Banking Act 1979, the Girobank, the Trustee Savings Banks, the Banking Department of the Bank of England and those institutions in the Channel Islands and the Isle of Man which have opted to participate in the new monetary control arrangements), those of the Finance Houses which are not part of the Monetary Sector and the Building Societies. The last two belong to what is called Other Financial Institutions (OFIs), but many of the Finance Houses became part of the monetary sector at the end of 1981.

1.4 Coverage of Sources

Data collected by both official agencies and professional associations will be covered. However, the bulk of these are produced by the former. The data are compiled through the completion of returns by the financial institutions. Table 1 shows which official agencies and professional bodies are responsible for the collection of statistics.

It should be noted that from the Professional Associations, only the Committee of London and Scottish Bankers (CLSB), the Building Societies Association (BSA) and the Finance Houses Association (FHA) are actively involved in the collection and dissemination of information.

The two main official publications are the *Bank of England Quarterly Bulletin* [QRL.5] and the monthly publication of *Financial Statistics* [QRL.24]. The main purpose of the CSO presentation is to show a lot of detail, thus providing building bricks for users to adapt to their own needs. For example, it contains the detailed statistics for most of the various groups of other Financial Institutions.

Three useful documents which have provided background information about the present structure of financial institutions are: the evidence by the CLCB [B.49] and

Table 1 : Responsibility for the Collection of Statistics

Group of Financial Institutions	Official Agencies	Professional Bodies
Monetary sector	Bank of England	British Bankers' Association, The Committee of London and Scottish Bankers
	Dept. of Trade and Industry	Irish Banks' Standing Committee, Accepting Houses' Committee, London Discount Market Association, American Banks' Association of London, Foreign Banks' Association, British-Overseas Commonwealth Banks' Association, Association of Consortium Banks, Japanese Banks' Association, Finance Houses Association
Finance Houses and other Consumer Credit Grantors	Dept. of Trade and Industry	Finance Houses Association
Building Societies	Bank of England	Building Societies Association
	Dept. of Environment	Chief Registrar of Friendly Societies

the evidence by the BSA [B.45] to the Wilson Committee on the Functioning of Financial Institutions; and the *Report* prepared by the Wilson Committee [B.53].

This review will give most attention to the presently available statistics. Historical data is covered in a separate chapter. The main sources of historical data suggested are: F. Capie and A. Webber, *A Monetary History of the UK, 1870-1982, Vol I: Data Sources and Methods* [B.3]; D.K. Sheppard, *The Growth and Role of UK Financial Institutions 1880-1962* [B.10]; and the *Compendium of Building Society Statistics* [QRL.17], published by the BSA.

With regard to geographical coverage, the whole of the United Kingdom will be covered. Sources of certain disaggregated data have been given as well.

1.5 Plan of the Review

Banking statistics mainly set out information in the form of levels of assets and liabilities, changes in those levels over time, and information on interest rates related to assets and liabilities. This type of information is examined for the different types of institutions.

Table 2 shows the plan of the review.

Chapter 6 looks at the monetary aggregates and their counterparts. This is one of the main purposes of the compilation of banking data. Chapter 7 summarises the sources of historical data. Finally, in Chapter 8, the various statistical sources are

Table 2: Plan of Review by Information and Institutions

Type of Information	Monetary Sector; various disaggragations	Finance Houses	Building Societies
Assets/Liabilities; infrastructure	Chapter 2	Chapter 3	Chapter 4
Interest Rates	Chapter 5	Chapter 5	Chapter 5

evaluated for coverage, reliability, and availability. It ends with a few recommendations.

1.6 Other Source Books

There are two other books which cover similar areas to the current study. These are the *Guide to Official Statistics* [B.47] and *Sources of World Financial and Banking Information* [B.4]. [B.47] covers financial and non-financial data. It either identifies the source for particular statistics or indicates where it might be found. There is neither detailed discussion of the data nor a comparison of the sources for particular statistics.

Sources of World Banking Information [B.4] includes a section on the UK. It lists regular and occasional sources on money and banking in alphabetical order. The sources are not disaggregated by either type of institution or by type of information. There is no commentary at all on the collection and presentation of data. The value of that book lies more with its worldwide coverage than with the actual information given on UK.

CHAPTER 2

ASSETS AND LIABILITIES: MONETARY SECTOR

2.1 Composition of the Monetary Sector

Following the new monetary control arrangements introduced in August 1981, a new definition of the monetary sector was introduced on 19th November 1981 for the monthly banking statistics and with effect from 31st December 1981 for the quarterly statistics. It comprises the UK offices of institutions, either recognised as banks or licenced to take deposits under the Banking Act 1979, together with the Girobank, the Trustee Savings Banks, the Banking Department of the Bank of England, and those institutions in the Channel Islands and the Isle of Man which have opted to participate in the new monetary control arrangements.

Previous to November 1981, the UK banking sector comprised those institutions included on the statistical list of banks and discount market institutions, together with the Banking Department of the Bank of England. Inclusion on the statistical lists, which had existed for many years, was based chiefly on informal appraisal of a bank's size and reputation and was usually closely associated with the granting of authorized bank status for exchange control purposes. It carried with it, moreover, an obligation to observe the reserve asset and credit control restrictions introduced in 1971 and subsequently.

The implementation of the Banking Act of 1979, which requires the Bank to issue formal lists of recognized banks and licensed deposit-takers (LDTs), and the removal of exchange control in the autumn of 1979, meant that the existence of separate statistical lists, which did not include some recognized banks and many LDTs, had become no longer appropriate. Moreover, the new monetary control arrangements were designed from the outset to apply in principle to all recognized banks and LDTs.

The complete list of institutions comprising the new monetary sector is given in the Additional Notes to the tables of the *Bank of England Quarterly Bulletin* [QRL.5] which appear in full in the March issue of each year. These notes are updated in the intervening issues. Appendix I gives the list of institutions as it stood in March 1986. The main groups of institutions are as follows:

A. Retail Banks These are banks which either have extensive branch networks in the United Kingdom or participate directly in a UK clearing system. This group includes branches in the Channel Islands and the Isle of Man, the parent banks of which have opted to participate in the monetary control arrangement introduced in August 1981. Thus, this group comprises the London Clearing Banks, the Scottish Clearing Banks, the Northern Ireland Banks, the Trustee Savings Bank, the Girobank, the Co-operative Bank, the Yorkshire Bank and the Banking Department of the Bank of England.

B. Accepting Houses This group comprises the sixteen members of the Accepting Houses Committee and certain of their subsidiaries in the Channel Islands and the Isle of Man.

C. Other British Banks These include all other UK-registered institutions and certain institutions in the Channel Islands and the Isle of Man which are either independent companies, or controlled by UK companies or by individuals. Banks controlled by overseas companies are classified as overseas banks. Thus, thc subsidiaries of Allied Irish Banks Ltd and The Bank of Ireland are included in the group of other overseas banks.

D. American Banks These include the branches and subsidiaries, including certain offices in the Channel Islands, of American banks. The branches and subsidiaries of American companies which are not banks in the United States are included in the group of other overseas banks.

E. Japanese Banks These include the branches and subsidiaries of Japanese banks.

F. Other Overseas Banks These include the branches and subsidiaries (including certain offices in the Channel Islands and the Isle of Man) of all foreign companies other than American and Japanese banks.

G. Consortium Banks These include UK-registered institutions which are owned by banks or financial institutions but in which no one institution has a direct shareholding of more than 50 per cent, and in which at least one shareholder is based overseas.

H. Discount Houses The London Discount Market Association (LDMA) consists of 19 members which account for most of the business in the discount market.

The relative importance of the above institutions within the monetary sector is given in Table 3.

Table 3: UK Banking Sector: Balance Sheet totals in February 1986

Monthly Reporting Institutions	Total Assets/Liabilities (millions)
Retail Banks	190,493
Accepting Houses	27,622
Other British Banks	66,567
American Banks	98,156
Japanese Banks	186,506
Other Overseas Banks	189,639
Consortium Banks	16,825
All Banks in UK	775,807
Listed Discount Market Institutions	8,377
Total	784,184

Source: Bank of England Quarterly Bulletin [QRL.5].

More information on the above institutions is given below.

2.1.1 *London Clearing Banks*

There are six London Clearing Banks operating in England and Wales: Barclays, Lloyds, Midland, National Westminster (the so-called "big four"). Coutts & Company and Williams & Glyn's. The big four banks are public companies quoted on the Stock Exchange, and their shares are held by a very wide range of investors, both individual and institutional. Williams & Glyn's is wholly owned by a publicly-quoted bank holding company, the Royal Bank of Scotland. Coutts is a wholly-owned subsidiary of National Westminster.

For several of the banks, the biggest changes in the past 20 years have been due to the mergers that took place at the end of the 1960s. At the time of the Radcliffe Report there were 11 London Clearing Banks. Three of them (Coutts, Lloyds and Midland) were not involved in the mergers, but the other eight have been reduced to three.

Firstly, in November 1968, Barclays acquired the share capital of Martin's Bank; the business of Martin's was transferred to Barclay's on 15th December 1969 by private Act of Parliament.

Secondly, National Westminster was formed in 1968 and acquired on 8th July 1968 the capital of Westminster Bank and National Provincial Bank; the latter had previously (in 1962) acquired District Bank. The business of all three banks was transferred to National Westminster on 1st January 1970. Coutts, which has been a wholly-owned subsidiary of National Provincial since 1920, became a subsidiary of National Westminster but retained its separate identity.

Thirdly, Williams & Glyn's was formed in 1969 and took over on 25th September 1970 the business of Glyn, Mills & Co., Williams Deacon's Bank and the National Bank. The first two had been subsidiaries of the Royal Bank of Scotland. The National Bank had been a public company until 1966, when it was acquired by National Commercial Bank of Scotland, having first sold its Irish business to the Bank of Ireland. The three banks fell under common ownership when their Scottish parents merged in 1968. The enlarged group was recognised so that the merged Royal Bank of Scotland and Williams & Glyn's each became a subsidiary of a common holding company, National and Commercial Banking Group. In September 1985, the Royal Bank of Scotland and Williams & Glyn's were merged under the Royal Bank of Scotland Group name.

In terms of their group balance sheet totals, Barclays and National Westminster are of similar size and together account for just 60 per cent of the total liabilities of the clearing banks, Lloyds and Midland for just under 40 per cent.

One of the basic functions of the clearing banks is the provision of the money transmission service which is the country's main payments mechanism. Cheques are exchanged between the banks at the Clearing House which is operated by The Cheque and Credit Clearing Company. High-value same-day clearings are operated by a different company, the CHAPS and TOWN Clearing Company.

Through yet another separate limited company, Bankers ' Automated Clearing Services, facilities are provided for the transfer of magnetic tapes containing details of customers' transactions. All three operational clearing companies are part of the Independent Association for Payment Clearing Services (APACS).

The growth of the banks' other two fundamental types of business –the acceptance of deposits and the supply of finance was considerably hampered over a number of years by a succession of official credit restraints. The situation changed with the introduction of "Competition and Credit Control" in September 1971. Although direct credit controls were re-imposed at intervals during the 1974-80 period, the banks have been able to expand lending and compete more actively for deposits, including bidding for funds in the various money markets. Traditionally, the clearing banks have concentrated on short-term finance for working capital but they are now much more flexible in both the length and purpose of their lending. For example, in the personal market the banks have entered the mortgage market offering secured loans for house purchase over periods up to 30 years, while over 40 per cent of their non-personal lending is now medium-term.

At the same time the banks have drifted away from the so-called "money banking" towards "service banking". This development started in 1958 when banks acquired shares in leading finance companies. In more recent years they have expanded considerably these financial services and are now in competition with financial institutions in various sectors. These include merchant banking, factoring, leasing, company registration, insurance-broking, computer payroll services, unit trusts and credit cards. The Access credit card is owned by National Westminster, Lloyds, Midland, Bank of Ireland, Clydesdale and the Royal Bank of Scotland, while Barclaycard is run by Barclays. Furthermore, the use of credit cards has been expanded overseas.

There have also been developments on the current account services. An important innovation since the mid-1960s is the cheque card. It is now issued in a standard form by all the clearers except Barclays, and it guarantees the payment of cheques up to £50 either in cash or in payment for goods or services. Other innovations include cash dispensers; automated tills (providing cash and account balances, plus taking orders for cheque books and statements), and budget accounts.

In addition to their domestic operations, the clearing banks are major international financial institutions. They are very active in the international financial markets and have extensive operations abroad. International representation has been obtained by either purchasing subsidiaries abroad or by direct representation by the banks or their subsidiaries. Furthermore, there has also been participation in consortium banks.

International banking activities account for a substantial proportion of the clearing banks' total assets and total profits.

2.1.2 *Scottish Clearing Banks*

There are three Scottish Clearing Banks: Bank of Scotland, Clydesdale, and the Royal Bank of Scotland. At the time of the Radcliffe Report there were five Scottish Clearing Banks but mergers in the 1960s reduced the number to three. All have links with the London Clearers, Clydesdale being 100 per cent owned by Midland, Bank of Scotland 35 per cent owned by Barclays, and Royal Bank of Scotland 16 per cent owned by Lloyds through the National and Commercial Banking Group (which also owns Williams and Glyns).

None of the Scottish banks has hived off its activities in the same way as some of the London Clearers, preferring to maintain international divisions in-house with branch representation in some important overseas centres.

2.1.3 *Northern Ireland Banks*

The Northern Ireland banking system is dominated by the Northern Ireland branches of the Northern Bank and Ulster Bank, both subsidiaries of London Clearing Banks, which engage in banking throughout Ireland. It also includes branches of three banks registered in the Republic of Ireland, Allied Irish Banks, the Bank of Ireland and the Trustee Savings Bank Northern Ireland (TSBNI).

2.1.4 *The Trustee Savings Bank*

The Trustee Savings Banks (TSBs) are unincorporated societies providing banking services to the personal and corporate sector. The older and earliest ones date from the beginning of the nineteenth century. The importance of TSBs has declined over the years, but they have now successfully improved their market share across a wide range of sectors. Having started off as depositories of small savings of private individuals, the TSBs now provide a full range of money transmission and personal borrowing and other banking facilities. Apart from current, deposit savings and investment accounts, the TSBs have introduced mortgage loans, travel cheques and foreign currency and the TSB Trustcard.

The big change in their activities began with the Trustee Savings Bank Act of 1976 which relaxed government control over the TSBs and removed the most restrictive statutory limitations on their activities. They were permitted to lend for the first time, and all the banks now offer a range of credit facilities including personal loan, overdrafts and card facilities.

In 1982, a major reorganization of the TSBs was announced. The purpose was to rearrange the then federal structure of sixteen unincorporated societies into something more appropriate to their new, more commercial stance and ambitions and, particularly, to meet the requirements of the Banking Act 1979 from which they had a specific exemption until 1985.

The proposal was that the TSB Group should have a Companies Act structure and will act as the holding company for all the group's activities. The ownership and accountability of the TSBs may be resolved by the issue of shares in the TSB Group PLC, depending on the House of Lords. For statistical purposes the TSBs as a whole were moved from the OFIs sector into the monetary sector at the end of 1981. Previous to November 1979, the TSBs' ordinary department belonged to the central government sector.

2.1.5 *The Girobank*

The Girobank was originally established as a bank within the Post Office in October 1968, after a long period of discussion following a recommendation by the Radcliffe Committee. Its original objectives were to provide a simple money transmission service and to extend the use of current account banking in the personal sector, and it was aimed principally at lower income groups who had traditionally been reluctant to use commercial banks.

The original concept of personal banking was extended in the early 1970s. The emphasis was put on business customers and on the provision of specialised services such as rent collection for public authorities, and cash collection from corporate customers. The range of personal customer services offered has broadened too. Girobank now offers deposit accounts, personal loans, limited overdraft facilities and cheque guarantee cards and is planning to move into areas such as the provision of mortgages. The bank depends for a large part of its deposit base on a few large customers e.g. the Department of Health and Social Security, British Telecom and on a large number of business customers in the retail trade sector. It has been obliged to maintain a high level of liquidity. Advances to customers, as yet, form only a small part of the assets side of the balance sheet. The treasury is empowered to require Girobank to invest a given proportion of its customer balances in certain specified classes of asset –particularly short-term marketable assets.

In 1978 The National Giro changed its name to National Girobank to reflect the wider range of banking services available and, in 1981, agreement was reached that it should become an operational member of the Clearing House. In October 1985 National Girobank became incorporated as Girobank PLC and as such was recognised as a bank under the 1979 Banking Act. The Girobank is investing in a five-year expansionary programme which includes the creation of seven new Regional Offices. It will, however, continue to direct most of its business through the 20,000 Post Office customers and through direct mail and telephone communications.

2.1.6 *The Banking Department of Bank of England*

The balance sheet of the Bank of England is divided, for accounting purposes between the issue department and the banking department. (The Bank's activities were divided in this way by the Bank Charter Act 1844, so as to separate the note issue function from all other functions). In the UK financial accounts, the issue department is included in the central government sector, while the banking department is in the monetary sector.

Through this department the Bank acts as banker to the government, to banks, to overseas central banks and international organisations, and to a smaller number of other domestic insitutions and private individuals, including staff.

2.1.7 *Accepting Houses*

The Accepting Houses traditional business is accepting, i.e. adding their name to bills of exchange issued by lesser known traders to finance trade which the latter had entered into. These acceptances are discountable at the finest rate by the Bank of England.

The Accepting Houses deal predominantly with the Corporate sector and are mainly engaged in wholesale banking. In addition to the full range of wholesale banking services the accepting houses also act as financial advisers and provide investment management services. They are members of the Issuing Houses Association and play a major role in organizing and underwriting capital issues in the UK domestic market.

2.1.8 *Overseas Banks*

There were 332 Overseas Banks in February, 1986 of which US and Japanese Banks are the most prevalent. An important reason for their presence is their desire to participate in the Euro-currency and Euro-bond markets. Some of them, however, are involved in domestic banking business.

Representation takes different forms. Some banks operate through subsidiaries whilst others have opened branches in their own names. There are also large numbers of representative offices which do not transact banking business but act as a focal point for building up business relationships.

2.1.9 *Consortium Banks*

There were 23 Consortium Banks in April, 1986. The Consortium Banks bring together leading banks from different countries, or from one country, combining resources and expertise predominantly to provide term loans in foreign currencies to corporate and public borrowers. They are also active in loan syndications and some banks manage or underwrite international bond issues.

2.1.10 *Discount Houses*

The London Discount Market represents an integral part of the financial mechanism of the City of London and is basically concerned with borrowing and investing short-term money. The market consists of 10 members of the London Discount Market Association (LDMA), a few small firms of bill brokers, and the money trading departments of 5 "listed" banks which carry out similar activities. Since November 1981, however, only the members of LDMA have formed part of the monetary sector.

The Discount Houses are a type of banking institution unique to the London market. They provide a home for banks' liquid funds by taking secured call deposits from them. These funds are then used for the purchase of a variety of assets including Treasury Bills, commercial bills and gilt-edged securities. The Discount Houses are the principal market makers in bills and the only institutions with direct borrowing access to the Bank of England.

For the company sector the houses' main function is providing liquidity to the commercial bill market through discounting bills of exchange, whilst as a secondary function the houses offer various forms of short-term investments for company portfolios.

The Discount Houses play an important role in the arrangements for financing the Government's short-term borrowing needs. As well as dealing in commercial bills they undertake collectively to cover in full the weekly Treasury bill tender which is part of the Government's short-term borrowing arrangements. They are also active dealers in short-dated Government stocks. Through their influence in those markets the houses provide the medium through which the Bank of England influences movements in short-term interest rates.

Prudential supervision has been strengthened in recent years. For many years,the houses observed some simple multipliers relating to the trading activities (assets held) to the capital and reserves held. In June 1982 new rules were introduced by the Bank of England which are designed to ensure that the Discount Houses can cover any losses they may sustain if the value of their assets drops. Under the new rules, a risk weighted sum of their assets must not be greater than 40 times their capital base, and a second ratio limits their holdings of higher risk assets.

2.2 Changes in Banking Statistics

The present system of banking statistics is based on the reporting system introduced during the course of 1975. Previous to that, banks were reporting on a wide variety of largely uncoordinated returns introduced at different times to meet specific statistical or operational requirements –such as the development of flow-of-funds statistics, the monitoring of credit control arrangements, the improvement of balance of payments statistics, or the introduction of new monetary aggregates. The clearing banks' and non-clearing banks' returns had evolved along different lines, with only clearing banks providing a full return of all assets and liabilities. The continuing development of financial analysis had emphasized the need for consistent banking information and a thorough review of the reporting system was undertaken in the early seventies with the help of various banking associations.

The reporting system, introduced in 1975, had stood the test of time well. For details see *New Banking Statistics* [B.24]. Nevertheless, there had been many changes and new developments over the period 1965-75, and by the late 1970s it had become clear that a review of banking statistics was desirable. However, the review was deferred in order to take into account the Banking Act which became law in 1979. The main provisions of the Act were implemented in the early part of 1980. The main implications of the Act for banking statistics were the formal extension of the Bank of England's supervisory role to a much wider range of institutions and an increase in the amount of information required for supervisory purposes.

Subsequent to that, an extensive review of monetary policy took place, to change the system of monetary control which had been in operation since 1971. This review of monetary policy, which is outlined in *Monetary Control Provisions* [B.23] required some immediate changes. Thus, many changes in banking statistics took place before the completion of the review of statistics in the autumn of 1982. Some of these earlier changes included a monetary aggregate more closely related to the concept of transactions balances, see *Transactions Balances –a New Monetary Aggregate* [B.33]; the abolition of the system of reserve ratios and the introduction of a uniform cash ratio; the extension of the banking sector to include all recognised banks and licensed deposit-taking institutions (LDTs); and, most important of all, the replacement of the narrowly defined banking sector with the monetary sector as the basis for statistical reporting.

The review of banking statistics recommended changes or improvements in the following areas:

(i) supervision of recognised banks and LDTs;
(ii) new areas of activity such as housing finance and leasing;
(iii) improvements to international banking statistics;
(iv) improvements to other statistics such as those used to compile the balance of payments.

The returns were revised accordingly to give more information in those areas. The main changes are summarised below. For a detailed explanation of the changes, see *Review of Banking Statistics*, [B.28].

2.2.1 *Supervision of recognised banks and LDTs under the Banking Act, 1979.*
The returns were revised and new form introduced to give more information in such areas as capital adequacy, liquidity, foreign currency exposure, profitability, provisions etc. The Bank of England has also published policy papers as articles in its *Quarterly Bulletin.* See "The Liquidity of Banks" [B.18], "Foreign Currency Exposure" [B.17] "The measurement of capital" [B.19] and "Consolidated Supervision" [B.14]. The extra detail is intended to assist in the assessment, both of an individual institution's capital adequacy of to its over-all performance and its exposure to certain types of risk.

2.2.2 *New areas of activity.*
The banks have greatly expanded their activities in recent years in lending for house purchase and leasing. In view of the banks increased share in the home loans market, it was seen as desirable to obtain information similar to that provided by building societies, insurance companies and local authorities for a proper analysis of the housing market. Accordingly, those banks which are actively engaged in housing finance have agreed to provide analyses of gross loans approved during the quarter. The analyses provide information on such things as the size of loan, purchase price of property, proportion of loans going to first time buyers and how much is for the purchase of new dwellings. These banks also provide figures for gross loans advanced during the quarter excluding bridging finance, but including topping-up and improvement loans. In addition, quarterly figures for net lending for house-purchase are now being provided by nearly all monetary sector institutions. With regard to leasing, the enlargement of the monetary sector in November 1981 resulted in bringing more businesses involved in leasing within it. At the same time, it seemed desirable that all the main institutions doing leasing business should submit returns to a single collecting body. It was, therefore, agreed that the Bank should assume responsibility for the collection of leasing statistics from those finance houses and specialist leasing companies which had up to that time reported to the Department of Trade. (See article *Recent Developments in Equipment of Leasing* [B.26]). The institutions involved were asked to submit a more detailed quarterly analysis (from 31st March 1983), covering capital expenditure on assets for their own use and on assets for leasing, hiring or renting out, and consisting of a breakdown by sector of lessee and by type of asset leased.

2.2.3 *Improvements to international banking statistics.*
The frequency with which geographical details of external business are reported has been reduced in return for substantially more detail of the activities of UK banks in the Euro-currency markets on the remaining reporting dates This change of emphasis was partly due to the increased use of Euro-sterling by UK residents

following the abolition of exchange control in October 1979. In order to monitor the nature and development of this market more closely, a form was introduced, to be completed quarterly by banks with majority UK ownership. The form covers Euro-sterling business of overseas banking, subsidiaries and affiliates and came into effect at the end of March 1983.

2.2.4 *Other improvements.*

The basis of the detailed industrial breakdown of bank lending is produced quarterly, and was changed as from November 1983 to the 1980 Standard Industrial Classification. The previous basis was 1968. The new analysis is more detailed than the previous one and at the same time should be more helpful when used in conjunction with other statistics. Details of the typical products and activities for each heading are found in the *Indexes to the Industrial Classification Revised 1980.* [B.48]. The majority of banking statistics are recorded at book value. However, balance sheets of the principal sectors of the UK economy have been compiled to complement the financial transactions accounts, and these measure assets and liabilities at market value or the nearest equivalent. For this purpose, banks are asked to report their holdings of certain assets at market value once a year.

2.2.5 *The 1982 Review*

The 1982 review involved radical changes in the presentation of figures for groups of British Banks. These groups have remained largely unchanged since 1975 and some go back considerably further. The composition of the groups reflected the membership of certain banking associations. The new groups published are more related to function. The old five-fold breakdown between London Clearing Banks, Scottish Clearing Banks, Northern Ireland Banks other British Banks and Accepting Houses was replaced by a threefold breakdown: retail banks which comprise the London Clearing Banks, Scottish Banks, Northern Ireland and certain other banks which conduct a mainly retail business (see Appendix I for a complete list of the institutions); Accepting Houses; and other British banks.

Separate figures for the London and Scottish Banks and their subsidiaries, and Northern Ireland Banks, are available from the representative banking associations.

2.3 The Reporting System

The bulk of banking data is covered by one reporting system comprising a set of interlocking returns under the responsibility of the Bank of England. Such an integrated system has the advantage of uniform definitions of items of information reported and facilitates the production of consistent statistics. In addition there is less duplication and, in the end, fewer returns.

The keystone to the system is a balance sheet (FORM BS). At present this is completed sixteen times a year, i.e. at mid-months and end-of-calendar quarters but from October 1986 it will be completed twelve times a year at end months only.

This return is important for monetary analysis and bank supervision. Its prompt submission and processing is thus essential and accordingly every effort is made to keep it at a manageable size. Even so, it contains over 250 cells because its users require detail by type of liability and asset, with separate figures for sterling and for foreign currency items –and a four-sector classification of certain items.

Liabilities and assets are reported at the value standing in the reporting institution's books. Liabilities and assets in currencies other than sterling are converted into sterling at the closing middle market spot rate on the reporting days.

2.3.1 *Liabilities*

The items comprising the liabilities side are as follows:

(i) Notes in circulation –these comprise the sterling notes issued by the reporting institution.

(ii) Deposits –these include all credit balances on customers' accounts, including deposits by other members of the monetary sector (except deposits in connection with syndicated lending), deposits by overseas offices of the reporting institution (except working capital provided by overseas offices which is included in capital and other funds), overdrawn accounts with UK and overseas correspondents and overseas offices of the reporting institutions and shareholders' deposits. They also include certificates of deposit issued (which are shown separately) and all liabilities in gold bullion or gold coin (which are included in other currency liabilities) except that deposited for safe custody. Deposits are split into sight deposits, time deposits, certificates of deposit and promisory notes issued by the reporting institution, and bills drawn by the reporting institution under acceptance credit facilities provided by another member of the monetary sector together with any other short-term paper issue. Sight deposits are deposits, whether interest bearing or not, which are transferable or withdrawable on demand without interest penalty. They include money at call (except where there is an agreement not to withdraw before a certain date or to call at a specific number of days notice) and money placed overnight. Time deposits comprise all other deposits (except certificates of deposit which are shown separately).

(iii) Items in suspense and transmission –these comprise credit balance not in customers' names but relating to customers' funds rather than the reporting institutions internal funds or to shareholders' funds, together with standing orders and credit transfers debited to customers' accounts, and other items for which the corresponding payment has not yet been made by the reporting institution. Also included are credits in course of transmission to UK branches of the reporting institution, to other members of the monetary sector, and to banks overseas.

(iv) Capital and other funds –these include shareholders' funds, working capital provided by overseas offices and all internal accounts (both liability and asset).

2.3.2 *Assets*

The items comprising the assets are as follows:

(i) Cash –that includes Bank of England notes and UK coin; sterling notes other than Bank of England notes; and balances with both the head office and branches of the Bank of England (except special deposits and cash ratio deposits which are shown separately).

(ii) Debit items in course of collection UK offices of the reporting institution and other monetary sector institutions in the UK and on banking offices overseas. These include cheques etc. drawn, and in course of collection on other members of the monetary sector. They include cheques that have been credited to customers' accounts but are held overnight before being presented or paid into the reporting institution's account with another member of the monetary sector; these exclude cheques already passed on to other members of the monetary sector for collection. They include all collections on banks overseas and items in transit to overseas offices of the reporting institution, where the reporting institution is acting as principal and not as an agent for collection and where it has already given credit or value for the items.

(iii) Market loans to banks (other than reserve assets) includes all balances (including correspondent balances) with, and funds lent to, monetary sector institutions and to banks overseas, apart from trade or portfolio investments; bills drawn by other members of the monetary sector under acceptance credit facilities and discounted by the reporting bank, promissory notes, CDs issued by the monetary sector institutions, other negotiable short-term paper. Other market loans include holdings of certificates of deposit issued by UK Building Societies, funds lent to UK local authorities through the local authority money markets, secured money at call with money brokers and gilt-edged jobbers. Market loans to overseas includes bills drawn on overseas offices of the reporting institution and banks overseas under acceptance credit facilities opened by the reporting institution which the reporting bank has itself discounted and certificates of deposit, promissory notes and other short term paper issued by overseas banks and owned by the reporting bank.

(iv) Balances with the Bank of England. Cash ratio deposits which are deposits with the Bank of England by reporting institutions with eligible liabilities of £10 million or more. These are non-operational and non-interest bearing and at present comprise half per cent of their eligible liabilities (quarter per cent of eligible liabilities of the Northern Ireland offices of institutions for which Northern Ireland is the main place of business in the UK). Special deposits. With effect from 20 August 1981, only monthly reporting institutions with average eligible liabilities of 10 million are liable for calls to lodge special deposits with the Bank of England. Interest is paid on special deposits at a rate adjusted weekly to the nearest one sixteenth per cent per annum on the average rate for Treasury Bills issued at the latest weekly tender. Other balances include those held with the Bank of England for operational purposes.

(v) Bills include bills, promissory notes and other negotiable paper (excluding certificates of deposit owned by the reporting institutions). They exclude the reporting institution's own acceptances which it has also discounted; bills connected with refinanceable lending under the special schemes exports and shipbuilding; and bills which the reporting institution has disposed of by rediscounting. Bills and notes are classified according to the drawee/acceptor and, as sterling or other currency according to the currency in which they are drawn.

(vi) Other loans and advances include all balances with, and funds lent (whether against collateral or not) to, customers not included elsewhere. They include the reporting institution's own acceptances which it has also discounted, except for those drawn by another monetary sector institution or by banks overseas, which are entered under market loans. Own acceptances discounted are shown as advances to the party that requested the acceptance credit to be opened. Provisions for bad and doubtful debts are not deducted. Where the reporting institution participates in (or acts as manager or co-manager of) a loan financed by more than one institution, it includes only the reporting institution's participation for its own account, the loan being classified according to the ultimate borrower. Advances to UK private sector include all medium and long-term advances (i.e. with an original maturity of two years or over); lending at fixed rates for shipbuilding for UK ownership under Department of Trade and Industry guarantee. They exclude any amounts which have been refinanced. Advances to overseas includes all medium and long-term lending, at fixed rates for exports under direct ECGD bank guarantee and all export lending at rates related to base rate under ECGD comprehensive bank bills note and open account guarantee schemes. They exclude any amounts which have been refinanced.

(vii) Investments include all securities beneficially owned by the reporting institution. It includes securities which the reporting institution has lent (or pledged) but still beneficially owns, but excludes securities which the reporting institution has borrowed and holds or has re-lent but which it does not beneficially own.

(viii) Items in suspense include all debit balances not in customers' names but related to customers' funds rather than to the reporting institution's own internal funds, for example debit balances awaiting transfer to customers' accounts.

(ix) Acceptances comprise all bills accepted by the reporting institution which are still outstanding excluding those which the reporting institution has itself discounted, but including any such discounts which have subsequently been rediscounted. Acceptances are classified according to the customer who has asked for the acceptance facility to be opened.

(x) Assets leased comprise all plant and equipment beneficially owned by the reporting institution which has been leased under finance lease agreements.

(xi) Other assets include unallocated gold bullion and gold coin; other commodities (e.g. silver); and land, premises, plant and equipment and other physical assets owned, or recorded as such, including assets leased under operating leases.

(xii) Eligible liabilities comprise, in broad terms sterling deposit liabilities, excluding deposits with an original maturity of over two years, plus any sterling resources obtained by switching foreign currencies into sterling. Inter-bank transactions (excluding cost ratio and special deposits with the Bank of England) are taken into calculation of an individual institution's eligible liabilities on a net basis irrespective of term.

2.3.3 *Further Notes on Returns*
It is important to note that for statistical purposes, the UK comprises Great Britain, Northern Ireland, the Channel Islands and the Isle of Man.

UK residents include: HM Government and other UK public authorities; enterprises which produce goods and services in the UK, including overseas enterprises branches and subsidiaries located and operating in the UK; individuals permanently resident in the UK (including temporary residents who have stayed, or who intend to stay for a year or more) together with individuals normally resident in the UK who are overseas for less than a year; and members of UK armed forces and officials of HM Government serving overseas, as well as their dependents.

Overseas residents include: overseas governments together with their diplomatic and military offices and representatives in the UK; international organisations, including their branches or representatives in the UK; UK representative offices of overseas banks; overseas offices of the reporting institution; enterprises located and operating overseas including branches and subsidiaries of businesses which are themsleves UK residents; and persons (including those of UK origin) who are residing outside the UK for a year or more. A copy of the return is given in Appendix III.

Information on selected balance sheet items is required from some banks in Form W1 which is at present completed at close of business each Wednesday, except in the week during which the last working day of the calendar month falls, when it is instead completed as at close of business on the last working day of the calendar month. After October 1986 completion will be on Wednesdays except for weeks when a month end occurs, then it will be completed with the BS return. A copy of the return is given in Appendix IV.

The balance sheet is supplemented by some twenty other returns with reporting dates ranging from monthly to triennial. Most of these are directly related to the balance sheet and contain more frequent or more detailed analyses of balance sheet items. Among these returns is Form Q1 which is completed quarterly at the end of March, June, September and December, and which contains sector details, e.g. the UK public sector is split into central government, public corporations and local authorities, other UK residents are split into other financial institutions, industrial and commercial companies, person, households and individual trusts.

Another return is Form Q1 (annex) which is completed by a small number of banks quarterly at the end of March, June, September and December, and contains an analysis of loans for house purchase, e.g. analysis by size of loan and analysis by purchase price of property.

Form Q3 contains an analysis of advances, acceptances and facilities to UK residents by economic activity. It is completed quarterly at present on the third Wednesday of February, May, August and November. From October 1986 the return will be completed at the end of these months. It is based on the 1980 Standard Industrial Classification.

Form Q6 contains maturity analysis of liabilities and assets in sterling by type. It is completed by monthly BS reporters on the third Wednesday, end quarters from November 1986 of February, May, August and November, and by quarterly BS reporters at the end of March, June, September and December. The same type of information but for liabilities and assets in currencies other than sterling is collected in Form S5.

For our purposes, the other relevant, external returns are: Form S1 (liabilities) Part 1 which contains external sterling liabilities by type and country, and is completed at end calender quarters; and Form S2 (section 2) which contains external foreign currency liabilities by type, and currency including forward positions and is completed quarterly. Copies of these returns are given in Appendices IV to XI.

It should be noted that not all the information which is collected is published. Part of the information which is not published can be made available to the public, occasionally in an aggregated form. Users are advised to write to the Financial Statistics Division of the Bank of England.

2.4 Sources of Statistics

It has already been mentioned that the two main sources of statistics are the *Bank of England Quarterly Bulletin* [QRL.5] and the CSO publication of *Financial Statistics* [QRL.24]. The two systems use the same data-sources, that is the system of integrated returns made to the Bank of England. In chapter 6, a brief account is given of how data are seasonally adjusted.

For general comments, however, on the method of seasonal adjustment of the quarterly figures see the Bank's publication of May 1978 *United Kingdom Flow of Funds Accounts; 1963-1976* [B.55]. The method of seasonal adjustment of the mid-month figures was described in the following publications of the *Quarterly Bulletin*: June 1978 [B.29], June 1981 [B.30] and June 1983 [B.31]. Information on the tables in the *Bank of England Quarterly Bulletin* [QRL.5] is given in the March issue of each year. These notes are updated in the intervening issues.

Background notes to the tables in *Financial Statistics* [QRL.24] are provided in the *Explanatory Handbook* [B.46] which is published by the CSO in April of each year. These two sources of background information are to some extent complementary. That necessitates the joint use of both of them for a thorough understanding of the tables in [QRL.5] and [QRL.24].

Data banks exist for the series included in both of the above sources. The data bank of the *Bank of England Quarterly Bulletin* [QRL.5] is handled by the Financial Statistics Division of the Bank of England. The majority of the series go back to May 1975. The data bank of the *Financial Statistics* [QRL.24] is handled by Cisi-Wharton, econometric forecasting associates. All series have the four digit identifier which is contained in [QRL.24]. The identifier is appended by the letters M. Q or A depending on whether they are available monthly, quarterly or annually respectively. The majority of the series go back to 1963. Specific reference to the series in the data banks is made in the Quick Reference List. The start of the series is also noted.

The CLSB publishes the *Abstract of Banking Statistics* [QRL.1]. This publication brings together annual statistics covering the London and Scottish Banks, paper and automated clearings and the use of credit cards.

Another publication of the CLSB is the *Monthly Statement* [QRL.28]. Furthermore the CLSB can make available books, articles and unrestricted reports, written by them.

Other regular sources of banking data are *Economic Trends* [QRL.21]; *Annual Abstract of Statistics* [QRL.2]; *Scottish Abstract of Statistics* [QRL.32]; and *Scottish Economic Bulletin* [QRL.33]; *Northern Ireland Annual Abstract of Statistics* [QRL.29]. An occasional source of data is the *Bank of England Statistical Abstract* [QRL.7].

The following journals also give information on banking statistics. *The Banker* [B.35] June issues, listing the top 500 banks; *The Banker's Magazine* [B.36] November issues, listing the Foreign Banks in London; *The Banking World* [B.37] November issues on the automated tele-machines; *Euromoney* [B.44] listing the top 500 banks. Information on the most aggregated concept of a group of institutions, i.e. the Monetary Sector is given below. Subsequent sections give disaggregated information.

2.4.1 *UK Monetary Sector*

2.4.1.1 *Consolidation Adjustments.* Data relating to the monetary sector are designed to show the position of the monetary sector as a whole in relation to third parties. Thus, transactions between institutions within the sector are excluded.

The following adjustments are made to the figures on consolidation to avoid double counting. Gross figures for deposits and advances are adjusted to allow for sterling transit items. These transit items appear in an individual bank's balance sheet both as credit items (e.g. standing orders) and debit items (e.g. cheques in course of collection). When figures are aggregated, these items may give rise to double counting of deposits received from customers outside the monetary sector or, where overdrawn or loan accounts are concerned, to the under-valuing of total lending made to such customers.

It is assumed that sixty per cent of the total value of debit less credit items affects deposits. This proportion is therefore deducted from gross deposits and the remaining forty per cent is added to deposits of, and lending to, the UK non-bank private sector. Some other 1975 sterling accounts on both sides of instiutions' balance sheets, which are unclassifiable by sector, are added to transit items and treated in the same way. Figures for sixty per cent of net debit transit items (levels and changes) are shown in tables on monetary aggregates in *Financial Statistics* [QRL.24]. As for foreign currency transit (and suspense) items, all credit items less all debit items are added to foreign currency deposits of the overseas sector.

Apart from transit and suspense items another consolidation adjustment concerns misclassified accounts. When excluding transactions between monetary sector institutions, residual errors can arise, i.e. inter-sector transactions as measured on the asset side of the balance sheet do not always equal intra-sector transactions measured on the liabilities side. Any sterling intra-sector residual errors are allocated to non-deposit liabilities (net) while foreign currency residuals are included as an adjustment to foreign currency deposits of the overseas sector.

2.4.1.2 *Breaks in the series.* Discontinuities in the series have occurred following a change in the number of contributors to the statistics or changes in the data collected. Whenever possible when a break occurs, for tables showing amount outstanding, two estimates are given at the changeover date, i.e. before and after. Where changes in balances are displayed, they may exclude the effect of the difference in coverage in the period in which it occurred. Footnotes will, whenever possible, be given quantifying the difference.

In the monetary sector statistics changes have yielded significant discontinuities in the series. These are outlined in the table below.

Recent Changes in Series

Date	Change
Mid –January 1971	: changes in accounting procedures
End –March 1972	: additional contributors
End –March 1973	: additional contributors
Mid –May 1975	: introduction of more comprehensive banking statistics
Mid –November 1981	: introduction of monetary sector
Mid –September 1983	: additional contributors

2.4.1.3 *Valuation Adjustments.* From the second calendar quarter of 1975, the changes in assets and liabilities in foreign currencies have been adjusted to exclude the effect of movements in exchange rates (to the extent that the total adjustments made to foreign currency assets does not equal the total of adjustments to foreign currency deposits, a net adjustment is made to non-deposit liabilities).

2.4.1.4 *Sources of Statistics.* Balance sheet information of the Monetary Sector for the latest month is first issued to the public in the *Bank of England Press Release* [QRL.4] which usually comes out on the fifth Thursday after the day to which they relate. The *Press Release* shows the UK monetary sector's transactions in liabilities and assets, some of the tables show seasonally adjusted and unadjusted splits, with deposits and lending split into public sector (with the Banking Department lending to central government sub-sector for sterling lending) private sector and overseas and sub-divided between sterling and other currencies, for periods ending mid-monthly for the latest 13 months. Under liabilities there is another item titled "Non-deposit liabilities (net)". It comprises changes in the Monetary Sector's Sterling capital and internal funds or reserves less their sterling investments in UK banks and other non-financial sterling assets. It also includes some residual errors arising from the exclusion of sterling transactions between institutions within the sector and the valuation adjustments described in previous sections.

The overseas sector deposits include estimated overseas holdings of negotiable dollar and sterling certificates of deposit. They also include some unclassified foreign currency accounts which are assumed to affect the total overseas liabilities of the monetary sector. The forms used in the compilation of that table are Forms BS, S1 (liabilities), and S2 (Section 2).

The above information of the monetary sector's transactions in liabilities and assets is reproduced in *Financial Statistics* [QRL.24]. Monthly data is shown for 2 years, quarterly for one and a half years and annual for 5 years. The same table gives the liabilities and assets outstanding at the end of period, quarterly for one and a half years and annually for 4 years. Quarterly (for 2 years) and annual (for 5 years) data are also shown in the *Bank of England Quarterly Bulletin* [QRL.5].

For longer run data of assets and liabilities of the Monetary Sector, one should consult the *Annual Abstract of Statistics* [QRL.2]. This shows the end-year levels, split into public sector, private sector and overseas sector, sterling and other currencies for the latest 10 years.

A second table in [QRL.24] titled "UK Monetary Sector: analysis of domestic deposit and lending" gives a further analysis of amounts outstanding. The public sector is split into the central government, local authorities, public corporations; the private sector into other financial institutions, industrial and commercial companies and the personal sector. The personal sector's figures are further disaggregated to show borrowing from and lending to persons, households and individual trusts. The information is given quarterly for 5 years and annually for a further 3 years.

A table in the *Bank of England Quarterly Bulletin* [QRL.5] titled "UK Monetary Sector and Other Financial Institutions: external liabilities and claims" gives an analysis of external liabilities and claims by currency and also geographical details of external liabilities and claims. Other financial institutions include banks in the Channel Islands and Isle of Man which have opted out of the Monetary Sector, three non-monetary sector gold dealers and a small number of other financial institutions located on the mainland that are outside the Monetary Sector but make loans to, or take deposits from, overseas residents. The figures show gross liabilities to, and claims on, overseas banks and other overseas customers, as recorded in the reporting institutions' books at the close of business on the last working day of each calendar quarter. Gross liabilities include unallocated London certificates of deposit, the holders of which are unknown but are thought to be non-residents. A further adjustment is made to gross liabilities in respect of certain other minor items which are not allocated sectorally by reporting institutions but which are assumed to relate to overseas residents.

External claims comprise loans and advances to non-residents; commercial bills and other negotiable paper drawn on non-residents; lending under special schemes for exports and sterling acceptances given on behalf of overseas residents and from December 1985, assets leased out to non-residents under finance leases and portfolio holdings of certain securities issued by non-residents.

From December 1983, the table includes liabilities and claims denominated in sterling as well as those denominated in foreign currencies. Since the ending of exchange control in October 1979, sterling deposits with UK banks and the banks' sterling lending to overseas residents have grown considerably in nominal terms. This change in coverage is explained in *UK Banks' external liabilities and claims in sterling; geographical analysis* [B.34] which appeared in September 1983. The information on this analysis is given for the latest 5 quarters, while the information on geographical analysis is given for the last two quarters. The relevant returns for this series are: Forms S1 (liabilities) Parts 1 and 2, S1 (claims) and S2 (liabilities) and (claims) for the country detail; Form S2 (section 2) for the foreign currency detail; Form BS and MFI (Q) for total liabilities and assets.

Another table in the *Bank of England Quarterly Bulletin* [QRL.5] titled "UK Monetary Sector: foreign currency business by maturity and sector" gives information on the analysis of business by maturity and sector. The coverage of this table is limited to monetary sector institutions. Institutions, however, with either small foreign currency or small sterling business, some of which report maturity analyses at end-quarters, are excluded from the table, as are members of the LDMA. The analyses primarily provide a measure of maturity transformation. As such, they do not take account of any of the adjustments necessary to measure the liquidity of banks, as set out in the Bank of England's paper "The measurement of liquidity" reprinted in the September 1982 *Bulletin* [B.20]. Although these surveys provide useful general information about the market as a whole, they are only snapshots of the position on particular days; and that position can rapidly change as market circumstances vary.

In these analyses, institutions are required to classify maturities by reference to the period remaining to maturity rather than to the original period of the deposit or loan. Most foreign currency lending and some sterling lending is in the form of "roll-overs", i.e. a loan made for, say, five years, but where the interest rate is refixed in line with prevailing market rates, typically every three to six months, depending on the agreement between the borrower and the lender. In these statistics such lending is classified according to the period remaining to the ultimate maturity date of the loan and not the next roll-over date. The "3 years and over" category also incorporates certain unallocated items, namely, overdrafts and any overdue repayments of loans. Deposit liabilities, on the other hand, are classified according to the period remaining to the earliest possible repayment date.

In the maturity analysis of foreign currency business data on the foreign currency position vis-a-vis UK residents is included. All figures are shown in dollars. Apart from certificates of deposit and other negotiable paper issued, intra-monetary sector liabilities do not equal intra-monetary sector claims. The table shows foreign currency business of all the banks and of the British banks. The foreign currency business of American banks, Japanese banks, other overseas banks and consortium banks are available from the Bulletin Group at the address given in the *Bank of England Quarterly Bulletin* [QRL.5].

The maturity analysis of sterling business, which is shown in the same table as the foreign business, was published for the first time in the September 1984 issue. As with the foreign currency section, intra-monetary sector liabilities do not equal intra-monetary sector claims apart from certificates of deposit and other negotiable paper issued. The sterling business of bank groups, other than the All Banks and the British Banks shown in the *Bulletin* can be obtained from the Bulletin Group. The additional groups for which sterling data are available are as follows: retail banks, accepting houses, other British banks, American banks, Japanese banks, other overseas banks and consortium banks.

Information on the above series is taken from Forms S5 and Q6.

An occasional source of banking data is the *Bank of England Statisitcal Abstract* No.1 1971 and No.2 1975 [QRL.7]. They contain long runs for the banking sector on the pre-1975 basis of presentation–No. 1 provides end year figures from 1945-69, monthly 1952-69, and quarterly figures from 1963-69 inclusive; Volume No. 2 contains quarterly figures from 1963 to the first quarter of 1975 and monthly figures from 1970-75.

2.4.2 *Banks: those reporting monthly*
This section discusses the business of the UK offices of those members of the Monetary Sector which report monthly (generally those with a total balance sheet of £100 million or more, or with eligible liabilities of 10 million or more), other than the members of the London Discount Market Association.

Information on assets and liabilities is first published in the *Bank of England Monthly Press Release* [QRL.4] and then reproduced in the *Financial Statistics* [QRL.24] and the *Bank of England Quarterly Bulletin* [QRL.5]. The data are given monthly according to the reporting day, which is, at present, the third Wednesday in each month, except in December when it is the second Wednesday. The data are given for the last 12 months. It is worth noting that adjustments are not made to eliminate interbank transactions and transit items.

Liabilities and assets are reported at the value standing in the reporting institutions' books. Liabilities and assets in currencies other than sterling are translated into sterling at the closing middle market spot rate on reporting days. The figures are therefore affected by movements in exchange rates.

Liabilities are split into sight deposits, time deposits, certificates of deposit, items in suspense and transmission, and capital and other funds and subdivided into sterling and other currency. Assets are split into balances with the Bank of England, market loans bills, advances, Banking Department lending to Central Government investments, miscellaneous assets and subdivided into sterling and other currencies. The definitions of these items have already been given in section 2.3 since the relevant monthly return is Form BS. Longer-run data are given in the *Annual Abstract of Statistics* [QRL.2]. The data are annual and given for 13 years.

Information on the analysis of advances and acceptances to UK residents by economic activity by banks in the UK is first published in the *Bank of England Quarterly Press Release* [QRL.6] and then in the *Financial Statistics* [QRL.24], and the *Bank of England Quarterly Bulletin* [QRL.5]. The relevant return is Form Q3. The reporting day is, at present, the third Wednesday in February, May, August and November. Since November 1983, the industrial analysis has been based on the Standard Industrial Classification of 1980 as opposed to 1968. The classification is based upon industries irrespective of owner (that is private, local authority or government). Loans are classified according to the main activity of the borrower –if necessary within the residual groups provided under the broad divisions. Lending to unincorporated businesses, etc. is allocated according to the trade or profession.

The analysis, which is not seasonally adjusted, covers loans, advances and acceptances in both sterling and other currencies provided by reporting institutions to their customers. The figures for loans and advances also include the following: secured money placed with money brokers and gilt-edged jobbers; holdings of time deposits placed with, and certificates of deposits issued by, building societies; amounts lent under the Department of Trade and Industry special scheme for domestic shipbuilding for UK buyers; and any funds lent through brokers or specialised financial markets to UK public corporations and to the UK private sector. It does not, however, include funds placed through the local authority money market or funds lent to monetary sector institutions or overseas residents. The figures for acceptances are for bills accepted by reporting institutions under facilities granted to UK residents (other than monetary sector institutions) which are still outstanding. Those acceptances discounted by the reporting institution itself are included under advances but not under acceptances.

The institutions report their other currency advances and acceptances outstanding after conversion into sterling at the closing middle market spot rate on the day of the report. The changes are derived from the amounts outstanding with adjustments to remove the effects of exchange rate movements. Data are given for amounts outstanding for the last 4 quarters in the *Quarterly Bulletin* [QRL.5] and for the last 5 in the *Financial Statistics* [QRL.24], for changes data is given for the last 4 quarters in both journals. Annual data are available in the *Annual Abstract of Statistics* [QRL.2], for the latest 10 years. In addition *Economic Trends* [QRL.21] includes a table showing net lending to UK residents by the UK Monetary Sector. Lending to the public and private sectors is shown separately and is split into sterling and other currencies. Figures are given quarterly and annually for about the latest 5 years.

It is worth noting that the *Bank of England Quarterly Press Release* [QRL.6] gives bank lending information for various banking groups. This group information is not reproduced by group in the *Quarterly Bulletin* [QRL.5].

2.4.3 *Retail Banks*

This group comprises the banks which have extensive branch networks in the United Kingdom or participate directly in a UK clearing system. It includes branches in the Channel Islands and the Isle of Man, the parent banks of which have opted to be included in the UK monetary control arrangements, and therefore in the UK Monetary sector introduced in August 1981.

Information on assets and liabilities is first published in the *Bank of England Monthly Press Release* [QRL.4] and then reproduced in the *Quarterly Bulletin* [QRL.5]. The latter gives data for the last 12 months. The relevant return is once more Form BS. For the definitions of items see section 2.3.

It has been noted in Section 2.4.1 that the analysis of sterling business by maturity and sector as presented in the *Bank of England Quarterly Bulletin* [QRL.5] for the monetary sector is available from the Bulletin Group for this group of banks. Furthermore, analysis of bank lending to UK residents by economic activity is available for this banking group as described in section 2.4.2.

2.4.3.1 *London and Scottish Banks.* This group comprises the members of the Committee of London and Scottish Bankers. Up until September 1983, the Bank of England published separate balance sheet figures for the six London Clearing Banks and the three Scottish Clearing Banks in its *Quarterly Bulletin* [QRL.5].

Data on the London and Scottish Banks' Groups (see Appendix II for the list of institutions) are collected centrally and published by CLSB in its *Monthly Statement* [QRL.28] and in its annual *Abstract of Banking Statistics* [QRL.1] which first came out in April 1984. In [QRL.1] the annual data goes back to 1975. More frequent data (i.e. monthly or quarterly) can be obtained upon application to the Statistical Unit of the CLSB. In particular, these sources give the following information on balance sheets, liabilities and advances.

Information on balance sheets is first published in the *Monthly Statement* [QRL.28]. Deposits are split into banking sector, private sector, public sector, overseas, and certificates of deposit, and subdivided between sterling and other currencies. Sterling assets are split into balances with the Bank of England, market loans, bills, advances and investments. Market loans are also further split into banking sector, private sector, public sector and certificates of deposit. Foreign assets are split into private, public and overseas sectors. The definitions of these instruments are similar to those of Form BS.

Individual groups of banks' balances are shown in a separate table. Information there is given for selected balance sheet items. It should be noted that these figures differ from the consolidated figures published by the banks in their annual accounts. The data published by CLSB are compiled on an aggregate basis and thus show intra-group deposits and loan gross. Detailed information on liabilities is given in the *Abstract of Banking Statistics* [QRL.1]. Such information on the London Clearing Banks was first published in the London Clearing Bank evidence to the Wilson Committee [B.49].

There is a table which gives an analysis of deposits by sector. The deposits are split into public sector deposits (with central government, public corporations, and local authorities sub-sectors) and personal sector deposits (with other financial institutions, industrial, commercial companies, and persons, households and individual trusts sub-sectors) and subdivided between sterling and other currencies.

Another table gives an analysis of deposits by type. The deposits are both sight and time deposits (with UK banks, other UK residents, overseas residents, and certificates of deposits sub-sectors) and subdivided into sterling and foreign currency.

A third table gives an analysis of deposits by outstanding maturity. Sterling and foreign currency deposits are analysed by residual period to earliest maturity date (ignoring roll-overs).

The following detailed information on advances is available.

(i) Analysis of advances to UK residents by sector comparable with the analysis of deposits. This presentation of advances data has not previously been published.

(ii) Industrial analysis of advances to UK residents. This information appears first every quarter starting in February of every year in the *Monthly Statement* [QRL.28]. The industry groups identified are based on the Standard Industrial Classification revised in 1980. (See section 2.2).

(iii) Analysis of advances by maturity.

(iv) Sterling lending for house purchase. Total sterling lending outstanding for house purchase is shown split between bridging finance and other house purchase, the latter including topping-up loans. Analyses by value bands of loans approved both by size of loan approved and by purchase price of the property, are also given. These figures are based on data obtained when the loan is approved and not when the loan is actually drawn: and therefore include some approvals which are never taken up. These figures appear first in the *Monthly Statement* [QRL.28] every quarter starting in January of every year.

(v) Advances and acceptances: total facilities outstanding and percentage utilisation. Total facilities outstanding include all loan overdraft and acceptance facilities whether or not they have been drawn, excluding market lending but including lending under special schemes for exports and shipbuilding. The percentage utilisation is the ratio of the amount drawn (i.e. advances and acceptances) to the total facility outstanding.

(vi) Lending under special scheme for exports and shipbuilding. Various schemes have existed over recent years under the terms of which the Export Credit Guarantee Department guarantee, and under the early schemes, refinance part of the loans made by banks to exporters (or to their overseas importers) to facilitate the export of UK manufactured goods. In all other analyses of bank lending this type of financing is classified as advances to overseas residents even if the direct recipient appears to be a UK exporter. The Department of Industry operates a scheme under which lending to finance shipbuilding in the UK for UK buyers is guaranteed at fixed interest rates. The scheme applies to lending with an original maturity of two years or over. This type of lending is classified as lending to the UK private sector in other analyses.

(vii) Loans and Commitments to Licences for North Sea Oil Development. These figures were first published in the London Clearing Banks' evidence to the Wilson Committee. Similar figures are also published in the December issue of the *Quarterly Bulletin* [QRL.5].

Further information on each of the London and Scottish and their subsidiaries and associate companies worldwide can be found in their individual annual "Report and Account" booklets. Information contained in these booklets includes: (a) Consolidated balance sheet; (b) Consolidated profit and loss account; and (c) Statement of source and application of funds. Some of this information is reproduced in the *Abstract of Banking Statistics* [QRL.1].

In the last couple of years, the Banks, due to their expansive approach abroad, have provided supplementary information on their activities in their "Report and Account" booklets. That includes:

Operating Profit
- by nature of income and expense
- by areas of operations
- by group structure;

Total Assets
- by nature of income and expense
- by area of operations
- by group structure

Interest Income;

Other Operating Income;

Provision for Bad and Doubtful Debts;

Current, Deposit and Other Accounts
- by type
- by geographical area
- by group structure

Summary of the Accounts Expressed in US Dollars
- consolidated balance sheet
- consolidated profit and loss account;

Lending to customers
- domestic customers, by type of customer and
by maturity of loan;
- international customers, i.e. UK, USA, South Africa
by type of customer
by maturity of loan.

Information on the infrastructure of each of the London and Scottish Banks is provided in the *Abstract of Banking Statistics* [QRL.1] going back to 1973. Quarterly figures can be made available from the CLSB.

Information on the infrastructure includes the following:

(i) Number of branches: figures include both full and sub-branches; the annual figures are given for the end of December;
(ii) Number of staff: figures include part-time workers counted as full-timers; the total number for all banks is split into male and female; the annual figures are given for the end of December;
(iii) Number of cash dispensers: the annual figures are given for the end of December; further details of types of cash dispensers and their usage is available on request from APACS;
(iv) Number of cards in issue: figures exclude cards radiated for use in ATM's;
(v) Volume of transactions which materialised during the year; figures are given for 1975 onwards; and
(vi) Value of cash: withdrawls which materialised during the year; figures are also given for 1975 onwards.

Information for all of London and Scottish Banks is given for the number of accounts, divided into current accounts and deposit and savings accounts, and on the number of cheque cards in issue. The latter figures include Barclaycards issued to customers of Barclays Bank, but exclude Eurocheque Encashment cards.

The *Abstract of Banking Statistics* [QRL.1] gives extensive information on Access and Visa. The Banks which issue Access cards are: Lloyds, Midland, National Westminster, Clydesdale, The Royal Bank of Scotland, and the Bank of Ireland (UK branches only). The Banks which issue Visa cards are Barclays, Bank of Scotland, Trustee Savings Banks, Co-operative Bank, Dunban & Co, Girobank, Save and Prosper Group, Standard Chartered and Yorkshire Bank. Information is given on the following:

(i) Credit outstanding
(ii) Number of cards issued
(iii) Number of accounts
(iv) Number of UK outlets
(v) Value of turnover in terms of millions of pounds; and
(vi) Value of turnover in terms of millions of transactions.

Separate figures are provided for Barclaycard back to 1972. In addition, earlier data on the major credit card companies are available from the *Report on the Supply of Credit Card Franchise Services in the United Kingdom* by the Monopolies and Mergers Commission [B.54] in 1980. Many of the figures shown there, though, are not comparable between different card companies.

Individual credit card companies collect detailed information. Barclays Bank collects information with regard to the Barclaycard which is found in *Barclaycard Fact Sheet* [QRL.9]. Figures are usually given for the last three years and possible details of:

(i) Cardholders: number of holders split into male and female, number of new Barclaycards issued monthly, average monthly lending; average monthly extended credit lending; number of cardholder payments to Barclaycard; average credit limit; and percentage of applications received.
(ii) Merchants: number of visa merchants in UK, average UK service charge; number of UK Visa merchant authorisation calls to Barclaycard

(iii) Interest charges
(iv) Cash Advances; cash advances through Barclaycard machines
(v) Cheque encashment
(vi) Fraud
(vii) Company Barclaycard
(viii)Barclays Premier Card.

The Trustee Savings Bank collects also information which is found in *The Feature Writer's Guide to Credit Cards*, [QRL.23]. Information however is given for Trustcard as well as for Barclaycard and Access for the latest year. The following areas are covered.

(i) Size of UK payments card market
(ii) UK Bank credit card market shares
(iii) Bank current account holders who also have credit cards
(iv) Regional breakdown of credit card ownership
(v) Socio-economic profiles of credit cardholders
(vi) Sex of credit cardholders
(vii) Age and income profiles
(viii)Methods of payment; as a percentage of total expenditure
(ix) Patterns of credit.

Data on clearing statistics can be found in the *Abstract of Banking Statistics* [QRL.1] and in the *Annual Abstract of Statistics* [QRL.2]. There are three main types of data.

Firstly, the *volume and value of debit and credit clearing*. It should be noted that the data do not only include the London and Scottish Banks, but the operational members of the Clearing House (Barclays Bank, Lloyds Bank, Midland Bank, National Westminster Bank, The Royal Bank of Scotland), Bank of England, Co-operative Bank (since December 1975), Trustee Savings

Bank (since December 1975) and Girobank (since February 1983)). There are plans however to open the clearing to all the banks and Building Societies.

Secondly, *automated-items* i.e. direct debits, standing orders, and other credits. These automated transactions are processed by a company called the Bankers' Automate Clearing Services (BACS) which has 12 members, the nine banks already listed plus Bank of Scotland, Clydesdale Bank and Coutts & Co. Non-clearing banks and other financial institutions have agency arrangements with BACS, while customers of the clearing banks and other banks are able to initiate payments by presenting magnetic tapes directly to BACS.

Thirdly, *Town Clearing*. In order for a cheque to be entered for Town Clearing it must be drawn on and paid into branches within the Town Clearing Area. The minimum value is now 10,000 and has been increased in the past, as follows; on 20th July 1970 from 2,000 to 5,000. on 20th June 1980 from 5,000 to 10,000.

There is also electronic credit transfers through CHAPS.

In both the *Abstract of Banking Statistics* [QRL.1] and the *Annual Abstract Statistics* [QRL.2] figures are given annually. In [QRL.1] figures run for 13 years and in [QRL.2] for 10 years. The automated items are only reported in the former source.

2.4.3.2 *Northern Ireland Banks*. This group comprises the members of the Northern Ireland Bankers' Association which includes two reporting institutions with head offices in the Republic of Ireland. Up until September 1983, the Bank of England published separate balance sheet figures for the Northern Ireland Banks in its *Quarterly Bulletin* [QRL.5]. More recent data can be found in *Northern Ireland Annual Abstract of Statistics* [QRL.29]. The latter also publishes information on advances to Northern Ireland residents.

2.4.3.3 *Trustee Savings Banks*. The TSBs became part of the new monetary sector in November 1981 and hence from January 1982 onwards, information on deposits is not shown separately. Prior to that, until December 1976, mid-month figures were interpolated from calendar month figures and from December 1976 until November 1981, figures were obtained from the mid-month returns.

Data for deposits with TSBs prior to January 1982 can be found in the *Bank of England Quarterly Bulletin* [QRL.5], in the table titled "Components of Private Sector Liquidity." The amounts outstanding are given annually at the end of the year, for the latest 6 years; the changes in periods are given in calendar quarters again for the latest six years. In addition, data are also given for both amounts outstanding and changes at the end month for the latest thirteen months.

From January 1982 onwards, TSBs lending figures are incorporated in the total lending figure for the monetary sector. Data, however, for consumer credit for TSBs prior to January 1982 can be found in *Financial Statistics* [QRL.24] in the table titled "Consumer Credit and Other Personal Sector Borrowing" Figures for amounts outstanding are given annually for the latest four years. Figures for net transactions are also given annually and quarterly for the latest five years.

Information on loans for house purchase prior to the first quarter of 1982 when the TSBs' figures were included indistinguishably within lending by the Monetary Sector can be found in the supplementary table of *Financial Statistics*, [QRL.24] entitled "Loans for House Purchase".

Information on annual accounts of the TSB Group can be found in the *Annual Report* [QRL.34]. Up until 1982, the TSB Central Board published a *Year Book* [QRL.35] which provided useful information on history, geographical distribution, services and statistics. In particular it gave annual data on the number of accounts and customer balances for cheque accounts, savings accounts and investment accounts for the latest fifteen years.

2.4.3.4 *The Banking Department of the Bank of England.* Information on the balance sheet is found in the *Quarterly Bulletin* [QRL.5]. Liabilities are divided into public deposits, special deposits, bankers' deposits and reserves and other accounts. Assets are divided into government securities, advances and other accounts, premises, equipment and other securities and notes and coin.

If we first examine *liabilities*, total liabilities included the Bank's capital of 14.6 million, held by the Treasury, which is not included in any of the sub-totals. Credit items in the course of transmission are included in deposits, and debt items in course of collection are deducted from deposits.

Public deposits are balances held by the central government at the Bank of England, including the accounts of the Exchequer, the National Loans Fund, the National Debt Commissioners and the Paymaster General, together with dividend accounts, accounts connected with tax collection and various other government funds. Deposits held by local authorities and public corporations are included under reserves and other accounts.

Special deposits are deposits of monthly reporting institutions with average eligible liabilities of £10 million or more. Interest is paid on special deposits at a rate adjusted weekly to the nearest one-sixteenth % per annum on the average rate for Treasury bills issued at the latest weekly tender.

Bankers' deposits consist of operational deposits held mainly by the clearing banks, and non-operational cash ratio deposits for which recognised banks and licensed deposit-takers are liable under the arrangements for monetary control introduced in August 1981. The split between these two elements is given in the table on Monetary Base.

Reserves and other accounts include deposit liabilities to overseas central banks, the dividend accounts of stocks managed by the Bank other than the direct obligations of the British government, local authority and public corporation accounts, and some private sector accounts.

On the *Assets* side, there are government securities which include government and government-guaranteed securities (valued at cost less provision for losses), and Treasury bills. Advances and other accounts include market advances to the discount market, loans to customers and support loans to deposit-taking institutions. Provisions for losses are deducted. Premises, equipment and other securities include equipment (at cost less accumulated depreciation) and premises (which have been valued professionally on the basis of an open-market value for existing use). Other securities include ordinary shares, local authority bills and bonds, and commercial bills. Both listed and unlisted securities are included at cost less provisions.

Figures are given monthly for the latest thirteen months. Longer runs of data can be found in the *Financial Statistics* [QRL.24]. Figures there are given annually for the latest four years and monthly for the latest three and a half years.

2.4.4 *Accepting Houses*

Information on balance sheets is first published in the *Bank of England Monthly Press Release* [QRL.4] and then reproduced in the *Quarterly Bulletin* [QRL.5]. The latter gives data for the last twelve months. The information for the compilation of this table is taken from Form BS.

As it has been noted in section 2.4.1 the analysis of sterling business by maturity and sector as presented in the *Quarterly Bulletin* [QRL.5] for the monetary sector is available from the Bulletin Group for this group of banks.

Information on bank lending to UK residents by economic activity is published in the *Bank of England Quarterly Press Release* [QRL.6]. For details see section 2.4.2.

2.4.5 *Other British Banks*

Information on this group of banks which comprises all other UK registered institutions and certain institutions in the Channel Islands and Isle of Man which either independent companies or controlled by UK companies or by individuals, is of exactly the same nature as that given in section 2.4.4 above.

2.4.6 *American Banks*

Information on balance sheets of the American banks which includes the branches and subsidiaries including certain offices in the Channel Islands of American Banks, is again first published in the *Bank of England Monthly Press Release* [QRL.4] and then reproduced in the *Quarterly Bulletin* [QRL.5]. The latter gives data for the last twelve months. Form BS is the relevant return for this table.

As has been noted in section 2.4.1 the analysis of sterling and foreign business by maturity and sector as presented in the *Quarterly Bulletin* [QRL.5] for the monetary sector is available from the Bulletin Group.

Information on bank lending to UK residents by economic activity is published in the *Bank of England Quarterlv Press Release* [QRL.6]. (For details see section 2.4.2.)

2.4.7 *Japanese Banks*

Information on this group of banks, which comprises the branches and subsidiaries of all Japanese Banks, is of exactly similar nature as that given in section 2.4.6.

2.4.8 *Other Overseas Banks*

Information on this group of banks which includes branches and subsidiaries (including certain offices in the Channel Islands and the Isle of Man) of foreign companies other than American and Japanese banks is of exactly similar nature as that given in section 2.4.6.

2.4.9 *Consortium Banks*

Information on this group of banks, which comprises UK registered institutions owned by banks or financial institutions but in which no one institution has a direct shareholding of more than 50 per cent and in which at least one shareholder is based overseas, is of exactly similar nature as that given in section 2.4.6.

2.4.10 *Discount Market*

The Discount Market currently consists of the nine discount houses that are members of the London Discount Market Association. Between 1975 and November 1981, this group included two discount brokers (who became members of LDMA in 1980) and the money trading departments of five banks which carried on a similar type of business.

The balance sheet is first published in the Bank of England *Press Monthly Release* [QRL.4] and then reproduced in the *Bank of England Quarterly Bulletin* [QRL.5] and the *Financial Statistics* [QRL.24]. The latter sources give data for the latest twelve months. Definitions of items are those accompanying Form BS. Longer-run data for assets can be found in the *Annual Abstract of Statistics* [QRL.2]. Figures are given annually for the latest ten years.

CHAPTER 3

ASSETS AND LIABILITIES: FINANCE HOUSES AND OTHERS

3.1 Introduction

The main business of the Finance Houses and other Consumer Credit Companies is the direct financing of instalment credit sales of motor vehicles, and durable goods, mainly to persons, together with a substantial amount of farm, industrial and building plant and equipment to business. The main source of funds for these companies is from other sectors, particularly the monetary sector and other financial institutions. Many of the Finance Houses have been classified as Licensed Deposit Takers (LDTs) under the Banking Act 1979. As LDTs they form part of the Monetary Sector and have to conform with the new monetary control provisions introduced in August 1981.

Many Finance Houses, although retaining a separate operating identity, are owned by banks and other financial institutions, and some are connected to manufacturing companies. A number, however, remain entirely independent.

The Finance Houses Association (FHA), the representative body for Finance Houses and major Consumer Credit Companies in the United Kingdom, was formed in 1945. In October 1985, it had 46 members. The FHA also collects statistics from its members about their business. The proportion of the non-consumer business has been increasing in recent years and around half of new instalment credit extended by the FHA is now to corporate bodies.

3.2 Regulation

There is no special legislation governing Finance Houses and other Consumer Credit Companies as such, although the nature of their business brings them under the aegis of a number of statutes. As an important source of finance for hire purchase and credit sale they have been affected by the Consumer Credit Act 1974, the final stage of which were implemented in May 1985.

The Consumer Credit Act was the result of the recommendations of the Crowther Committee. This was set up in 1963 to examine the law and practice governing the provision of credit to individuals for financing the purchase of goods and services for personal consumption, and to consider the advantages and disadvantages of existing and possible alternative arrangements for providing such credit.

The main thrust of the Act is in three areas: the control of credit granting and hiring institutions; the supply of information to debtors and hirers; and the protection of the consumer debtor and hirer. A summary of the Act is given in

Drury and Ferrier [B.5]. The present structure of the Act and its subordinate Statutory instruments will need to be changed in 1986/7 to be in accord with the European Community Consumer Credit Directive which is now reaching fruition having been approved by the European Parliament.

3.3 Method of Compilation

3.3.1 *Assets and Liabilities of Finance Houses in Great Britain*
A sample of Finance Houses and other consumer credit grantors which are outside the Monetary Sector in Great Britain send off end-quarter forms on assets and liabilities to the Department of Trade and Industry. It should be noted that figures for the Finance Houses, which are part of the Monetary Sector, are included in chapter 2 of this book.

The figures on assets and liabilities are based on a panel of Finance Houses and other consumer credit grantors because of the large number of institutions involved in this type of business. However, the Department of Trade and Industry conducts occasionally a "benchmark" inquiry to obtain, for a particular year, information on total credit advanced by consumer credit grantors, and, for companies granting credit, details of their balance sheets. The "benchmark" inquiry is used to provide base figures for regular sample inquiries. The last "benchmark" inquiry was conducted in 1976; it also covered credit grantors now in the monetary sector. The quarterly inquiry form was revised at the beginning of 1982 to collect figures for all assets and liabilities rather than figures for selected assets and liabilities. Since the first quarter of 1983, the figures have been grossed up using the results of the 1976 benchmark.

Details of the inquiry were published in the *Business Monitor* M13 "Consumer Credit Grantors" [B.43]. Earlier data were based on the results of the "benchmark" inquiry in respect of business in 1965.

The companies report levels, that is, holdings and amounts outstanding, of their assets and liabilities. Net acquisitions are obtained by subtracting the level at the beginning of the quarter from the level at the end. When a company joins or leaves the sector, net acquisitions in the quarter are estimated on the basis of the new coverage For this reason the figures for net acquisitions during the year do not always equal the differences in levels at the beginning and end of year.

A major break in the series took place at the end of 1981 when several companies joined the monetary sector as LDTs under the terms of the Banking Act 1979.

3.3.2 *Credit Business Statistics of Finance Houses in Great Britain*
The Department of Trade and Industry compiles statistics on new credit extended by all Finance Houses and other specialist consumer credit grantors in Great Britain, including Finance Houses in the monetary sector (but not clearing banks) and unincorporated credit grantors. Data are collected monthly for new credit extended by the kind of purchase and for amounts outstanding at the end of the month. The series are based on the 1976 "benchmark" inquiry. The panel consists of a representative sample of consumer credit grantors, stratified so that the majority of large credit grantors are included.

The principal ways in which the new series differs from the old are summarized in table 4.

Table 4: Coverage of DoT's 'old' and 'new' monthly series

Category	Implied change in debt 'old'	Implied change in debt 'new'
Lenders		
Banking sector		
Former finance houses	X	X
Other banks	-	-
Trustee savings banks	-	-
Finance houses and other consumer credit grantors		
Finance Houses	X	X
Check traders	1	X
Money lenders	-	X
Others specialising in personal loans and second mortgage business	-	X
Others specialising in lending to companies	X	-
Insurance companies	-	-
Retailers	X	X
Types of Credit		
Fixed sum instalment		
Fixed interest rate	X	X
Variable interest rate	-	X
Fixed sum non-instalment	-	X
Running account	2	2
Borrowers		
Personal sector		
Individuals	X	X
Unincorporated business	X	X
Non-profit-making bodies serving persons	X	X
Companies	X	X

1 –Separate information was available.
2 –Certain business of retailers only, but in the new series, additional information is available on outstanding debt of financial houses, etc.
X –included

For details on the inquiry and on consumer credit in general see *Economic Trends* [QRL.21].

3.3.3 *Hire Purchase Statistics of Finance Houses in Northern Ireland*
The Department of Economic Development in Belfast compile statistics on hire purchase and other instalment credit (including personal loans since 1975) extended by and repaid to Finance Houses which have headquarters or offices in Northern Ireland. Data are collected through a monthly return.

3.4 Sources of Statistics

3.4.1 *Great Britain*
There are two main sources of data: *Financial Statistics* [QRL.24] and two *Business Monitors* [QRL.15] and [QRL.16].

As it was mentioned in chapter 2, there is a data bank of [QRL.24] and this is handled by Cisi-Wharton, econometric forecasting associations. All series have the four digit identifier which is contained in [QRL.24]. The identifier is appended by the letters M, Q or A depending on whether they are available monthly, quarterly or annually, respectively. Specific reference to the series in the data bank will be made in the Quick Reference List. The start of the series will also be noted.

The first table in *Financial Statistics* [QRL.24] entitled "Non-monetary sector Consumer Credit Companies" covers assets and liabilities of Finance Houses and other consumer credit companies *excluding* those which were recognised as banks before implementation of the Banking Act 1979 and, from the first quarter of 1982, *excluding* those licensed to take deposits under the Banking Act 1979, which are included in the monetary sector.

Assets are split into current assets, loans and advances, company and government securities, other financial assets, and physical assets. Current assets are further split into cash and balances with the monetary sector, into certificates of deposit (which include promissory notes and any other negotiable paper issued by the monetary sector), and into a residual category which includes items in suspense and debit items in course of collection.

Loans and advances covers all types of lending, including instalment credit vouchers, etc. issued but not redeemed. It includes loans to unconsolidated subsidiary and associate companies of contributors to the inquiry. It excludes unearned credit charges which comprise the interest payments due over the remaining loan period for fixed-sum agreements with fixed interest rates. Loans and advances are split into block discounts which comprise finance provided to retailers against the security credit agreements initiated by them; into loans of other financial institutions; into loans of industrial and commercial companies; into loans to persons which include unincorporated businesses; and into loans overseas. Company and government securities include investment in other companies in the contributors' group. Physical assets are divided into UK and overseas.

Liabilities are split into borrowing, other current liabilities, capital issues and reserves. All are quoted at book value and include borrowing from unconsolidated parent, subsidiary and associated companies of contributors to the quarterly inquiry. Borrowing is split into commercial bills, which include promissory notes and other negotiable paper; into short-term borrowing from the monetary sector which excludes deposits; into longer-term borrowing from the monetary sector which includes deposits; into other financial institutions; into other UK; and into overseas. Other current liabilities includes items in suspense and credit items in the course of transmission while capital issues include preference shares and debentures as well as ordinary shares. This table as well as the one on hire purchase and other credit business covers two broad forms of credit:

(a) A loan for a fixed sum to finance a particular purchase; and
(b) A drawing on an existing credit arrangement, often termed a running account.

They do not include figures for accounts which should normally be settled in full by the end of the account period and where there are no formal credit arrangements.

With a fixed sum account the purchaser normally makes a down payment and pays the balance in equal instalments, which includes interest charges, over an agreed period. Fixed sum credit can be provided by a Finance House or other specialist consumer credit grantor either directly or with a retailer (or motor trader) acting as agent, or it can be provided by a retailer from his own resources. It may also be provided by a check trader, where the purchaser uses a trading cheque drawn on his account with the check trader, though this is becoming less common.

With running account credit the purchaser normally receives his account monthly, when he has the option of not paying in full, with interest being charged on any balance left unpaid. A common arrangement is for the purchaser to pay a fixed amount each month by standing order. The purchases may be made in a variety of ways. For example, the purchaser may sign the bill, or he may use some form of credit card (some of which are valid only for a particular retailer and some more generally) or he may use a special cheque book (normally valid only for a particular retailer). As for fixed sum credit, running account credit may be provided by a finance house or other specialist consumer credit grantor. Credit from specialist grantors includes much of the credit obtained by cards for use only with particular retailers, because many retailers have arrangements for specialist grantors to run schemes for them.

Credit by means of cards issued by high street banks, such as Visa or Access, is not included in the figures for retailers or specialist consumer credit grantors. It is included indistinguishably in the figures for lending by the monetary sector. (See section 2.4.1.2.)

Figures on assets and liabilities are given annually for holdings at book value at the end of the year for the last seven years; and figures for net acquisitions are given annually (for the last five years) and quarterly (for the last thirteen quarters).

Similar information is also given in *Business Monitor* SDQ7 [QRL.16] 'Assets and Liabilities of Finance Houses and other consumer credit companies', and in the *Annual Abstract of Statistics* [QRL.2]. In the latter the table is titled 'Selected Assets and Liabilities of Finance Houses and other consumer credit companies'.

Information on hire purchase and other credit business is given in another table in *Financial Statistics* [QRL.24] titled "Hire Purchase and Other Credit Business". The figures relate to all Finance Houses and other specialist credit grantors and to selected kinds of retail business. They differ from the figures in the previous table in *Financial Statistics* [QRL.24] in that, as well as retailers, they include specialist consumer credit companies in the monetary sector and unincorporated consumer credit grantors.

The figures for Finance Houses and other specialist consumer credit grantors relate only to agreements where the finance comes from the specialist credit grantor from the start. They exclude, for example, agreements which retailers have block discontinued with specialist grantors, which are included in the figures for retailers. The figures do not cover clearing banks so they exclude credit provided through Barclaycard or Access. The table gives information on new credit extended on fixed agreements in total and separately for regulated fixed-sum agreements and for other fixed-sum agreements. Regulated fixed-sum agreements are as defined in the Consumer Credit Act 1974 and cover credit advance to individuals (which here include unincorporated businesses) for amounts not exceeding a specified limit (increased from £5,000 to £15,000 on 20th May 1985).

Other fixed-sum agreements cover credit advanced to companies, as well as to individuals for amounts over the £5,000 limit. New credit extended covers only fixed-sum credit (i.e. excludes running account credit) and excludes charges. That series covers both fixed sum and running account credit, and excludes charges. The table shows also the change in amounts outstanding. For retailers the table shows new credit extended and the change in amounts outstanding, both exclusive of charges. Both unadjusted and seasonally adjusted figures are given. The unadjusted figures are given annually for the last five years, quarterly for the last thirteen quarters, and monthly for the last twelve months. The seasonally adjusted data are given quarterly for the last thirteen quarters and monthly for the last twelve months.

It is worth noting that the latest month's figures, seasonally adjusted, are first published in a Department of Trade and Industry press notice about five weeks after the end of the month. Detailed statistics appear also in *Business Monitor* SDM6 [QRL.15], 'Finance Houses and other specialist Consumer Credit Grantors', in *Economic Trends* [QRL.21] and in the *Monthly Digest of Statistics* [QRL.27]. A longer-run of annual figures is given in the *Annual Abstract of Statistics* [QRL.2].

The FHA publishes also some data in its quarterly review *Credit* [QRL.18]. There are two tables: One on outstanding credit to FHA members; and the other on new credit extended by FHA members. The figures in both tables are split up to show credit to consumers, to business customers (excluding leasing) and to leasing. These figures differ from the ones in *Financial Statistics* [QRL.24]. The data in *Credit* [QRL.18] cover FHA members only; some of these members are companies who primarily grant credit to other companies and are therefore not covered by the tables in *Financial Statistics* [QRL.24]. The table on credit business in [QRL.24] covers many more credit grantors including non-corporate credit grantors and retailers, although the business of the latter is shown separately. It excludes those who do not primarily lend to consumers. Data in *Credit* [QRL.18] are shown for the last five quarters.

3.4.2 *Northern Ireland*

The main source of data is the *Northern Ireland Annual Abstract of Statistics* [QRL.29]. There are two tables on Finance Houses. The first one titled "Finance Houses: Hire Purchase and Other Credit Business" excludes transactions financed by money lenders, retailers and other merchants and which are not subsequently block discounted. It gives figures for the total value of hire purchase and other credit instalments outstanding at end of period, figures for new credit extended (including interest changes) and for repayments. Information is given annually for the last ten years and quarterly for the last thirteen quarters.

The second table in [QRL.29] is titled "Finance Houses: New Credit Extended by Type of Goods." The goods are divided into four categories. The first category includes private cars, motor cycles, power assisted cycles and caravans; the second category includes commercial motor vehicles; the third category includes tractors; and the fourth category includes industrial and building plant equipment. The figures are given for "new" goods and "used" goods and are presented annually for the last ten years and quarterly for the last thirteen quarters.

CHAPTER 4

ASSETS AND LIABILITIES: BUILDING SOCIETIES

4.1 Introduction

Building Societies are mutual organisations which have mostly borrowed personal savings (wholesale funding only being introduced in 1980) and lend most of them to individuals buying their own homes. In the early days of Building Societies the contributors to Societies were the same people as the borrowers. Now, savers and borrowers are more separate, but many Societies still give preference in their lending to those who have previously saved with the society.

Personal savings can be invested in Building Societies by a means of a deposit account or a share account, the latter forming the biggest proportion. There are two differences between deposits and shares. First, shares rank behind deposits in the event of liquidation and, second, because of the Building Societies status as mutual organisations, shares convey voting rights.

Building Societies make mortgage advances for house purchase at a variable rate of interest usually repayable over a period of 20-25 years. Repayment can be made in the form of a regular monthly sum in respect of both interest and repayment of principal, the interest being calculated on the declining balance outstanding at the beginning of the society's financial year. In the early life of the mortgage, interest accounts for the greater part of the monthly payment. Alternatively, societies are prepared to combine a mortgage with an endowment assurance policy; only interest payments are made to the Building Society during the life of the mortgage, the outstanding debt being repaid when the endowment policy matures.

4.1.1 *Assets and Liabilities*

An important characteristic of the operations of Building Societies is that they borrow short and lend long. Shares and deposits form a major part (86.4% at the end of 1985) of Building Societies' liabilities and reserves and the bulk of them can be withdrawn at a relatively short notice.

Other liabilities include interest accrued, but not yet credited to accounts, tax and other payment due and provisions, and, on two occasions, loans made to Building Societies by the government for special purposes.

Looking now at the Building Societies' assets, 80% of them are held as mortgage advances. A proportion of Building Societies' assets are held in liquid investment to provide working capital and to cover any short term excess of withdrawals and lending over deposits. Trustee status and membership of the Building Societies Association require a minimum liquidity ratio (cash and investment as a percentage of total assets) of 7.5 per cent. In practice, however, societies work on much higher ratios. At the end of 1985, the average liquidity ratio for all societies stood at 18.9% seasonally adjusted, and 18.1% unadjusted.

Building Societies' reserves are built from the small surplus usually made each year from their operations. Reserves represent the excess of assets over liabilities (at book values) and provide a solvency margin for societies to cover the risk of loss on mortgages or on investments. Minimum reserve ratios (general reserves as a percentage of total assets) are required on a sliding scale for trustee status and for membership of BSA. Currently these ratios are:

2.5 per cent for societies with assets not exceeding 100 million.

2 per cent for societies with assets exceeding 100 million but not exceeding 500 million.

1.5 per cent for societies with assets exceeding 500 million but not exceeding 1,000 million.

1.25 per cent for societies with assets exceeding 1,000 million.

4.1.2 *Developments in the Building Society Structure*

During the last thirty years the Building Societies have experienced extraordinary growth. In December 1985, their total deposits amounted to £104 billion. Their assets grew about five times in real terms. The Building Societies responded to conditions which were working in their favour. Rent controls were damaging the private sector rented accommodation so the choice effectively for most households was between rented municipal accommodation and owner occupation. In the view of many commentators the tax system has been favouring the latter.

During this period the recommended Building Societies rate system, established in 1939, was one of the factors leading to non-price competition. Branch networks grew together with supporting expenditure on advertising. The total number of offices grew from just over 750 in 1955 to 2,016 in 1970, and to 6,816 at the end of 1984 (although this was still only about half as many as the clearing banks). For an analysis of Building Society Branching see Mark Boleat [B.1].

The number of Building Societies declined from over 2,000 at the turn of the century to 783 in 1955 and to 167 in 1985. Table 5 shows the rate of decline in the number of Building Societies between 1900 and 1984.

The table shows that between 1900 and 1930 the number of societies declined at a fairly steady rate. Between 1930 and 1960 the rate of decline fell but since 1960 there has been a significant acceleration. In fact the reduction of 12.1 per cent in 1985 was the greatest since 1897.

Up to the early 1950s, the number of societies declined predominantly as a result of the dissolution of societies but since that time transfers of engagements have been more important. Thus, of the 796 societies on the register at the beginning of 1953, 536 had transferred their engagements to other societies by the end of 1983, and a further 55 had been involved in unions.

For the most part those societies which have transferred their engagements have been small societies, and mergers between large societies have been comparatively rare. Since 1928, when the Halifax Permanent Benefit Building Society amalgamated with the Halifax Equitable Benefit Building Society to form the Halifax Building

Table 5: Rate of Decline in Number of Building Societies 1900 - 1982

Decade	Annual Rate of Decline %
1900 –1910	2.8
1910 –1920	3.0
1920 –1930	2.1
1930 –1940	0.7
1940 –1950	1.5
1950 –1960	1.2
1960 –1970	4.0
1970 –1980	5.5
1980 –1982	8.0
1982 –1984	8.3

Source: "Concentration and Mergers in the Building Society Industry" [B.41], and *BSA Bulletin* [QRL.11].

Society, there have been only 13 other mergers which have involved societies who each had more than 0.5 per cent of the industry's assets.

The decline in the number of societies has been accompanied by increasing concentration within the industry. The five largest societies increased their share of total assets from 37.3 per cent in 1950 to 56.6 per cent in 1985 and the market share of the twenty largest societies increased over the same period from 62.5 per cent to 88.6 per cent. It is believed that the growth of the societies has been internally generated since the largest five societies have not recently been involved in merger activity. For an extensive analysis of the issues on concentration and mergers see [B.41].

Apart from the above structural changes, the Building Societies responded to the competitive pressures developed in recent years from the clearing banks on the mortgage loan side, and from the government sector on the borrowing side, with a list of innovations. Among these are the entry by the larger societies into wholesale money markets borrowing (see [B.42] for a discussion), the introduction of new forms of high interest accounts and the use of new electronic technology.

4.1.3 *Regulation of Building Societies*

Legislation on Building Societies is currently consolidated by the Building Societies Act 1962 which contains detailed provisions relating to the management of Building Societies and gives responsibility for their prudential supervision to the Chief Registrar of Friendly Societies. The Chief Registrar is appointed by the Chancellor of the Exchequer but is responsible directly to Parliament in some respects.

A society must register with the Chief Registrar before it can do business. The Registrar is responsible for ensuring that existing societies continue to comply with the Act, and monitors their financial performance on the basis of annual quarterly and monthly returns. He has two major statutory powers over existing societies: he can prevent them from advertising for new investments and can prohibit them from taking new investments. The Registrar also makes regulations under the Act specifying which liquid assets societies may hold. These are mostly short and medium term stock issued by the government or by local authorities.

The Chief Registrar has the power to designate the societies in which trustees may invest. Designation is greatly valued by societies as an indicator of security. The minimum requirements are:

(i) Assets of at least £10.0m.
(ii) Liquidity ratio of at least 7.5 per cent.
(iii) Reserves of 2.5 per cent of total assets not exceeding £100 million reducing by steps to 1.25 per cent of assets exceeding £1,000 million. (see section 4.1.1)

Even when these requirements are met, designation is at the Registrar's discretion.

In recent years, the character of supervision has begun to change. The Authorization Regulations which give effect to the European Community's First Banking Directive came into operation on 1 December 1981. These regulations require positive authorization of Societies by the Registry and introduce criteria related to management. As a result it has become more difficult to form a new society.

In 1980 the Government indicated that there would be new primary legislation on Building Societies in the present Parliament. In July 1984 the Government published a Green Paper *Building Societies: A New Framework* [B.39] following the BSA proposals on the issue. The Green Paper recognised that societies need wider powers if they are to meet the demands of their members and to thrive in increasingly competitive markets. However, it also stressed that societies should maintain their basic characteristics as mutual housing finance institutions, and it proposes changes to bring their legal framework up-to-date. The BSA's response to the Green Paper which was summarised in [B.38] was in general agreement to the approach of the Green Paper.

The Building Societies Bill, based on those recommendations, was published on 6th December 1985 and received an unopposed second reading in the House of Commons on 19th December. The report stage and third reading took place on June 4th 1986. The Bill is expected to be effective from January 1987. The new legislation will replace both the 1962 Act and the 1967 Act covering Northern Ireland and will therefore produce an Act dealing with the whole United Kingdom.

4.1.4 *Taxation*

Building Societies pay a composite rate of income tax on behalf of their investors, which represents the average marginal liability to basic rate tax of their investors. If not liable to tax the investor cannot claim any repayment and investors must directly discharge any liability to rates higher than the basic rate and to investment income surcharge (abolished in the 1984 Budget). The advantage of the composite rate for the Inland Revenue is that it receives the tax due without having to deal individually with each investor. In the financial year 1985/86, the agreed composite rate of tax was 25.25 per cent. It is worth noting that in October 1982 the BSA agreed with the Inland Revenue to raise the limits for composite rate investments. The previous limits of £20,000 and £40,000 (for joint accounts) were increased to

£30,000 and £60,000 respectively. Building Societies as all other financial institutions pay a corporate tax rate of 35 per cent on their surpluses.

4.2 Method of Compilation of Statistics

4.2.1 *Assets and Liabilities*

Until the early 1950s, the only wholly reliable source of statistics on Building Societies were the annual *Reports of the Chief Registrar of Friendly Societies* [QRL.31]. With the increasing importance of the role which Building Societies were playing in the economy, a new monthly return covering receipts and withdrawals of shares, deposits, mortgage advances, repayments, and liquidity, was introduced in 1955. In addition, quarterly and annual financial returns were also introduced in 1955. The basic forms have been retained although the quantity of information being sought has increased over the years. The result is a long-run of compatible statistics.

The monthly return is by far the most important which Building Societies make. Currently, each month a panel of about 83 Societies, with assets amounting to 97% of total assets of the industry, make a return to the BSA which is responsible for processing the returns, grossing them up to represent the whole industry and for distributing the results. Seasonally adjusted figures are also calculated in accordance with adjustment procedures worked out by the Bank of England. A similar procedure is used for the quarterly and annual returns, which are processed and aggregated by the Bank of England. For the quarterly and annual returns, the panel of societies consists of about 38 societies with assets amounting to over 93% of total Building Society assets. Because the figures are based on a sample, when the final annual statutory returns, made to the Registrar of Friendly Societies by all Building Societies, become available, the figures from the three financial returns have to be adjusted retrospectively in order to make them compatible. In general, however, the adjustments are of a fairly minor nature.

A sample of the above return as well as of those of the quarterly returns on the monitoring of assets and liabilities are given in Appendix XII. In addition a full list of the current statistical returns, together with details of the sample, the frequency of the return, the date by which the return should be received and the purpose of the return can be found in a leaflet sent to Building Societies by the BSA in January of every year and named "Building Society Statistical Returns". (See Appendix XIII)

4.2.2 *Lending*

In 1975, a new return was introduced to provide a detailed breakdown of both advances and commitments, as well as statistics on house prices. Previous to that, the statistics recorded made possible an accurate calculation of lending on new houses only. Some 52 Societies, representing 90 per cent of the total assets of the industries, completed the return. The return was made directly to the Department of Environment which was responsible for processing the statistics. In 1981, the details of the return were altered, and the sample was reduced to the largest 17 (now 15) societies, representing over 84 per cent of the total assets of the industry. A sample of the return is given in Appendix XII.

A major source of statistics on lending is the five per cent sample survey of lending society mortgage completions. Reference to this sample survey has already been made in another volume of this series of Reviews [B.7] in section 6.2.4. A copy of the questionnaire was also included in the Appendix. The sample survey is the principal source of detailed statistics on the distribution of building society mortgage loans. The survey is run by the Department of Environment in co-operation with the BSA. The survey began in late 1965 and coverage was increased to its present level in the second quarter of 1968, although various additional analyses have been introduced from time to time. The larger Building Societies are asked to complete questionnaires on a sample of five per cent of new mortgage advances they make to home buyers. The smaller Building Societies provide a slightly larger sample. Questionnaires covering mortgage advances completed during each month are returned by each Building Society after the end of the month. The data are processed by the Department of the Environment. For more information about the survey, see Evans [B.6].

The information provided by the questionnaire covers:

(a) The mortgage advance: the amount advanced; whether the advance is to be used wholly for the purchase of the property; the period over which the advance is due to be repaid; the gross interest rate charged initially; the initial monthly repayment; and the method of repayment.

(b) The dwelling: purchase price, location; period of construction; type of dwelling; freehold or leasehold; number of habitable rooms; whether there is a bathroom; whether there is a garage; and net rateable value.

(c) The main applicant: sex; age; basic income; any other income on which the mortgage is based; and previous tenure.

4.2.3 *Seasonal Adjustment*

Some of the building society statistics are seasonally adjusted. Building Society statistical series exhibit seasonal variation primarily for the following reasons:

(i) receipts and withdrawals are influenced by the seasonal pattern of consumer expenditure;

(ii) lending is influenced by the slight concentration of house purchase activity into the summer months; and

(iii) interest credited and paid out and the liquidity ratio are influenced by institutional factors which concentrate payments into certain months of the year.

The seasonal adjustment of Building Societies is the responsibility of the Bank of England. It was formerly the responsibility of the CSO. The general philosophy behind the adjustments is the same although a different computer program is used. The Bank's program is based on a recently developed method known as Signal Extraction, whereas the CSO used the X-11 program based on moving average techniques. The new method (see Burman [B.2]) enables the seasonal and trading day adjustments to be estimated simultaneously.

The model used for the majority of the series is still a multiplicative one.

Y	=	T x S x I
where Y	=	observed value of the series at a particular time
T	=	value of trend cycle
S	=	value of seasonal factor (including trading day factor, where appropriate)
I	=	value of irregular part of the series

However, each multiplicative seasonal factor in the series is converted into an equivalent additive seasonal component for ease of use. This has the advantage that the forecast seasonal components can be made to sum to zero over the calendar year, and hence the total of the adjusted series will automatically equal the total of the unadjusted series.

For a detailed analysis of the method used to seasonally adjust building society statistics, see the fifth and sixth editions of the *BSA Compendium Building Society Statistics* [QRL.17].

4.3 Sources of Statistics

Financial statistics on Building Societies are published by the CSO in the monthly publications of *Financial Statistics* [QRL.24] and *Economic Trends* [QRL.21]. In the latter some of the data are given for long periods.

A wealth of statistics is given in the BSA publications. The BSA is responsible for four publications. It publishes quarterly the *BSA Bulletin* [QRL.11] (January, April, July and October). Each issue contains a commentary on Building Societies and the housing market in the preceding quarter, regular tables on trends in building society activity and in the housing market and special articles on subjects of topical interest and underlying trends. A few of the tables relate to the information published in the *Financial Statistics* [QRL.24], and to the information made available in the *BSA Monthly Press Release* [QRL.12].

The BSA publishes the *Building Society Fact Book* [QRL.14] which used to be called the *Annual Report* [QRL.3], on the activities of Building Societies. The first issue was published in July 1980. The introduction of the report followed the decision of the Chief Registrar of Friendly Societies to cease publishing a separate report on the activities of Societies. The data published, which are of interest here, relate to information published in the *BSA Bulletin* [QRL.11] and the *Financial Statistics* [QRL.24] Statistics on the major operating variables are drawn from societies' annual returns.

Finally, the BSA publishes a *Compendium of Building Society Statistics* [QRL.17]. The first edition came out in September 1978, and since then there have been five more editions. In future the Building Societies Association intends to publish the *Compendium* annually. It is a valuable source of data because it brings together data from various sources and for long periods. For example, information published in *Financial Statistics* for the period 1955-84; statistics collected by the Registry of Friendly Societies for the period 1890-1984; and some of the results of the five per cent sample survey of Building Society Mortgages.

In addition to the BSA, the Department of the Environment, in conjunction with the Scottish Development Department and the Welsh Office, publish every quarter the *Housing and Construction Statistics* [QRL.26]. A longer run of figures is published in *Housing and Construction Statistics* 1973-83 [QRL.26].

The relevant tables from the above sources are given below, commencing with the general information on liabilities and assets, and continuing with more detailed information on the various types of liabilities and assets. One of the three relevant tables in *Financial Statistics* [QRL.24] entitled 'Building Societies: Liabilities and Assets', gives end year annual holdings at book values and annual and quarterly transactions at cash values. The former is reproduced in a table entitled 'Building Societies: Assets and Liabilities (book value) end of period', and the latter in another table entitled 'Building Societies: Sources and Uses of Funds (cash transactions)', *BSA Bulletin* [QRL.11].

Liabilities are divided into shares and deposits, interest accrued but not credited, official loans, and reserves. Assets are divided into mortgages, which comprise lending for house purchase to persons and a very small amount to industrial and commercial companies; into short-term assets, British government securities, local authority long-term debt and overseas government securities. Further analysis of assets as well as of shares and deposits is given in an accompanying table. In that table short-term assets and British government securities are shown by type of asset, while shares and deposits are shown by type of owner.

In [QRL.24] and [QRL.11] data are given for long periods. Another source of long-run annual data which gives general information on balance sheets as well as the number of societies on register is the table titled "Building Societies: Number and Balance Sheets" in the *Annual Abstract of Statistics* [QRL.2].

Information on receipts of principal, withdrawals, net inflow and interest on shares and deposits is given in another table in [QRL.24] titled 'Shares and deposits, mortgages and investments'. In the same table, there is a breakdown of mortgages in terms of new commitments, which cover gross commitments (i.e. formal offers of mortgage loans by building societies) less cancellations, which may relate to commitments from earlier periods; in terms of advances, which are gross mortgage advances made at purchase completion dates; in terms of repayments of principal and interest, the former including repayments on the premature winding up of mortgages which occur when dwellings are sold, as well as contractual repayments; and in terms of net advances of principal. There are also figures for the liquidity ratio. The ratio is based on unpublished figures in the monthly returns of receipts and payments. It is calculated as the ratio of holdings of cash and investments to total assets at the end of the month.

The figures appear both seasonally adjusted and unadjusted. Figures are given annually for the last 5 years, quarterly for the last 13 quarters and monthly for the last 16 months. The figures for shares and deposits appear also in the *BSA Bulletin* [QRL.11] in a table entitled 'Building Societies: shares and deposits'; and those for mortgages in a table entitled 'Building Societies: mortgages'.

A third table in *Financial Statistics* [QRL.24] entitled 'Building Society commitments and mortgage advances' gives an analysis of new commitments and advances by type of dwelling i.e. new dwelling, existing dwelling and other dwellings. The figures appear both seasonally adjusted and unadjusted. They are given annually for the last five years, quarterly for the last thirteen quarters and monthly for the last fifteen months. The figures for advances are reproduced in a table titled

'Building Societies: advances' in *BSA Bulletin* [QRL.11] and in *Housing and Construction Statistics* [QRL.26]. Unadjusted figures for new commitments also appear in a table titled 'Building Societies: new net commitments' in the *BSA Bulletin* [QRL.11].

Detailed information on loans for house purchase can be found in one of the supplementary tables in [QRL.24] titled 'Loans for house purchase'. The table is published quarterly, appearing in the January, April, July and October issues. It brings together the contribution of various types of institutions in lending for housing. It gives figures for Building Societies, Local Authorities, Insurance Companies, the Monetary Sector and TSBs up to the end of 1981 when they became part of the Monetary Sector. Gross advances and repayments are also shown for Building Societies. The figures for repayments are split between regular repayments, repayments on redemption and other lump-sum repayments. From the second quarter 1978 these figures have been based on a sample representing over 95% of total assets of all societies; before 1978 the estimates were from samples which varied between 50% and 80% of total assets. In addition, the table shows annual figures split between annuity and endowment mortgages from the end of 1978.

Parts of the table are reproduced in *BSA Bulletin* [QRL.11] in the table titled "Loans for House Purchase". There is a wealth of information on loans which is drawn from the five per cent sample survey and is given in either *BSA Bulletin* [QRL.11] or in *A Compendium of Building Society Statistics* [QRL.17] or in both.

In [QRL.17] there is a table titled "The Distribution of Building Society loans by Region", which gives figures, both annual and quarterly, for the number of loans in thousands given in the specific time period, and the distribution of these loans by geographical region, as percentages of the total.

In [QRL.11] the table titled "Distribution of Mortgages" gives information on the age of borrower, previous tenure of borrower, type of mortgage, income of borrower, age of dwellings, type of dwellings, mortgage amounts, and on deposits of borrowers. Another table in [QRL.11] titled "Building Society Loans: Regional Figures" gives regional figures broken down into the percentage to first time buyers, the percentage of loans on new houses, the average house price, the average advance and the average percentaqe advance, and the average income of borrowers. Similar information, but over a longer period, is given in Table E2: Building Society Lending - Regional Figures, *Compendium of Building Society Statistics* [QRL.17].

Another table in [QRL.11] titled "Building Societies: First-Time buyers" gives information on loans to first time buyers, including, their total number, the percentage of all mortgages, the average dwelling price, advance and income, as well as the average percentage advance, and the ratio of average advance over average income. Figures are given annually and quarterly. Similar information is given in Table E3: Loans to first time buyers, *Compendium of Building Societies Statistics* [QRL.17]. The same data are given for former owner-occupiers in [QRL.11] in the table titled "Building Societies: Former Owner-Occupiers."

Information on the structure of Building Societies is given annually in the Building Society Fact Book [QRL.14]. The information covers changes in the Register of Building Societies, changes in the distributions of assets, and changes in the degree of concentration. In a separate section of [QRL.14] information is given on the number of account holders (shareholders, creditors and borrowers), branches and staff.

Apart from the above main sources of Building Society statistics, the following sources give useful information: *The Digest of Welsh Statistics* [QRL.20], gives details of the number of mortgages granted annually in Wales. These are analysed by size, deposit, income of borrowers and price dwelling. Comparative U.K. figures are also given.

The *Report of the Chief Registrar of Friendly Societies* [QRL.31] contains related statistics from the aggregation of Building Societies' statutory annual returns, which are for various accounting years ending between 1st February and the following 31st January.

The Building Societies Year Book [QRL.13] provides a long-run of the data published in the annual *Report of the Chief Registrar of Friendly Societies* [QRL.31].

The *Northern Ireland Annual Abstract of Statistics* [QRL.29] which has replaced the *Digest of Statistics, Northern Ireland* [QRL.19] gives figures on shares and deposits, interest, replacements and mortgages in Northern Ireland. The *Northern Ireland Housing Statistics* [QRL.30] contains figures for shares and deposits, mortgages, repayments and building society mortgages completed.

CHAPTER 5

INTEREST RATES

5.1 Introduction

This chapter analyses the sources on data available on the rates of interest charged by and paid by the different financial institutions. The financial institutions are divided into three groups: UK Banks which are further divided into Selected Retail Banks and Discount Houses–Finance Houses and the Building Societies. Some of the interest rates refer to instruments which are traded between the institutions. In such cases the sources on those interest rates are included under the group of institutions which deals extensively in those instruments.

The main sources on interest rates are the *Bank of England Quarterly Bulletin* [QRL.5], the *Financial Statistics* [QRL.24] and the *BSA Bulletin* [QRL.11]. As it has been stated in the previous chapters, a data bank exists for the *Financial Statistics* [QRL.24] and the *Bank of England Quarterly Bulletin* [QRL.5] series. Specific reference to the series in the data bank is made in the Quick Reference List. The start of the series is also noted. The publications that are mentioned in this study quote an interest rate range whenever there is a discrepancy between the institutions.

5.2 UK Banks

Figures for inter-bank rates and sterling certificates of deposit can be found in *Financial Statistics* [QRL.24] in the *Bank of England Quarterly Bulletin* [QRL.5] and in the *Annual Abstract of Statistics* [QRL.2].

The *Financial Statistics* [QRL.24] in the table titled "Short-Term Money Rates" provides figures for inter-bank rates for overnight lending, seven days, one, two and three months (spread of rates over the day) and three months sterling certificates of deposit (mean of lowest bid and highest offer rates at 10.30 a.m.). The figures are for the last Friday of the month and are given annually for the past six years and monthly for the past twenty-eight months. Weekly figures are given in [QRL.5] in the table titled "Treasury Bill Tender and Short-Term Money Rates" for the overnight three months inter-bank rate and the three months sterling certificate of deposit.

Daily figures for rates of interest for sterling certificates of deposit (one month, two months, three months, six months, nine months, and one year) and inter-bank rates (seven day, one month, two months, three months, six months, nine months, and one year) can be found in the *Financial Times* [QRL.25].

Average quarterly figures for the three month inter-bank rate (average of working days) can be found in a supplementary table titled "Average Money Rates" in *Financial Statistics* [QRL.24]. This table is published quarterly (February, May,

August and November). Average monthly figures for the past twelve years can be found in the *Annual Abstract of Statistics* [QRL.2].

5.2.1 *Selected Retail Banks*

The retail banks covered in this section are: Barclays Banks, Lloyds Bank, Midland Bank and National Westminster Bank.

Figures for base rates, deposit account rates and call money can be found in the table titled "Short-Term Money Rates" in *Financial Statistics* [QRL.24] and in the table titled "Treasury Bill Tender and Short-Term Money Rates" in the *Bank of England Quarterly Bulletin* [QRL.5].

Each of the retail banks has a single base rate, which may sometimes differ from those of the other banks. The rates of interest charged by the banks on much of their lending to customers are set at margins over their own base rates: the size of the margin depends on the nature and status of the customer. A change in base rate normally follows a market change in the level of short-term market rates. There is no strict formula, however, linking the two. Some bank lending is more closely related to money market rates which vary daily and some, for example, to persons for house purchase, are at rates which vary less frequently than base rate. The only loans for which the banks charge uniform rates are those for ECGD guaranteed exports and for domestic shipbuilding. Changes in their base rate are announced individually by the banks and are published in the financial press.

Figures for the banks' base rate can be found in *Financial Statistics* [QRL.24] and in the *Bank of England Quarterly Bulletin* [QRL.5]. In [QRL.24] information is given on the date of change and on the new rate for the past nine years. The *Annual Abstract of Statistics* [QRL.2] provides similar information. In [QRL.5] the figures for base rates relate to the Friday of every week.

Figures for the banks' deposit accounts at seven days' notice and call money, i.e. the secured loans made to the discount market (mid-morning rate), can also be found in *Financial Statistics* [QRL.24]. The figures are for the last Friday of the month and are given annually for the past five years and monthly for the past forty-one months. Weekly figures are given in [QRL.5] for the past five months.

It is worth noting that average quarterly figures for the seven-day deposit rate (average of working days), and the call rate (closing rate until June 1982 and the mid-morning rate thereafter) can be found in a supplementary table entitled "Average Money Rates" in *Financial Statistics* [QRL.24]. This table is published quarterly (February, May, August and November). The banks' rates can also be found in a table titled "Interest Rates, Security Prices and Yields", in *Economic Trends* [QRL.21]. The figures are given annually and monthly.

From May 1985 the quoted rates by banks are net of income tax where this is paid by the banks at an agreed composite rate.

5.2.2 *Discount Houses*

Discount rates for the Treasury bill tender and commerical bills are published in *Financial Statistics* [QRL.24] in the table titled "Short-Term Money Rates" and in the *Bank of England Quarterly Bulletin* [QRL.5] in the table entitled "Treasury Bill Tender and Short-Term Money Rates".

The figures on the Treasury tender refer to the average rate of discount on allotment for 91-day bills at the weekly tender, and the yield which is the average discount rate expressed as the rate at which interest is earned during the life of the bills. Figures on Treasury bill yield are given in [QRL.24] only. The figures on commercial bill rates refer to eligible bank bills and to trade bills.

Eligible bank bills are those bills which have been accepted by those banks whose acceptances are eligible for rediscount at the Bank of England. The rate shown is the average of the discount market's buying and selling rates for three-month bills. Trade bills are those bills accepted by parties other than banks. The rate shown is the discount market's buying rate for three-month bills of good quality.

In *Financial Statistics* [QRL.24] the figures are for the last Friday of each month and are given annually for the past five years and monthly for the past forty one months. In [QRL.5] the figures are given weekly for the past five months. Average monthly figures for the past twelve years can be found in the *Annual Abstract of Statistics* [QRL.2].

5.3 Finance Houses

The base rate was first published by the Finance Houses's Association on 1st September 1970, and is calculated monthly. The rate is calculated by averaging the weekly averages of the three-month inter-bank rate in the preceding eight weeks, and rounding to the nearest one-half per cent above. Changes in the base rate are announced by the Finance Houses' Association and published in the press. The change takes effect on the first of the month and the new rate is normally published in *Financial Statistics* [QRL.24] about the end of the month. Figures are given for the past two and a half years.

Daily figures (mid morning) for Finance House Deposit rates (one month, two months, three months, six months, nine months and one year) are published in the *Financial Times* [QRL.25].

5.4 Building Societies

There are two types of information on Building Society interest rates: average rates paid on Building Societies' shares, deposits and charged on mortgage advances; and those recommended or advised by the BSA. (BSA advised rates, which replaced recommended rates were discontinued from November 1984).

The average rates paid on shares, deposits and charged on mortgage advances are based on the mean of amounts outstanding of shares, deposits, and mortgages advances at the end of successive accounting years. Figures for each year relate to accounts falling between 1st February of that year and 31st January of the following year. The quoted rates on shares and deposits are net of income tax where this is paid by Societies at the agreed composite rate. The latest composite rate is given in the *Financial Statistics Explanatory Handbook* [B.46].

The average rates paid on shares, deposits and charged on mortgage advances is published in *Financial Statistics* [QRL.24] in the table titled "Building Societies: rates of interest." The figures are given monthly for the last two years.

The new rates on new mortgages to owner occupiers, deposits and ordinary shares recommended or advised by the BSA are shown for the recommended or advised effective date. Recommended rates were replaced by advised rates in October 1983. The information is published in *BSA Bulletin* [QRL.11] in the table entitled "Building Society Rates of Interest". The figures are given for the last thirteen years.

CHAPTER 6

MONETARY AGGREGATES AND THEIR COUNTERPARTS

6.1 Introduction

One of the main purposes for which financial statistics are collected from banking institutions is "the compilation of statistics to permit the formulation of up-to-date assessments of developments as a basis for tactical policy decisions, including, for example, the monitoring of monetary targets". ("Purposes of Banking Statistics" [B.25]).

This emphasis on monetary aggregates in macro-economic policy is a relatively recent phenomenon which has occurred not only in the United Kingdom but in many other industrial countries. This has culminated in publicly declared targets for monetary growth. The money aggregates are often seen by financial markets as a barometer of the success of goverment financial policy and markets may react if they suspect that policy is inconsistent with the declared target.

There are several definitions of monetary aggregates and this reflects the differences of opinions as to what is the appropriate basis for defining money. Furthermore, there is a good deal of uncertainty as to what empirical definition best fits the various theoretical approaches.

There is the traditional approach which defines money as assets serving as media of exchange; or in other words, those which can be used to buy goods or services or discharge debts. M*0*, M*1*, and M*2* fall in this approach. There is another approach, employed by Friedman, which defines money as a "temporary abode of purchasing power", that is to say assets held relatively briefly when a firm or individual has receipts exceeding expenditure. The broader definitions of money fall into this category.

The interpretation of monetary aggregates is a complex subject too. The Green Paper on *Monetary Control* [B.50] published in March 1980, stated that "No single statistical measure of the money supply can be expected fully to encapsulate monetary conditions, and so provide a uniquely correct basis for controlling the complex relationships between monetary growth and prices and nominal incomes. A degree of substitutability between forms of money or liquidity just inside or outside their respective measures means that it is insufficient to rely on one measure alone".

In interpreting the behaviour of monetary aggregates, in order to implement monetary policy, the authorities pay attention to a variety of indicators. The declared targets apply to a number of monetary aggregates. Information on the evolution of monetary targeting and an analysis of the difficulties encountered in the use of monetary targets can be found in "Setting Monetary Objectives", [B.32], June 1983.

6.2 Definitions of Monetary Aggregates and their Supply Side Counterparts

6.2.1 *Definitions of Monetary Aggregates*

There are five definitions of the money stock and two liquidity measures altogether. Chart 1 shows the relationship among the monetary and liquidity aggregates and their components.

The first definition is M*0* which is a wide monetary base comprising notes and coin, both in circulation with the public and held in banks' tills, and banks' operational balances with the Bank of England. For more details see "The Monetary Base–A Statistical Note" [B.21] and "Changes to Monetary Aggregates and the Analysis of Bank Lending" [B.11].

The second definition M*1* is a narrow one consisting of notes and coin in circulation with the public, that is all holdings of notes and coin other than by the Monetary Sector, plus sterling sight deposits held by the UK private sector only. The third definition, Sterling M*3*, comprises notes and coin in circulation with the public, together with all sterling deposits (including certificates of deposit) held by UK residents in the private sector. Until March 1984, the series included public sector deposits as well. See "Changes to monetary aggregates and the analysis of bank lending" [B.11] March 1984. The fourth definition M*3* equals sterling M*3* plus all deposits held by UK residents in other currencies. These additional deposits amount at present to some 10 per cent, although the figures are uncertain because of possibly incomplete coverage of holdings by UK residents of foreign currency certificates of deposit. The reasons for paying less attention to these deposits and switching emphasis from total M*3* to sterling M*3*, can be found in 'DCE and the Money Supply. A Statistical Note' [B.16].

The fifth definition M*2* was introduced in the summer of 1982. M*2* was designed to be more directly related to transactions in goods and services than sterling M*3* and less sensitive to relative interest rates than M*1*. M*2* is defined as notes and coin in circulation with the public, non- interest bearing private sector sterling sight deposits, private sector interest bearing retail sterling bank deposits and private sector holdings of retail building society deposits and national savings bank ordinary accounts. Greater details of the construction of M*2* can be found in the "Transactions Balances–and New Monetary Aggregate" [B.33]. The series introduced in 1982 differs from the old M*2* series which was dropped in 1971 following the introduction of Competition and Credit Control. The old series consisted of M*2* plus private sector deposit accounts with deposit banks (which comprised the clearing banks and a handful of other banks doing similar business) and Discount Houses.

It should be noted that in all of these definitions, except M*2*, deposits are confined to those with institutions included in the UK monetary sector, and 60 per cent of the net debit value of sterling transit and suspense items is deducted.

6.2.2 *Definitions of Counterparts to Changes in Money Stock*

Looking at cash and banks' deposits is one way of assessing trends in monetary conditions. Another useful framework is to look at the other side of the balance sheet of the monetary sector, namely, the banks' assets. By grouping the banks' assets according to the sector of the borrower (i.e. public, private or overseas) it is possible to associate changes in the money supply with bank lending to the public and private sectors and external transactions. Movements in the money stock can thus be analysed in terms of these counterpart transactions: the Public Sector Borrowing Requirement, purchases of public sector debt by the non-bank private sector, bank lending in sterling to the private and overseas sectors, and external and foreign currency transaction of the public and banking sectors.

Money creation takes different forms, it can be discretionary when the monetary sector lends to the private sector and overseas, and automatic when it lends to the government. The latter type of lending is automatic because the discount market, which is part of the monetary sector, has undertaken to underwrite the Treasury bill tender each week. That assures the government of an automatic source of residual finance.

Another counterpart is the Domestic Credit Expansion (DCE). It has two elements:

(i) that part of the PSBR which is not offset by purchases of public sector debts by the UK non-bank private sector;

(ii) and, the increase in monetary sector lending in sterling to the UK private and overseas sectors.

Monetary sector lending in sterling to overseas residents is included in DCE because at least until the abolition of exchange controls it was largely connected with the finance of UK exports and therefore has much the same effect on domestic liquidity as direct bank lending to a UK exporter. Following the abolition of exchange controls and the subsequent removal of the supplementary special deposits scheme in June 1980, bank lending in sterling to overseas residents has also reflected the UK banks' transactions with the Euro-markets. Such transactions led to less emphasis being placed on the DCE, and to the inclusion of sterling lending to overseas residents among external and foreign currency counterparts to changes in sterling M*3*. Furthermore, this change in the format implied that DCE could no longer be directly calculated. Thus after December 1981 figures for the DCE were shown as a memorandum item.

Since June 1983, figures for the DCE have been completely discontinued. Apart from the reasons given there was always some scepticism regarding the interpretation of DCE which stemmed from the wide use of the pound by non-residents, albeit less now than in the past, and the change to a floating exchange rate system. For a discussion of these points see "Domestic Credit Expansion" [B.15].

6.2.3 *Seasonal Adjustment*

The monthly money series, M*1*, Sterling M*3* and, total M*3*, are seasonally adjusted to remove first the fluctuations which broadly recur each at the same time each year and secondly the effect of recurrent variations in government receipts and payments.

The first type of seasonal adjustment is carried out by looking at the deviations of the series from its trend over several years and deriving the average deviations appropriate to the different months of the year. These averages provide adjustments which can be added to or subtracted from the current values of the original series. The resulting series contains long- term trend and any irregular components, e.g. removal of lending restrictions.

The second type of seasonal adjustment is undertaken for two reasons. First, the month-to-month changes in bank deposits and lending are very much influenced by the monthly flows of government revenue and expenditure.

The pattern of government receipts might change suddenly because of the introduction of a new tax or of new arrangements for disbursing government expenditure. These may cause sudden large changes in the regular monthly pattern of bank deposits and advances, which the traditional methods of seasonal adjustment, depending on averaging the past, will not pick up for two or three years. Thus, the seasonal adjustment of the banking statistics, and hence of the money stock, is linked to the seasonal adjustment of the Central Government Borrowing Requirement. This implies that revisions to recent seasonal adjustments will be larger than usual later on, when the change has worked its way through the moving averages of the standard method. It is worth noting that it is not the purpose of seasonal adjustment to correct for "all" fluctuations in government receipts and payments, but only for those of a regular recurrent nature.

The second reason for undertaking the second type of seasonal adjustment is to take account of the differing dates in the month on which banking months are –the third Wednesday (except in December, when it is the second Wednesday). These dates are of great importance because of the influence on government transactions. If revenue and expenditure flowed evenly through the month, the varying length of banking month would effect both about equally, and their influence of the banking system would largely cancel out. However, this is not the case. Certain taxes are due to be paid, monthly or quarterly, around the banking statistics make-up date; and large payments are made from the Consolidated Fund to local authorities on fixed dates in respect of housing subsidies and the Rate Support Grant, the totals varying considerably from one month of the year to another. Thus, the money and banking figures are adjusted for an estimated correction for recurrent patterns associated with the varying reporting dates, as well as for the more "nominal" seasonal factors which cancel out within the year.

The above characteristics of seasonal adjustment as applied to the money and banking figures lead to the following two unusual features. First, the adjustments to be applied to individual months in any year often differ substantially from those of the same month in the year before. Second, the seasonal adjustments do not necessarily precisely cancel out over a period of twelve months.

This seasonal adjustment of banking and money figures is based on the financial transactions matrix and therefore takes account of the additional constraints imposed by the process. In particular:

(a) in any month, the sum of the adjustments of all sectors for a particular asset or liability is zero;
(b) in any month, the sum of the adjustments for the identified assets and liabilities of a particular sector is related, where possible, to the adjustment for the net acquisition of financial assets for that sector.

The seasonal adjustments for the monthly series are less reliable than those for the quarterly series because there is less information available on banking months from which to calculate the financial transactions matrix. For further details of the monthly seasonal adjustment of the money series, see [B.29], [B.30] and [B.31]. Account is now taken of the seasonal pattern of surrenders of certificates of tax deposit to pay corporation tax, and of a three-monthly "seasonal" cycle in interest bearing sight deposits.

With regard to the quarterly seasonal adjustment of the money series, comments are given in *United Kingdom flow of funds accounts: 1963-1976*, [B.55] published by the Bank of England in May 1978.

6.2.4 *Availability of Data*

Statistical data for the money stock and its counterparts are available as follows:

M*0*: Monthly figures from March 1981; annual averages back to 1919 and monthly figures back to 1961 are given in "*The Monetary Base–A Statistical Note*" [B.21]. Since March 1984 monthly figures are constructed from averaging weekly levels (see *Bank of England Quarterly Bulletin* [QRL.5] March 1984).

M*1*: Monthly figures from October 1971 and quarterly figures from the first quarter of 1963.

M*2*: Monthly figures from November 1981.

M*3* and sterling M*3*: Monthly figures from July 1971 and quarterly figures from the first quarter of 1963.

Counterparts: Monthly figures from August 1971 and quarterly figures from the first quarter of 1963.

6.2.5 *Breaks in the Series*

Breaks in the series have occurred from time to time as a result of changes in the reporting populations. The main changes are outlined below:

(i) End-March 1972 and 1973 as new contributors were included in the banking statistics.

(ii) End-March 1973 as dollar certificates of deposits held by UK residents were included; the coverage of these holdings was expanded from end-December 1977.

(iii) Mid-May 1975 as a result of the introduction of new statistical returns. For detailed information see *New Banking Statistics* [B.24].

(iv) End-December 1975 due to the exclusion of one contributor.

(v) Mid-November 1981 for the monthly series and end-December 1981 for the quarterly series as a result of the introduction of the new monetary sector basis and this has enabled levels on both bases to be produced in the money stock statistical tables.

(vi) End-March 1983 due to the addition of 43 contributors following the completion of the banking statistics review.

6.3 Definitions of Liguidity Aggregates

The two private sector liquidity measures PSL1 and PSL2 were assembled and first published in the *Bank of England Quarterly Bulletin* [QRL.5] September 1979. Any definition of liquidity is inevitable arbitrary and it will depend to some extent on the particular purpose for which the information is required. There are four main blocks of items that comprise the private sector liquidity; these are: (i) money, (ii) other money–market instruments, (iii) savings deposits and securities, and (iv) certificates of tax deposits. Only liquid assets held by the UK private sector are included (other than banks). All public sector holdings have been omitted.

The items comprising each block, which may be viewed as alternatives by their main holders, are as follows:

(i) *Money*: includes M*1*, certificates of deposits, time deposits, excluding deposits with maturity of more than two years original maturity. The only difference, therefore, of the 'money' block from the 'sterling M*3*' is that £M*3* includes all time deposits irrespective of maturity and (until March 1984) all public sector deposits.

(ii) *Other money market instruments*: gross holdings comprise Treasury Bills, bank bills, local authority temporary debt, and deposits with finance houses held by the non-bank private sector. The latter is only included until 18th November 1981 since thereafter it is included in the 'money' block as part of the monetary sector. Net holdings are estimated by deducting from the gross figures indentified holdings of money market instrument of those finance houses which are subject to credit control.

(iii) *Savings Deposits and Securities*: this block contains deposits with savings institutions. In particular the gross holdings include shares and deposits with building societies, deposits with Trustee savings banks (until 18th November 1981 when the Trustee savings banks became part of the Monetary sector), deposits with the National Savings Bank, and National Savings securities. From the gross total of the above, the following are subtracted–savings institutions' holdings of money, saving institutions' holdings of other money market instruments, and Building Societies' deposit with other savings institutions.

(iv) *Certificates of tax deposit*: includes all the certificates of tax deposit less the holdings by building societies.

More information on the components of private sector liquidity can be found in "Components of Private Sector Liquidity" [B.13]. A major change in the PSL1 has occurred with the introduction of the monetary sector, 18th November 1981 when the money block was increased substantially in size incorporating finance houses and Trustee Savings bank data which ceased to be identified separately elsewhere.

There exist two summary measures of Private Sector Liquidity, PSL1 and the PSL2. The PSL1 includes 'money', other money market instruments, and certificates of tax deposits. By including the main instruments in which wholesale liquid funds are invested it is likely to be relatively unaffected by large movements of company sector funds as a result of interest rate differentials between sterling assets. PSL2, in addition to the wholesale items in PSL1 includes what can be described as the retail liquidity of the personal sector in the form of building society shares and deposits and other similar forms of liquid savings instruments. Building Societies' holdings of money, other money market instruments and certificates of tax deposit (included in PSL1) are excluded from PSL2. The relationships among the monetary and liquidity aggregates are shown in Chart 1.

The only items that have been seasonally adjusted are "money", building society shares and deposits, and certificates of tax deposit. The seasonal adjustments for building society shares and deposits relate to interest credited to accounts only.

Chart 1. Source: *Bank of England Quarterly Bulletin* [B.11]

Bank of England Quarterly Bulletin: March 1984

Table A
MO, the wide monetary base—average amounts outstanding

£ millions; *percentage changes in italics*

Month ended	Notes and coin in circulation outside the Bank of England		Banks' deposits(a) with the Banking Department	MO			
	Unadjusted	Seasonally adjusted	Unadjusted	Unadjusted	Seasonally adjusted	Change in month: Seasonally adjusted	
1969 June 18	3,534	3,535	287	3,821	3,822		
July 16	3,570	3,535	294	3,864	3,829	7	*0.2*
Aug. 20	3,622	3,554	257	3,879	3,811	− 18	*−0.5*
Sept. 17	3,581	3,570	245	3,826	3,815	4	*0.1*
Oct. 15	3,591	3,626	253	3,844	3,879	64	*1.7*
Nov. 19	3,587	3,626	224	3,811	3,850	− 29	*−0.7*
Dec. 10	3,678	3,636	232	3,910	3,868	18	*0.5*
1970 Jan. 21	3,750	3,690	205	3,955	3,895	27	*0.7*
Feb. 18	3,585	3,682	208	3,793	3,890	− 5	*−0.1*
Mar. 18	3,629	3,702	186	3,815	3,888	− 2	*−0.1*
Apr. 15	3,723	3,731	176	3,899	3,907	19	*0.5*
May 20	3,708	3,739	170	3,878	3,909	2	*0.1*
June 17	3,768	3,771	163	3,931	3,934	25	*0.6*
July 15	3,835	3,805	178	4,013	3,983	49	*1.2*
Aug. 19	3,931	3,859	152	4,083	4,011	28	*0.7*
Sept. 16	3,901	3,889	155	4,056	4,044	33	*0.8*
Oct. 21	3,861	3,903	174	4,035	4,077	33	*0.8*
Nov. 18	3,874	3,915	184	4,058	4,099	22	*0.5*
Dec. 9	3,939	3,903	188	4,127	4,091	− 8	*−0.2*
1971 Jan. 20	4,006	3,935	189	4,195	4,124	33	*0.8*
Feb. 17	4,016	4,125	259	4,275	4,384	260	*6.3*
Mar. 17	4,089	4,175	217	4,306	4,392	8	*0.2*
Apr. 21	4,083	4,102	192	4,275	4,294	− 98	*−2.2*
May 19	4,040	4,072	187	4,227	4,259	− 35	*−0.8*
June 16	4,093	4,093	216	4,309	4,309	50	*1.2*
July 21	4,133	4,093	216	4,349	4,309	—	—
Aug. 18	4,179	4,104	187	4,366	4,291	− 18	*−0.4*
Sept. 15	4,127	4,114	213	4,340	4,327	36	*0.8*
Oct. 20	4,069	4,113	178	4,247	4,291	− 36	*−0.8*
Nov. 17	4,099	4,144	193	4,292	4,337	46	*1.1*
Dec. 8	4,158	4,132	167	4,325	4,299	− 38	*−0.9*
1972 Jan. 19	4,228	4,150	159	4,387	4,309	10	*0.2*
Feb. 16	4,066	4,174	159	4,225	4,333	24	*0.6*
Mar. 15	4,107	4,199	147	4,254	4,346	13	*0.3*
Apr. 19	4,224	4,239	193	4,417	4,432	86	*2.0*
May 17	4,248	4,298	202	4,450	4,500	68	*1.5*
June 21	4,369	4,399	218	4,587	4,617	117	*2.6*
July 19	4,435	4,392	190	4,625	4,582	− 35	*−0.8*
Aug. 16	4,471	4,387	204	4,675	4,591	9	*0.2*
Sept. 20	4,456	4,471	211	4,667	4,682	91	*2.0*
Oct. 18	4,441	4,498	232	4,673	4,730	48	*1.0*
Nov. 15	4,483	4,532	224	4,707	4,756	26	*0.5*
Dec. 13	4,661	4,616	210	4,871	4,826	70	*1.5*
1973 Jan. 17	4,785	4,696	212	4,997	4,908	82	*1.7*
Feb. 21	4,585	4,706	230	4,815	4,936	28	*0.6*
Mar. 21	4,641	4,786	202	4,843	4,988	52	*1.1*
Apr. 18	4,719	4,820	232	4,951	5,052	64	*1.3*
May 16	4,811	4,871	246	5,057	5,117	65	*1.3*
June 20	4,854	4,927	241	5,095	5,168	51	*1.0*
July 18	4,955	4,971	222	5,177	5,193	25	*0.5*
Aug. 15	5,039	5,005	288	5,327	5,293	100	*1.9*
Sept. 19	4,957	5,012	273	5,230	5,285	− 8	*−0.2*
Oct. 17	4,895	4,997	254	5,149	5,251	− 34	*−0.6*
Nov. 21	4,952	5,065	279	5,231	5,344	93	*1.8*
Dec. 12	5,144	5,123	228	5,372	5,351	7	*0.1*
1974 Jan. 16	5,325	5,183	293	5,618	5,476	125	*2.3*
Feb. 20	5,025	5,205	312	5,337	5,517	41	*0.7*
Mar. 20	5,070	5,229	296	5,366	5,525	8	*0.1*
Apr. 17	5,219	5,280	302	5,521	5,582	57	*1.0*
May 15	5,225	5,336	263	5,488	5,599	17	*0.3*
June 19	5,313	5,398	271	5,584	5,669	70	*1.3*
July 17	5,438	5,463	253	5,691	5,716	47	*0.8*
Aug. 21	5,593	5,556	296	5,889	5,852	136	*2.4*
Sept. 18	5,606	5,659	285	5,891	5,944	92	*1.6*
Oct. 16	5,610	5,727	264	5,874	5,991	47	*0.8*
Nov. 20	5,691	5,822	302	5,993	6,124	133	*2.2*
Dec. 11	5,902	5,884	302	6,204	6,186	62	*1.0*
1975 Jan. 15	6,124	5,938	287	6,411	6,225	39	*0.6*
Feb. 19	5,789	5,998	276	6,065	6,274	49	*0.8*
Mar. 19	5,883	6,062	330	6,213	6,392	118	*1.9*
Apr. 16	6,050	6,119	347	6,397	6,466	74	*1.2*
May 21	6,062	6,200	360	6,422	6,560	94	*1.5*
June 18	6,214	6,289	318	6,532	6,607	44	*0.7*
July 16	6,304	6,339	305	6,609	6,644	35	*0.5*
Aug. 20	6,455	6,407	267	6,722	6,674	29	*0.4*
Sept. 17	6,401	6,459	307	6,708	6,766	88	*1.3*
Oct. 15	6,357	6,490	287	6,644	6,777	9	*0.1*
Nov. 19	6,390	6,539	301	6,691	6,840	55	*0.8*
Dec. 10	6,562	6,561	299	6,861	6,860	15	*0.2*
1976 Jan. 21	6,772	6,650	329	7,101	6,979	114	*1.7*
Feb. 18	6,506	6,644	296	6,802	6,940	− 38	*−0.5*
Mar. 17	6,602	6,726	318	6,920	7,044	104	*1.5*
Apr. 21	6,772	6,784	277	7,049	7,061	17	*0.2*
May 19	6,810	6,886	300	7,110	7,186	123	*1.7*
June 16	6,954	6,973	286	7,240	7,259	72	*1.0*
July 21	7,090	7,050	345	7,435	7,395	135	*1.9*
Aug. 18	7,280	7,186	334	7,614	7,520	127	*1.7*
Sept. 15	7,266	7,236	297	7,563	7,533	12	*0.2*
Oct. 20	7,183	7,255	329	7,512	7,584	50	*0.7*
1976 Nov. 17	7,213	7,317	323	7,536	7,640	46	*0.6*
Dec. 8	7,343	7,301	316	7,659	7,617	− 18	*−0.2*
1977 Jan. 19	7,610	7,358	361	7,971	7,719	109	*1.4*
Feb. 16	7,269	7,427	301	7,570	7,728	12	*0.2*
Mar. 16	7,323	7,462	326	7,649	7,788	61	*0.8*
Apr. 20	7,503	7,511	341	7,844	7,852	66	*0.8*
May 18	7,499	7,594	343	7,842	7,937	86	*1.1*
June 15	7,778	7,703	355	8,133	8,058	119	*1.5*
July 20	7,832	7,791	339	8,171	8,130	75	*0.9*
Aug. 17	7,958	7,847	303	8,261	8,150	24	*0.3*
Sept. 21	7,948	7,932	354	8,302	8,286	137	*1.7*
Oct. 19	7,881	7,961	335	8,216	8,296	7	*0.1*
Nov. 16	7,922	8,037	387	8,309	8,424	126	*1.5*
Dec. 14	8,363	8,248	405	8,768	8,653	227	*2.7*
1978 Jan. 18	8,605	8,322	374	8,979	8,696	50	*0.6*
Feb. 15	8,239	8,419	430	8,669	8,849	156	*1.8*
Mar. 15	8,372	8,526	331	8,703	8,857	8	*0.1*
Apr. 19	8,609	8,625	445	9,054	9,070	212	*2.4*
May 17	8,659	8,728	385	9,044	9,113	40	*0.4*
June 21	8,821	8,859	428	9,249	9,287	176	*1.9*
July 19	9,083	8,985	471	9,554	9,456	171	*1.8*
Aug. 16	9,274	9,111	364	9,638	9,475	22	*0.2*
Sept. 20	9,191	9,171	390	9,581	9,561	89	*0.9*
Oct. 18	9,162	9,253	370	9,532	9,623	57	*0.6*
Nov. 15	9,229	9,362	428	9,657	9,790	162	*1.7*
Dec. 13	9,535	9,425	417	9,952	9,842	53	*0.5*
1979 Jan. 17	9,882	9,538	399	10,281	9,937	99	*1.0*
Feb. 21	9,486	9,693	446	9,932	10,139	209	*2.1*
Mar. 21	9,611	9,792	362	9,973	10,154	17	*0.2*
Apr. 18	9,857	9,845	405	10,262	10,250	97	*1.0*
May 16	9,900	9,962	449	10,349	10,411	149	*1.5*
June 20	9,983	10,028	417	10,400	10,445	39	*0.4*
July 18	10,124	10,036	453	10,577	10,489	56	*0.5*
Aug. 15	10,340	10,161	473	10,813	10,634	138	*1.3*
Sept. 19	10,247	10,221	512	10,759	10,733	101	*0.9*
Oct. 17	10,288	10,383	491	10,779	10,874	134	*1.2*
Nov. 21	10,386	10,532	553	10,939	11,085	216	*2.0*
Dec. 12	10,695	10,519	511	11,206	11,030	− 57	*−0.5*
1980 Jan. 16	11,083	10,671	518	11,601	11,189	158	*1.4*
Feb. 20	10,412	10,641	541	10,953	11,182	− 2	—
Mar. 19	10,515	10,714	454	10,969	11,168	− 10	*−0.1*
Apr. 16	10,822	10,794	445	11,267	11,239	65	*0.6*
May 21	10,820	10,885	431	11,251	11,316	80	*0.7*
June 18	10,840	10,907	520	11,360	11,427	113	*1.0*
July 16	10,994	10,951	487	11,481	11,438	11	*0.1*
Aug. 20	11,118	10,954	589	11,707	11,543	113	*1.0*
Sept. 17	11,009	10,990	593	11,602	11,583	40	*0.3*
Oct. 15	10,934	11,035	533	11,467	11,568	− 13	*−0.1*
Nov. 19	10,916	11,073	596	11,512	11,669	95	*0.8*
Dec. 10	11,224	11,090	554	11,778	11,644	− 35	*−0.3*
1981 Jan. 21	11,551	11,203	502	12,053	11,705	74	*0.6*
Feb. 18	10,993	11,230	618	11,611	11,848	147	*1.3*
Mar. 18	11,082	11,292	600	11,682	11,892	40	*0.3*
Apr. 15	11,396	11,424	567	11,963	11,991	97	*0.8*
May 20	11,587	11,479	571	12,158	12,050	49	*0.4*
June 17	11,409	11,479	500	11,909	11,979	− 71	*−0.6*
July 15	11,533	11,506	662	12,195	12,168	190	*1.6*
Aug. 19	11,701	11,535	559	12,260	12,094	− 74	*−0.6*
Sept. 16	11,651	11,607	263	11,914	11,870	99	*0.8*
Oct. 21	11,528	11,644	232	11,760	11,876	6	*0.1*
Nov. 18	11,500	11,665	203	11,703	11,868	− 8	*−0.1*
Dec. 9	11,752	11,661	181	11,933	11,842	− 27	*−0.2*
1982 Jan. 20	12,210	11,821	239	12,449	12,060	223	*1.9*
Feb. 17	11,551	11,799	197	11,748	11,996	− 64	*−0.5*
Mar. 17	11,489	11,706	196	11,685	11,902	− 94	*−0.8*
Apr. 21	11,660	11,667	243	11,903	11,910	8	*0.1*
May 19	11,602	11,697	164	11,766	11,861	− 49	*−0.4*
June 16	11,739	11,770	216	11,955	11,986	125	*1.1*
July 21	11,878	11,817	171	12,049	11,988	2	—
Aug. 18	11,985	11,829	162	12,147	11,991	3	—
Sept. 15	11,992	11,942	196	12,188	12,138	147	*1.2*
Oct. 20	11,888	12,005	172	12,060	12,177	39	*0.3*
Nov. 17	11,879	12,048	221	12,100	12,269	92	*0.8*
Dec. 8	12,207	12,140	164	12,371	12,304	35	*0.3*
1983 Jan. 19	12,647	12,232	178	12,825	12,410	106	*0.9*
Feb. 16	11,999	12,255	145	12,144	12,400	− 10	*−0.1*
Mar. 16	12,133	12,359	176	12,309	12,535	135	*1.1*
Apr. 20	12,424	12,436	205	12,629	12,641	106	*0.8*
May 18	12,411	12,510	131	12,542	12,641	20	*0.2*
June 15	12,556	12,589	149	12,705	12,738	97	*0.8*
July 20	12,669	12,619	105	12,774	12,724	− 14	*−0.1*
Aug. 17	12,772	12,599	162	12,934	12,761	37	*0.3*
Sept. 21	12,773	12,749	154	12,927	12,903	142	*1.1*
Oct. 19	12,685	12,810	166	12,851	12,976	73	*0.6*
Nov. 16	12,689	12,867	171	12,860	13,038	62	*0.5*
Dec. 14	13,106	12,931	155	13,261	13,086	48	*0.4*
1984 Jan. 18	13,345	12,915	222	13,567	13,137	51	*0.4*
Feb. 15	12,686	12,955	202	12,888	13,157	20	*0.2*

(a) Up to 20 August 1981, these deposits comprised all deposits other than special deposits; subsequently they comprised operational deposits only (for further detail, see the March 1981 and September 1981 *Bulletins*).

Seasonal adjustments for "money" and certificates of tax deposit are taken from the appropriate parts of seasonal adjustments for sterling M*3* and its counterparts. Quarterly data for the components of private sector liquidity are available from the first quarter of 1963 and monthly data from mid-May 1975.

6.4 Sources of Statistics

Several sources are drawn upon to produce the various monetary aggregates. The main ones include the monthly and quarterly balance sheet returns submitted by banks and LOTs in the monetary sector, similar returns from some other financial institutions and statistics of public sector finance.

Two main sources of data are the *Bank of England Quarterly Bulletin* [QRL.5] and the *Financial Statistics* [QRL.24]. However, monthly figures for the monetary aggregates and their counterparts are issued to the public for the first time in the *Bank of England Monthly Press Release* [QRL.4], usually on the fifth Thursday after the mid-month make-up day. In addition, preliminary money supply figures are also published, normally on the third Tuesday after make-up day. As it was already mentioned in previous chapters, there is a data bank for both [QRL.5] and [QRL.24], (see 2.4 and 3.4.1).

6.4.1 *Monetary Aggregates*

Figures for amounts outstanding for the components of M*1*, sterling M*3*, and M*2* next appear in *Financial Statistics* [QRL.24] and then in the *Bank of England Quarterly Bulletin* [QRL.5]. Both sources give figures for end of quarters and banking months, seasonally adjusted and unadjusted. [QRL.24] however, does not give details for M*0* but it includes quarterly figures for the velocity of circulation, as well as percentage changes. The velocity of circulation for a quarter is calculated as the ratio of gross national product at current market prices, seasonally adjusted, expressed at an annual rate to the quarterly average of money stock seasonally adjusted. Monthly figures for M*0* are given in a separate table in [QRL.5] titled 'M*0* the wide monetary base'. Figures are given for amounts outstanding and for changes.

Figures for the changes in money stock are given in separate tables in [QRL.5] and [QRL.24]. The changes in money stock may not equal the differences between the amounts outstanding. This is because changes in bank liabilities arising directly from alterations in the composition of the monetary sector, or from the use of new sources of information, are excluded from the tables showing changes. Small discrepancies in the quarterly figures also arise. The changes in notes and coin in circulation with the public do not allow for wastage and hoarding of coin; the amounts outstanding do allow for this. Also, quarterly notes and coin figures differ in their construction from those for banking months by excluding an estimated amount for overseas residents' holdings. Banking month estimates of overseas residents' holdings of notes and coin are not available.

Finally, the seasonally adjusted changes in M*1* and M*3* may not be the same as the differences between seasonally adjusted amounts outstanding, in part because the latter are rounded whereas the former are not, but also because of the slight technical differences in the approach used to adjust the two series. All foreign currency items in all the tables in this section are adjusted to exclude the effects of movements in exchange rates.

6.4.2 *Counterparts to changes in money stock*

The accounting identities between (a) domestic counterparts, (b) external and foreign currency counterparts, (c) changes in net non-deposit, and (d) changes in sterling M*3* are shown in both [QRL.5] and [QRL.24]. Figures are presented by banking months, by calendar quarter and by financial year. In [QRL.7] figures for calendar years are also given. Figures appear both unadjusted and seasonally adjusted.

6.4.3 *Liquidity Aggregates*

The sterling components of private sector liquidity are brought together in separate tables from the other monetary aggregates in both [QRL.5] and [QRL.24]. The figures run quarterly, monthly and annually. Changes are also given for monthly and quarterly periods.

CHAPTER 7

HISTORICAL DATA

7.1 Introduction

Historical data are important for the analysis of the financial system. They are important for the examination of various economic theories put forward to explain either the growth or the role of the financial sector. In this chapter the major sources that include historical financial information are reported. The objective is to give information on how far back the relevant financial series go without attempting to evaluate these sources. Comments on the series can be found in Forrest Capie and Alan Webber (1984) [B.3].

The first data on bank deposits collected and published in a standardised form appeared in "The Economist" in 1877. However, this was not a complete survey. It is possible using other printed sources and archive material to produce estimates of bank deposits, and other items on banks' balance sheets, from 1870. From 1870 the largest banks presented either annual or semi-annual accounts usually in June and/or only in December of each year. There were though, a number of banks that did not disclose their accounts. In addition to the annual accounts, 16 banks began to publish monthly balance sheets in 1891.

From 1919 the London Clearing Banks, having already been established as the dominant banks in the United Kingdom, started publishing an average of their monthly balance sheets for each month. From the beginning of January 1922 until July 1939, data for all series were presented as a monthly average figure. In August 1939 these banks began to publish a figure for a date towards the end of the month, varying from bank to bank, except in June and December when all banks reported on the last day of the month. This reduction in coverage was done, presumedly, as a wartime economy measure and this manner of reporting lasted until 1946.

In December 1946, the London Clearing Banks, decided to draw up their balance sheets on a common day in the month. The third Wedensday was agreed upon as a day least affected by monthly or weekly cycles in bank assets and liabilities, and because it was also a Bank of England day account. This practice changed to the end of the month, in October 1986.

Immediately after the war, the main emphasis was placed on the development of economic, rather than monetary statistics. As the Radcliffe Committee reported "there had been a steady improvement in the collection and publication of statistics of national income and output, the statistical coverage of financial assets and liabilities had not received the same attention either from the monetary authorities or outside commentators". (*Committee on the Working of the Monetary Systems*, [B.51]). The Radcliffe *Report* went on to advocate the collection and publications of a wider range of statistics. This change of emphasis reflected a growing interest in money and monetary policy in the 1950s. Following the recommendations of the Radcliffe Report, the Bank of England introduced their *Quarterly Bulletin* [QRL.5] in 1960 and the CSO *Financial Statistics* [QRL.24] in 1962.

The Radcliffe Report had also called for statistics which would measure the effects of monetary pressure on demand. In 1966 figures of money stock, which had one definition in those days, and the factors influencing money supply, were first published.

The major revision of banking data since the early 1960s, took place in 1975. During that period, the returns had developed to meet particular needs, for example, to monitor bank lending: to compile figures of the money supply and domestic credit, to calculate the banks' eligible liabilites, reserve ratios and special deposits. The result had been a profusion of returns, not always consistent. In particular, the returns collected from the clearing and non-clearing banks, respectively, had tended to evolve along different lines, making it difficult to compile integrated figures for the banking sector as a whole. There had also been serious inconsistencies–both in concept and coverage–in the information provided by the banks for internal banking statistics and for external statistics.

The system introduced in 1975 provided for integrated figures made on common reporting dates and based on common definitions. The principal form was a balance-sheet type of return which all banks were required to submit at mid-months and at end-quarters (previously, only the London and Scottish Clearing Banks gave full details of their assets and liabilites). For details see "New banking statistics" [B.24].

The current system is based on the one introduced in 1975. However, there have been some comparatively minor revisions to allow for developments in the financial system. These changes have already been outlined in previous chapters.

7.2 Sources of Historical Data

The best known study of financial institutions which presents annual aggregate data for the UK over a long period is Sheppard's study [B.10] published in 1971. However, there are many inaccuracies in the series for money aggregates and their components. Prior to that, the coverage of the UK's financial statistics was grossly inadequate. When H.G. Johnson was reviewing the situation in 1959, he observed "...it is remarkable how incomplete and inadequate monetary statistics available in this country are..." (H.G. Johnson, [B.9]). As a consequence, until quite recently, empirical studies of the growth and role of the financial system have been difficult, especially in the period before 1945.

A recent extensive coverage is that of Forrest Capie and Alan Webber [B.3] published in 1985. It provides monthly annual and quarterly average data for monetary aggregates and their components for the period 1870-1982. Other publications include the *Bank of England Statistical Summary* [QRL.8] produced for the directors as a result of the Macmillan Committee; *The British Economy Key Statistics* 1900-1970 [QRL.10] which gives basic annual national statistics for the 20th Century; the *Bank of England Statistical Abstract* [QRL.7] which was first published in 1971, giving figures starting in 1951; *Annual Abstract of Statistics* [QRL.2] published annually by the CSO.

There are additional sources which are specific to the building societies. The chief Registrar of Friendly Societies was obliged to provide annual *Reports on Building Societies* [QRL.31] by the 1894 Building Societies Act. These reports provide detailed statistics. However, in interpreting these figures, it should be borne in mind that the statistics for the earlier years are not as reliable as those for more recent years. The Chief Registrar of Friendly Societies ceased to publish a separate report on the activities of societies in 1980. As a result, the BSA started publishing *Annual Reports* [QRL.3] during the same year. These annual reports are now called *Building Society Fact Book* [QRL.14]. Further, the BSA publishes a *Compendium of Building Society Statistics* [QRL.17]. The first one came out in September 1978, and since then there have been five more editions.

Detailed information on the major sources mentioned in this section is given below. Reference to the tables in those sources is given in the Quick Reference List.

7.2.1 *The Growth and Role of UK Financial Institutions, 1880-1962*

In the first three chapters of [B.10], an attempt is made to identify the most important financial developments such as the growing importance of non-bank financial institutions, the revealed instability of certain important asset preferences, and the close correspondence between the growth of certain financial claims and the growth of economic activity. In the next two chapters some of the theories which have been put forward to explain the changes in these asset preferences are tested against the data through the use of an ordinary least squares estimating procedure as applied to a single equation.

The main text is supported by annual data given in the appendix. The appendix is divided into three sections. The first section covers UK banks. In particular the tables refer to end-year balance sheet figures of the joint-stock banks of the UK, The joint-stock banks of England, Wales and Ireland, and (from 1920) of Northern Ireland, the joint-stock banks of Scotland, and a consolidation of the balance sheet figures of some private banks. End-year as well as annual average balance sheets of the London Clearing Banks are given for the period 1919-1966. Finally, data on bank advances in Great Britain, bank clearings in Great Britain, discount houses and the Bank of England are also provided. The second section gives data on the non-bank financial intermediaries 1880-1966. It provides data for the Post Office, Trustee Savings Banks, Building Societies, Friendly Societies and Finance Houses. The third section deals with the National Savings, coin and currency in circulation, money supply and interest rates.

7.2.2 *A Monetary History of the UK, 1870-1982 Vol I.*

This study [B.3] provides monthly, quarterly, half-yearly and annual average data for the UK for 1870-1982 for the monetary aggregates, proximate determinants, and other monetary and banking data series. Previous studies presented only annual average or end-year figures. The historical development of the items represented by each series and the method used in deriving and calculating the data is also discussed. Part of the data presented has been derived and calculated by the authors themselves.

The study is divided into the following parts:

(i) Monetary aggregates and determinants. The series presented in this part are derived from the calculations of the authors. An explanation of the calculations is given in the relevant parts. The series described are for M*1*, M*3*, monetary base, money multipliers, cash deposit ratios, reserve deposit ratios and the income velocity of circulation. The data for the money multiplier for M*1* is presented for the period between 1921 and 1969, and for the money multiplier for M*3* from 1870 to 1969. The series are presented either, half-yearly and annually, or monthly, quarterly and annually for 1870- 1921; and monthly, quarterly, and annually for 1921-1969. The Bank of England has made the figures available for end-quarter series from March 1963, and for monthly series from June 1971. The Bank of England has also made available a series for the monetary base which is an annual average from 1919-1980 and a monthly figure from January 1961 to February 1981. These figures are reproduced in the volume. Part Ib provides a comprehensive survey of all previous attempts to estimate monetary variables and component data series, and illuminates the deficiences associated with all previously constructed data.

(ii) Components of the Monetary Aggregates and Monetary Measures. This section treats the components of the monetary measures which are computed from the detailed series discussed in (iii).

(iii) This gives series for bank deposits, cash, the Bank of England balance sheet, notes, interest rates, retail prices, and other financial data. A short historical discussion is provided for each series, followed by a detailed description of how the series has been constructed.

7.2.3 *Annual Abstract of Statistics*

The *Annual Abstract of Statistics* [QRL.2] is produced by the CSO. It deals with all aspects of statistics and has separate sections dedicated to financial statistics. The data are similar to that included in the *Financial Statistics* [QRL.24] but are mainly annual figures. Depending on availability, both adjusted and unadjusted data are given.

Apart from the *Financial Statistics* [QRL.24], other contributing sources to the *Annual Abstract* are the Bank of England, the Building Societies Association, the Department of Trade, the Finance Houses Association, and the Friendly Societies Association.

The *Annual Abstract of Statistics* was first published in 1946, although up to World War II it was preceded by the *Statistical Abstract*, the first issue of which came out in 1840. Each edition includes data of the last ten years prior to publication.

The first section on financial statistics is on Home Finance: Central Government. It gives tables on: Public Sector Financial Account, Public Sector Borrowing Requirement, Financing Public Sector Borrowing Requirement, and on National Savings.

The second section deals with banking as well as other series of financial statisitcs that are not relevant to us. On the Banking and Capital Markets, tables are given on: Assets of the Monetary Sector and of the various disaggregated group of banks;

Advances and Acceptances to UK residents by UK Banks; the Discount Market; and interest rates.

Under the "Other Financial Institutions" section, data on the following types of financial institutions are given: Trustee Savings Banks; Building Societies; Finance Houses; and selected assets of Finance Houses.

7.2.4 *Bank of England Statistical Abstract*

The *Bank of England Statistical Abstract* [QRL.7] was published by the Economic Intelligence Department of the Bank of England (now called the Financial Statistics Division). Two editions have been published so far. The first edition was published in 1971 covering 1945-1969. The second issue was published in 1975 and it covers the period 1970 to 1974, or, where financial years are more appropriate, from March 1970 to March 1975. However, the banking figures have been extended to mid-April 1975. Where figures in the first *Abstract* have been revised significantly, the appropriate tables in this issue extend further back than 1970. For example, the tables on the money stock go as far back as 1963. The tables that are provided in the *Abstract* are the following: Central Government Borrowing Requirement and its financing, (annual figures from 1963 and quarterly figures from 1963), Discount Houses from 1963, Banks in the United Kingdom (summary tables, as well as tables on UK banks giving aggregated and disaggregated figures of Accepting Houses, Overseas Banks, and other Banks, from 1970). Tables on eligible liabilities, reserve assets, reserve ratios and special deposits on Banks and Finance House are given monthly from 1971. In addition disaggregated figures of Analysis of Advances and Acceptances in the United Kingdom from February 1970 are included for the London Clearing Banks, Scottish Clearing Banks, Other Banks in Great Britian, Banks in Northern Ireland.

A further set of tables on the UK banking sector give strictly aggregated figures on liabilities and assets, changes in liabilities and assets, analysis of current and deposit accounts and analysis of advances. These figures run from 1963.

7.2.5 *Bank of England Statistical Summary*

Following a recommendation of the Macmillan Committee, the *Statistical Summary* [QRL.8], previously compiled by the Bank of England for internal use and private circulation, was issued to the public for the first time in January 1932, and it appeared monthly until it was superseded by the *Monthly Digest of Statistics* [QRL.27] at the beginning of 1946.

Among the data published in the *Statistical Summary* which are relevant to the current study are balance sheets of the Bank of England Banking Department and London Clearing Banks. Monthly figures for certain items of the London Clearing Banks, were contained in Appendix I of the Macmillan *Report* [B.52] for the period January 1919, to March 1931 inclusive and for six Scottish banks in Appendix II. Annual averages of London Clearing Bank figures were reproduced in the July 1932 issue of the *Statistical Summary*, together with a series of monthly figures commencing in January 1931. This latter series was continued in the issue of February 1933, and from April 1933 onward appeared monthly until the suspension of publication. In these figures, offices outside England and Wales were excluded up to December 1937. For the post-war period the series has been continued in the *Monthly Digest of Statistics* [QRL.27].

7.2.6 *The British Economy Key Statistics 1900-1970*

The British Economy Key Statistics [QRL.10] gives figures in as comparable form as possible from 1900-1970. The data which are relevant to the current study include net deposits of London Clearing and Scottish banks as a percentage of gross domestic product at current factor cost; gross deposits, liquid assets, the liquidity ratio, investments advances, special deposits, and advances to the private sector by the London Clearing Banks; and shares and deposits outstanding of Building Societies.

Information is given on the definitions especially when there is a break in the continuity of the series.

7.2.7 *A Compendium of Building Society Statistics*

Reference to the *Compendium* has already been given in section 4.3. Apart from current data, historical data are also given going back to 1890, and relate to statistics collected by the Registrar of Friendly Societies. As was mentioned earlier, the Chief Registrar of Friendly Societies was obliged by law to produce a report on the activity of Building Societies. These reports provide fairly detailed information but it should be borne in mind that the statistics for the earlier years are not as reliable as those for more recent years.

Historical data are given on the following:

(a) the number of Building Societies, investors and borrowers;
(b) assets and liabilities–balance sheet figures;
(c) advances and management expenses;
(d) rates of interest: average rates actually paid and charged by Building Societies; and BSA recommended interest rates.

7.2.8 *Building Society Fact Book*

The *Building Society Fact Book* [QRL.14] replaced in 1984 the *Annual Report* [QRL.3] which had been published since 1980. This publication draws on information published by the *BSA Bulletin* [QRL.11] and *Financial Statistics* [QRL.24]. Apart from current data, historical data are also shown. There is a table titled 'Building Societies: Progress' which gives important data going back to 1900 e.g. number of Societies, number of shareholders, number of depositers, number of borrowers, share balances, deposit balances, mortgage balances, average mortgage rate, and average share rate.

CHAPTER 8

IMPROVEMENTS AND FUTURE DEVELOPMENTS

The Bank of England and the CSO have developed financial data extraordinarily well following the initiative of the Radcliffe Committee. Data have been developed in response not only to changes in monetary control, but also to developments in the structure of financial institutions and financial markets.

Changes in financial statistics have been taking place in consultation with the financial institutions, more specifically with the different professional associations. The two main associations involved have been the Committee of London and Scottish Bankers (CLSB) and the British Bankers Association (BBA). The BBA embraced, up until April 1983, almost all UK financial institutions "listed" as banks by the Bank of England. Since April 1983, only institutions recognised as banks under the Banking Act 1979 have been eligible for membership of the BBA. The association ensures that the information requested by the Bank of England is necessary and the returns are drawn up in the way most convenient to the banking community.

The financial data are not only used by the Bank of England but by the financial institutions themselves in monitoring their performance and developing their marketing strategies. However, the requirements of these two main users of financial data might not coincide. Hence consideration is given to the fact that the collection of data is a costly affair in terms of money and time.

The Bank of England, in conjunction with the Standing Committee of Statistics Users, an independent body representative of various national organisations and professional associations, held two conferences on the theme of financial statistics. The first one took place in November 1977 and the second one in November 1985. The aim of the conferences was to bring together a wide cross-section of different groups of users and suppliers of statistics, in conjunction with the Government Statistical Service, to examine possible new developments and improvements.

Many issues were raised at the conference and many suggestions were made. Some of the suggestions made in the 1977 conference have been implemented. For example, there was a widespread demand for more monetary indicators including a series for the monetary base irrespective of which indicators the authorities pay greater attention to. Since then, no less than five monetary aggregates and two liquidity ones have been published regularly.

Another suggestion concerned the introduction of a reliability grading system for published financial statistics. This has partially materialised in so far as the CSO now publishes in *Financial Statistics Explanatory Handbook* [B.42] a table of reliability gradings for variables in the financial accounts.

A third suggestion concerned the fact that the banking month dates did not coincide with the calendar month dates. From October 1986 all statistical reporting of banks will be at end-calendar months and not on the third Wednesday of every month.

Another issue which yet remains unresolved relates to the availability of statistics. In particular, it relates to the weekly monetary series which is not made available to the public. The Bank of England's reason for that centres on the difficulties encountered in seasonally adjusting it. Quoting from C.A.E. Goodhart's (Bank of England) contribution to the conference: "At present details of the figures are not being provided to anyone, neither to the market nor to higher authorities within the Bank. The reason for this self-denying ordinance within the Bank is that we felt that we ourselves –just as much as the market –could well misinterpret the figures in the first few months when we could not, for example, assess the regular (seasonal) intra-monthly patterns. So we are not providing them to the market nor, for the time being, are we providing them to ourselves for exactly the same reasons". However, many years have passed since this statement was made. At the same time, it should be recognised that the greater the amount of information made available, the less the speculation about what the latest figures might show. The market will learn to discount a lot of the "noise". A market needs a continuous flow of information in order to be able to react smoothly to changing events. If data are published infrequently and new data differ from that expected, the stock market has no way of knowing whether the expected deviation is a random fluctuation (that may already have reversed) or the start of a new trend. (See *Bank of England Quarterly Bulletin* [QRL.5], page 152 June 1977), for more details on the authorities' difficulties.

Some new suggestions were made in the 1985 conference. For example, with regard to the breaks in series, dates should be shown on the old and new basis for the quarter when the breaks occur. For some series (e.g. the monetary sector dates which were affected by the TSB) the size of the break can only be found by consulting old copies of the publication.

On the whole, statistics aimed at the marketing side of financial institutions seem to be lacking, more so in the banking sector than in the Building Societies' sector. For example, there are no official data relating to the size of deposits and loans, or to the social class of transactor, and there are only annual data relating to the type of business of loan recipients. There is also no information on interest rates paid on different types of assets. Such data might not be of use to the monetary authorities but they will be appreciated by users of statistics in industry and commerce.

The following statistical changes which are of special interest to bank supervisors are expected to take place in the next year or so. These are consolidated supervision (in this context, taking the business of group companies, both bank and non-bank, into account in assessing a bank's position), and business not directly represented by items on a bank's balance sheet (that is, contingent liabilities and committments).

At the same time, the usefulness of certain published statistics has diminished in recent years and may need examination. A particular example is the split of deposits into "sight" and "time". This dichotomy has become less meaningful as the major banks have introduced interest bearing accounts available at sight and bearing little or no interest penalty for withdrawal. Further complications arise with those accounts which are also chequeable and with some which nominally require seven days' notice of withdrawal, but where in practice cash can be withdrawn immediately and without loss of interest through a cash dispenser. Thus, interest-bearing sight deposits are no longer basically overnight funds in the money markets, nor are non-interest bearing sight deposits a measure of current chequeable accounts.

There will always be room for improvement in response to developments in banking activities. It is unlikely though that the suggestions will be for rebuilding the existing edifice.

QUICK REFERENCE LIST - TABLE OF CONTENTS

QUICK REFERENCE LIST

Type of data	Breakdown	Area	Frequency	QRL Publication	Text Reference
Assets and Liabilities: Monetary Sector					
Monetary Sector					
Balance Sheets	Deposits and lending split into public sector, private sector and overseas and subdivided between sterling and other currencies	UK	Monthly	[QRL.4]	2.4.1.4 Other sources include [QRL.5], [QRL.24] and [QRL.2]. Databank [QRL.5] quarterly from 1963; databank [QRL.24] monthly from 1963. Historical data in [B.10] 1880-1966 and for deposits, notes, inter-bank deposits, clearings, reserves and bankers' balances in [B.3] 1870-1982
Analysis of Domestic Deposits and Lending	The public sector is split into the central government local authorities public corporations; the private sector is split into financial institutions, industrial and commercial companies and the personal sector	UK	Quarterly	[QRL.24]	2.4.1.4 Historical data on UK gross and net Bank Deposits in [B.3] 1870-1982
Analysis of Business	By maturity and sector	UK	Quarterly	[QRL.5]	2.4.1.4
External Liabilities and Claims	By currency, by sector; and country detail	UK	Quarterly	[QRL.5]	2.4.1.4 Includes the monetary sector and some other institutions
Banks: those reporting monthly					

Balance sheets	Liabilities are split into sight deposits, time deposits, items in suspense and transmission, capitol and other funds and sub divided into sterling and other currencies. Assets are split into balances with the Bank of England, market loans and bills, advances and investments and subdivided into sterling and other currencies	UK	Monthly	[QRL.4]	2.4.2 Other sources include [QRL.2] and [QRL.5] Databank [QRL.5] monthly from May 1975; databank [QRL.24] monthly from November 1981. Historical data for the London clearing, non-clearing, Scottish and Irish banks in [B.3] 1870-1982
Analysis of advances and acceptances	By economic activity and by banks	UK	Quarterly	[QRL.6]	2.4.2 Other sources include [QRL.24], [QRL.5], [QRL.2] and [QRL.21]. Databank [QRL.5] quarterly from May 1975. Historical dates on GB in [B.5] 1936-8, 1946-66
Retail Banks					
Balance Sheet	Liabilities are split into monetary, public, private and overseas sectors and certificates of deposit and sub divided into sterling and other currencies. Assets are split into balances with the Bank of England, market loans, bills, advances and investments and subdivided between sterling and other currencies	UK	Monthly	[QRL.4]	2.4.3 Another source is [QRL.5]. Databank monthly since Sept 1983. Historical dates on Joint-Stock Banks of England and Wales in 1880-1960. Historical data for selected items, deposits, notes, reserves and other items in [B.3] 1870-1982
Analysis of sterling business	By maturity and by sector	UK	Quarterly	[QRL.5]	2.4.3
Analysis of advances and acceptances	By economic activity	UK	Quarterly	[QRL.6]	2.4.3 and 2.4.2
London Clearing Banks					

Type of data	Breakdown	Area	Frequency	QRL Publication	Text Reference
Balance Sheet	Liabilities are split into monetary, public, private and overseas sectors and certificates of deposit and subdivided into sterling and other currencies. Assets are split into balances with the Bank of England, market loans, bills, advances, and investments and subdivided between sterling and other currencies	UK	Monthly	[QRL.5]	2.4.3.1 This series ended in September 1983. Databank [QRL.5] monthly May 1975 - Aug 1983. Historical dates in [B.10] 1919-1966; in [QRL.10] 1900-70; Historical data for deposits, inter-bank deposits, clearings and reserves in [B.3] 1921-1982
Scottish Clearing Banks					
Balance Sheet	Same	UK	Monthly	[QRL.5]	2.4.3.1 This series ended in September 1983. Databank [QRL.5] monthly May 1975 - August 1983. Historical dates on Joint-Stock of Banks of Scotland in [B.10] 1880-1966 and for deposits, notes, interbank deposits, clearings and reserves in [B.3] 1870-1982
London and Scottish Banks' Groups					
Balance Sheet	Same	UK	Monthly	[QRL.28]	2.4.3.1 Another source is [QRL.1]
Analysis of deposits	By sector, by type and by outstanding maturity	UK	Annual	[QRL.1]	2.4.3.1
Analysis of advances	By sector, by industry and by maturity	UK	Quarterly	[QRL.28]	2.4.3.1 Another source is [QRL.1]
Sterling lending for house purchase	Total sterling lending split into bridging finance and other house purchase; analyses of value bands of loans appeared by size of loan and by purchase price of the property	UK	Quarterly	[QRL.28]	2.4.3.1 Another source is [QRL.1]

Advances and acceptances: total facilities outstanding and percentage utilisation		UK	Annual	[QRL.1]	2.4.3.1
Lending under special scheme for exports and shipbuilding		UK	Annual	[QRL.1]	2.4.3.1
Loans and commitments to Licenses for North Sea Oil Development		UK	Annual	[QRL.1]	2.4.3.1 Another source is [QRL.5]
Number of accounts	Current, deposit and savings accounts	UK	Annual	[QRL.1]	2.4.3.1
Number of cheque controls in issue		UK	Annual	[QRL.1]	2.4.3.1
Credit Card: Barclaycard	Cardholders, merchants, interest charges, cash advances, cheque encashment, fraud, company Barclaycard and Barclays Premier Card	UK	Annual	[QRL.9]	2.4.3.1 Other sources are [QRL.1] and [QRL.23]
Credit Card: Access	Credit outstanding, number of cards issued, number of accounts, number of UK outlets and value of turnover	UK	Annual	[QRL.1]	2.4.3.1 Another source is [QRL.23]
Credit Card: Trustcard	Cardholders, regional breakdown of credit card ownership, socieconomic profiles of credit cardholders; sex of credit cardholders and age and income profiles	UK	Annual	[QRL.23]	2.4.3.1
Clearing statistics	Volume and value of credit and debit clearing, town clearing, automated items and electronic credit transfers through CHAPS	UK	Annual	[QRL.1]	2.4.3.1 Another source is [QRL.2]. Historical dates in GB. in [B.10] 1880-1966 and UK data in [B.3] 1870-1982
Information on each of the London and Scottish Banks					

Type of data	Breakdown	Area	Frequency	QRL Publication	Text Reference
Annual accounts: individual group data	Group pretax profits and outstanding group provisions	UK	Annual	[QRL.1]	2.4.3.1 Another source is the individual bank Annual Reports and Accounts
Number of branches	Full and sub-branches	UK	Annual	[QRL.1]	2.4.3.1
Number of staff	Male and female	UK	Annual	[QRL.1]	2.4.3.1
Number of cash dispensers		UK	Annual	[QRL.1]	2.4.3.1
Volume of transactions		UK	Annual	[QRL.1]	2.4.3.1
Volume of cash withdrawals		UK	Annual	[QRL.1]	2.4.3.1
Northern Ireland Banks					
Balance sheet	Liabilites are split into monetary, public, private and overseas sectors and certificates of deposit and subdivided into sterling and other currencies. Assets are split into balances with the Bank of England, market loans, bills, advances and investments and subdivided between sterling and other currencies	UK	Monthly	[QRL.29]	2.4.3.2 [QRL.5] gives also data up to Sept 1983. Databank [QRL.1] monthly May 1975 - Aug 1983. Historical dates on Joint-Stock Banks of Ireland in [B.10] 1880-1920 Historical data for deposits, notes, inter-bank deposits, clearings and reserves in [B.3] 1870-1982
Advances	By sector	NI	Monthly	[QRL.29]	2.4.3.2
Trustee Savings Banks					
Deposits		UK	Monthly	[QRL.5]	2.4.3.3 This series ended in January 1982. Historical dates in [B.3] 1880-1967
Consumer Credit		UK	Quarterly	[QRL.24]	2.4.3.3 This series ended in January 1982
Loans of house purchase		UK	Quarterly	[QRL.24]	2.4.3.3 This series ended in January 1982
Number of accounts		UK	Annual	[QRL.36]	2.4.3.3 This series ended in 1982
Customer balances	Cheque accounts, savings accounts, and investment accounts	UK	Annual	[QRL.36]	2.4.3.3 This series ended in 1982

The Banking Department of the Bank of England					
Balance sheet	Liabilities are split into public deposits, special deposits, bankers' deposits, and reserves and other accounts. Assets are split into government securities, advances and other accounts, premises, equipment and other securities and notes and coins	UK	Monthly	[QRL.5]	2.4.3.4 Another source is [QRL.24] Historical dates in [B.10] 1880-1966 and for certain items in [B.3] 1870-1982
Accepting Houses					
Balance sheet	Liabilities are split into monetary, public, private and overseas sectors and certificates of deposit and subdivided into sterling and other currencies; assets are split into balances with the Bank of England, market loans, bills, advances and investments and subdivided between sterling and other currencies	UK	Monthly	[QRL.4]	2.4.4 Another source is [QRL.5] Databank [QRL.5] monthly from May 1975
Analysis of sterling business	By maturity and sector	UK	Quarterly	[QRL.5]	2.4.4 and 2.4.1
Bank lending to UK residents	By economic activity	UK	Quarterly	[QRL.6]	2.4.4 and 2.4.2
Other British Banks					
Balance sheet	Liabilities are split into monetary, public, private and overseas sectors and certificates of deposit and subdivided into sterling and other currencies; assets are split into balances with the Bank of England, market loans, bills, advances and investments and subdivided between sterling and other currencies	UK	Monthly	[QRL.4]	2.4.5 and 2.4.4. Other sources include [QRL.5]. Databank [QRL.5] monthly from May 1975. Historical data for the principal non-clearing retail banks for deposits, reserves and some other items are available from [B.3] 1870-1982
Analysis of sterling business	By maturity and by sector	UK	Quarterly	[QRL.5]	2.4.5 and 2.4.4

Type of data	Breakdown	Area	Frequency	QRL Publication	Text Reference
Bank lending to UK residents	By economic activity	UK	Quarterly	[QRL.6]	2.4.5 and 2.4.4
American Banks					
Balance sheet	Liabilities are split into monetary, public, private and overseas sectors and certificates of deposit are subdivided into sterling and other currencies, assets are split into balances with the Bank of England, market loans, bills, advances and investments and subdivided between sterling and other currencies	UK	Monthly	[QRL.4]	2.4.6 Another source is [QRL.5]. Databank [QRL.5] monthly from May 1975
Analysis of Sterling and foreign currency business	By maturity and by sector	UK	Quarterly	[QRL.5]	2.4.6 and 2.4.1
Bank lending to UK residents	By economic activity	UK	Quarterly	[QRL.6]	2.4.6 and 2.4.2
Japanese Banks					
Balance sheet	Liabilities are split into monetary, public, private and overseas sectors and certificates of deposit are subdivided into sterling and other currencies. Assets are split into balances with the Bank of England etc.	UK	Monthly	[QRL.4]	2.4.7 Another source is [QRL.5]. Databank [QRL.5] monthly from May 1975
Analysis of sterling and foreign currency business	By maturity and by sector	UK	Quarterly	[QRL.5]	2.4.7 and 2.4.1
Bank lending to UK residents	By economic activity	UK	Quarterly	[QRL.6]	2.4.7 and 2.4.2
Other Overseas Banks					

Balance sheet	Liabilities are split into monetary, public, private and overseas sectors and certificates of deposit and subdivided into sterling and other currencies; assets are split into balances with the Bank of England, market loans, bills, advances and investments and subdivided between sterling and other currencies	UK	Monthly	[QRL.4]	2.4.8 Another source is [QRL.5]. Databank [QRL.5] monthly from May 1975
Analysis of sterling and foreign currency business	By maturity and by sector	UK	Quarterly	[QRL.5]	2.4.8 and 2.4.1
Bank lending to UK residents	By economic activity	UK	Quarterly	[QRL.6]	2.4.8 and 2.4.2
Consortium Banks					
Balance sheet	Libailities are split into monetary, public, private and overseas sectors and certificates of deposit and subdivided into sterling and other currencies; assets are split into balances with the Bank of England, market loans, bills, advances and investments and subdivied between sterling and other currencies	UK	Monthly	[QRL.4]	2.4.9 Another source is [QRL.5]. Databank [QRL.5] monthly from May 1975
Analysis of sterling and foreign currency business	By maturity and by sector	UK	Quarterly	[QRL.5]	2.4.9 and 2.4.1
Bank lending to UK residents	By economic activity	UK	Quarterly	[QRL.6]	2.4.9 and 2.4.2
Discount Market					
Balance sheet	Liabilities are split into monetary sector, other UK and overseas and subdivied between sterling and other currencies; assets are split into bills, funds lent, investments and subdivided between sterling and other currencies	UK	Monthly	[QRL.4]	2.4.10 Other sources include [QRL.5], [QRL.24] and [QRL.2]. Databank [QRL.5] monthly from May 1975

Type of data	Breakdown	Area	Frequency	QRL Publication	Text Reference
Assets and Liabilities: Finance Houses					
Finance Houses in GB					
Balance sheets	Assets are split into current assets, loans and advances, company and government securities, other financial assets and physical assets. Liabilites are split into borrowing, other current liabilities, capital issues and reserves	GB	Quarterly	[QRL.24]	3.3.1 and 3.4.1 Other sources include [QRL.16] and [QRL.2]. Historical data in [B.10] 1920-1966
Hire Purchase and Other Credit Business	By type of agreement	GB	Monthly	[QRL.24]	3.3.2 and 3.4.1 Other sources include [QRL.15], [QRL.21], [QRL.27], [QRL.2] and [QRL.18]
Finance Houses in NI					
Hire Purchase and Other Credit Business	New credit extended and repayments	NI	Quarterly	[QRL.29]	3.3.3 and 3.4.2
New Credit Extended	By type of good	NI	Quarterly	[QRL.29]	3.3.3 and 3.4.2
Assets and Liabilites: Building Societies					
Liabilities and Assets	Liabilities are divided into shares and deposits, interest accrued but not credited, official loans and currencies. Assets are divided into mortgages, short-term assets, British government securities, local authority long-term debt and overseas government securities	UK	Quarterly	[QRL.24]	4.2.1 and 4.3 Other sources include [QRL.11] and [QRL.2]. Historical data in GB in [B.10] 1880-1967; in [QRL.17] 1890-
Shares and deposits	Receipts of principal, withdrawals, net inflow and interest	UK	Monthly	[QRL.24]	4.2.1 and 4.3 Other sources include [QRL.11]. Historical data in [QRL.30] 1900-1970
Commitments and mortgage advances	By type of dwelling	UK	Monthly	[QRL.24]	4.2.2 and 4.3 Other sources include [QRL.11] and [QRL.26]
Loans for house purchase	By type of institution	UK	Quarterly	[QRL.24]	4.2.2 and 4.3 Other sources include [QRL.11] and [QRL.17]

Distribution of mortgages	With respect to age of borrower, previous tenure of borrower, type of mortgage, income of borrower, age of dwellings, type of dwellings, mortgage amounts and deposits of borrowers	UK	Annual	[QRL.11]	4.3
Regional loan figures	By first-time buyers, new houses, average house price, average advance and average income of borrowers	UK	Quarterly	[QRL.11]	4.3 Other sources include [QRL.17]
Loans to first-time buyers	By the average dwelling price, average advance and average income	UK	Quarterly	[QRL.11]	4.3 Other sources include [QRL.17]
Structure of Building Societies	Changes in the Register of Building Societies, changes in the distributions of assets and changes in the degree of concentration	UK	Annual	[QRL.14]	4.3
Number of Building Societies, investors and borrowers		UK	Annual	[QRL.17]	7.2.7 and 7.2.8 Historical data in [QRL.17] and [QRL.14] 1890 onwards
Branches		UK	Annual	[QRl.14]	4.1.2 and 4.3
Staff		UK	Annual	[QRL.14]	4.3
Number of mortgages	Size, deposit, income of borrowers and price of dwelling	W	Annual	[QRL.20]	4.3
Shares and deposits	Receipts of principal, withdrawals and interest	NI	Quarterly	[QRL.29]	4.3
Advances	New houses, other houses	UK	Quarterly	[QRL.29]	4.3
Repayments	Principal, interest	NI	Quarterly	[QRL.29]	4.3
Interest Rates					
UK Banks					
Interbank rate		UK	Daily	[QRL.25]	5.2 Other sources include [QRL.5], [QRL.24] and [QRL.2]. Databank [QRL.5] weekly from Oct 1977
Sterling Certificate and Deposit		UK	Daily	[QRL.25]	5.2 Other sources include [QRL.5] and [QRL.24]. Databank [QRL.5] weekly from Oct 1977
Selected Retail Banks					
Base Rates		UK	Date of change	[QRL.24]	5.2 Other sources include [QRL.5] and [QRL.2]. Databank [QRL.5] weekly from October 1977

Type of data	Breakdown	Area	Frequency	QRL Publication	Text Reference
Seven day deposit rate		UK	Weekly	[QRL.24]	5.2 Other sources include [QRL.5]. Databank [QRL.5] weekly from Oct 1977. Historical data in [B.3] 1870-1982
Call Money		UK	Weekly	[QRL.24]	5.2 Other sources include [QRL.5]. Databank [QRL.5] weekly from October 1977. Historical data in [B.3] 1870-1982 and [B.10] 1891-1908 and 1919-1966
Discount Houses					
Treasury Bill Tender		UK	Weekly	[QRL.24]	5.2.2 Other sources include [QRL.5] and [QRL.2]. Databank [QRL.5] weekly from October 1977. Historical data in [B.3] 1870-1982 and [B.10] 1900-1966
Trade' Bill rate		UK	Weekly	[QRL.24]	5.2.2 Other sources include [QRL.5] and [QRL.24]. Databank [QRL.5] weekly from October 1977
Eligible bank bill rate		UK	Weekly	[QRL.24]	5.2.2 Other sources include [QRL.5] and [QRL.2]. Databank [QRL.5] weekly from October 1977
Finance Houses					
Base Rate		UK	Monthly	[QRL.24]	5.3 Other sources include [QRL.25]
Shares, Deposits and Mortgage Advances		UK	Annual	[QRL.24]	5.4 Historical data in [QRL.17] 1900-
Building Societies					
New rates on new mortgages to owner occupiers; deposits and ordinary shares		UK	Recommended or advised effective date	[QRL.24]	5.4 Other sources include [QRL.16]. Historical data in [QRL.17] 1900-
Monetary Aggregates and Their Counterparts					

Average rates paid on shares, deposits and charged on mortgage advances	UK	Monthly	[QRL.24]	5.4 Historical data in [QRL.17] 1920-
Amounts Outstanding, M0, M1, Sterling M3, M3 and M2	UK	Monthly	[QRL.5]	6.2.1, 6.2.3, 6.2.4, 6.2.5, 6.4 and 6.4.1. Other sources include [QRL.24]. Databank [QRL.5] monthly M0 from July 1969; monthly M, and Sterling M3 from Jan 1972; monthly M3 from May 1975; monthly M2 from Nov 1981. Quarterly figures are available for M1, Sterling M3 and M3 from 1963. The same information applies to databank [QRL.24]. Historical data in [B.3] going back to 1870
Changes in M0, M1, sterling M3, M3 and M2	UK	Monthly	[QRL.5]	6.2.1, 6.2.3, 6.2.4, 6.2.5, 6.4 and 6.4.1. Other sources include [QRL.24]. Information on databank as given above
Counterparts to changes in money stock	UK	Monthly	[QRL.5]	6.2.2, 6.2.4, 6.4 and 6.4.1. Other sources include [QRL.24]. Databank [QRL.5] quarterly from 1963; monthly May 1975
Amounts outstanding, PSL, and PSL2	UK	Monthly	[QRL.5]	6.3, 6.4 and 6.4.3. Other sources include [QRL.24]. Databank [QRL.5] quarterly from 1963; monthly from June 1975
Changes, PSL1 and PSL2	UK	Monthly	[QRL.5]	6.3, 6.4 and 6.4.3. Other sources include [QRL.24]

QUICK REFERENCE LIST KEY TO PUBLICATIONS

Reference	Author or Organisation	Title	Publisher	Frequency or Date	Remarks
[QRL.1]	Committee of London and Scottish Bankers Statistical Unit	*Abstract of Banking Statistics*	Committee of London and Scottish Bankers	Annual	First came out in April 1984
[QRL.2]	Central Statistical Office	*Annual Abstract of Statistics*	HMSO, London	Annual	
[QRL.3]	The Economics and Statistics Department, The Building Societies Association	*Annual Report*	The Building Societies Association	Annual 1980-1983	In 1984 it was superseded by *Building Society Fact Book* [QRL.14]
[QRL.4]	Financial Statistics Division of the Bank of England	*Bank of England Monthly Press Release*	Bank of England	Monthly	
[QRL.5]	Financial Statistics Division of the Bank of England	*Bank of England Quarterly Bulletin*	Bank of England	Quarterly	First published in 1960
[QRL.6]	Financial Statistics Division of the Bank of England	*Bank of England Quarterly Press Release*	Bank of England	Quarterly	
[QRL.7]	Financial Statistics Division of the Bank of England	*Bank of England Statisical Abstract*	Bank of England	1971, 1975	
[QRL.8]	Economic Intelligence Dept, Bank of England	*Bank of England Statistical Summary*	Bank of England	Monthly	In 1946 it was superceded by the *Monthly Digest of Statistics* [QRL.27]
[QRL.9]	Barclays Bank	*Barclaycard Fact Sheet*	Barclays Bank	Annual	
[QRL.10]	London Cambridge Economic Service	*The British Economy key Statistics*	Times Newspapers Ltd	One publication	
[QRL.11]	The Economics and Statistics Dept, The Buildings Societies Association	*Building Societiies Association Bulletin*	The Building Societies Association	Quarterly	From October 1978. Formerly *Facts and Figures* [QRL.22]

[QRL.12]	Economics and Statistics Dept, The Buildings Society Association	*Building Societies Association Monthly Press Release*	The Building Societies Association	Monthly	
[QRL.13]		*Building Societies Year Book*	Franey and Co Ltd	Annual	
[QRL.14]	The Economics and Statistics Dept, The Buildings Societies Association	*Building Society Fact Book*	The Building Societies Association	Annual	From 1984. Formerly *Annual Report.* [QRL.3]
[QRL.15]	Department of Trade and Industry	*Business Monitor SDM6*	HMSO, London	Monthly	
[QRL.16]	Department of Trade and Industry	*Business Monitor SDQ7*	HMSO, London	Quarterly	
[QRL.17]	Economics and Statistics Department, The Building Societies Association	*Conpendium of Building Societies Statistics*	The Building Societies Association	1978, 1979, 1980, 1982, 1984, 1985	
[QRL.18]	Finance Houses Association	*Credit*	Finance Houses Association	Quarterly	
[QRL.19]	Dept of Finance and Personnel for Northern Ireland	*Digest of Statistics Northern Ireland*	HMSO Northern Ireland Office	Annual	In 1982 it was superseded by *Northern Ireland Annual Abstract of Statistics* [QRL.29]
[QRL.20]	Welsh Office	*Digest of Welsh Statistics*	HMSO Cardiff	Annual	
[QRL.21]	Central Statistical Office	*Economic Trends*	HMSO London	Monthly	
[QRL.22]	The Economics and Statistics Dept, The Building Societies Association	*Facts and Figures*	The Buildings Societies Association	Quarterly	In Oct 1978 it was superseded by BSA Bulletin
[QRL.23]	Trustee Savings Bank	*The Feature Writer's Guide to Credit Cards*	Trustee Saving Bank	Annual	
[QRL.24]	Central Statistical Office	*Financial Statistics*	HMSO London	Monthly	First published in 1962
[QRL.25]		*Financial Times*	Financial Times Ltd	Daily	

Reference	Author or Organisation	Title	Publisher	Frequency or Date	Remarks
[QRL.26]	Department of Environment	*Housing and Construction Statistics*	HMSO London	Quarterly	
[QRL.27]	Central Statistical Office	*Monthly Digest of Statistics*	HMSO London	Monthly	
[QRL.28]	Committee of London and Scottish Bankers	*Monthly Statement of the London and Scottish Banks*	Committee of London and Scottish Bankers	Monthly	
[QRL.29]	Dept of Finance and Personnel for Northern Ireland	*The Northern Ireland Annual Abstract of Statistics*	HMSO Northern Ireland Office	Annual	From 1982. Formerly *Digest of Statistics Northern Ireland* [QRL.19]
[QRL.30]	Dept of Finance and Personnel for Northern Ireland	*The Northern Ireland Housing Statistics*	HMSO Belfast	Annual	
[QRL.31]		*Report of the Chief Registrar of Friendly Societies*	HMSO London	Annual	
[QRL.32]	Government Statistical Service	*Scottish Abstract of Statistics*	HMSO for Scottish Office	Annual	
[QRL.33]	Scottish Office	*Scottish Economic Bulletin*	HMSO Edinburgh	Biannual	
[QRL.34]	HM Treasury	*TSBs: Annual Report*	HMSO London	Annual	
[QRL.35]	TSB Central Branch	*TSB's Year Book*	TSB Central Board	Annual	The last publication was in 1982

BIBLIOGRAPHY

[B.1] Boleat, M. *The Building Society Industry*. Allen and Unwin, London, 1982

[B.2] Burman, J.P. *Journal of Royal Statistical Society*. Series A, Vol. 143, Part 3, 1980 P.321

[B.3] Capie, F. and Webber, A. *A Monetary History of the U.K, 1870-1982, Vol I: Dates, Sources and Methods*. George Allen & Unwin, 1985

[B.4] Dicks, G.R. *Sources of World Financial and Banking Information*. Gower Publishing Company Limited, 1981

[B.5] Drury, A.C and Ferrier C.W. *Credit Cards*. Butterworths & Co. Ltd, London, 1984

[B.6] Evans, A.W. "The Five Per Cent Sample Survey of Building Society Mortgages." *Studies in Official Statistics*, HMSO. No.26, 1975

[B.7] Farthing, S.M. "Housing in Great Britain" in *Reviews of UK Statistical Sources* Heinemannn Educational Books, 1974

[B.8] Fforde, J.S. "Competition, Innovation and Regulation in British Banking." *Bank of England Quarterly Bulletin*. Vol.23, No 3, 1983

[B.9] Johnson, H. *British Monetary Statistics*. Economica, Vol. XXIV, February 1959

[B.10] Sheppard, D.K. *The Growth and Role of U.K Financial Institutions, 1880-1962*. Methuen & Co. Ltd, London 1971

[B.11] *Bank of England Quarterly Bulletin*. "Changes in Monetary Aggregates and the Analysis of Bank Lending. "Vol.24, No.1, 1984

[B.12] *Bank of England Quarterly Bulletin*. "Competition and Credit Control." Vol.11, No.2, 1971

[B.13] *Bank of England Quarterly Bulletin*. "Components of Private Sector Liquidity." Vol.19, No.3, 1979

[B.14] *Bank of England Quarterly Bulletin* "Consolidated Supervision of Institutions Authorised under the Banking Act 1979". Vol 26, No 1, 1986

[B.15] *Bank of England Quarterly Bulletin*. "Domestic Credit Expansion." Vol.23, No.2, 1983

[B.16] *Bank of England Quarterly Bulletin*. "DCE and the Money Supply. A Statistical Note." Vol.17, No.1, 1977

[B.17] *Bank of England Quarterly Bulletin*. "Foreign Currency Exposure." Vol.21, No.2, 1981

[B.18] *Bank of England Quarterly Bulletin*. "The Liquidity of Banks." Vol.21, No.1, 1981

[B.19] *Bank of England Quarterly Bulletin*. "The measurement of Capital." Vol.20, No.3, 1980

[B.20] *Bank of England Quarterly Bulletin* "The Measurement of Liquidity" Vol 22, No 3, 1982

[B.21] *Bank of England Quarterly Bulletin*. "The Monetary base - A Statistical Note." Vol.21, No.1, 1981

[B.22] *Bank of England Quarterly Bulletin* "Monetary Control: Next Steps" Vol 21, No 1, 1981

[B.23] *Bank of England Quarterly Bulletin*. "Monetary Control Provisions." Vol.21, No.3, 1981

[B.24] *Bank of England Quarterly Bulletin*. "New Banking Statistics." Vol.15, No.2, 1975

[B.25] *Bank of England Quarterly Bulletin* " Purposes of Banking Statistics". Vol 21, No 3, 1981

[B.26] *Bank of England Quarterly Bulletin*. "Recent Developments in Equipment Leasing." Vol.22, No.3, 1982

[B.27] *Bank of England Quarterly Bulletin*. "Reserve Ratios: Further Definitions." Vol.11, No.4, 1971

[B.28] *Bank of England Quarterly Bulletin.* "Review of Banking Statistics." Vol.23, No.1, 1983
[B.29] *Bank of England Quarterly Bulletin.* "Seasonal Adjustment of Monthly Money Series." Vol.18, No.2, 1978
[B.30] *Bank of England Quarterly Bulletin.* "Seasonal Adjustment of Money and its Counterparts." Vol.21, No.3, 1981
[B.31] *Bank of England Quarterly Bulletin.* "Seasonal Adjustment of Money and its Counterparts." Vol.23, No.2, 1983
[B.32] *Bank of England Quarterly Bulletin.* "Setting Monetary Objectives." Vol.23, No.2, 1983
[B.33] *Bank of England Quarterly Bulletin.* "Transactions Balances - a New Monetary Aggregate." Vol.22, No.2, 1982
[B.34] *Bank of England Quarterly Bulletin.* "U.K Banks' External Liabilities and Claims in Sterling: Geographical Analysis." Vol.23, No.3, 1983
[B.35] *The Banker.* The Banker Division of Financial Times Ltd.
[B.36] *The Bankers' Magazine.* BPC (The Bankers' Magazine) Ltd.
[B.37] *The Banking World.* Journal of the Institute of Bankers, Waterlow Publishers
[B.38] Building Societies Association. *Building Societies: A New Framework.* October, 1984
[B.39] Government Green Paper. *Building Societies: A New Framework.* Cmnd 9316. HMSO, London, July 1984
[B.40] *Building Societies Association Bulletin.* "Building Society Branching," No.36, 1983
[B.41] *Building Societies Association Bulletin.* "Concentration and Mergers in the Building Society Industry," No.36, 1983
[B.42] *Building Societies Association Bulletin.* "Wholesale Funding" No.36, 1983
[B.43] *Business Monitor: Consumer Credit Grantors.* M13
[B.44] *Euromoney* Euromoney publications, London
[B.45] *Evidence Submitted to the Building Societies Association to the Committee to Review the Functioning of Financial Institutions* The Building Societies Association. 1978.
[B.46] Central Statistical Office. *Financial Statistics Explanatory Handbook.* HMSO, London, 1986
[B.47] Central Statistical Office. *Guide to Official Statistics.* HMSO, London, 1982
[B.48] Cental Statistical Office. *Indexes to the Industrial Classification, Revised 1980.* HMSO, London, 1980
[B.49] Committee of London Clearing Bankers. *The London Clearing Banks.* Longmans Group Ltd, London, 1978
[B.50] Government Green Paper. *Monetary Control.* Cmnd 7858. HMSO, London, March 1980
[B.51] Radcliffe Committee. *Report of the Committee on the Workings of the Monetary System.* Cmnd 827. HMSO, London 1959
[B.52] Macmillan Committee.*Report on Finance and Industry.* Cmnd 3897. HMSO, London, 1931.
[B.53] Wilson Committee. *Report on the Functioning of Financial Institutions,* Cmnd 7937. HMSO 1980
[B.54] Monopolies and Mergers Commission. *Report on the Supply of Credit Card Franchise Services in the United Kingdom* Cmnd 8034. HMSO, London, 1980
[B.55] Bank of England. *United Kingdom Flow of Funds Account: 1963-1976.* May 1978.

LIST OF APPENDICES

APPENDIX I

INSTITUTIONS FORMING THE MONETARY SECTOR (at 16 February 1984)

Retail Banks
Adam & Company plc
Allied Irish Banks Ltd
The Bank of Ireland
Bank of Scotland
Banking Dept of the Bank of England
Barclays Bank plc
Central Trustee Savings Bank Ltd
Clydesdale Bank plc
Co-operative Bank plc
Coutts & Co
Lloyds Bank plc
Midland Bank plc
National Girobank
National Westminster Bank plc
Northern Bank Ltd
The Royal Bank of Scotland plc
Trustee Savings Banks
Ulster Bank Ltd
Williams & Glynn's Bank plc
Yorkshire Bank plc

Accepting Houses
Baring Brothers & Co Ltd
Brown, Shipley & Co Ltd
Brown, Shipley (Guernsey) Ltd
Brown, Shipley (Jersey) Ltd
Charterhouse Japhet plc
Charterhouse Japhet (Jersey) Ltd
Robert Fleming & Co Ltd
Guinness Mahon & Co Ltd
Guinness Mahon Guernsey Ltd
Hambros Bank Ltd
Hambros Bank (Guernsey) Ltd
Hambros Bank (Jersey) Ltd
Hill Samuel & Co Ltd
Hill Samuel & Co (Guernsey) Ltd
Hill Samuel & Co (Jersey) Ltd
Kleinwort, Benson Ltd
Kleinwort, Benson (Channel Islands) Ltd
Kleinwort, Benson (Guernsey) Ltd
Kleinwort, Benson (Isle of Man) Ltd
Lazard Brothers & Co Ltd
Lazard Brothers & Co (Jersey) Ltd
Samuel Montagu & Co Ltd
Samuel Montagu & Co (Jersey) Ltd
Morgan Grenfell & Co Ltd
Morgan Grenfell & (Guernsey) Ltd
Morgan Grenfell (Jersey) Ltd
Rea Brothers plc
Rea Brothers (guernsey) Ltd
Rea Brothers (Isle of Man) Ltd
N.M. Rothschild & Sons Ltd
N.M. Rothschild & Sons (C.I.) Ltd
J. Henry Schroder Wagg & Co Ltd
Singer & Friedlander Ltd
Singer & Friedlander (Isle of Man) Ltd
S.G. Warburg & Co Ltd
S.G. Warburg & Co (Jersey) Ltd

Other British Banks
A1 (Investments) Ltd
A P Bank Ltd
Abbey Finance Co Ltd
Aitken Hume Ltd
Aitken Hume (Guernsey) Ltd
Al Baraka International Ltd
The Alliance Trust plc
Henry Ansbacher & Co Ltd
Armada Investments Ltd
Assemblies of God Property Trust
Associated Credits Ltd
Auban Finance Ltd
B.C.F. Finance Co Ltd
BMI (Hampshire) Ltd
Bank of London & South America Ltd
The Baptist Union Corporation Ltd
Barclays Bank Finance Company (Jersey) Ltd
Barclays Bank International Ltd
Barclays Bank Trust Company Ltd
Barclays Bank UK Ltd
Barclays Finance Company (Guernsey) Ltd
Barclays Finance Company (Isle of Man) Ltd
Barclays Merchant Bank Ltd
Thomas Barlow & Bros Ltd
Beaver Investments Ltd
Bradford Investments
Bremar Holdings Ltd
Bridgeover Ltd

Bridgeway Finance Ltd
The British Linen Bank Ltd
Brook Securities & Co Ltd
Buchanan Securities Ltd
Bucks Land & Building Co Ltd
Bunge & Co Ltd
Burns-Anderson Trust Company Ltd
Business Mortgages Trust plc
Calculus Finance plc
Castle Court Trust Ltd
Castle Philips Finance Co Ltd
Cattles Holdings Finance Ltd
Cayzer Ltd
Cedar Holdings Ltd
Century Factors Ltd
Chancery Securities plc
Charter Consolidated Financial Services Ltd
The Chartered Bank
Chartered Trust plc
Charterhouse Japhet Credit Ltd
Chesterfield Street Trust Ltd
CP Choularton, Sons & Partners Ltd
City Trust Ltd
Close Brothers Ltd
Clydesdale Bank Finance Corporation Ltd
Cobnar Finance Co Ltd
Combined Capital Ltd
Commercial Bank of Wales plc
Consolidated Credits & Discounts Ltd
The Continental Trust Ltd
Co-operative Bank (Commercial) Ltd
County Bank Ltd
Coutts Finance Co
Craneheath Securities Ltd
Cross & Bevingtons (Finance) Ltd
Cue & Co
Dalbeattie Finance Co Ltd
Darlington Merchant Credits Ltd
Dartington & Co Ltd
The Dorset, Somerset & Wilts Investment Society Ltd
Dryfield Finance Ltd
Dunbar & Co Ltd
Duncan Lawrie Ltd
Dunsterville Allen plc
E.T. Trust Ltd
Eagil Trust & Co Ltd
East Anglian Securities Trust Ltd
East Midlands Finance Co Ltd
Eastcheap Investments Ltd
Eccles Savings and Loans Ltd
The English Association Trust Ltd
Ensign Discount Co Ltd
Equatorial Trust Corporation Ltd
Everett Chettle Associates
Exeter Trust Ltd
F & C Management Ltd
Fairmount Trust Ltd
Family Finance Ltd
Farmers (WCF) Finance Ltd
Federated Trust Corporation Ltd
Financial and General Securities Ltd
James Finlay Corporation Ltd
Finova Finance Ltd
First Co-operative Finance Ltd
First Indemnity Credit Ltd
First National Securities Ltd
Forward Trust Ltd
Robert Fraser & Partners Ltd
Gillespie Bros & Company Ltd
Goode Durrant Trust plc
Granville Finance Ltd
H.T. Greenwood Ltd
Greetwell Finance Ltd
Gresham Trust plc
Grindlay Brandts Ltd
Grindlays Bank plc
Grindlays Bank (Jersey) Ltd
Grindlays Humberclyde Ltd
Grindlays Industrial Finance Ltd
Grosvenor Acceptances Ltd
Gulf Guarantee Trust Ltd
H & J Finance Co (Midlands) Ltd
Hanson Guernsey Ltd
The Hardware Federation Finance Co Ltd
Harrods Trust Ltd
Harton Securities Ltd
The Heritable & General Trust Ltd
C. Hoare & Co
Hobart Securities Ltd
Holdenhurst Securities Ltd
Industrial Finance and Investment Corporation plc
Industrial Funding Trust Ltd
International Westminster Bank plc
Investment Trustees Ltd
Investors in Industry plc
Investors in Industry Group plc
Jabac Finances Ltd
Johnson Matthey Bankers Ltd
Leopold Joseph & Sons Ltd
Leopold Joseph & Sons (Guernsey) Ltd
Kingsnorth Trust Ltd
Kintyre Securities Ltd
Knowsley & Co Ltd
K.S. Consumer Credit Finance Ltd
LBI Finance (Jersey) Ltd
Little Lakes Finance Ltd
Lloyds Bowmaker Ltd
Lloyds & Scottish plc
Lloyds Bank International Ltd
Lloyds Bank International (France) Ltd

Lloyds Bank (LABCO) Ltd
Lodhi Finance Ltd
Lombard Acceptances Ltd
Lombard & Ulster Ltd
Lombard Bank (Isle of Man) LTtd
Lombard Banking (Jersey) Ltd
Lombard North Central plc
Lombard Street Investment Trust Co Ltd
London and Arab Investments Ltd
London Law Securities Ltd
London Scottish Finance Corporation plc
Lordsvale Finance Ltd
McNeill Pearson Ltd
Mallinhall Ltd
Manchester Exchange Trust Ltd
W.M. Mann & Co (Investments) Ltd
Edward Manson & Co Ltd
The Mardun Investment Co Ltd
Medens Trust Ltd
Meghraj & Sons Ltd
Mercantile Credit Company Ltd
Mercury Provident Society Ltd
Merseyside Finance Ltd
The Methodist Chapel Aid Association Ltd
Midland Bank Finance Corporation Ltd
Midland Bank Industrial Equity Holdings Ltd
Midland Bank Trust Company Ltd
Midland Bank Trust Corporation (Guernsey) Ltd
Midland Bank Trust Corporation (Isle of Man) Ltd
Midland Bank Trust Corporation (Jersey) Ltd
Milford Mutual Facilities Ltd
Minster Trust Ltd
Moneycare Ltd
Moorgate Mercantile Holdings plc
Mortgage Management & Investments Ltd
Mount Credit Corporation Ltd
Musket Finance Ltd
Mynshul Trust Ltd
N.I.I.B. Group Ltd
The National Bank of New Zealand Ltd
National Commercial & Glyns Ltd
National Guardian Finance Corporation Ltd
National Westminster Bank Finance (C.I.) Ltd
Noble Grossart Ltd
The North of Scotland Finance Co Ltd
North West Securities Ltd
Northern Bank Development Corporation ltd
Northern Bank Executor & Trustee Company Ltd
Northern Ireland Industrial Bank (I.O.M.) Ltd
Norwich General Trust Ltd
Oppenheimer Money Management Ltd
PL Investments & Savings Ltd
P.S. Refson & Co Ltd
Park Street Securities Ltd
The People's Trust & Savings Ltd
Pointon York Ltd
Prestwick Investment Trust plc
Ralli Investment Compant Ltd
R. Raphael & Sons plc
Rathbone Bros. & Co
Reliance Trust Ltd
Rhone Trust Ltd
Roxburghe Guarantee Corporation Ltd
S.P. Finance Ltd
St. Margaret's Trust Ltd
Schroder Leasing Ltd
Shawlands Securities Ltd
Smith & Williamson Securities
South Notts Finance Ltd
Southsea Mortgage & Investment Co Ltd
Spring Gardens Securities plc
Spry Finance Ltd
The Standard Bank plc
Standard Chartered Bank plc
Standard Chartered Merchant Bank Ltd
Standard Credit Services Ltd
Standard Property Investment plc
Sterling Trust Ltd
TCB Ltd
The Teachers & General Investment Co Ltd
Thorncliffe Finance Ltd
Treloan Ltd
Trucanda Trusts Ltd
Tullet and Riley Money Management Ltd
Tyndall & Co
Ulster Bank Trust Company
Ulster Investment Bank Ltd
United Dominions Trust Ltd
Universal Credit Ltd
Barrie Vanger & Co Ltd
Venture Finance Ltd
Vernons Trust Corporation
Wagon Finance Ltd
Wallace, Smith Trust Co Ltd
Welbeck Finance plc
West Riding Securities Ltd
Whiteaway Laidlaw & Co Ltd
Wimbledon & South West Finance Co Ltd
Wintrust Securities Ltd
N.H. Woolley & Co Ltd
Yorkshire Bank Finance Ltd
H.F. Young & Co Ltd

American Banks

Allied Bank International
American National Bank and Trust

Company of Chicago
Bank of America International Ltd
Bank of America N.T & S.A.
The Bank of California N.A.
The Bank of New York
The Bank of Tokyo Trust Company
Bankers Trust Company
Bankers Trust International Ltd
Boston Trust & Savings Ltd
Carolina Bank Ltd
Centerre Bank N.A.
Chase Bank & Trust Company (C.I.) Ltd
Chase Bank (Ireland) Ltd
The Chase Manhatten Bank N.A.
Chase Manhatten Ltd
Chemical Bank
Chemical Bank International Ltd
Citibank N.A.
Citibank Trust Ltd
Citicorp International Bank Ltd
Comerica Bank-Detroit
Continental Illinois Ltd
Continental Illinois National Bank and Trust Company of Chicago
Crocker National Bank
The Fidelity Bank
First City National Bank of Houston
First Interstate Bank of California
The First National Bank of Boston
The First National Bank of Boston (Guernsey) Ltd
First National Bank of Chicago (C.I.) Ltd
The Fisrt National Bank of Chicago
First National Bank of Maryland
First National Bank of Minneapolis
First National Boston Ltd
First Pennsylvania Bank N.A.
First Wisconsion National Bank of Milwaukee
Fleet National Bank
Harris Trust and Savings Bank
Interfirst Bank Dallas N.A.
Irving Trust Company
M.H. Credit Corporation Ltd
Manufacturers Hanover Ltd
Manufacturers Hanover Export Finance Ltd
Manufacutrers Hanover Industrial Finance Ltd
Manufacturers Hanover Trust Company
Marine Midland Bank N.A.
Mellon Bank N.A.
Morgan Guaranty Trust Company of New York
NCNB National Bank of North Carolina
National Bank of Detroit
National Bank of Fort Sam Houston
The Northern Trust Company
Republic Bank Dallas N.A.
Republic National Bank of New York
The Riggs National Bank of Washington D.C.
Seattle-First National Bank
Security Pacific National Bank
Security Pacific Trust Ltd
Texas Commerce Bank N.A.
Texas Commerce International Ltd
Wells Fargo Ltd
Wells Fargo Bank N.A.

Japanese Banks

The Bank of Tokyo Ltd
Bank of Tokyo International Ltd
The Bank of Yokohama Ltd
The Chuo Trust & Banking Company Ltd
The Dai-Ichi Kangyo Bank Ltd
The Daiwa Bank Ltd
The Fuji Bank Ltd
The Hokkaido Takushoku Bank Ltd
IBJ International Ltd
The Industrial Bank of Japan Ltd
The Kyowa Bank Ltd
The Long-Term Credit Bank of Japan Ltd
The Mitsubishi Bank Ltd
The Mitsubishi Trust and Banking Corporation
The Mitsui Bank Ltd
The Mitsui Trust & Banking Company Ltd
The Nippon Credit Bank Ltd
The Saitama Bank Ltd
The Sanwa Bank Ltd
The Sumitomo Bank Ltd
The Sumitomo Trust and Banking Company Ltd
The Taiyo Kobe Bank Ltd
The Tokai Bank Ltd
The Toyo Trust & Banking Company Ltd
The Yasuda Trust and Banking Co Ltd

Other Overseas Banks

Afghan National Credit & Finance Ltd
African Continental Bank Ltd
AK International Ltd
Al Saudi Banque S.A.
Algemene Bank Nederland N.V.
Allied Arab Bank Ltd
Allied Bank of Pakistan Ltd
Allied Banking Corporation
Allied Irish Banks (C.I.) Ltd
Allied Irish Banks (I.O.M.) Ltd
Allied Irish Finance Co Ltd
Allied Irish Investment Bank Ltd
Altajir Ltd
American Express International Banking Corporation

Amsterdam-Rotterdam Bank N.V.
Arab Bank Ltd
Arab Bank Investment Co ltd
Arab Banking Corporation B.S.C.
Arbuthnot Latham Bank Ltd
Armco Trust Ltd
Associates Captial Corporation Ltd
Australia & New Zealand Banking Group Ltd
Australia & New Zealand Banking Group (Channel Islands) Ltd
Avco Trust Ltd
Badische Kommunale Landesbank Girozentrale
Banca Commerciale Italiana
Banca Nazionale del Lavoro
Banca Serfin S.A.
Banco Central S.A.
Banco de Bilbao S.A.
Banco de Jerez S.A.
Banco de la Nacion Argentina
Banco de Santander S.A.
Banco de Vizcaya S.A.
Banco di Roma S.P.A.
Banco di Sicilia
Banco do Brasil S.A.
Banco do Estado de Sao Paulo S.A.
Banco Espirito Santo e Comercial de Lisboa
Banco Exterior-U.K. S.A.
Banco Mercantil de Sao Paulo S.A.
Banco Nacional de Mexico S.N.C.
Banco Portugues do Atlantico
Banco Real S.A.
Banco Totta & Acores E.P.
Bancomer S.N.C.
Bangkok Bank Ltd
Bank Julius Baer & Co Ltd
Bank Bumiputra Malaysia Berhad
Bank Cantrade Switzerland (C.I.) Ltd
Bank fur Gemeinwirtschaft A.G.
Bank Handlowy w Warszawie S.A.
Bank Hapoalim B.M.
Bank Leumi (U.K.) Ltd
Bank Mees & Hope N.V.
Bank Mellat
Bank Melli Iran
Bank of Baroda
Bank of Ceylon
Bank of China
Bank of Credit and Commerce International S.A.
Bank of Cyprus (London) Ltd
Bank of India
Bank of Ireland Finance Ltd
Bank of Ireland Finance (N.I.) Ltd
Bank of Ireland (Jersey) Ltd
Bank of Montreal
Bank of New Zealand
The Bank of Nova Scotia
The Bank of Nova Scotia Channel Islands Ltd
The Bank of Nova Scotia Trust Company (United Kingdom) Ltd
Bank of Oman Ltd
Bank of Seoul & Trust Co
Bank Saderat Iran
Bank Sepah
Bank Tejarat
Banque Belge Ltd
Banque Belgo-Zairoise S.A.
Banque Bruxelles Lambert S.A.
Banque Bruxelles Lambert S.A.
Banque du Liban et d'Outre-Mer
Banque du Rhone et de la Tamise S.A.
Banque Francaise du Commerce Exterieur
Banque Indosuez
Banque Internationale pour l'Afrique Occidentale S.A.
Banque Nationale de Paris plc
Banque Nationale de Paris S.A.
Banque Paribas
Barbados National Bank
Bayerische Hypotheken-und Wechsel-Bank A.G.
Bayerische Landesbank Girozentrale
Bayerische Vereinsbank
Beirut Riyad Bank S.A.L.
Beneficial Trust Ltd
Berliner Bank A.G.
Bilbao International Bank (Jersey) Ltd
The British Bank of Middle East
British Credit Trust Ltd
Byblos Bank S.A.L.
Canadian Imperial Bank of Commerce
Canada Permanent Trust Co (U.K.) Ltd
Cassa di Risparmio delle Provincie Lombarde
Central Bank of India
The Cho-Heung Bank Ltd
CE Coates & Co Ltd
Commercial Bank of Korea Ltd
The Commercial Bank of the Near East plc
Commercial Credit Services Ltd
Commerzbank A.G.
Commonwealth Savings Bank of Australia
Commonwealth Trading Bank of Australia
Credit Commercial de France
Credit du Nord
Credit Industrial et Commercial
Credit Lyonnais
Credit Lyonnais Bank Nederland N.V.
Credit Suisse
Credit Suisse First Boston Ltd

Creditanstalt-Bankverein
Creito Italiano
Cyprus Credit Bank Ltd
Cyprus Finance Corporation (London) Ltd
The Cyprus Popular Bank
Den Danske Bank af 1871 Aktieselskab
Deutsche Bank A.G.
Deutsche Genossenschaftsbank
The Development Bank of Singapore Ltd
Discount Bank (Overseas) Ltd
Dresdner Bank A.G.
FIBI Financial Trust Ltd
First Bank of Nigeria Ltd
Ford Financial Trust Ltd
Ford Motor Credit Co Ltd
French Bank of Southern Africa Ltd
Ghana Commercial Bank
Antony Gibbs & Sons Ltd
Girozentrale und Bank der Osterreichischen Sparkassen A.G.
Goldman Sachs Ltd
Gray Dawes plc
Greyhound Guaranty Ltd
Gulf International Bank B.S.C.
HFC Trust & Savings Ltd
Habib Bank A.G. Zurich
Habib Bank Ltd
Hanil Bank
Havana International Bank Ltd
Hessische Landesbank-Girozentrale
The Hongkong & Shanghai Banking Corporation
The Hongkong & Shanghai Banking Corporation (C.I.) Ltd
Houston Financial Services Ltd
Hungarian International Bank Ltd
International Energy Bank Ltd
The Investment Bank of Ireland Ltd
Isituto Bancario San Paolo di Torino
Italian International Bank Ltd
Italian International (Channel Islands) Ltd
Keesler Federal Credit Union
Korea Exchange Bank
Korea First Bank
Malayan Banking Berhad
Matheson Trust Co Ltd
Mercantile Bank Ltd
Merril Lynch International Bank Ltd
MiddLe East Bank Ltd
Moscow Narodny Bank Ltd
Multibanco Comermex S.N.C.
Muslim Commercial Bank Ltd
National Bank of Abu Dhabi
National Bank of Canada
National Bank of Egypt
National Bank of Greece S.A.
The National Bank of Kuwait S.A.K.
National Bank of Nigeria Ltd
National Bank of Pakistan
National Commercial Banking Corporation of Australia Ltd
Nedbank Ltd
Nederlandsche Middenstansbank N.V.
New Migeria Bank Ltd
Oriental Credit Ltd
Orion Royal Bank Ltd
Orion Royal Bank (Guernsey) Ltd
Oversea-Chinese Banking Corporation Ltd
Overseas Trust Bank Ltd
Overseas Union Bank Ltd
PSP & Company (UK) Ltd
Phibrobank A.G.
Philippine National Bank
Privatbanken Ltd
Punjab & Sind Bank
Punjab National Bank
Qatar National Bank S.A.Q.
Rafidain Bank
Reserve Bank of Australia (London Branch only)
The Royal Bank of Canada
The Royal Bank of Canada (Channel Islands) Ltd
The Royal Trust Company of Canada
The Rural and Industries Bank of Western Australia
Savings Bank of South Australia
Shanghai Commercial Bank Ltd
The Siam Commercial Bank Ltd
Societe de Banque Occidentale
Societe Generale
Societe Generale Bank Ltd
Sonali Bank
State Bank of India
State Bank of New South Wales
State Bank of Victoria
Swiss Bank Corporation
Swiss Bank Corporation International Ltd
Syndicate Bank
The Thai Farmers Bank Ltd
The Toronto-Dominion Bank
Trade Development Bank
Turkish Bank ltd
Turkiye Is Bankasi A.S.
Union Bank of India
Union Bank of Nigeria Ltd
Union Bank of Switzerland
United Bank Ltd
United Commercial Bank
United Mizrahi Bank Ltd
United Overseas Bank Ltd
Volkskas International Ltd

Westdeutsche Landesbank Girozentrale
Western Trust & Savings Ltd
Westpac Banking Corporation
Wurttembergische Kommunale Landesbank Girozentrale
Zambia National Commercial Bank Ltd
Zivnostenska Banka National Corporation

Consortium Banks

Anglo-Romanian Bank Ltd
Anglo-Yugoslav (LDT) Ltd
Associated Japanese Bank (International) Ltd
Atlantic International Bank Ltd
Banco Urquijo Hispano Americano Ltd
Euro-Latinamerican Bank Ltd
European Arab Bank Ltd
European Banking Company Ltd
European Brazilian Bank Ltd
Fenno Scandia Ltd
International Commercial Bank plc
International Mexican Bank Ltd
Iran Overseas Investment Corporation Ltd
Japan International Bank Ltd
Libra Bank Ltd
London & Continental Bankers Ltd
London Interstate Bank Ltd
Nordic Bank plc
PK Christiania Bank (UK) Ltd
Saudi International Bank (Al-Bank Al-Saudi Al-Alami Ltd)
Scandanavian Bank Ltd
UBAF Bank Ltd
The United Bank of Kuwait Ltd

Discount Market

Alexanders Discount plc
Cater Allen Ltd
Clive Discount Company Ltd
Gerrard & National plc
Jessel, Toynbee & Gillett plc
King & Shaxson plc
Gerald Quin, Cope & Co Ltd
Seccombe Marshall & Campion plc
Smith St. Aubyn & Co Ltd
The Union Discount Company of London plc

APPENDIX II

LONDON CLEARING BANKS

Barclays Bank PLC
Barclays Bank International Ltd
Barclays Merchant Bank Ltd
Barclays Bank Finance Co (Jersey) Ltd
Barclays Finance Co (Guernsey) Ltd
Barclays Finance Co (Isle of Man) Ltd
Mercantile Credit Co Ltd
Barclays Bank Trust Company Ltd (from November 1981)
Lloyds Bank PLC
Lloyds Bank (LABCO) Ltd
Lloyds Bank International Ltd (inc. LBI Finance (Jersey) Ltd)
The National Bank of New Zealand Ltd
Lloyds & Scottish Ltd (from November 1981)
Lloyds & Scottish Trust Ltd (from November 1981) merged in January 1984 as Lloyds Bowmaker Ltd
Bowmaker Ltd (from January 1982)
Cedar Holdings Ltd (from November 1981)
Midland Bank PLC
Midland Bank Trust Corporation (Guernsey) Ltd
Midland Bank Trust Corporation (Jersey) Ltd
Midland Bank Trust Corporation (I.O.M.) Ltd (excluded November 1981 –June 1983)
Forward Trust Ltd
Samuel Montagu & Co Ltd
Samuel Montagu (Jersey) Ltd (excluded November 1981 –June 1983)
Crocker National Bank (from November 1981)
National Westminster Bank PLC
Coutts & Co
Coutts Finance Company
County Bank Ltd
Lombard North Central PLC
Lombard Bank (Isle of Man) Ltd (excluded November 1981 –June 1983)
Lombard Banking Jersey (excluded November 1981 –June 1983)
National Westminster Bank Finance (C.I.) Ltd
International Westminster Bank Ltd
Williams & Glynn's PLC

St. Margaret's Trust Ltd (from November 1981)

SCOTTISH CLEARING BANKS

Bank of Scotland
The British Linen Bank Ltd
North-West Securities Ltd (from November 1981)
Clydesdale Bank PLC
The Royal Bank of Scotland PLC
National Commercial & Glyn's Ltd

APPENDIX III
FORM BS

Private and confidential **Form BS**

Balance sheet

as at ______________________________

Reporting institution ______________________________

____

Name (block letters please) and signature of authorised official of reporting institution

In the event of a query, the Bank of England may contact (block letters please)

______________________ Tel no ______________________ Ext ________

Notes on completion

If you have any difficulty in completing this form, please telephone 01-601 4218/4544/4598.

1 Monthly reporters should complete the form as at the last day of the calendar month. Quarterly reporters should complete the form as at the end of March, June, September and December.

2 For definition of items refer to the *Banking statistics definitions folder.*

3 Enter amounts to nearest thousand, omitting £000s.

4 Enter the sterling equivalent of the total of other currencies in Column 2.

5 Items marked * are required for the calculation of eligible liabilities.

6 Return form within **SEVEN CALENDAR DAYS** of reporting date, clearly addressed, to:

FINANCIAL STATISTICS DIVISION
GROUP 2/2 (BB-1)
BANK OF ENGLAND
THREADNEEDLE STREET
LONDON EC2R 8AH

7 Forms may also be delivered to the Reception Desk at the Threadneedle Street entrance of the Bank of England between 9.00 am and 5.00 pm, Monday to Friday. Envelopes should be clearly addressed as above.

(7805)

Bank of England use only

Logged in	Data entered	Amendment book	Amendment input

October 1986

Liabilities

Item no		Sterling: Interest-bearing	Sterling: Non-interest-bearing	£000s Column 1 Sterling	£000s Column 2 Other currencies
1	**Notes in circulation**				
2	**Deposit liabilities**				
2·1	Sight deposits				
2·2	UK monetary sector	•	•	•	
2·4	UK public sector	•	•	•	
2·5	Other UK residents	•	•	•	
2·6	Overseas offices of the reporting institution: gross deposits (excluding working capital)	•	•	•	
2·7	Other overseas residents	•	•	•	
2·8	Time deposits				
2·9	UK monetary sector			•	
2·10	UK public sector				
2·11	Deposits with original maturity of 2 years or less			•	
2·12	Other deposits				
2·13	Other UK residents				
2·14	Deposits with original maturity of 2 years or less			•	
2·15	Other deposits				
2·16	Overseas offices of the reporting institution: gross deposits (excluding working capital)			•	
2·17	Other overseas residents				
2·18	Deposits with original maturity of 2 years or less			•	
2·19	Other deposits				
2·20	Certificates of deposit issued			•	
2·21	Promissory notes, bills and other short-term paper issued			•	
3	**Items in suspense** (excluding internal accounts)			•	
4	**Credit items in course of transmission to**				
4·1	UK offices of the reporting institution			•	
4·2	Other monetary sector institutions in the United Kingdom			•	
4·3	Banks and banking offices overseas				
5	**Capital and other funds**				
5·1	Working capital provided by overseas offices: in form of deposits			•	
5·2	: not in form of deposits				
5·3	Other capital and other funds (including all internal accounts)				
6	**TOTAL LIABILITIES** (equals item 21 Total assets)				•

Assets

Item no		Column 1 Sterling (£000s)	Column 2 Other currencies (£000s)
10	**Cash**		
10·1	Bank of England notes and UK coin		
10·2	Other notes and coin		
10·3	Balances with Bank of England (excluding special deposits and cash ratio deposits)	•	
11	**Debit items in course of collection on**		
11·1	UK offices of the reporting institution	•	
11·2	Other monetary sector institutions in the United Kingdom	•	
11·3	Banks and banking offices overseas		
12	**Market loans**		
12·2	Secured money with members of the London Discount Market Association	•	
12·3	Unsecured money with members of the London Discount Market Association	•	
12·4	Secured money at call with money brokers and gilt-edged jobbers	•	
12·6	Balances with and loans and advances to other UK monetary sector institutions	•	
12·8	Certificates of deposit issued by other UK monetary sector institutions	•	
12·9	Promissory notes, bills and other short-term paper issued by other UK monetary sector institutions	•	
12·10	Certificates of deposit issued by and time deposits placed with building societies		
12·10A	Certificates of deposit		
12·10B	Time deposits		
12·11	Placed with UK local authorities		
12·14	Placed overseas: balances with, and loans and advances to, overseas offices of the reporting institution	•	
12·15	: balances with, and loans and advances to, other banks overseas		
13·1	Special deposits and cash ratio deposits with Bank of England: special		
13·2	: cash ratio		
14	**Bills** (excluding lending under special schemes–item 15 below)		
14·1	UK Treasury bills		
14·2	Northern Ireland Treasury bills		
14·3	UK local authority bills: eligible for rediscount at Bank of England		
14·4	: other		
14·5	Other public sector bills		
14·6	UK monetary sector bills: eligible for rediscount at Bank of England		
14·7	: other		
14·8	Other UK bills		
14·9	Overseas bills		
14·10	Sterling commercial paper issued by UK residents		
14·10A	: of which guaranteed by UK monetary sector institutions		
14·11	Sterling commercial paper issued by overseas residents		
14·11A	: of which guaranteed by UK monetary sector institutions		
15·1	ECGD special scheme lending for exports		
15·2	Medium and long-term lending		
15·3	Lending at rates related to base rate		
15·4	DTI special scheme lending for shipbuilding for UK ownership		

Assets

Item no		Column 1 Sterling (£000s)	Column 2 Other currencies (£000s)
16	**Other loans and advances**		
16·1	Northern Ireland Government		
16·2	UK local authorities		
16·3	Public corporations		
16·4	Other public sector		
16·5	Other UK residents		
16·6	Overseas residents		
17	**Assets leased out under finance leases**		
18	**Investments**		
18·1	British government stocks		
18·2	Index-linked		
18·3	Other		
18·6	Northern Ireland government stocks		
18·7	Certificates of Tax Deposit		
18·8	UK local authority stocks and bonds		
18·9	Other public sector stocks and bonds		
18·10	Investments in monetary sector institutions		
18·11	Other UK investments		
	Overseas investments:		
18·12	Working capital provided for overseas offices in form of deposits		
18·13	Other working capital		
18·14	Other		
19	**Items in suspense** (excluding internal accounts)		
20·1	Gold bullion		
20·2	Other assets		
21	**TOTAL ASSETS** (equals item 6 Total liabilities)		

Supplementary items

Item no		Column 1 Sterling (£000s)	Column 2 Other currencies (£000s)
22·1	Acceptances		
22·2	UK monetary sector		
22·3	Public sector		
22·4	Banks overseas		
22·5	Other overseas residents		
22·6	Other UK residents		
22·7	Refinanced lending at fixed rates: under ECGD special export schemes		
22·8	: under the DTI special shipbuilding scheme		
23	**Total amount of overdraft, loan and acceptance facilities outstanding**		
24	**Total eligible liabilities**	•	

UK liabilities in sterling and foreign currencies to overseas residents — formerly Form BS (annex)

Levels		Column 1 Sterling (£000s)	Column 2 Other currencies (£000s)
A	Sight and time deposit liabilities to:		
A1	Banks overseas (inc central monetary institutions)		
A2	Other overseas non-bank residents		
A3	Central monetary institutions		
B	Certain other liabilities to overseas residents in sterling		
B1	UK monetary sector sterling certificates of deposit lodged (inc those issued by the reporting institution)		
B2	UK Treasury bills lodged		
B3	Local authority temporary money and bills held for overseas residents		
B4	UK monetary sector sterling bills held for overseas residents		
B5	Sterling commercial paper held for overseas residents, issued by UK residents		
B5A	:of which guaranteed by UK monetary sector institutions		
B6	Sterling commercial paper held for overseas residents, issued by overseas residents		
B6A	:of which guaranteed by UK monetary sector institutions		
Transactions			
C	Transactions in British government and government-guaranteed stocks for overseas residents		
C1	International organisations		
C2	Central monetary institutions		
C3	Banks overseas, other than CMIs and international organisations, plus other overseas non-bank residents		

To be completed by weekly-reporting banks only (instead of Form W1)

Sterling deposit liabilities

Item no		£000s
2·4	Sight deposits: UK public sector	
	Central government	
	Public corporations	
	Local authorities	
2·10	Time deposits: UK public sector	
	Central government	
	Public corporations	
	Local authorities	

Retail deposits in sterling

Item no	£000s Non-interest-bearing sight	Other chequable	Other
Part of 2·4 & 2·10 UK public sector			
Part of 2·5 & 2·13 Other UK residents			
Part of 2·7 & 2·17 Overseas residents *(excluding banks)*			

APPENDIX IV
FORM WI (BS WEEKLY)

Private and Confidential

Form W1 (BS weekly)

Selected balance sheet items

as at ______________________________

Reporting institution ______________________________

____

Name (block letters please) and signature of authorised official of reporting institution

In the event of a query, the Bank of England may contact (block letters please)

______________________ Tel no ______________ Ext ____________

Notes on completion

If you have any difficulty in completing this form, please telephone 01-601 4218/4544/4598.

1 This form should be completed as at close of business each Wednesday **except** in the week during which the last working day of the calendar month falls, when it should, instead, be completed as at close of business on the last day of the calendar month. The form need not be completed on the last day of a calendar month (when Form BS is also due), **provided that** the Form BS is submitted within the prescribed **seven calendar days**, and the final section of Form BS (the breakdown of sight and time deposits from the UK public sector and the retail deposits data) is completed.

2 Items are numbered as in Form BS. For definition of items refer to the appropriate section of the *Banking statistics definitions* folder.

3 Enter amounts to nearest thousand, omitting £000s.

4 The form should be returned within **FOUR WORKING DAYS** of the reporting date, using the pre-addressed envelopes provided, to:

FINANCIAL STATISTICS DIVISION
GROUP 2/2 (BB-1)
BANK OF ENGLAND
THREADNEEDLE STREET
LONDON EC2R 8AH

5 Forms may also be delivered to the Reception Desk at the Threadneedle Street entrance of the Bank of England between 9.00 a.m. and 5.00 p.m., Monday to Friday.

Bank of England use only

Logged in	Data entered	Amendment book	Amendment input

October 1986

(504)

Sterling liabilities

Form BS item no		£000s
1	Notes in circulation	
	Deposit liabilities	
2.4	Sight deposits: UK public sector	
	Central government	
	Public corporations	
	Local authorities	
2.5	: Other UK residents	
2.10	Time deposits: UK public sector	
	Central government	
	Public corporations	
	Local authorities	
2.13	: Other UK residents	
Total of items 2.4 + 2.5 + 2.10 + 2.13		
2.6 + 2.7 + 2.16 + 2.17	Overseas deposits	
2.20 + 2.21	CDs, promissory notes, bills, etc issued	
3	**Items in suspense (excluding internal accounts)**	
4	**Credit items in course of transmission**	

Retail deposits in sterling

£000s

Form BS item no		Non-interest-bearing sight	Other chequable	Other
Part of 2.4 & 2.10	UK public sector			
Part of 2.5 & 2.13	Other UK residents			
Part of 2.7 & 2.17 (excluding banks)	Overseas residents			

Foreign currency deposit position (net)

Form BS item no		£000s
(6 − 5) − 21	Total currency liabilities, other than capital and other funds, *less* total currency assets	

Sterling assets

Form BS item no		£000s
	Cash	
10.1 + 10.2	All notes and coin	
11	**Debit items in course of collection**	
	Market Loans	
12.4	Secured money at call with money brokers and gilt-edged jobbers	
12.8 + 12.9	CDs, promissory notes, bills, etc, issued by other monetary sector institutions	
12.11	Placed with UK local authorities	
12.14 + 12.15	Placed overseas with own offices and other banks	
Total of items 12.4 + 12.8 + 12.9 + 12.11 +12.14 + 12.15		
	Bills etc.	
14.1	UK Treasury bills	
14.3 + 14.4	All UK local authority bills	
14.5	Other public sector bills	
14.6 + 14.7 + 14.8 + 14.10	All UK monetary sector bills and other UK bills	
14.9 + 14.11	Overseas bills	
Total of items 14.3 to 14.11		
	Lending under special schemes for exports and shipbuilding	
15.1	ECGD special scheme lending for exports	
15.4	DTI special scheme lending for shipbuilding for UK ownership	
	Other loans and advances	
16.2	UK local authorities	
16.1 + 16.3 + 16.4	Other public sector	
16.5	Other UK residents	
16.6	Overseas	
Total of items 16.1 to 16.6		

Sterling assets (continued)

Form BS item no		£000s
	Investments	
18.1	British government stocks	
18.7	Certificates of Tax Deposit	
18.8	UK local authority stocks and bonds	
18.9	Other public sector stocks and bonds	
18.11	Other UK investments	
18.12 + 18.13 + 18.14	All overseas investments including working capital	
Total items 18.7 to 18.14 except 18.10		
19	**Items in suspense (excluding internal accounts)**	

Supplementary items

Form BS item no		£000s
	Sterling acceptances	
22.2	UK monetary sector	
22.3	Public sector	
22.4 + 22.5	All overseas residents (including banks)	

Overseas customers' holdings

Form BS item no		£000s
B2	UK Treasury bills lodged (total)	
C1	Transactions, since the date of the previous W1 return (or any intervening BS return, which was submitted in place of a W1 return), in British government and government-guaranteed stocks for international organisations (purchase + /sales –)	
C2	Transactions, since the date of the previous W1 return (or any intervening BS return, which was submitted in place of a W1 return), in British government and government-guaranteed stocks for CMIs (purchases + /sales –)	
C3	Transactions, since the date of the previous W1 return (or any intervening BS return, which was submitted in place of a W1 return), in British government and government-guaranteed stocks for banks overseas and other overseas residents other than CMIs and international organisations (purchases + /sales –)	

APPENDIX V - FORM Q1

This return is completed quarterly at the end of March, June, September and December and contains sector details.

The following comments should be borne in mind when reading the return:

(i) In item 5.3 ordinary shares include voting and non-voting ordinary shares and deferred shares; preference shares include cumulative participating, redemable and convertible preference shares; other capital comprises bonds, debentures, secured and unsecured loan stocks, convertible loan stocks and floating rate notes with an original maturity of one year or more; reserves and other internal accounts comprise all accounts both liability and asset, i.e. profit and loss accounts (including profit and loss expense accounts), reserves, provisions (including provisions for bad and doubtful debts), share premium accounts, accounts relating to interest accruing (both to be paid and received) and to the operating expenses of the reporting institution, such as salaries and wages, other renumerations, rent, rates, stationery, water charges, heating and lighting, insurance, hire of euipment and maintenance.

(ii) In item 12.11 short-term lending comprises market lending repayable in less then twelve months from its inception, including longer term lending repayable within twelve months of its inception by invoking a break clause; and other lending comprises market lending having an original term of twelve months or more which is not repayable in less than twelve months from its inception by invoking a break clause.

(iii) In item 16.2 short-term lending comprises all overdrafts, together with other lending repayable in less than twelve months from its inception, including longer term lending repayable within twelve months from its inception by invoking a break clause; and other lending comprises other lending having an original term of twelve months or more which is not repayable in less than twelve months from its inception by invoking a break clause.

(iv) In other items, cash receipts and cash repayments in respect of transactions in capital, comprise issues and redemptions including any share premium paid or received but excluding transactions such as issues of securities in exchange for other securities during take-overs or conversions, or bonus issues; and commodities beneficially owned refer to the net spot position in silver and other commodities (excluding gold) beneficially owned by the reporting institution, as shown in the institution's books on the day of the report.

Private and confidential

Form Q1

Sector details

Analysis of certain items on balance sheet return (Form BS)

as at ______________________________

Reporting institution ______________________________

____

Name (block letters please) and signature of authorised official of reporting institution

In the event of a query, the Bank of England may contact (block letters please)

______________________________ Tel no ______________ Ext ______________

Notes on Completion

If you have any difficulty in completing this form, please telephone 01-601 4218/4544/4598.

1 Complete form quarterly as at the end of March, June, September and December.
2 For definition of items refer to *Banking statistics definitions* folder.
3 Enter amounts to nearest thousand, omitting £000s.
4 Ensure items in shaded areas agree with related items on Form BS.
5 Return form within **SEVENTEEN CALENDAR DAYS** of reporting date, clearly addressed, to:

FINANCIAL STATISTICS DIVISION
GROUP 2/2 (BB-1)
BANK OF ENGLAND
THREADNEEDLE STREET
LONDON EC2R 8AH

6 Forms may also be delivered to the Reception Desk at the Threadneedle Street entrance of the Bank of England between 9.00 am and 5.00 pm, Monday to Friday. Envelopes should be clearly addressed as above.

Bank of England use only

Logged in	Data entered	Amendment book	Amendment input

October 1986

(6227)

Liabilities

		£000s	
		Sterling	Other currencies
2	**Deposit liabilities**		
	Sight deposits		
2.4	UK public sector	[BS 2.4]	
2.41	Central government		
2.42	Public corporations		
2.43	Local authorities		
2.5	Other UK residents	[BS 2.5]	
2.52	Other financial institutions		
2.53	Industrial and commercial companies		
2.53A	Interest-bearing		
2.53B	Non-interest-bearing		
2.54	Persons, households and individual trusts		
2.55	Other		
	Time deposits		
2.10	UK public sector	[BS 2.10]	
2.101	Central government		
2.102	Public corporations		
2.103	Local authorities		
2.13	Other UK residents	[BS 2.13]	
2.132	Other financial institutions		
2.133	Industrial and commercial companies		
2.134	Persons, households and individual trusts		
2.135	Other		
5.3	**Other capital and other funds (including all internal accounts)**	[BS 5.3]	
5.31	Ordinary shares		
5.31A	Preference shares		
5.32	Other capital (excluding working capital)		
5.33	Reserves, other internal accounts, etc		

Assets

		£000s	
		Sterling	Other currencies
12.11	**Market loans, placed with UK local authorities**		
		[BS 12.11]	
12.111	Short-term		
12.112	Other		
14.8 & 14.10	**Other UK bills and sterling commercial paper issued by UK residents**		
		[BS 14.8 & 14.10]	
14.82 & 14.102	Other financial institutions		
14.83 & 14.103	Industrial and commercial companies		
14.85 & 14.105	Other		
16	**Other loans and advances**		
16.2	UK local authorities		
		[BS 16.2]	
16.21	Short-term		
16.22	Other		
16.5	Other UK residents		
		[BS 16.5]	
16.52	Other financial institutions		
16.53	Industrial and commercial companies		
16.531	Overdrafts		
16.532	Other loans and advances		
16.54	Persons, households and individual trusts		
16.54A	Bridging finance		
16.54B	Other house purchase		
16.541	Credit card credit		
16.542	Other, of which: overdrafts		
16.543	loans and advances		
16.55	Other		
16.551	Overdrafts		
16.552	Other loans and advances		
17	**Assets leased out under finance leases**		
		[BS 17]	
17.1	To UK residents		
17.2	To overseas residents		
18.11	**Investments: other UK investments**		
		[BS 18.11]	
18.112	Other financial institutions		
18.113	Industrial and commercial companies and other		
18.14	**Investments: other overseas investments**		
		[BS 18.14]	
18.141	Direct investments		
18.142	Portfolio investments		
18.143	Debt with a contractual repayment date		
18.144	Other portfolio investments		

Other items

		£000s Sterling	£000s Other currencies
22.6	**Acceptances: other UK residents**	(BS 22.6)	
22.62	Other financial institutions		
22.63	Industrial and commercial companies		
22.65	Other		

Cash receipts and cash payments in respect of transactions in capital **£000s**

		Gross issues Sterling	Gross issues Other currencies		Gross redemptions Sterling	Gross redemptions Other Currencies
Ordinary shares	I1A			R1A		
Preference shares	I1B			R1B		
Other capital (exc. working capital)	I1C			R1C		
Total						

Net spot position in commodities beneficially owned (long +/short −)

		Sterling & other currencies
N2A	Silver	
N2B	Other (excluding gold)	

APPENDIX VI - FORM Q1 (ANNEX)

This return seeks various analyses of reporting institutions' gross loans to individuals for house purchase other than bridging finance.

The following points should be borne in mind:

(i) In item 1 total gross loans for house purchase advanced during the quarter exclude bridging finance but include amounts lent as topping-up and improvement loans. In the case of an existing borrower who increases his loan in order to purchase a different house, this borrowing is treated as though the existing loan has been redeemed and a new loan for the gross advanced.

(ii) In items 2 and 3 gross loans to individuals for house purchase exclude bridging finance and topping-up and improvement loans. Loans are reported at the approval stage rather than when the funds are actually advanced, and only information on "primary loans" for owner-occupation are included.

(iii) In item 2 the total value of gross advances and the total number of loans approved during the quarter in each of the size bands are reported. Both totals are analysed to indentify loans to the first-time purchasers and loans for the purchase of new dwellings. (First-time purchasers are buyers who were not previously owner-occupiers, not just purchasers who did not previously have a mortgage with the reporting institution concerned.) Where the loan is to be advanced in instalments the total amount approved is reported.

(iv) In item 3 the total number of loans approved during the quarter for the purchase of properites in each of the price bands is reported.

Private and confidential

Form Q1 (annex)

Further analysis of loans for house purchase

as at ______________________________

Reporting institution ______________________________

____

Signature of authorised official of reporting institution

In the event of a query, the Bank of England may contact (block letters please)

______________________________ Tel no ______________ Ext ______________

Notes on Completion

If you have any difficulty in completing this form, please telephone 01-601 4218/4544/4598.

1 Complete form quarterly as at end of March, June, September and December.

2 Enter amounts to nearest thousand, omitting £000s.

3 Return form together with main Form Q1 within **FOURTEEN** calendar days of reporting date to:

Financial Statistics Division (HO-4)
Group 2/2
Bank of England
Threadneedle Street
London EC2R 8AH

Bank of England use only

Logged in	Data entered	Amendment book	Amendment input

December 1982

(221)

Further analysis of loans for house purchase - other than bridging finance

1 Gross loans for house purchase

Note Report here total **gross** loans for house purchase **advanced** during the quarter, **including** amounts lent as topping-up and improvement loans.

£000s

Note In analyses 2 and 3 below, **the total amount approved** should be reported, even when the loan is advanced in instalments. **Exclude** topping-up and improvement loans.

2 Analysis by size of loan

	Amount £000s	Number of loans
Under £10,000		
£10,000 to £11,999		
£12,000 to £13,999		
£14,000 to £15,999		
£16,000 to £17,999		
£18,000 to £19,999		
£20,000 to £21,999		
£22,000 to £23,999		
£24,000 to £25,999		
£26,000 to £27,999		
£28,000 to £29,999		
£30,000 to £39,999		
£40,000 to £49,999		
£50,000 and over		
TOTAL*		

*Of which:

First-time purchasers		
New dwellings		

3 Analysis by purchase price of property

	Number of loans
Under £15,000	
£15,000 to £17,499	
£17,500 to £19,999	
£20,000 to £22,499	
£22,500 to £24,999	
£25,000 to £27,499	
£27,500 to £29,999	
£30,000 to £34,999	
£35,000 to £39,999	
£40,000 to £44,999	
£45,000 to £49,999	
£50,000 to £59,999	
£60,000 to £69,999	
£70,000 to £79,999	
£80,000 and over	
TOTAL	

(221)

APPENDIX VII - FORM Q3

This is an industrial analysis of loans and advances, acceptances and facilities granted to UK residents (excluding monetary sector institutions) according to the main activity of the borrower. Where, however, the borrower is either an industrial holding company or a subsidiary whose prime function is to raise finance on behalf of the other group companies or divisions, then the loan is classified according to the main activity of the ultimate beneficiary.

It should be noted that facilities outstanding comprise all outstanding overdraft, loan and acceptance facilities granted to UK residents, whether or not drawn. The unutilised portion of a facility which may be drawn in either sterling or another currency at the option of the borrower, is entered under the 'other currencies' column.

Private and confidential

Form Q3

Analysis of loans and advances, acceptances and facilities to UK residents
including holdings of sterling commercial paper issued by UK residents

as at ______________________________

Reporting institution ______________________________

____

Name (block letters please) and signature of authorised official of reporting institution

In the event of a query, the Bank of England may contact (block letters please)

______________________________ Tel no ______________ Ext ______________

Notes on Completion

If you have any difficulty in completing this form, please telephone 01-601 4218/4544/4598.

1. Complete form quarterly as at the end of February, May, August and November.
2. For definition of items refer to *Banking statistics definitions* folder.
3. Enter amounts to nearest thousand, omitting £000s.
4. Ensure items in shaded areas agree with related items on Form BS.
5. Return form within **FOURTEEN CALENDAR DAYS** of reporting date clearly addressed to:

   FINANCIAL STATISTICS DIVISION
   GROUP 2/2 (BB-1)
   BANK OF ENGLAND
   THREADNEEDLE STREET
   LONDON EC2R 8AH

6. Forms may also be delivered to the Reception desk at the Threadneedle Street entrance of the Bank of England between 9.00 am and 5.00 pm, Monday to Friday. Envelopes should be clearly addressed as above.

Bank of England use only

Logged in	Data entered	Amendment book	Amendment input

October 1986

(3780)

£000s	Loans & advances outstanding		Acceptances outstanding		Facilities outstanding		Holdings of sterling commercial paper
	Sterling	Other currencies	Sterling	Other currencies	Sterling	Other currencies	Sterling
1 Agriculture, forestry and fishing							
2 Energy and water supply industries							
(a) Oil and extraction of natural gas							
(b) Other energy industries							
(c) Water supply							
3 Manufacturing industry							
(a) Extraction of minerals and ores (other than fuels)							
(b) Metal manufacturing							
(c) Manufacture of non-metallic mineral products							
(d) Chemical industry							
(e) Mechanical engineering							
(f) Electrical & electronic engineering							
(g) Motor vehicles							
(h) Other transport equipment							
(i) Other engineering and metal goods							
(j) Food, drink and tobacco							
(k) Textiles, leather, clothing and footwear							
(l) Other manufacturing							
4 Construction							
5 Garages, distribution, hotels and catering							
(a) Garages and retail distribution of motor vehicles							
(b) Other retail distribution							
(c) Wholesale distribution							
(d) Hotels and catering							

6 **Transport**				
(a) Air transport				
(b) Other transport				
7 **Postal services and telecommunications**				
8 **Financial**				
(a) Building societies				
(b) Investment and unit trusts etc				
(c) Insurance companies, pension funds etc				
(d) Leasing enterprises				
(e) Other financial				
(f) Securities dealers, stockbrokers, jobbers, etc				
9 **Business and other services**				
(a) Central and local government				
(b) Property companies				
(c) Hiring of movables				
(d) Other services				
10 **Persons**				
(a) Bridging finance for house purchase				
(b) Other house purchase				
(c) Other advances to persons				
Total to UK residents	(BS 16.1 to 16.5)	(BS 22.3 + 22.6)		(BS 14.10)
Of which: overdrafts		Of which: overdraft facilities immediately available		
other loans and advances		other facilities		

APPENDIX VIII - FORM Q6

This return analyses, by residual maturity, sterling liabilities and assets contained in the monthly balance sheet return (Form BS).

Liabilities and assets are classified according to their remaining maturity.

Deposits with the reporting institution are entered according to their earliest repayment dates. In this context, the earliest repayment date means the first roll-over date or the shortest period of notice required to call or exercise a break clause, where applicable. (This rule applies, for example, even where a guarantee has been received that certificates of deposit will be taken up on roll-over.)

"Next day" is every liability and asset due, available or maturing on 16 February;

"2 days-less than 8 days" is every item maturing between 17 February and 22 February inclusive;

"8 days-less than 1 month" is every item maturing between 23 February and 14 March inclusive;

"1 month-less than 3 months" is every item maturing between 15 March and 14 May inclusive;

"3 months-less than 6 months" is every item maturing between 15 May and 14 August inclusive;

"6 months-less than 1 year" is every item maturing between 15 August and 14 February inclusive; and so on.

Overdue items refer to an asset, or part of it, which has passed the due date for repatment by fourteen days or more (or, in the case of ECGD special scheme lending for exports, by thirty day or more), on the reporting date. The amount of principal which is in arrears is entered in the "Overdue" column. Assets (other than overdrafts) having passed the due date by less than fouteen days (less than thirty days for ECGD special scheme lending for exports) are entered under "Next day".

Overdrafts are not analysed by maturity in this form.

"Other commitments" includes commiments to lend, or to take up bills, certificates of deposit, investments, etc., where there has been an agreed date (or dates) for the draw-down of the facility.

"Floating rate notes" includes marketable securities where the interest payable varies according to current market rates.

Investments where the interest rate varies initially but may, if triggered by specific market conditions, subsequently be changed to a fixed rate (commonly known as "drop lock bonds") are treated as floating rate notes until such time as the fixed interest rate is triggered; thereafter they are treated as "other investments".

Private and confidential

Form Q6

Maturity analysis of liabilities and assets in sterling

as at ______________________________

Reporting institution ______________________________

____

Name (block letters please) and signature of authorised official of reporting institution

In the event of a query, the Bank of England may contact (block letters please)

______________________________ Tel no ______________ Ext ______________

Notes on Completion

If you have any difficulty in completing this form, please telephone 01-601 4218/4544/4598.

1 Monthly BS reporters should complete Form Q6 as at the end of January, April, July and October. Quarterly BS reporters should complete Form Q6 as at the end of March, June, September and December.
2 For definition of items refer to the *Banking statistics definitions* folder.
3 Enter amounts to nearest thousand, omitting £000s.
4 Ensure that the items in the shaded areas agree with related items on Form BS column 1 (sterling).
5 Return form within **FOURTEEN CALENDAR DAYS** of reporting date, clearly addressed, to:

FINANCIAL STATISTICS DIVISION
GROUP 2/2 (BB-1)
BANK OF ENGLAND
THREADNEEDLE STREET
LONDON EC2R 8AH

6 Forms may also be delivered to the Reception Desk at the Threadneedle Street entrance of the Bank of England, between 9.00 am and 5.00 pm, Monday to Friday. Envelopes should be clearly addressed as above.

Bank of England use only

Logged in	Data entered	Amendment book	Amendment input

October 1986

(482)

STERLING MATURITY ANALYSIS (£000s) Item	Figures in shaded areas must agree with referenced items on Form BS column 1	Total
LIABILITIES		
1 Deposit liabilities		
1.1 UK monetary sector	2.2 + 2.9	
1.2 Other UK residents	2.4 + 2.5 + 2.10 + 2.13	
1.3 Banks overseas 1.4 Other overseas residents	2.6 + 2.7 + 2.16 + 2.17	
1.5 Certificates of deposit and other short-term paper issued	2.20 + 2.21	
SUB TOTAL	2	
2 All other liabilities*	1 + 3 + 4 + 5	
TOTAL STERLING LIABILITIES	6	
3 Other commitments		
ASSETS		
4 Market loans		
4.1 Balances with and advances to UK monetary sector, money brokers and gilt-edged jobbers	12.2 to 12.6	
4.2 Balances with banks overseas	12.14 + 12.15	
4.3 Placed with UK local authorities	12.11	
4.4 Certificates of deposit and other short-term paper issued by other UK monetary sector institutions and certificates of deposit issued by building societies	12.8 + 12.9 + 12.10	
5 Bills		
5.1 Treasury and eligible bills	14.1 + 14.2 + 14.3 + 14.6	
5.2 Other bills and short-term paper (other than issued by UK monetary sector or in respect of special schemes for export/shipbuilding)	14.4 + 14.5 + 14.7 to 14.11	
6 Lending under special schemes for exports and shipbuilding	15.1 + 15.4	
7 Other loans and advances to:		
7.1 Other UK residents: loans 7.2 overdrafts	16.1 to 16.5	
7.3 Overseas residents: loans 7.4 overdrafts	16.6	
8 Assets leased out under finance leases	17	
9 Investments		
9.1 British government stocks and bonds	18.1	
9.2 Other public sector stocks and bonds	18.6 to 18.9	
9.3 Floating rate notes 9.4 Other investments	18.10 to 18.14	
SUB TOTAL†	12 + 14 + 15.1 + 15.4 + 16 + 17 + 18	
10 All other assets*	10 + 11 + 13.1 + 13.2 + 19 + 20.2	
TOTAL STERLING ASSETS	21	
See Section overleaf on irrevocable standby credit facilities		

*Analysed by maturity if relevant (see reporting instructions).

† The entry in the 'Total' column will exceed the sum of the entries in the subsequent columns by the amount of overdrafts not yet 'overdue' (ie those for which repayment dates have not yet been fixed, and those where repayment has been fixed for dates up to 13 days before the reporting date, or later than the reporting date).

(482)

Overdue	Next day	Less than 8 days (excluding next day)	8 days - less than 1 month	1 month - less than 3 months	3 months - less than 6 months	6 months - less than 1 year	1 year - less than 3 years	3 years - less than 5 years	5 years and over (incl undated)

Formal irrevocable standby credit facilities in sterling given to and received from other UK monetary sector institutions and banks overseas.

			£000s
11	**Facilities received**		
11.1	from UK monetary sector	drawn	
11.2		undrawn	
11.3	from banks overseas	drawn	
11.4		undrawn	
12	**Facilities given**		
12.1	to UK monetary sector	drawn	
12.2		undrawn	
12.3	to banks overseas	drawn	
12.4		undrawn	

APPENDIX IX - FORM S5

This return analyses by maturity liabilities and assets in currencies other than sterling contained in the monthly balance sheet returns (Form BS).

Comments made on Form Q6 apply here as well.

Private and confidential

Form S5

Maturity analysis of liabilities and assets in currencies other than sterling

as at ______________________________

Reporting institution ______________________________

____

Signature of authorised official of reporting institution

In the event of a query, the Bank of England may contact (block letters please)

______________________________ Tel no ______________ Ext ______________

Notes on Completion

If you have any difficulty in completing this form, please telephone 01-601 4885/4870 unless directed otherwise in the notes to the form.

1 Monthly BS reporters should complete form quarterly as at 3rd Wednesday of February, May, August and November.
 Quarterly BS reporters should complete quarterly as at end of March, June, September and December
2 For definition of items refer to the *Banking statistics definitions* folder.
3 Enter amounts to nearest thousand, omitting £000s.
4 Ensure that the items in the shaded areas agree with related items in column 2 (other currencies) of Form BS.
5 Return form within **FOURTEEN** calendar days of reporting date to:

Financial Statistics Division HO-3
Group 3/2
Bank of England
Threadneedle Street
London EC2R 8AH

Bank of England use only

Logged	Data entered	Pending	Query	Awaiting update	Revision book	Revision input

February 1983

(3783)

NON-STERLING MATURITY ANALYSIS (£000s) Item	Figures in shaded areas must agree with referenced items on Form BS column 2	Total
LIABILITIES		
1 Deposit liabilities		
1.1 UK monetary sector	2.2 + 2.9	
1.2 Other UK residents	2.4 + 2.5 + 2.10 + 2.13	
1.3 Banks overseas 1.4 Other overseas residents	2.6 + 2.7 + 2.16 + 2.17	
1.5 Certificates of deposit and other short-term paper issued	2.20 + 2.21	
SUB TOTAL	2	
2 All other liabilities*	3 + 4 + 5	
TOTAL NON-STERLING LIABILITIES	6	
3 Other commitments		
ASSETS		
4 Market loans		
4.1 Balances with and advances to UK monetary sector, money brokers and gilt-edged jobbers	12.2 to 12.6	
4.2 Balances with banks overseas	12.14 + 12.15	
4.3 Placed with UK local authorities	12.11	
4.4 Certificates of deposit and other short-term paper issued by other UK monetary sector institutions and certificates of deposit issued by building societies	12.8 + 12.9 + 12.10	
5 Bills		
5.1 Bills and short-term paper (other than issued by UK monetary sector or in respect of special schemes for exports)	14	
6 ECGD special scheme lending for exports	15.1	
7 Other loans and advances to:		
7.1 Other UK residents: loans 7.2 overdrafts	16.1 to 16.5	
7.3 Overseas residents: loans 7.4 overdrafts	16.6	
8 Assets leased out under finance leases	17	
9 Investments		
9.1 British government stocks	18.1	
9.2 Other public sector stocks and bonds	18.8 + 18.9	
9.3 Floating rate notes 9.4 Other investments	18.10 to 18.14	
SUB TOTAL†	12 + 14 + 15.1 + 16 + 17 + 18	
10 All other assets*	10 + 11 + 19 + 20.1 + 20.2	
TOTAL NON-STERLING ASSETS	21	
See Section overleaf on irrevocable standby credit facilities		

*Analysed by maturity if relevant (see reporting instructions)

† The entry in the 'Total' column will exceed the sum of the entries in the subsequent columns by the amount of overdrafts not yet 'overdue' (ie those for which repayment dates have not yet been fixed, and those where repayment has been fixed for dates up to 13 days before the reporting date, or later than the reporting date).

(3783)

Overdue	Next day	2 days – less than 8 days	8 days – less than 1 month	1 month – less than 3 months	3 months – less than 6 months	6 months – less than I year	1 year – less than 3 years	3 years – less than 5 years	5 years and over (incl undated)

Formal irrevocable standby credit facitities in currencies other than sterling given to and received from other UK monetary sector institutions and banks overseas.

			£000s
11	**Facilities received**		
11.1	from UK monetary sector	drawn	
11.2		undrawn	
11.3	from banks overseas	drawn	
11.4		undrawn	
12	**Facilities given**		
12.1	to UK monetary sector	drawn	
12.2		undrawn	
12.3	to banks overseas	drawn	
12.4		undrawn	

APPENDIX X - FORMS S1

These returns analyse certain of the reporting institition's liabilities to and claims on overseas residents. They are concerned solely with liabilities and claims denominated in sterling. The sterling component of liabilities and claims denominated in composite currencies should not be included.

In form S1 (liabilities) part 2, sterling certificates of deposit include sterling certificates of deposit issued by monetary sector institutions including those issued by the reporting institution which are held on behalf of overseas residents, including those lodged as collateral by overseas residents. UK Tresury bills include United Kingdom Treasury bills held on behalf of overseas residents, including those lodged as collateral by overseas residents.

Transactions in British government stocks include only transactions in British government stocks for banks overseas, international organisations or central monetary institutions during the period since the immediately preceding reporting date on Form S1, whether mid-quarter or end-quarter. Transactions in stocks of the has and electricity industries guaranteed by HM Government are also included.

In form S1 (claims) syndicated loans include only the reporting institution's participating for its own account (excluding lending covered by ECGD bank guarantees which is included in column 5).

Overseas bills include all commercial bills, promissory notes and other negotiable paper drawn on overseas residents and owned by the reporting institution, except those covered by ECGD bank guarantees.

ECGD special scheme lending for exports includes all lending in sterling covered by ECGD bank guatantees, including lending under supplier credit. The country analysis of such lending is normally made according to the destination of the exports. Where payment is due from a resident of another overseas country, however, the lending is entered against that country.

Private and confidential **Form S1 (liabilities) Part 1**

UK external sterling liabilities

Country analysis of overseas residents' sterling deposits

as at ____________________

Reporting institution ____________________

____

Signature of authorised official of reporting institution

In the event of a query, the Bank of England may contact (block letters please)

____________________ Tel. no ____________________ Ext. ________

Notes on completion

If you have any difficulty in completing this form, please telephone 01-601 4463/4070.

1 Complete form as at third Wednesday of February, May, August and November and as at end of March, June, September and December, unless otherwise requested by the Bank of England.

2 For definition of items refer to the *Banking statistics definitions* folder.

3 Complete both sections of the return.

4 Enter amounts to nearest thousand omitting £000s.

5 Ensure that the items in the shaded areas agree with related items in column 1 (sterling) of Form BS, or the relevant balance sheet return.

6 Return form within **TEN** calendar days of reporting date to:

Financial Statistics Division HO-3
Group 3/2
Bank of England
Threadneedle Street
London EC2R 8AH

Bank of England use only

Logged	Data entered	Pending	Query	Awaiting update	Revision book	Revision input

(52/1) February 1983

Sterling deposit liabilities to overseas residents

£000s

Section 1 — Analysis by country		1	2	3
		Reporting institution's sight and time deposit liabilities to:		
		Overseas offices of the reporting institution	Other banks overseas (including central monetary institutions)	Other overseas residents

Figures in shaded areas must agree with referenced items on Form BS column 1 †

		1	2	3
Total of all overseas customers (A + B + C) below				
		[2·6+2·16]	[A1] [2·7+2·17]	[A2]
A International organisations	EC institutions			
	Other institutions			
B Unallocated by country				
C Country breakdown				

		1	2	3
Abu Dhabi	ABUD			
Afghanistan	AFGH			
Albania	ALBA			
Algeria	ALGE			
Andorra	ANDO			
Angola	ANGO			
Anguilla	ANGU			
Antigua	ANTI			
Argentina	ARGE			
Australia	AUSL			
Austria	AUSR			
Bahamas	BAHA			
Bahrain	BAHR			
Bangladesh	BANG			
Barbados	BARB			
Belgium	BELG			
Belize	BELI			
Benin	DAHO			
Bermuda	BERM			
Bhutan	BHUT			

Section 1 — Analysis by country *(continued)*		1	2	3
		Reporting institution's sight and time deposit liabilities to:		
		Overseas offices of the reporting institution	Other banks overseas (including central monetary institutions)	Other overseas residents
France	FRAN			
French Guiana	FGUI			
French Polynesia	FPOL			
French Southern and Antarctic Territories	FSAT			
Gabon	GABO			
Gambia	GAMB			
German Democratic Republic	EGER			
Germany, Federal Republic of	WGER			
Ghana	GHAN			
Gibraltar	GIBR			
Greece	GREE			
Greenland	GRND			
Grenada	GREN			
Guadeloupe	GUAD			
Guatemala	GUAT			
Guinea	GUIN			
Guinea-Bissau	PGUI			
Guyana	GUYA			
Haiti	HAIT			
Honduras	HOND			
Hong Kong	HONG			
Hungary	HUNG			
Iceland	ICEL			
India	INDI			
Indonesia	INDO			
Iran	IRAN			
Iraq	IRAQ			
Ireland	EIRE			
Israel	ISRA			
Italy	ITAL			

Bolivia	BOLI			
Botswana	BOTS			
Brazil	BRAZ			
British Antarctic Territory	BRAT			
British Indian Ocean Territory	BIOT			
British Virgin Islands	BRVI			
Brunei	BRUN			
Bulgaria	BULG			
Burma	BURM			
Burundi	BURU			
Cameroon, United Republic of	CAME			
Canada	CANA			
Canton and Enderbury Islands	CANT			
Cape Verde	CAPE			
Cayman Islands	CAYM			
Central African Republic	CEAR			
Chad	CHAD			
Chile	CHIL			
China, People's Republic	CHIN			
Colombia	COLO			
Comoros	COMO			
Congo	CONG			
Costa Rica	COSR			
Cuba	CUBA			
Cyprus	CYPR			
Czechoslovakia	CZEC			
Denmark	DENM			
Djibouti	AFIS			
Dominica	DOMA			
Dominican Republic	DOMR			
Dubai	DUBA			
Ecuador	ECUA			
Egypt	EGYP			
El Salvador	ELSA			
Equatorial Guinea	EQUA			
Ethiopia	ETHI			
Faeroe Islands	FARO			
Falkland Islands	FALK			
Fiji	FIJI			
Finland	FINL			

Ivory Coast	IVCO			
Jamaica	JAMA			
Japan	JAPA			
Jordan	JORD			
Kampuchea, Democratic	KHME			
Kenya	KENY			
Kiribati (formerly Gilbert Islands)	GILB			
Korea, Democratic People's Republic of	NKOR			
Korea, Republic of	SKOR			
Kuwait	KUWA			
Lao People's Democratic Republic	LAOS			
Lebanon	LEBA			
Lesotho	LESO			
Liberia	LIBE			
Libyan Arab Jamahiriya	LIBY			
Liechtenstein	LICH			
Luxembourg	LUXE			
Macau	MACA			
Madagascar (Malagasy Republic)	MADA			
Malawi	MALW			
Malaysia	MALA			
Maldives	MALD			
Mali	MALI			
Malta	MALT			
Martinique	MART			
Mauritania	MTAN			
Mauritius	MAUR			
Mexico	MEXI			
Monaco	MONA			
Mongolia	MONG			
Montserrat	MONT			
Morocco	MORO			
Mozambique	MOZA			
Namibia (SW Africa)	NAMI			
Nauru	NAUR			
Nepal	NEPA			
Netherlands	NETH			
Netherlands Antilles	NETA			
New Caledonia	NWCL			
New Zealand	NEWZ			

† Institutions reporting on Form BS(DM), Form MFI(Q) or Form GD(Q) should refer to the notes on the back cover.

Sterling deposit liabilities to overseas residents *(continued)*

£000s

Section 1 — Analysis by country *(continued)*		1	2	3
		Reporting institution's sight and time deposit liabilities to:		
		Overseas offices of the reporting institution	Other banks overseas (including central monetary institutions)	Other overseas residents
Nicaragua	NICA			
Niger	NIGR			
Nigeria	NIGE			
Norway	NORW			
Oman	OMAN			
Other United Arab Emirates	OUAE			
Pakistan	PAKI			
Panama	PANA			
Papau New Guinea	PNGU			
Paraguay	PARA			
Peru	PERU			
Philippines	PHIL			
Pitcairn Island	PITC			
Poland	POLA			
Portugal	PORT			

Section 1 — Analysis by country *(continued)*		1	2	3
		Reporting institution's sight and time deposit liabilities to:		
		Overseas offices of the reporting institution	Other banks overseas (including central monetary institutions)	Other overseas residents
Switzerland	SWIT			
Syrian Arab Republic	SYRI			
Taiwan	TAIW			
Tanzania, United Republic of	TANZ			
Thailand	THAI			
Togo	TOGO			
Tonga	TONG			
Trinidad and Tobago	TRIN			
Tunisia	TUNI			
Turkey	TURK			
Turks and Caicos Islands	TUCA			
Tuvalu (formerly Ellice Islands)	TUVA			
Uganda	UGAN			
United States	USA			
US Trust Territories in the Pacific	USTP			

Qatar	QATA			
Reunion	REUN			
Romania	ROMA			
Rwanda	RWAN			
St Helena	SAHE			
St Kitts-Nevis	SCRN			
Saint Lucia	SLUC			
St Pierre and Miquelon	SPMI			
Saint Vincent and the Grenadines	SVIN			
Samoa (formerly Western Samoa)	WSAM			
Sao Tome and Principe	SATP			
Saudi Arabia	SAUA			
Senegal	SENE			
Seychelles	SEYC			
Sierra Leone	SILE			
Singapore	SING			
Solomon Islands	BRSI			
Somalia	SOMA			
South Africa	SAFR			
Spain	SPAI			
Sri Lanka	SRIL			
Sudan	SUDA			
Suriname	SURI			
Swaziland	SWAZ			
Sweden	SWED			

US Virgin Islands	USVI			
Upper Volta	UVOL			
Uruguay	URUG			
USSR	USSR			
Vanuatu (fomerly New Hebrides)	NWHB			
Vatican City State (Holy See)	VATI			
Venezuela	VENE			
Vietnam, Socialist Republic of	VNMN			
Wallis and Futuna Islands	WALF			
Western Sahara	WSAH			
Yemen Arab Republic	YEME			
Yemen, People's Democratic Republic of	YEMS			
Yugoslavia	YUGO			
Zaire	ZAIR			
Zambia	ZAMB			
Zimbabwe	RHOD			

Sterling deposit liabilities to overseas central monetary institutions

£000s

Section 2 Analysis by area central monetary institutions in:		Total sight and time deposits (a)
European Community	EEC	
Other Western Europe	OWEN	
Other OECD countries	OECN	
Eastern Europe	EEUR	
Latin America and Caribbean	LACN	
Middle East oil exporting countries	MEOX	
Other oil exporting countries	OILN	
Other Africa	OAFN	
Far East	FEAN	
Other	OTHN	

The total of the above must agree with item A3 in column 1 (sterling) of Form BS.

(a) Part of Section 1, column 2.

Private and confidential

Form S1 (liabilities) Part 2

UK external sterling liabilities
Country analysis of sterling custody holdings for overseas residents

as at ____

Reporting institution __________________________________

____

Signature of authorised official of reporting institution

In the event of a query, the Bank of England may contact (block letters please)

____________________ Tel. no ____________________ Ext. ______

Notes on completion

If you have any difficulty in completing this form, please telephone 01-601 4463/4070.

1 Complete form as at third Wednesday of February, May, August and November and as at end of March, June, September and December, unless otherwise requested by the Bank of England.

2 For definition of items refer to the *Banking statistics definitions* folder.

3 Complete both sections of the return.

4 Enter amounts to nearest thousand omitting £000s.

5 Ensure that the items in the shaded areas agree with related items in column 1 (sterling) of Form **BS**

6 Return form within **TEN** calendar days of reporting date to:

Financial Statistics Division HO-3
Group 3/2
Bank of England
Threadneedle Street
London EC2R 8AH

Bank of England use only

Logged	Data entered	Pending	Query	Awaiting update	Revision book	Revision input

(52/2) February 1983

Sterling custody holdings for account of overseas residents

£000s

Section 1 Analysis by country		1 Amount outstanding of: Sterling certificates of deposit (inc. those issued by reporting institution)	2 Amount outstanding of: UK Treasury bills	3 Transactions in: British Government and government-guaranteed stocks for banks overseas (including CMI) and international organisations only (purchases +/sales —)
Total of all overseas customers (A + B + C) below		[B1]	[B2]	
A International organisations	EC institutions			
	Other institutions			
B Unallocated by country				
C Country breakdown				
Abu Dhabi	ABUD			
Afghanistan	AFGH			
Albania	ALBA			
Algeria	ALGE			
Andorra	ANDO			
Angola	ANGO			
Anguilla	ANGU			
Antigua	ANTI			
Argentina	ARGE			
Australia	AUSL			
Austria	AUSR			
Bahamas	BAHA			
Bahrain	BAHR			
Bangladesh	BANG			
Barbados	BARB			
Belgium	BELG			
Belize	BELI			
Benin	DAHO			
Bermuda	BERM			
Bhutan	BHUT			

Figures in shaded areas must agree with referenced items on Form BS column 1.

Section 1 Analysis by country *(continued)*		1 Amount outstanding of: Sterling certificates of deposit (inc. those issued by reporting institution)	2 Amount outstanding of: UK Treasury bills	3 Transactions in: British Government and government-guaranteed stocks for banks overseas (including CMI) and international organisations only (purchases +/sales —)
France	FRAN			
French Guiana	FGUI			
French Polynesia	FPOL			
French Southern and Antarctic Territories	FSAT			
Gabon	GABO			
Gambia	GAMB			
German Democratic Republic	EGER			
Germany, Federal Republic of	WGER			
Ghana	GHAN			
Gibraltar	GIBR			
Greece	GREE			
Greenland	GRND			
Grenada	GREN			
Guadeloupe	GUAD			
Guatemala	GUAT			
Guinea	GUIN			
Guinea-Bissau	PGUI			
Guyana	GUYA			
Haiti	HAIT			
Honduras	HOND			
Hong Kong	HONG			
Hungary	HUNG			
Iceland	ICEL			
India	INDI			
Indonesia	INDO			
Iran	IRAN			
Iraq	IRAQ			
Ireland	EIRE			
Israel	ISRA			
Italy	ITAL			

Bolivia	BOLI			
Botswana	BOTS			
Brazil	BRAZ			
British Antarctic Territory	BRAT			
British Indian Ocean Territory	BIOT			
British Virgin Islands	BRVI			
Brunei	BRUN			
Bulgaria	BULG			
Burma	BURM			
Burundi	BURU			
Cameroon, United Republic of	CAME			
Canada	CANA			
Canton and Enderbury Islands	CANT			
Cape Verde	CAPE			
Cayman Islands	CAYM			
Central African Republic	CEAR			
Chad	CHAD			
Chile	CHIL			
China, People's Republic	CHIN			
Colombia	COLO			
Comoros	COMO			
Congo	CONG			
Costa Rica	COSR			
Cuba	CUBA			
Cyprus	CYPR			
Czechoslovakia	CZEC			
Denmark	DENM			
Djibouti	AFIS			
Dominica	DOMA			
Dominican Republic	DOMR			
Dubai	DUBA			
Ecuador	ECUA			
Egypt	EGYP			
El Salvador	ELSA			
Equatorial Guinea	EQUA			
Ethiopia	ETHI			
Faeroe Islands	FARO			
Falkland Islands	FALK			
Fiji	FIJI			
Finland	FINL			

Ivory Coast	IVCO			
Jamaica	JAMA			
Japan	JAPA			
Jordan	JORD			
Kampuchea, Democratic	KHME			
Kenya	KENY			
Kiribati (formerly Gilbert Islands)	GILB			
Korea, Democratic People's Republic of	NKOR			
Korea, Republic of	SKOR			
Kuwait	KUWA			
Lao People's Democratic Republic	LAOS			
Lebanon	LEBA			
Lesotho	LESO			
Liberia	LIBE			
Libyan Arab Jamahiriya	LIBY			
Liechtenstein	LICH			
Luxembourg	LUXE			
Macau	MACA			
Madagascar (Malagasy Republic)	MADA			
Malawi	MALW			
Malaysia	MALA			
Maldives	MALD			
Mali	MALI			
Malta	MALT			
Martinique	MART			
Mauritania	MTAN			
Mauritius	MAUR			
Mexico	MEXI			
Monaco	MONA			
Mongolia	MONG			
Montserrat	MONT			
Morocco	MORO			
Mozambique	MOZA			
Namibia (SW Africa)	NAMI			
Nauru	NAUR			
Nepal	NEPA			
Netherlands	NETH			
Netherlands Antilles	NETA			
New Caledonia	NWCL			
New Zealand	NEWZ			

Sterling custody holdings for account of overseas residents *(continued)*

Section 1 **Analysis by country** *(continued)*		1	2	3
		Amount outstanding of:		**Transactions in:**
		Sterling certificates of deposit (inc. those issued by reporting institution)	UK Treasury bills	British Government and government-guaranteed stocks for banks overseas (including CMI) and international organisations only (purchases +/sales —)
Nicaragua	NICA			
Niger	NIGR			
Nigeria	NIGE			
Norway	NORW			
Oman	OMAN			
Other United Arab Emirates	OUAE			
Pakistan	PAKI			
Panama	PANA			
Papau New Guinea	PNGU			
Paraguay	PARA			
Peru	PERU			
Philippines	PHIL			
Pitcairn Island	PITC			
Poland	POLA			
Portugal	PORT			

Section 1 **Analysis by country** *(continued)*		1	2	3
		Amount outstanding of:		**Transactions in:**
		Sterling certificates of deposit (inc. those issued by reporting institution)	UK Treasury bills	British Government and government-guaranteed stocks for banks overseas (including CMI) and international organisations only (purchases +/sales —)
Switzerland	SWIT			
Syrian Arab Republic	SYRI			
Taiwan	TAIW			
Tanzania, United Republic of	TANZ			
Thailand	THAI			
Togo	TOGO			
Tonga	TONG			
Trinidad and Tobago	TRIN			
Tunisia	TUNI			
Turkey	TURK			
Turks and Caicos Islands	TUCA			
Tuvalu (formerly Ellice Islands)	TUVA			
Uganda	UGAN			
United States	USA			
US Trust Territories in the Pacific	USTP			

Qatar	QATA			
Reunion	REUN			
Romania	ROMA			
Rwanda	RWAN			
St Helena	SAHE			
St Kitts-Nevis	SCRN			
Saint Lucia	SLUC			
St Pierre and Miquelon	SPMI			
Saint Vincent and the Grenadines	SVIN			
Samoa (formerly Western Samoa)	WSAM			
Sao Tome and Principe	SATP			
Saudi Arabia	SAUA			
Senegal	SENE			
Seychelles	SEYC			
Sierra Leone	SILE			
Singapore	SING			
Solomon Islands	BRSI			
Somalia	SOMA			
South Africa	SAFR			
Spain	SPAI			
Sri Lanka	SRIL			
Sudan	SUDA			
Suriname	SURI			
Swaziland	SWAZ			
Sweden	SWED			

US Virgin Islands	USVI			
Upper Volta	UVOL			
Uruguay	URUG			
USSR	USSR			
Vanuatu (fomerly New Hebrides)	NWHB			
Vatican City State (Holy See)	VATI			
Venezuela	VENE			
Vietnam, Socialist Republic of	VNMN			
Wallis and Futuna Islands	WALF			
Western Sahara	WSAH			
Yemen Arab Republic	YEME			
Yemen, People's Democratic Republic of	YEMS			
Yugoslavia	YUGO			
Zaire	ZAIR			
Zambia	ZAMB			
Zimbabwe	RHOD			

Sterling custody holdings for account of overseas central monetary institutions

£000s

Section 2 **Analysis by area central monetary institutions in:**		1 Sterling certificates of deposit (including those issued by reporting institution) (a)	2 UK Treasury bills (b)	3 Transactions in government and government-guaranteed stocks (purchases +/ sales —) (c)
European Community	EEC			
Other Western Europe	OWEN			
Other OECD countries	OECN			
Eastern Europe	EEUR			
Latin America and Caribbean	LACN			
Middle East oil exporting countries	MEOX			
Other oil exporting countries	OILN			
Other Africa	OAFN			
Far East	FEAN			
Other	OTHN			

(a) Part of Section 1, column 1.
(b) Part of Section 1, column 2.
(c) Part of Section 1, column 3.

Private and confidential **Form S1 (claims)**

Country analysis of
UK external sterling claims

as at ____

Reporting institution ____

____
Signature of authorised official of reporting institution

In the event of a query, the Bank of England may contact (block letters please)

________________________ Tel. no ________________________ Ext. ________

Notes on completion

If you have any difficulty in completing this form, please telephone 01-601 4463/4070.

1 Complete form as at third Wednesday of February, May, August and November and as at end of March, June, September and December, unless otherwise requested by the Bank of England.

2 For definition of items refer to the *Banking statistics definitions* folder.

3 Complete both sections of the return.

4 Enter amounts to nearest thousand omitting £000s.

5 Ensure that the items in the shaded areas agree with related items in column 1 (sterling) of Form BS, or the relevant balance sheet return.

6 Return form within **TEN** calendar days of reporting date to:

Financial Statistics Division HO-3
Group 3/2
Bank of England
Threadneedle Street
London EC2R 8AH

Bank of England use only

Logged	Data entered	Pending	Query	Awaiting update	Revision book	Revision input

(5575) February 1983

Sterling claims on overseas residents

£000s

Section 1 Analysis by country		1 Loans and advances to and balances with: Overseas offices of the reporting institution	2 Other banks overseas (including central monetary institutions)	3 Other overseas residents	4 Overseas bills	5 ECGD special scheme lending for exports and refinanced lending at fixed rates	6 Acceptances given under credit facilities opened on behalf of overseas residents
Total of all overseas customers (A+B+C below)		[12.14]	[12.15]	[16.6]	[14.9]	[15.1+22.7]	[22.4+22.5]
A International organisations	EC institutions	X	X				
	Other institutions	X	X				
B Unallocated by country							
C Country breakdown							
Abu Dhabi	ABUD						
Afghanistan	AFGH						
Albania	ALBA						
Algeria	ALGE						
Andorra	ANDO						
Angola	ANGO						
Anguilla	ANGU						
Antigua	ANTI						
Argentina	ARGE						
Australia	AUSL						
Austria	AUSR						
Bahamas	BAHA						
Bahrain	BAHR						
Bangladesh	BANG						
Barbados	BARB						
Belgium	BELG						
Belize	BELI						
Benin	DAHO						
Bermuda	BERM						
Bhutan	BHUT						
Bolivia	BOLI						

Figures in shaded areas must agree with referenced items on Form BS column 1†

Botswana	BOTS						
Brazil	BRAZ						
British Antarctic Territory	BRAT						
British Indian Ocean Territory	BIOT						
British Virgin Islands	BRVI						
Brunei	BRUN						
Bulgaria	BULG						
Burma	BURM						
Burundi	BURU						
Cameroon, United Republic of	CAME						
Canada	CANA						
Canton and Enderbury Islands	CANT						
Cape Verde	CAPE						
Cayman Islands	CAYM						
Central African Republic	CEAR						
Chad	CHAD						
Chile	CHIL						
China, People's Republic	CHIN						
Colombia	COLO						
Comoros	COMO						
Congo	CONG						
Costa Rica	COSR						
Cuba	CUBA						
Cyprus	CYPR						
Czechoslovakia	CZEC						
Denmark	DENM						
Djibouti	AFIS						
Dominica	DOMA						
Dominican Republic	DOMR						
Dubai	DUBA						
Ecuador	ECUA						
Egypt	EGYP						
El Salvador	ELSA						
Equatorial Guinea	EQUA						
Ethiopia	ETHI						
Faeroe Islands	FARO						
Falkland Islands	FALK						
Fiji	FIJI						
Finland	FINL						

† Institutions reporting on Form BS(DM), Form MFI(Q) or Form GD(Q) should refer to the notes on the back cover.

Sterling claims on overseas residents

£000s

Section 1 **Analysis by country** *(continued)*		1 Loans and advances to and balances with: Overseas offices of the reporting institution	2 Other banks overseas (including central monetary institutions)	3 Other overseas residents	4 Overseas bills	5 ECGD special scheme lending for exports and refinanced lending at fixed rates	6 Acceptances given under credit facilities opened on behalf of overseas residents
France	FRAN						
French Guiana	FGUI						
French Polynesia	FPOL						
French Southern and Antarctic Territories	FSAT						
Gabon	GABO						
Gambia	GAMB						
German Democratic Republic	EGER						
Germany, Federal Republic of	WGER						
Ghana	GHAN						
Gibraltar	GIBR						
Greece	GREE						
Greenland	GRND						
Grenada	GREN						
Guadeloupe	GUAD						
Guatemala	GUAT						
Guinea	GUIN						
Guinea-Bissau	PGUI						
Guyana	GUYA						
Haiti	HAIT						
Honduras	HOND						
Hong Kong	HONG						
Hungary	HUNG						
Iceland	ICEL						
India	INDI						
Indonesia	INDO						
Iran	IRAN						
Iraq	IRAQ						
Ireland	EIRE						
Israel	ISRA						
Italy	ITAL						

Ivory Coast	IVCO						
Jamaica	JAMA						
Japan	JAPA						
Jordan	JORD						
Kampuchea, Democratic	KHME						
Kenya	KENY						
Kiribati (formerly Gilbert Islands)	GILB						
Korea, Democratic People's Republic of	NKOR						
Korea, Republic of	SKOR						
Kuwait	KUWA						
Lao People's Democratic Republic	LAOS						
Lebanon	LEBA						
Lesotho	LESO						
Liberia	LIBE						
Libyan Arab Jamahiriya	LIBY						
Liechtenstein	LICH						
Luxembourg	LUXE						
Macau	MACA						
Madagascar (Malagasy Republic)	MADA						
Malawi	MALW						
Malaysia	MALA						
Maldives	MALD						
Mali	MALI						
Malta	MALT						
Martinique	MART						
Mauritania	MTAN						
Mauritius	MAUR						
Mexico	MEXI						
Monaco	MONA						
Mongolia	MONG						
Montserrat	MONT						
Morocco	MORO						
Mozambique	MOZA						
Namibia (SW Africa)	NAMI						
Nauru	NAUR						
Nepal	NEPA						
Netherlands	NETH						
Netherlands Antilles	NETA						
New Caledonia	NWCL						
New Zealand	NEWZ						

Sterling claims on overseas residents

£000s

Section 1 **Analysis by country** *(continued)*		1 Loans and advances to and balances with: Overseas offices of the reporting institution	2 Other banks overseas (including central monetary institutions)	3 Other overseas residents	4 Overseas bills	5 ECGD special scheme lending for exports and refinanced lending at fixed rates	6 Acceptances given under credit facilities opened on behalf of overseas residents
Nicaragua	NICA						
Niger	NIGR						
Nigeria	NIGE						
Norway	NORW						
Oman	OMAN						
Other United Arab Emirates	OUAE						
Pakistan	PAKI						
Panamá	PANA						
Papau New Guinea	PNGU						
Paraguay	PARA						
Peru	PERU						
Philippines	PHIL						
Pitcairn Island	PITC						
Poland	POLA						
Portugal	PORT						
Qatar	QATA						
Reunion	REUN						
Romania	ROMA						
Rwanda	RWAN						
St Helena	SAHE						
St Kitts-Nevis	SCRN						
Saint Lucia	SLUC						
St Pierre and Miquelon	SPMI						
Saint Vincent and the Grenadines	SVIN						
Samoa (formerly Western Samoa)	WSAM						
Sao Tome and Principe	SATP						
Saudi Arabia	SAUA						
Senegal	SENE						
Seychelles	SEYC						
Sierra Leone	SILE						

Singapore	SING						
Solomon Islands	BRSI						
Somalia	SOMA						
South Africa	SAFR						
Spain	SPAI						
Sri Lanka	SRIL						
Sudan	SUDA						
Suriname	SURI						
Swaziland	SWAZ						
Sweden	SWED						
Switzerland	SWIT						
Syrian Arab Republic	SYRI						
Taiwan	TAIW						
Tanzania, United Republic of	TANZ						
Thailand	THAI						
Togo	TOGO						
Tonga	TONG						
Trinidad and Tobago	TRIN						
Tunisia	TUNI						
Turkey	TURK						
Turks and Caicos Islands	TUCA						
Tuvalu (formerly Ellice Islands)	TUVA						
Uganda	UGAN						
United States	USA						
US Trust Territories in the Pacific	USTP						
US Virgin Islands	USVI						
Upper Volta	UVOL						
Uruguay	URUG						
USSR	USSR						
Vanuatu (fomerly New Hebrides)	NWHB						
Vatican City State (Holy See)	VATI						
Venezuela	VENE						
Vietnam, Socialist Republic of	VNMN						
Wallis and Futuna Islands	WALF						
Western Sahara	WSAH						
Yemen Arab Republic	YEME						
Yemen, People's Democratic Republic of	YEMS						
Yugoslavia	YUGO						
Zaire	ZAIR						
Zambia	ZAMB						
Zimbabwe	RHOD						

Sterling claims on overseas central monetary institutions

£000s

Section 2 **Analysis of claims on central monetary institutions**	**1** **Loans and advances to and balances with central monetary institutions (a)**	**2** **Overseas bills (b)**	**3** **ECGD special scheme lending for exports and refinanced lending at fixed rates (c)**	**4** **Acceptances given under credit facilities opened on behalf of overseas residents (d)**
TOTAL				

(a) Part of Section 1 column 2
(b) Part of Section 1 column 4
(c) Part of Section 1 column 5
(d) Part of Section 1 column 6

Cross-form references for institutions reporting on Form BS(DM), Form MFI(Q) or Form GD(Q).

The entries in the "Total of all overseas customers" row in this form should agree with, or should be consistent with, the items in column 1 (sterling) of the relevant balance sheet return indicated below, if completed for the reporting date:

	Loans and advances to and balances with: Overseas offices of the reporting institution (Col 1)	Loans and advances to and balances with: Other banks overseas (incl. CMI) (Col 2)	Loans and advances to and balances with: Other overseas residents (Col 3)	Overseas bills (Col 4)	ECGD special scheme lending for exports (Col 5)	Acceptances (Col 6)
Reporters on Form BS(DM)		11.10		12.10	†	†
Reporters on Form MFI(Q)		2.1.7 (part)		2.2.3	2.1.7 (part)	†
Reporters on Form GD(Q)		2.1.7 (part)		2.3.3 (part)	†	†

† Not applicable

APPENDIX XI - FORMS S2

Forms S2 (liabilities) and (claims) analyse certain of the reporting institution's liabilities to and claims on overseas residents by country (or geographical area) and by currency. Form S2 (section 2) analyses total spot liabilities and claims by currency and by sector; and total forward sales and purchases by currency. These forms are concerned solely with liabilities and claims in currencies other than sterling.

With the exception of London certificates of deposit lodged by overseas residents, liabilities and claims denominated in composite currencies are disaggregated into their component national currencies and reported under those national currencies. The sterling component of such business, and any other national currency components which are not separately specified on the form, are included under "other currencies".

In addition on Form S2 (section 2) in the memorandum items the whole amount of SDR-denominated business and ECU-denominated business, are shown after they have been translated into sterling, under each column which is relevant (including forward sales and purchases).

Private and confidential **Form S2 (claims)**

Currencies other than sterling

Country analysis of UK external claims

as at ____________________

Reporting institution ____________________

____

Signature of authorised official of reporting institution

In the event of a query, the Bank of England may contact (block letters please)

____________________ Tel. no ____________________ Ext. ________

Notes on completion

If you have any difficulty in completing this form, please telephone 01-601 4885/4870.

1 Complete form quarterly as at end of March, June, September, and December unless otherwise requested by the Bank of England.

2 For definition of items refer to the *Banking statistics definitions* folder.

3 Enter amounts in sterling to nearest thousand omitting £000s.

4 Ensure that the items in the shaded areas agree with related items in column 2 (other currencies) of Form BS, or the relevant balance sheet return, and with the relevant currency entries on Form S2 (section 2).

5 Return form within **TEN** calendar days of reporting date to:

Financial Statistics Division HO-3
Group 3/2
Bank of England
Threadneedle Street
London EC2R 8AH

Bank of England use only

Logged	Data entered	Pending	Query	Awaiting update	Revision book	Revision input

December 1983
(64)

UK external claims in

Analysis by country (Sheet 1)		Claims on overseas residents (excluding acceptances): Total analysed by type of asset: Loans and advances 1	Overseas bills 2	ECGD special scheme lending for exports 3	Total (1 + 2 + 3) 4	Total analysed: Loans and advances to banks overseas* 5
Total of all overseas customers (A + B + C) below						
Figures in shaded areas must agree with referenced items on Form BS column 2 and on Form S2 (section 2).†		[BS 12.14+12.15+16.6]	[BS 14.9]	[BS 15.1]		[BS 12.14+12.15]
A International organisations	EC institutions					
	Other institutions					
B Unallocated by country						
C Country breakdown						
Abu Dhabi	ABUD					
Afghanistan	AFGH					
Albania	ALBA					
Algeria	ALGE					
Andorra	ANDO					
Angola	ANGO					
Anguilla	ANGU					
Antigua	ANTI					
Argentina	ARGE					
Australia	AUSL					
Austria	AUSR					
Bahamas	BAHA					
Bahrain	BAHR					
Bangladesh	BANG					
Barbados	BARB					
Belgium	BELG					
Belize	BELI					
Benin	DAHO					
Bermuda	BERM					
Bhutan	BHUT					
Bolivia	BOLI					
Botswana	BOTS					
Brazil	BRAZ					
British Antarctic Territory	BRAT					
British Indian Ocean Territory	BIOT					
British Virgin Islands	BRVI					
Brunei	BRUN					
Bulgaria	BULG					
Burma	BURM					
Burundi	BURU					
Cameroon, United Republic of	CAME					
Canada	CANA					
Canton and Enderbury Islands	CANT					
Cape Verde	CAPE					
Cayman Islands	CAYM					
Central African Republic	CEAR					
Chad	CHAD					
Chile	CHIL					
China, People's Republic	CHIN					
Colombia	COLO					
Comoros	COMO					
Congo	CONG					
Costa Rica	COSR					
Cuba	CUBA					
Cyprus	CYPR					
Czechoslovakia	CZEC					
Denmark	DENM					

† Institutions reporting on Form BS(DM), Form MFI(Q) or Form GD(Q) should refer to the notes on the back cover.

*Including CMI

currencies other than sterling

£000s

by sector	Country	Total analysed by currency and sector					
		US dollars		Deutschemarks		Swiss francs	
Other		Loans and advances to banks overseas*	Other	Loans and advances to banks overseas*	Other	Loans and advances to banks overseas*	Other
6		7	8	9	10	11	12
[BS 14.9 + 15.1 + 16.6]		[S2 (2) Claims Cols. 3 + 4 for US $]		[S2 (2) Claims Cols. 3 + 4 for DM]		[S2 (2) Claims Cols. 3 + 4 for Sw. Fcs.]	
	ABUD						
	AFGH						
	ALBA						
	ALGE						
	ANDO						
	ANGO						
	ANGU						
	ANTI						
	ARGE						
	AUSL						
	AUSR						
	BAHA						
	BAHR						
	BANG						
	BARB						
	BELG						
	BELI						
	DAHO						
	BERM						
	BHUT						
	BOLI						
	BOTS						
	BRAZ						
	BRAT						
	BIOT						
	BRVI						
	BRUN						
	BULG						
	BURM						
	BURU						
	CAME						
	CANA						
	CANT						
	CAPE						
	CAYM						
	CEAR						
	CHAD						
	CHIL						
	CHIN						
	COLO						
	COMO						
	CONG						
	COSR						
	CUBA						
	CYPR						
	CZEC						
	DENM						

UK external claims in

Analysis by country (Sheet 2)	Claims on overseas residents (excluding acceptances)				
	Total analysed by currency and sector (continued)				
	Japanese yen		French francs		Netherlands
	Loans and advances to banks overseas*	Other	Loans and advances to banks overseas*	Other	Loans and advances to banks overseas*
	13	14	15	16	17
Total of all overseas customers (A + B + C) below					
Figures in shaded areas must agree with referenced items on Form BS column 2 and on Form S2 (section 2).†	[S2 (2) Claims Cols. 3 + 4 for Yen]		[S2 (2) Claims Cols. 3 + 4 for Fr. Fcs.]		[S2 (2) Claims
A EC institutions					
A Other institutions					
B					
C					
ABUD					
AFGH					
ALBA					
ALGE					
ANDO					
ANGO					
ANGU					
ANTI					
ARGE					
AUSL					
AUSR					
BAHA					
BAHR					
BANG					
BARB					
BELG					
BELI					
DAHO					
BERM					
BHUT					
BOLI					
BOTS					
BRAZ					
BRAT					
BIOT					
BRVI					
BRUN					
BULG					
BURM					
BURU					
CAME					
CANA					
CANT					
CAPE					
CAYM					
CEAR					
CHAD					
CHIL					
CHIN					
COLO					
COMO					
CONG					
COSR					
CUBA					
CYPR					
CZEC					
DENM					

† Institutions reporting on Form BS(DM), Form MFI(Q) or Form GD(Q) should refer to the notes on the back cover.

* Including CMI

currencies other than sterling

£000s

guilders	Country	Italian lire		Belgian francs		Other † currencies	Acceptances given under credit facilities opened on behalf of overseas residents
Other		Loans and advances to banks overseas*	Other	Loans and advances to banks overseas*	Other		
18		19	20	21	22	23	24
Cols. 3 + 4 for Guilders]		[S2 (2) Claims Cols. 3 + 4 for Lire]		[S2 (2) Claims Cols. 3 + 4 for B. Fcs.]			[BS 22.4 + 22.5]
	ABUD						
	AFGH						
	ALBA						
	ALGE						
	ANDO						
	ANGO						
	ANGU						
	ANTI						
	ARGE						
	AUSL						
	AUSR						
	BAHA						
	BAHR						
	BANG						
	BARB						
	BELG						
	BELI						
	DAHO						
	BERM						
	BHUT						
	BOLI						
	BOTS						
	BRAZ						
	BRAT						
	BIOT						
	BRVI						
	BRUN						
	BULG						
	BURM						
	BURU						
	CAME						
	CANA						
	CANT						
	CAPE						
	CAYM						
	CEAR						
	CHAD						
	CHIL						
	CHIN						
	COLO						
	COMO						
	CONG						
	COSR						
	CUBA						
	CYPR						
	CZEC						
	DENM						

† Including the sterling components of SDR and ECU claims

UK external claims in

Analysis by country (Sheet 1) *(continued)*		Claims on overseas residents (excluding acceptances)				
		Total analysed by type of asset			Total (1 + 2 + 3)	Total analysed
		Loans and advances	Overseas bills	ECGD special scheme lending for exports		Loans and advances to banks overseas*
		1	2	3	4	5
Djibouti	AFIS					
Dominica	DOMA					
Dominican Republic	DOMR					
Dubai	DUBA					
Ecuador	ECUA					
Egypt	EGYP					
El Salvador	ELSA					
Equatorial Guinea	EQUA					
Ethiopia	ETHI					
Faeroe Islands	FARO					
Falkland Islands	FALK					
Fiji	FIJI					
Finland	FINL					
France	FRAN					
French Guiana	FGUI					
French Polynesia	FPOL					
French Southern and Antarctic Territories	FSAT					
Gabon	GABO					
Gambia	GAMB					
German Democratic Republic	EGER					
Germany, Federal Republic of	WGER					
Ghana	GHAN					
Gibraltar	GIBR					
Greece	GREE					
Greenland	GRND					
Grenada	GREN					
Guadeloupe	GUAD					
Guatemala	GUAT					
Guinea	GUIN					
Guinea-Bissau	PGUI					
Guyana	GUYA					
Haiti	HAIT					
Honduras	HOND					
Hong Kong	HONG					
Hungary	HUNG					
Iceland	ICEL					
India	INDI					
Indonesia	INDO					
Iran	IRAN					
Iraq	IRAQ					
Ireland	EIRE					
Israel	ISRA					
Italy	ITAL					
Ivory Coast	IVCO					
Jamaica	JAMA					
Japan	JAPA					
Jordan	JORD					
Kampuchea, Democratic	KHME					
Kenya	KENY					
Kiribati (formerly Gilbert Islands)	GILB					
Korea, Democratic People's Republic of	NKOR					
Korea, Republic of	SKOR					
Kuwait	KUWA					

*Including CMI

currencies other than sterling

£000s

by sector	Country	Total analysed by currency and sector					
		US dollars		Deutschemarks		Swiss francs	
Other		Loans and advances to banks overseas*	Other	Loans and advances to banks overseas*	Other	Loans and advances to banks overseas*	Other
6		7	8	9	10	11	12
	AFIS						
	DOMA						
	DOMR						
	DUBA						
	ECUA						
	EGYP						
	ELSA						
	EQUA						
	ETHI						
	FARO						
	FALK						
	FIJI						
	FINL						
	FRAN						
	FGUI						
	FPOL						
	FSAT						
	GABO						
	GAMB						
	EGER						
	WGER						
	GHAN						
	GIBR						
	GREE						
	GRND						
	GREN						
	GUAD						
	GUAT						
	GUIN						
	PGUI						
	GUYA						
	HAIT						
	HOND						
	HONG						
	HUNG						
	ICEL						
	INDI						
	INDO						
	IRAN						
	IRAQ						
	EIRE						
	ISRA						
	ITAL						
	IVCO						
	JAMA						
	JAPA						
	JORD						
	KHME						
	KENY						
	GILB						
	NKOR						
	SKOR						
	KUWA						

UK external claims in

Analysis by country (Sheet 2) *(continued)*	Claims on overseas residents (excluding acceptances)				
	Total analysed by currency and sector (continued)				
	Japanese yen		French francs		Netherlands
	Loans and advances to banks overseas*	Other	Loans and advances to banks overseas*	Other	Loans and advances to banks overseas*
	13	14	15	16	17
AFIS					
DOMA					
DOMR					
DUBA					
ECUA					
EGYP					
ELSA					
EQUA					
ETHI					
FARO					
FALK					
FIJI					
FINL					
FRAN					
FGUI					
FPOL					
FSAT					
GABO					
GAMB					
EGER					
WGER					
GHAN					
GIBR					
GREE					
GRND					
GREN					
GUAD					
GUAT					
GUIN					
PGUI					
GUYA					
HAIT					
HOND					
HONG					
HUNG					
ICEL					
INDI					
INDO					
IRAN					
IRAQ					
EIRE					
ISRA					
ITAL					
IVCO					
JAMA					
JAPA					
JORD					
KHME					
KENY					
GILB					
NKOR					
SKOR					
KUWA					

*Including CMI

currencies other than sterling

£000s

guilders	Country	Italian lire		Belgian francs		Other † currencies
Other		Loans and advances to banks overseas*	Other	Loans and advances to banks overseas*	Other	
18		19	20	21	22	23
	AFIS					
	DOMA					
	DOMR					
	DUBA					
	ECUA					
	EGYP					
	ELSA					
	EQUA					
	ETHI					
	FARO					
	FALK					
	FIJI					
	FINL					
	FRAN					
	FGUI					
	FPOL					
	FSAT					
	GABO					
	GAMB					
	EGER					
	WGER					
	GHAN					
	GIBR					
	GREE					
	GRND					
	GREN					
	GUAD					
	GUAT					
	GUIN					
	PGUI					
	GUYA					
	HAIT					
	HOND					
	HONG					
	HUNG					
	ICEL					
	INDI					
	INDO					
	IRAN					
	IRAQ					
	EIRE					
	ISRA					
	ITAL					
	IVCO					
	JAMA					
	JAPA					
	JORD					
	KHME					
	KENY					
	GILB					
	NKOR					
	SKOR					
	KUWA					

† Including the sterling components of SDR and ECU claims

£000s

Acceptances given under credit facilities opened on behalf of overseas residents
24

UK external claims in

Analysis by country (Sheet 1) *(continued)*		Claims on overseas residents (excluding acceptances): Total analysed by type of asset				Total analysed
		Loans and advances	Overseas bills	ECGD special scheme lending for exports	Total (1 + 2 + 3)	Loans and advances to banks overseas*
		1	2	3	4	5
Lao People's Democratic Republic	LAOS					
Lebanon	LEBA					
Lesotho	LESO					
Liberia	LIBE					
Libyan Arab Jamahiriya	LIBY					
Liechtenstein	LICH					
Luxembourg	LUXE					
Macau	MACA					
Madagascar (Malagasy Republic)	MADA					
Malawi	MALW					
Malaysia	MALA					
Maldives	MALD					
Mali	MALI					
Malta	MALT					
Martinique	MART					
Mauritania	MTAN					
Mauritius	MAUR					
Mexico	MEXI					
Monaco	MONA					
Mongolia	MONG					
Montserrat	MONT					
Morocco	MORO					
Mozambique	MOZA					
Namibia (SW Africa)	NAMI					
Nauru	NAUR					
Nepal	NEPA					
Netherlands	NETH					
Netherlands Antilles	NETA					
New Caledonia	NWCL					
New Zealand	NEWZ					
Nicaragua	NICA					
Niger	NIGR					
Nigeria	NIGE					
Norway	NORW					
Oman	OMAN					
Other United Arab Emirates	OUAE					
Pakistan	PAKI					
Panama	PANA					
Papau New Guinea	PNGU					
Paraguay	PARA					
Peru	PERU					
Philippines	PHIL					
Pitcairn Island	PITC					
Poland	POLA					
Portugal	PORT					
Qatar	QATA					
Reunion	REUN					
Romania	ROMA					
Rwanda	RWAN					
St Helena	SAHE					
St Kitts-Nevis	SCRN					
Saint Lucia	SLUC					
St Pierre and Miquelon	SPMI					

*Including CMI

currencies other than sterling

£000s

by sector	Country	Total analysed by currency and sector					
		US dollars		Deutschemarks		Swiss francs	
Other		Loans and advances to banks overseas*	Other	Loans and advances to banks overseas*	Other	Loans and advances to banks overseas*	Other
6		7	8	9	10	11	12
	LAOS						
	LEBA						
	LESO						
	LIBE						
	LIBY						
	LICH						
	LUXE						
	MACA						
	MADA						
	MALW						
	MALA						
	MALD						
	MALI						
	MALT						
	MART						
	MTAN						
	MAUR						
	MEXI						
	MONA						
	MONG						
	MONT						
	MORO						
	MOZA						
	NAMI						
	NAUR						
	NEPA						
	NETH						
	NETA						
	NWCL						
	NEWZ						
	NICA						
	NIGR						
	NIGE						
	NORW						
	OMAN						
	OUAE						
	PAKI						
	PANA						
	PNGU						
	PARA						
	PERU						
	PHIL						
	PITC						
	POLA						
	PORT						
	QATA						
	REUN						
	ROMA						
	RWAN						
	SAHE						
	SCRN						
	SLUC						
	SPMI						

UK external claims in

Analysis by country (Sheet 2) *(continued)*	Claims on overseas residents (excluding acceptances)				
	Total analysed by currency and sector (continued)				
	Japanese yen		French francs		Netherlands
	Loans and advances to banks overseas*	Other	Loans and advances to banks overseas*	Other	Loans and advances to banks overseas*
	13	14	15	16	17
LAOS					
LEBA					
LESO					
LIBE					
LIBY					
LICH					
LUXE					
MACA					
MADA					
MALW					
MALA					
MALD					
MALI					
MALT					
MART					
MTAN					
MAUR					
MEXI					
MONA					
MONG					
MONT					
MORO					
MOZA					
NAMI					
NAUR					
NEPA					
NETH					
NETA					
NWCL					
NEWZ					
NICA					
NIGR					
NIGE					
NORW					
OMAN					
OUAE					
PAKI					
PANA					
PNGU					
PARA					
PERU					
PHIL					
PITC					
POLA					
PORT					
QATA					
REUN					
ROMA					
RWAN					
SAHE					
SCRN					
SLUC					
SPMI					

*Including CMI

currencies other than sterling

£000s

guilders Other 18	Country	Italian lire: Loans and advances to banks overseas* 19	Italian lire: Other 20	Belgian francs: Loans and advances to banks overseas* 21	Belgian francs: Other 22	Other † currencies 23
	LAOS					
	LEBA					
	LESO					
	LIBE					
	LIBY					
	LICH					
	LUXE					
	MACA					
	MADA					
	MALW					
	MALA					
	MALD					
	MALI					
	MALT					
	MART					
	MTAN					
	MAUR					
	MEXI					
	MONA					
	MONG					
	MONT					
	MORO					
	MOZA					
	NAMI					
	NAUR					
	NEPA					
	NETH					
	NETA					
	NWCL					
	NEWZ					
	NICA					
	NIGR					
	NIGE					
	NORW					
	OMAN					
	OUAE					
	PAKI					
	PANA					
	PNGU					
	PARA					
	PERU					
	PHIL					
	PITC					
	POLA					
	PORT					
	QATA					
	REUN					
	ROMA					
	RWAN					
	SAHE					
	SCRN					
	SLUC					
	SPMI					

£000s

Acceptances given under credit facilities opened on behalf of overseas residents 24

† Including the sterling components of SDR and ECU claims

UK external claims in

Analysis by country (Sheet 1) *(continued)*		Claims on overseas residents (excluding acceptances)				
		Total analysed by type of asset			Total (1 + 2 + 3)	Total analysed
		Loans and advances	Overseas bills	ECGD special scheme lending for exports		Loans and advances to banks overseas*
		1	2	3	4	5
Saint Vincent and the Grenadines	SVIN					
Samoa (formerly Western Samoa)	WSAM					
Sao Tome and Principe	SATP					
Saudi Arabia	SAUA					
Senegal	SENE					
Seychelles	SEYC					
Sierra Leone	SILE					
Singapore	SING					
Solomon Islands	BRSI					
Somalia	SOMA					
South Africa	SAFR					
Spain	SPAI					
Sri Lanka	SRIL					
Sudan	SUDA					
Suriname	SURI					
Swaziland	SWAZ					
Sweden	SWED					
Switzerland	SWIT					
Syrian Arab Republic	SYRI					
Taiwan	TAIW					
Tanzania, United Republic of	TANZ					
Thailand	THAI					
Togo	TOGO					
Tonga	TONG					
Trinidad and Tobago	TRIN					
Tunisia	TUNI					
Turkey	TURK					
Turks and Caicos Islands	TUCA					
Tuvalu (formerly Ellice Islands)	TUVA					
Uganda	UGAN					
United States	USA					
US Trust Territories in the Pacific	USTP					
US Virgin Islands	USVI					
Upper Volta	UVOL					
Uruguay	URUG					
USSR	USSR					
Vanuatu (fomerly New Hebrides)	NWHB					
Vatican City State (Holy See)	VATI					
Venezuela	VENE					
Vietnam, Socialist Republic of	VNMN					
Wallis and Futuna Islands	WALF					
Western Sahara	WSAH					
Yemen Arab Republic	YEME					
Yemen, People's Democratic Republic of	YEMS					
Yugoslavia	YUGO					
Zaire	ZAIR					
Zambia	ZAMB					
Zimbabwe	RHOD					

*Including CMI

currencies other than sterling

£000s

by sector	Country	Total analysed by currency and sector					
		US dollars		Deutschemarks		Swiss francs	
Other		Loans and advances to banks overseas*	Other	Loans and advances to banks overseas*	Other	Loans and advances to banks overseas*	Other
6		7	8	9	10	11	12
	SVIN						
	WSAM						
	SATP						
	SAUA						
	SENE						
	SEYC						
	SILE						
	SING						
	BRSI						
	SOMA						
	SAFR						
	SPAI						
	SRIL						
	SUDA						
	SURI						
	SWAZ						
	SWED						
	SWIT						
	SYRI						
	TAIW						
	TANZ						
	THAI						
	TOGO						
	TONG						
	TRIN						
	TUNI						
	TURK						
	TUCA						
	TUVA						
	UGAN						
	USA						
	USTP						
	USVI						
	UVOL						
	URUG						
	USSR						
	NWHB						
	VATI						
	VENE						
	VNMN						
	WALF						
	WSAH						
	YEME						
	YEMS						
	YUGO						
	ZAIR						
	ZAMB						
	RHOD						

UK external claims in

Analysis by country (Sheet 2) *(continued)*	Claims on overseas residents (excluding acceptances) — Total analysed by currency and sector (continued)				
	Japanese yen		French francs		Netherlands
	Loans and advances to banks overseas*	Other	Loans and advances to banks overseas*	Other	Loans and advances to banks overseas*
	13	14	15	16	17
SVIN					
WSAM					
SATP					
SAUA					
SENE					
SEYC					
SILE					
SING					
BRSI					
SOMA					
SAFR					
SPAI					
SRIL					
SUDA					
SURI					
SWAZ					
SWED					
SWIT					
SYRI					
TAIW					
TANZ					
THAI					
TOGO					
TONG					
TRIN					
TUNI					
TURK					
TUCA					
TUVA					
UGAN					
USA					
USTP					
USVI					
UVOL					
URUG					
USSR					
NWHB					
VATI					
VENE					
VNMN					
WALF					
WSAH					
YEME					
YEMS					
YUGO					
ZAIR					
ZAMB					
RHOD					

*Including CMI

currencies other than sterling

£000s | £000s

guilders	Country	Italian lire		Belgian francs		Other † currencies	Acceptances given under credit facilities opened on behalf of overseas residents
Other		Loans and advances to banks overseas*	Other	Loans and advances to banks overseas*	Other		
18		19	20	21	22	23	24
	SVIN						
	WSAM						
	SATP						
	SAUA						
	SENE						
	SEYC						
	SILE						
	SING						
	BRSI						
	SOMA						
	SAFR						
	SPAI						
	SRIL						
	SUDA						
	SURI						
	SWAZ						
	SWED						
	SWIT						
	SYRI						
	TAIW						
	TANZ						
	THAI						
	TOGO						
	TONG						
	TRIN						
	TUNI						
	TURK						
	TUCA						
	TUVA						
	UGAN						
	USA						
	USTP						
	USVI						
	UVOL						
	URUG						
	USSR						
	NWHB						
	VATI						
	VENE						
	VNMN						
	WALF						
	WSAH						
	YEME						
	YEMS						
	YUGO						
	ZAIR						
	ZAMB						
	RHOD						

† Including the sterling components of SDR and ECU claims

Private and confidential **Form S2 (liabilities)**

Currencies other than sterling

Country analysis of UK external liabilities

as at ______________________

Reporting institution ______________________

____

Signature of authorised official of reporting institution

In the event of a query, the Bank of England may contact (block letters please)

______________________ Tel. no ______________________ Ext. ________

Notes on completion

If you have any difficulty in completing this form, please telephone 01-601 4885/4870.

1 Complete form quarterly as at end of March, June, September, and December unless otherwise requested by the Bank of England.

2 For definition of items refer to the *Banking statistics definitions* folder.

3 Enter amounts in sterling to nearest thousand omitting £000s.

4 Ensure that the items in the shaded areas agree with related items in column 2 (other currencies) of Form BS, or the relevant balance sheet return, and with the relevant currency entries on Form S2 (section 2).

5 Return form within **TEN** calendar days of reporting date to:

Financial Statistics Division HO-3
Group 3/2
Bank of England
Threadneedle Street
London EC2R 8AH

Bank of England use only

Logged	Data entered	Pending	Query	Awaiting update	Revision book	Revision input

December 1983
(65)

UK external liabilities in

PART A Analysis by country (Sheet 1)		Sight and time deposit liabilities to overseas residents: Total analysed by sector: Banks overseas (including CMI) 1	Other overseas residents 2	Total (1 + 2) 3	Total analysed by US: Banks overseas (including CMI) 4
Total of all overseas customers (A + B + C) below Figures in shaded areas must agree with referenced items on Form BS column 2 and on Form S2 (section 2).†		[BS - A1]	[BS - A2]	[BS 2.6 + 2.7 + 2.16 + 2.17]	[S2 (2) Liabs. Col.
A International organisations	EC institutions				
	Other institutions				
B Unallocated by country					
C Country breakdown					
Abu Dhabi	ABUD				
Afghanistan	AFGH				
Albania	ALBA				
Algeria	ALGE				
Andorra	ANDO				
Angola	ANGO				
Anguilla	ANGU				
Antigua	ANTI				
Argentina	ARGE				
Australia	AUSL				
Austria	AUSR				
Bahamas	BAHA				
Bahrain	BAHR				
Bangladesh	BANG				
Barbados	BARB				
Belgium	BELG				
Belize	BELI				
Benin	DAHO				
Bermuda	BERM				
Bhutan	BHUT				
Bolivia	BOLI				
Botswana	BOTS				
Brazil	BRAZ				
British Antarctic Territory	BRAT				
British Indian Ocean Territory	BIOT				
British Virgin Islands	BRVI				
Brunei	BRUN				
Bulgaria	BULG				
Burma	BURM				
Burundi	BURU				
Cameroon, United Republic of	CAME				
Canada	CANA				
Canton and Enderbury Islands	CANT				
Cape Verde	CAPE				
Cayman Islands	CAYM				
Central African Republic	CEAR				
Chad	CHAD				
Chile	CHIL				
China, People's Republic	CHIN				
Colombia	COLO				
Comoros	COMO				
Congo	CONG				
Costa Rica	COSR				
Cuba	CUBA				
Cyprus	CYPR				
Czechoslovakia	CZEC				
Denmark	DENM				

† Institutions reporting on Form BS(DM), Form MFI(Q) or Form GD(Q) should refer to the notes on the back cover.

currencies other than sterling

£000s

currency and sector

dollars	Country	Deutschemarks		Swiss francs		Japanese yen	
Other overseas residents		Banks overseas (including CMI)	Other overseas residents	Banks overseas (including CMI)	Other overseas residents	Banks overseas (including CMI)	Other overseas residents
5		6	7	8	9	10	11
3 for US $]		[S2 (2) Liabs. Col. 3 for DM]		[S2 (2) Liabs. Col. 3 for Sw. Fcs.]		[S2 (2) Liabs. Col. 3 for Yen]	
	ABUD						
	AFGH						
	ALBA						
	ALGE						
	ANDO						
	ANGO						
	ANGU						
	ANTI						
	ARGE						
	AUSL						
	AUSR						
	BAHA						
	BAHR						
	BANG						
	BARB						
	BELG						
	BELI						
	DAHO						
	BERM						
	BHUT						
	BOLI						
	BOTS						
	BRAZ						
	BRAT						
	BIOT						
	BRVI						
	BRUN						
	BULG						
	BURM						
	BURU						
	CAME						
	CANA						
	CANT						
	CAPE						
	CAYM						
	CEAR						
	CHAD						
	CHIL						
	CHIN						
	COLO						
	COMO						
	CONG						
	COSR						
	CUBA						
	CYPR						
	CZEC						
	DENM						

UK external liabilities in

PART A Analysis by country (Sheet 2)	Sight and time deposit liabilities to overseas residents Total analysed by currency and sector (continued) French francs		Netherlands guilders		Italian lire	
	Banks overseas (including CMI)	Other overseas residents	Banks overseas (including CMI)	Other overseas residents	Banks overseas (including CMI)	Other overseas residents
	12	13	14	15	16	17
(A + B + C) below Figures in shaded areas must agree with referenced items on Form S2 (section 2).†	[S2 (2) Liabs. Col. 3 for Fr. Fcs.]		[S2 (2) Liabs. Col. 3 for Guilders]		[S2 (2) Liabs. Col. 3 for Lire]	
A EC institutions						
Other institutions						
B						
C						
ABUD						
AFGH						
ALBA						
ALGE						
ANDO						
ANGO						
ANGU						
ANTI						
ARGE						
AUSL						
AUSR						
BAHA						
BAHR						
BANG						
BARB						
BELG						
BELI						
DAHO						
BERM						
BHUT						
BOLI						
BOTS						
BRAZ						
BRAT						
BIOT						
BRVI						
BRUN						
BULG						
BURM						
BURU						
CAME						
CANA						
CANT						
CAPE						
CAYM						
CEAR						
CHAD						
CHIL						
CHIN						
COLO						
COMO						
CONG						
COSR						
CUBA						
CYPR						
CZEC						
DENM						

currencies other than sterling

£000s

Country	Belgian francs		Other * currencies	London certificates of deposit lodged by overseas residents			
				Denominated in US dollars		Denominated in other currencies	
	Banks overseas (including CMI)	Other overseas residents		Banks overseas (including CMI)	Other overseas residents	Banks overseas (including CMI)	Other overseas residents
	18	19	20	21	22	23	24
	[S2 (2) Liabs. Col. 3 for B. Fcs.]						
ABUD							
AFGH							
ALBA							
ALGE							
ANDO							
ANGO							
ANGU							
ANTI							
ARGE							
AU[illegible]							
AUSR							
BAHA							
BAHR							
BANG							
BARB							
BELG							
BELI							
DAHO							
BERM							
BHUT							
BOLI							
BOTS							
BRAZ							
BRAT							
BIOT							
BR[illegible]							
BR[illegible]							
BULG							
BURM							
BURU							
CAME							
CANA							
CANT							
CAPE							
CAYM							
CEAR							
CHAD							
CHIL							
CHIN							
COLO							
COMO							
CONG							
COSR							
CUBA							
CYPR							
CZEC							
DENM							

£000s

* Including the sterling components of SDR and ECU liabilities

UK external liabilities in

PART A **Analysis by country (Sheet 1)** *(continued)*		Sight and time deposit liabilities to overseas residents: Total analysed by sector: Banks overseas (including CMI)	Other overseas residents	Total (1 + 2)	Total analysed by US: Banks overseas (including CMI)
		1	2	3	4
Djibouti	AFIS				
Dominica	DOMA				
Dominican Republic	DOMR				
Dubai	DUBA				
Ecuador	ECUA				
Egypt	EGYP				
El Salvador	ELSA				
Equatorial Guinea	EQUA				
Ethiopia	ETHI				
Faeroe Islands	FARO				
Falkland Islands	FALK				
Fiji	FIJI				
Finland	FINL				
France	FRAN				
French Guiana	FGUI				
French Polynesia	FPOL				
French Southern and Antarctic Territories	FSAT				
Gabon	GABO				
Gambia	GAMB				
German Democratic Republic	EGER				
Germany, Federal Republic of	WGER				
Ghana	GHAN				
Gibraltar	GIBR				
Greece	GREE				
Greenland	GRND				
Grenada	GREN				
Guadeloupe	GUAD				
Guatemala	GUAT				
Guinea	GUIN				
Guinea-Bissau	PGUI				
Guyana	GUYA				
Haiti	HAIT				
Honduras	HOND				
Hong Kong	HONG				
Hungary	HUNG				
Iceland	ICEL				
India	INDI				
Indonesia	INDO				
Iran	IRAN				
Iraq	IRAQ				
Ireland	EIRE				
Israel	ISRA				
Italy	ITAL				
Ivory Coast	IVCO				
Jamaica	JAMA				
Japan	JAPA				
Jordan	JORD				
Kampuchea, Democratic	KHME				
Kenya	KENY				
Kiribati (formerly Gilbert Islands)	GILB				
Korea, Democratic People's Republic of	NKOR				
Korea, Republic of	SKOR				
Kuwait	KUWA				

currencies other than sterling

£000s

currency and sector

dollars	Country	Deutschemarks		Swiss francs		Japanese yen	
Other overseas residents		Banks overseas (including CMI)	Other overseas residents	Banks overseas (including CMI)	Other overseas residents	Banks overseas (including CMI)	Other overseas residents
5		6	7	8	9	10	11
	AFIS						
	DOMA						
	DOMR						
	DUBA						
	ECUA						
	EGYP						
	ELSA						
	EQUA						
	ETHI						
	FARO						
	FALK						
	FIJI						
	FINL						
	FRAN						
	FGUI						
	FPOL						
	FSAT						
	GABO						
	GAMB						
	EGER						
	WGER						
	GHAN						
	GIBR						
	GREE						
	GRND						
	GREN						
	GUAD						
	GUAT						
	GUIN						
	PGUI						
	GUYA						
	HAIT						
	HOND						
	HONG						
	HUNG						
	ICEL						
	INDI						
	INDO						
	IRAN						
	IRAQ						
	EIRE						
	ISRA						
	ITAL						
	IVCO						
	JAMA						
	JAPA						
	JORD						
	KHME						
	KENY						
	GILB						
	NKOR						
	SKOR						
	KUWA						

UK external liabilities in

PART A Analysis by country (Sheet 2) *(continued)*	Sight and time deposit liabilities to overseas residents Total analysed by currency and sector (continued) French francs Banks overseas (including CMI) 12	French francs Other overseas residents 13	Netherlands guilders Banks overseas (including CMI) 14	Netherlands guilders Other overseas residents 15	Italian lire Banks overseas (including CMI) 16	Italian lire Other overseas residents 17
AFIS						
DOMA						
DOMR						
DUBA						
ECUA						
EGYP						
ELSA						
EQUA						
ETHI						
FARO						
FALK						
FIJI						
FINL						
FRAN						
FGUI						
FPOL						
FSAT						
GABO						
GAMB						
EGER						
WGER						
GHAN						
GIBR						
GREE						
GRND						
GREN						
GUAD						
GUAT						
GUIN						
PGUI						
GUYA						
HAIT						
HOND						
HONG						
HUNG						
ICEL						
INDI						
INDO						
IRAN						
IRAQ						
EIRE						
ISRA						
ITAL						
IVCO						
JAMA						
JAPA						
JORD						
KHME						
KENY						
GILB						
NKOR						
SKOR						
KUWA						

currencies other than sterling

£000s

Country	Belgian francs		Other * currencies	London certificates of deposit lodged by overseas residents: Denominated in US dollars		Denominated in other currencies	
	Banks overseas (including CMI)	Other overseas residents		Banks overseas (including CMI)	Other overseas residents	Banks overseas (including CMI)	Other overseas residents
	18	19	20	21	22	23	24
AFIS							
DOMA							
DOMR							
DUBA							
ECUA							
EGYP							
ELSA							
EQUA							
ETHI							
FARO							
FALK							
FIJI							
FINL							
FRAN							
FGUI							
FI[illegible]							
FSAT							
GABO							
GAMB							
EGER							
WGER							
GHAN							
GIBR							
GREE							
GRND							
GREN							
GUAD							
GUAT							
GUIN							
PGUI							
GUYA							
HA[illegible]T							
H[illegible]							
HONG							
HUNG							
ICEL							
INDI							
INDO							
IRAN							
IRAQ							
EIRE							
ISRA							
ITAL							
IVCO							
JAMA							
JAPA							
JORD							
KHME							
KENY							
GILB							
NKOR							
SKOR							
KUWA							

£000s (columns 21–24)

* Including the sterling components of SDR and ECU liabilities

UK external liabilities in

PART A **Analysis by country** **(Sheet 1)** *(continued)*		Sight and time deposit liabilities to overseas residents: Total analysed by sector: Banks overseas (including CMI) 1	Other overseas residents 2	Total (1 + 2) 3	Total analysed by US: Banks overseas (including CMI) 4
Lao People's Democratic Republic	LAOS				
Lebanon	LEBA				
Lesotho	LESO				
Liberia	LIBE				
Libyan Arab Jamahiriya	LIBY				
Liechtenstein	LICH				
Luxembourg	LUXE				
Macau	MACA				
Madagascar (Malagasy Republic)	MADA				
Malawi	MALW				
Malaysia	MALA				
Maldives	MALD				
Mali	MALI				
Malta	MALT				
Martinique	MART				
Mauritania	MTAN				
Mauritius	MAUR				
Mexico	MEXI				
Monaco	MONA				
Mongolia	MONG				
Montserrat	MONT				
Morocco	MORO				
Mozambique	MOZA				
Namibia (SW Africa)	NAMI				
Nauru	NAUR				
Nepal	NEPA				
Netherlands	NETH				
Netherlands Antilles	NETA				
New Caledonia	NWCL				
New Zealand	NEWZ				
Nicaragua	NICA				
Niger	NIGR				
Nigeria	NIGE				
Norway	NORW				
Oman	OMAN				
Other United Arab Emirates	OUAE				
Pakistan	PAKI				
Panama	PANA				
Papau New Guinea	PNGU				
Paraguay	PARA				
Peru	PERU				
Philippines	PHIL				
Pitcairn Island	PITC				
Poland	POLA				
Portugal	PORT				
Qatar	QATA				
Reunion	REUN				
Romania	ROMA				
Rwanda	RWAN				
St Helena	SAHE				
St Kitts-Nevis	SCRN				
Saint Lucia	SLUC				
St Pierre and Miquelon	SPMI				

currencies other than sterling

£000s

currency and sector							
dollars	Country	Deutschemarks		Swiss francs		Japanese yen	
Other overseas residents		Banks overseas (including CMI)	Other overseas residents	Banks overseas (including CMI)	Other overseas residents	Banks overseas (including CMI)	Other overseas residents
5		6	7	8	9	10	11
	LAOS						
	LEBA						
	LESO						
	LIBE						
	LIBY						
	LICH						
	LUXE						
	MACA						
	MADA						
	MALW						
	MALA						
	MALD						
	MALI						
	MALT						
	MART						
	MTAN						
	MAUR						
	MEXI						
	MONA						
	MONG						
	MONT						
	MORO						
	MOZA						
	NAMI						
	NAUR						
	NEPA						
	NETH						
	NETA						
	NWCL						
	NEWZ						
	NICA						
	NIGR						
	NIGE						
	NORW						
	OMAN						
	OUAE						
	PAKI						
	PANA						
	PNGU						
	PARA						
	PERU						
	PHIL						
	PITC						
	POLA						
	PORT						
	QATA						
	REUN						
	ROMA						
	RWAN						
	SAHE						
	SCRN						
	SLUC						
	SPMI						

UK external liabilities in

PART A Analysis by country (Sheet 2) *(continued)*	Sight and time deposit liabilities to overseas residents Total analysed by currency and sector (continued) French francs Banks overseas (including CMI) 12	French francs Other overseas residents 13	Netherlands guilders Banks overseas (including CMI) 14	Netherlands guilders Other overseas residents 15	Italian lire Banks overseas (including CMI) 16	Italian lire Other overseas residents 17
LAOS						
LEBA						
LESO						
LIBE						
LIBY						
LICH						
LUXE						
MACA						
MADA						
MALW						
MALA						
MALD						
MALI						
MALT						
MART						
MTAN						
MAUR						
MEXI						
MONA						
MONG						
MONT						
MORO						
MOZA						
NAMI						
NAUR						
NEPA						
NETH						
NETA						
NWCL						
NEWZ						
NICA						
NIGR						
NIGE						
NORW						
OMAN						
OUAE						
PAKI						
PANA						
PNGU						
PARA						
PERU						
PHIL						
PITC						
POLA						
PORT						
QATA						
REUN						
ROMA						
RWAN						
SAHE						
SCRN						
SLUC						
SPMI						

currencies other than sterling

£000s

£000s

Country	Belgian francs		Other * currencies	London certificates of deposit lodged by overseas residents: Denominated in US dollars		Denominated in other currencies	
	Banks overseas (including CMI)	Other overseas residents		Banks overseas (including CMI)	Other overseas residents	Banks overseas (including CMI)	Other overseas residents
	18	19	20	21	22	23	24
LAOS							
LEBA							
LESO							
LIBE							
LIBY							
LICH							
LUXE							
MACA							
MADA							
MALW							
MALA							
MALD							
MALI							
MALT							
MART							
M[illegible]							
MAUR							
MEXI							
MONA							
MONG							
MONT							
MORO							
MOZA							
NAMI							
NAUR							
NEPA							
NETH							
NETA							
NWCL							
NEWZ							
NICA							
NIGR							
NI[illegible]							
NORW							
OMAN							
OUAE							
PAKI							
PANA							
PNGU							
PARA							
PERU							
PHIL							
PITC							
POLA							
PORT							
QATA							
REUN							
ROMA							
RWAN							
SAHE							
SCRN							
SLUC							
SPMI							

* Including the sterling components of SDR and ECU liabilities

UK external liabilities in

PART A Analysis by country (Sheet 1) *(continued)*		Sight and time deposit liabilities to overseas residents: Total analysed by sector: Banks overseas (including CMI)	Other overseas residents	Total (1 + 2)	Total analysed by: US: Banks overseas (including CMI)
		1	2	3	4
Saint Vincent and the Grenadines	SVIN				
Samoa (formerly Western Samoa)	WSAM				
Sao Tome and Principe	SATP				
Saudi Arabia	SAUA				
Senegal	SENE				
Seychelles	SEYC				
Sierra Leone	SILE				
Singapore	SING				
Solomon Islands	BRSI				
Somalia	SOMA				
South Africa	SAFR				
Spain	SPAI				
Sri Lanka	SRIL				
Sudan	SUDA				
Suriname	SURI				
Swaziland	SWAZ				
Sweden	SWED				
Switzerland	SWIT				
Syrian Arab Republic	SYRI				
Taiwan	TAIW				
Tanzania, United Republic of	TANZ				
Thailand	THAI				
Togo	TOGO				
Tonga	TONG				
Trinidad and Tobago	TRIN				
Tunisia	TUNI				
Turkey	TURK				
Turks and Caicos Islands	TUCA				
Tuvalu (formerly Ellice Islands)	TUVA				
Uganda	UGAN				
United States	USA				
US Trust Territories in the Pacific	USTP				
US Virgin Islands	USVI				
Upper Volta	UVOL				
Uruguay	URUG				
USSR	USSR				
Vanuatu (fomerly New Hebrides)	NWHB				
Vatican City State (Holy See)	VATI				
Venezuela	VENE				
Vietnam, Socialist Republic of	VNMN				
Wallis and Futuna Islands	WALF				
Western Sahara	WSAH				
Yemen Arab Republic	YEME				
Yemen, People's Democratic Republic of	YEMS				
Yugoslavia	YUGO				
Zaire	ZAIR				
Zambia	ZAMB				
Zimbabwe	RHOD				

currencies other than sterling

£000s

currency and sector

dollars	Country	Deutschemarks		Swiss francs		Japanese yen	
Other overseas residents		Banks overseas (including CMI)	Other overseas residents	Banks overseas (including CMI)	Other overseas residents	Banks overseas (including CMI)	Other overseas residents
5		6	7	8	9	10	11
	SVIN						
	WSAM						
	SATP						
	SAUA						
	SENE						
	SEYC						
	SILE						
	SING						
	BRSI						
	SOMA						
	SAFR						
	SPAI						
	SRIL						
	SUDA						
	SURI						
	SWAZ						
	SWED						
	SWIT						
	SYRI						
	TAIW						
	TANZ						
	THAI						
	TOGO						
	TONG						
	TRIN						
	TUNI						
	TURK						
	TUCA						
	TUVA						
	UGAN						
	USA						
	USTP						
	USVI						
	UVOL						
	URUG						
	USSR						
	NWHB						
	VATI						
	VENE						
	VNMN						
	WALF						
	WSAH						
	YEME						
	YEMS						
	YUGO						
	ZAIR						
	ZAMB						
	RHOD						

UK external liabilities in

PART A Analysis by country (Sheet 2) *(continued)*	Sight and time deposit liabilities to overseas residents Total analysed by currency and sector (continued) French francs Banks overseas (including CMI) 12	French francs Other overseas residents 13	Netherlands guilders Banks overseas (including CMI) 14	Netherlands guilders Other overseas residents 15	Italian lire Banks overseas (including CMI) 16	Italian lire Other overseas residents 17
SVIN						
WSAM						
SATP						
SAUA						
SENE						
SEYC						
SILE						
SING						
BRSI						
SOMA						
SAFR						
SPAI						
SRIL						
SUDA						
SURI						
SWAZ						
SWED						
SWIT						
SYRI						
TAIW						
TANZ						
THAI						
TOGO						
TONG						
TRIN						
TUNI						
TURK						
TUCA						
TUVA						
UGAN						
USA						
USTP						
USVI						
UVOL						
URUG						
USSR						
NWHB						
VATI						
VENE						
VNMN						
WALF						
WSAH						
YEME						
YEMS						
YUGO						
ZAIR						
ZAMB						
RHOD						

currencies other than sterling

£000s

Country	Belgian francs: Banks overseas (including CMI)	Belgian francs: Other overseas residents	Other * currencies	London certificates of deposit lodged by overseas residents — Denominated in US dollars: Banks overseas (including CMI)	Denominated in US dollars: Other overseas residents	Denominated in other currencies: Banks overseas (including CMI)	Denominated in other currencies: Other overseas residents
	18	19	20	21	22	23	24
SVIN							
WSAM							
SATP							
SAUA							
SENE							
SEYC							
SILE							
SING							
BRSI							
SOMA							
SAFR							
SPAI							
SRIL							
SUDA							
SURI							
SV							
SWED							
SWIT							
SYRI							
TAIW							
TANZ							
THAI							
TOGO							
TONG							
TRIN							
TUNI							
TURK							
TUCA							
TUVA							
UGAN							
USA							
USTP							
US							
UVOL							
URUG							
USSR							
NWHB							
VATI							
VENE							
VNMN							
WALF							
WSAH							
YEME							
YEMS							
YUGO							
ZAIR							
ZAMB							
RHOD							

£000s

* Including the sterling components of SDR and ECU liabilities

UK external liabilities to overseas central monetary institutions in currencies other than sterling

£000s

PART B Analysis by area central monetary institutions in:		Sight and time deposit liabilities to overseas central monetary institutions							London certificates of deposit lodged by overseas central monetary institutions (b) (£000s)	
		Total (a)	of which liabilities in selected currencies							
			US dollars	Deutsche-marks	Swiss francs	Japanese yen	French francs	Netherlands guilders	Denominated in US dollars	Denominated in other currencies
Total (c)										
European Community	EEC									
Other Western Europe	OWEN									
Other OECD Countries	OECN									
Eastern Europe	EEUR									
Latin America and Caribbean	LACN									
Middle East oil exporting countries	MEOX									
Other oil exporting countries	OILN									
Other Africa	OAFN									
Far East	FEAN									
Other	OTHN									

(a) Contained within Part A, column 1. The total must agree with the total reported in column 6 of the liabilities part of Form S2 (section 2)

(b) Contained within Part A, Columns 21 and 23.

(c) Figures in the shaded areas must agree with the relevant currency items in column 6 of Form S2 (section 2) Liabilities and, for reporters on Form BS, the total must agree with Item A3 in column 2 (other currencies).

Private and confidential

Form S2 (section 2)

Currencies other than sterling
Currency analysis of liabilities and claims

as at ______________________________

Reporting institution ______________________________

____
Signature of authorised official of reporting institution

In the event of a query, the Bank of England may contact (block letters please)

______________________________ Tel no ______________ Ext ______________

Notes on Completion

If you have any difficulty in completing this form, please telephone 01-601 4885/4870.

1 Complete form quarterly as at end of March, June, September and December.
2 For definition of items refer to the *Banking statistics definitions* folder.
3 Enter amounts in sterling to nearest thousand, omitting £000s.
4 Ensure that the items in the shaded areas agree with the related items in column 2 (other currencies) of Form BS, or with the relevant currency items in Form S2 (liabilities) or in Form S2 (claims), as indicated.
5 Return form within **TEN** calendar days of reporting date to:

Financial Statistics Division HO-3
Group 3/2
Bank of England
Threadneedle Street
London EC2R 8AH

Bank of England use only

Logged	Data entered	Pending	Query	Awaiting update	Revision book	Revision input

December 1983

(153)

LIABILITIES IN CURRENCIES OTHER THAN STERLING

£000's

Analysis by currency		Sight and time deposit liabilities to:			Other liabilities	Total spot liabilities	of which: sight and time deposit liabilities to overseas central monetary institutions (b)	Total forward sales
		UK monetary sector	Other UK residents	Overseas residents (a)				
		1	2	3	4	5	6	7
TOTAL *								
*Figures in shaded areas in columns 1 to 5 must agree with referenced items on Form BS column 2		(2.2 + 2.9)	(2.4 + 2.5 + 2.10 + 2.13)	(2.6 + 2.7 + + 2.16 + 2.17)	(2.20 + 2.21 + 3 to 5)	(6)		
US dollars	USA							
Belgian francs	BELG							
Canadian dollars	CANA							
Danish kroner	DENM							
Deutschemarks	WGER							
French francs	FRAN							
Irish pounds	EIRE							
Italian lire	ITAL							
Japanese yen	JAPA							
Netherlands guilders	NETH							
Saudi riyals	SAUA							
Swedish kronor	SWED							
Swiss francs	SWIT							
Gold bullion	GOLD							
Gold coin	RCON							
Other foreign currencies (c)	OTHC				(d)			

Memorandum items: liabilities and forward sales denominated in composite currencies

£000's

Special drawing rights	SDRS							
European currency units	ECUS							

(a) Figures in the shaded areas must equal the sum of the "Banks overseas" and "Other overseas residents" entries for the relevant currency in the "Total of all overseas customers" line of Form S2 (liabilities) Part A.

(b) Figures in the shaded areas must equal the relevant currency entries (including the total) in the total line of Form S2 (liabilities) Part B.

(c) Enter here the total of all other currencies including the sterling components of SDR- and ECU- denominated liabilities.

(d) Include here the translation/revaluation adjustment contained within item 5.3 in column 2 of Form BS (see notes).

(153)

CLAIMS IN CURRENCIES OTHER THAN STERLING

£000's

Analysis by currency		Loans and advances to: UK monetary sector (including certificates of deposit)	Loans and advances to: Other UK residents	Loans and advances to: Overseas residents (e)	ECGD special scheme lending for exports; overseas bills (e)	Other assets	Total spot claims	of which: claims on overseas central monetary institutions	Total forward purchases
		1	2	3	4	5	6	7	8
TOTAL *									
*Figures in shaded areas must agree with referenced items on Form BS column 2		(12.2 + 12.3 + 12.6 to 12.9)	(12.4 + 12.10 + 12.11 + 16.1 to 16.5)	(12.14 + 12.15 + 16.6)	(14.9 + 15.1)	(10 + 11 + 14.5 + 14.7 + 14.8 + 17to 19 + 20.1 + 20.2)	(21)		
US dollars	USA								
Belgian francs	BELG								
Canadian dollars	CANA								
Danish kroner	DENM								
Deutschemarks	WGER								
French francs	FRAN								
Irish pounds	EIRE								
Italian lire	ITAL								
Japanese yen	JAPA								
Netherlands guilders	NETH								
Saudi riyals	SAUA								
Swedish kronor	SWED								
Swiss francs	SWIT								
Gold bullion	GOLD								
Gold coin	RCON								
Other foreign currencies (f)	OTHC								

Memorandum items: claims and forward purchases denominated in composite currencies

£000's

Special drawing rights	SDRS								
European currency units	ECUS								

(e) For each currency having shaded areas in columns 3 and 4, the sum of these two entries should equal the sum of the "Loans and advances to banks overseas" and "Other" entries for that currency in the "Total of all overseas customers" line of Form S2 (claims).

(f) Enter here the total of all other currencies including the sterling components of SDR- and ECU- denominated claims.

(153)

APPENDIX XII - SPECIMENS OF BUILDING SOCIETY STATISTICAL RETURNS

APPENDIX XII SPECIMENS OF BUILDING SOCIETY STATISTICAL RETURNS

PRIVATE AND CONFIDENTIAL **BS1**

BUILDING SOCIETIES

MONTHLY RETURN OF RECEIPTS AND PAYMENTS

Return of RECEIPTS and PAYMENTS during the month of ______________________

Completed returns should be sent by the 6th of the month, covering the activities of the previous month to:

THE SECRETARY GENERAL, THE BUILDING SOCIETIES ASSOCIATION, 3 SAVILE ROW, LONDON W1X 1AF.

Telephone enquiries may be made to 01-437 0655.

Name of building society ______________________

Key number ______________________ Size group code ______________________

Notes to the return are below.

In the event of a query, the BSA may contact: ______________________ Tel no ______________

All amounts should be entered to the nearest thousand pounds, omitting 000s.

NOTES AND DEFINITIONS

1 BALANCES

Figures at the beginning of the month should equal balances at end of previous month.

1.1 Cash

Include bank balances.

1.2 Holdings of investments

Exclude interest accrued on investments.

RECEIPTS AND PAYMENTS

2 Shares and deposits

2.2 Interest credited to accounts

Represents interest capitalised at normal due rates.

2.3 Interest paid out

Exclude any interest already counted as interest 'credited to accounts' under item 2.2 in this or previous returns.

3 Mortgages

3.2 Interest

Repayments of interest will be an estimated figure including interest recoverable from HM Government under option mortgage scheme and MIRAS.

3.3 Advances made

For instalment advances, only instalments made during the month should be included.

4 INVESTMENTS

If book value of realisations exceeds proceeds, there is a loss on sale, this should be shown as a minus under Total profit (loss). In the case of unquoted investments, proceeds and book values will normally be the same figure.

7 Other borrowing

7.4 Time deposits and 7.6.4 interest paid on time deposits

Include only time deposits of £50,000 or more on which interest is paid gross.

TOTALS (1-7)

The totals shown in both columns should be equal.

8 APPROVALS OUTSTANDING

8.1 Approvals outstanding at beginning of month

Figures should equal approvals outstanding at end of previous month.

Bank of England

December 1983

(3151)

	At beginning of month	At end of month
1 BALANCES		
1.1 Cash (less bank loans and overdrafts)		
1.2 Holdings of investments excluding building society CDs (book values)		
1.3 Building society certificates of deposit held		
TOTAL (1)		
RECEIPTS AND PAYMENTS	Receipts	Payments
2 SHARES AND DEPOSITS		
2.1 Shares and deposits		
2.2 Interest credited to accounts		
2.3 Interest paid out		
TOTAL INTEREST (2.2 + 2.3)		
3 MORTGAGES		
3.1 Repayments: principal		
3.2 : interest		
TOTAL REPAYMENTS (3.1 + 3.2)		
3.3 Advances made		
4 INVESTMENTS		
4.1 Proceeds of realisations		
4.2 Book cost		
TOTAL PROFIT (LOSS) (4.1-4.2)		
5 TAXATION		
6 OTHER		
7 OTHER BORROWING		
7.1 Negotiable bonds		
7.2 Certificates of deposit		
7.3 Loans from banks etc		
7.4 Time deposits		
7.5 Other		
TOTAL (7.1 to 7.5)		
7.6 Interest paid	Paid gross	Paid net
7.6.1 Negotiable bonds		
7.6.2 Certificates of deposit		
7.6.3 Loans from banks etc		
7.6.4 Time deposits		
7.6.5 Other		
TOTAL (7.6)		
TOTAL RECEIPTS AND PAYMENTS (2 to 7)		
TOTALS (1 to 7)		

	Value
8 APPROVALS OUTSTANDING	
8.1 Approvals outstanding at beginning of month	
8.2 Approvals during month (less cancelled)	
8.3 Advances during month (as above)	
TOTAL APPROVALS OUTSTANDING AT END OF MONTH (8.1 + 8.2)	
9 INVESTMENTS MADE AT COST	

(3151)

PRIVATE AND CONFIDENTIAL **BS 2**

BUILDING SOCIETIES

QUARTERLY RETURN OF TRANSACTIONS

Return of TRANSACTIONS during the quarter ended ______________________

Completed returns should be sent (if possible, within 2 weeks from the end of the quarter concerned) to:

GROUP 5/4, FINANCIAL STATISTICS DIVISION, HO-4, BANK OF ENGLAND, THREADNEEDLE STREET, LONDON, EC2R 8AH

Telephone enquiries may be made to 01-601 4988.

Name of building society ______________________

Key number ______________________ Size group code ______________________

In the event of a query, the Bank of England may contact: ______________________ Tel no ______________________

Notes to the return begin on page 3.

All amounts should be entered to the nearest thousand pounds, omitting 000s. Please show the last three figures of each entry to the right of each dividing line.

	At beginning of quarter		At end of quarter	
A LIABILITIES (outstanding amounts)				
1 Shares and deposits				
1.1 Industrial and commercial companies				
1.2 Insurance companies				
1.3 Pension funds				
1.4 Persons and trusts				
1.5 Overseas residents				
1.6 Unidentified				
TOTAL SHARES AND DEPOSITS (1)				
2 Interest accrued but not credited to share and deposit accounts (2)				
3 Time deposits on which interest is paid gross				
3.1 UK monetary sector				
3.2 Industrial and commercial companies				
3.3 Insurance companies				
3.4 Pension funds				
3.5 Persons and trusts				
3.6 Overseas residents				
3.7 Unidentified				
TOTAL TIME DEPOSITS (3)				
4 Other liabilities				
4.1 Taxation				
4.2 Reserves				
4.3 Other liabilities				
TOTAL OTHER LIABILITIES (4)				

(2846)

- 2 -

All amounts should be entered to the nearest thousand pounds omitting 000s.

		Receipts		Payments	
B	**TRANSACTIONS IN CERTAIN OTHER LIABILITIES**				
5	**Short-term borrowing**				
5.1	Overdrafts and advances from UK monetary sector				
5.2	Certificates of deposit				
5.3	Other (please specify items over £500,000)				
	TOTAL SHORT-TERM BORROWING (5)				
6	**Longer-term borrowing**				
6.1	Advances from Central Government				
6.1.1	Under House Purchase and Housing Act 1959				
6.1.2	Other				
6.2	Negotiable bonds				
6.3	Loans from UK monetary sector institutions				
6.4	Other (please specify individually)				
	TOTAL LONGER-TERM BORROWING (6)				

		At beginning of quarter		At end of quarter	
C	**SHORT-TERM ASSETS (outstanding amounts)**				
7.1	Notes and coin				
7.2	Deposits with UK monetary sector				
7.3	Deposits with National Savings Bank				
7.4.1	Sterling certificates of deposit: monetary sector				
7.4.2	: building society				
7.5	UK Treasury bills				
7.6.1	UK local authority: bills				
7.6.2	: other temporary money				
7.7	Certificates of tax deposit				
7.8	Bills of exchange				
7.9	Other short-term assets (please specify items over £50,000)				
	TOTAL SHORT-TERM ASSETS (7)				

		Assets realised		Assets acquired	
D	**TRANSACTIONS IN INVESTMENTS**				
8.1.1	British government securities: index-linked				
8.1.2	: other: up to and including 5 years				
8.1.3	: over 5 and up to and including 15 years				
8.1.4	: over 15 years and undated				
8.2.1	UK local authority listed securities and bonds				
8.2.2	Other UK local authority long-term debt				
8.3	Overseas government etc securities				
8.4	Other investments (please specify items over £100,000)				
	TOTAL INVESTMENTS (8)				

(2846)

- 3 -

All amounts should be entered to the nearest thousand pounds omitting 000s.

		Assets realised	Assets acquired
E	**TRANSACTIONS IN OTHER ASSETS**		
9	**Fixed assets**		
9.1	Office premises		
9.2	Other fixed assets		
10	**Other financial assets**		
10.1	Loans to Northern Ireland Housing Executive		
10.2	Other		
	TOTAL OTHER ASSETS (10)		
		Advanced	Repaid
F	**MORTGAGES**		
11	**Analysis by borrower**		
11.1	Housing associations		
11.2	Bodies Corporate		
11.3	Owner occupiers and other borrowers		
	TOTAL MORTGAGES (11)		
12	**Repayments**		
12.1	Regular repayments of principal		
12.2	Repayments of principal on redemption		
12.3	Other lump sum repayments		
	TOTAL REPAYMENTS (12)		

NOTES AND DEFINITIONS

A LIABILITIES

1 Shares and Deposits

Exclude time deposits on which interest is paid gross. Amounts should include interest credited to accounts. Where societies are unable to provide a full analysis by depositor, single figures bracketing more than one item together are acceptable.

1.1 Industrial and Commercial Companies

Deposits by limited, unlimited and other corporate bodies, other than financial institutions and those in the public sector, on which interest payments are taxable at basic rates. Insurance companies and charities should be included under item 1.2 and 1.4 respectively.

1.2 Insurance Companies

Deposits by insurance companies, including those connected with linked life assurance schemes.

1.4 Persons and Trusts

Individuals' and joint accounts; accumulating, discretionary and other trusts; charities, clubs and unincorporated businesses.

1.5 Overseas Residents

Accounts held by non-UK residents. Residents of the Channel Islands and Isle of Man and individuals visiting the UK for more than a year are regarded as UK residents.

3 Time Deposits on which interest is paid gross

Amounts should include interest credited. Interest accrued should be included under item 4.3.

3.1 UK Monetary Sector

Deposits by recognised banks, licensed deposit-taking institutions, National Girobank, trustee savings banks, the Banking Department of the Bank of England, and those banks in the Channel Islands and the Isle of Man which opted to join the UK monetary sector.

3.1.1 to 3.7

See definintions under note 1 above.

(2846)

3 Interest accrued but not credited
Estimates are acceptable where quarterly information is not available. Include provision for bonus under the Contractual Savings Scheme (SAYE).

4 Other liabilities

4.1. Taxation
Changes in tax liability arising from corporation tax on profits and net capital gains and income tax at the composite or basic rate paid on behalf of shareholders and depositors.

4.3 Other liabilities
Interest accruing on negotiable bonds, certificates of deposit, time deposits and other borrowing, should be included here.

B TRANSACTIONS IN CERTAIN OTHER LIABILITIES

Loans with an original maturity of less than twelve months should be included under item 5 and longer term loans under item 6.

C SHORT TERM ASSETS

Those with an **original** maturity of less than one year, except for bank deposits and certificates of deposit, which should be included here irrespective of maturity.

7.1 Notes and Coin
UK coin and bank notes, including those received on last day of the quarter and held overnight in branch safes or bank night safes.

7.3 Deposits with National Savings Banks
Include holdings of Income Bonds and Deposit Bonds.

7.6.2 Other UK local authority temporary money
All loans to local authorities with an **original** maturity of less than twelve months, whether secured by mortgage or not, including longer term loans and mortgages repayable at lender's option within one year. Local authority stocks, bonds and mortgages with a **stress** clause should be reported under item 8.2.

D TRANSACTION IN INVESTMENTS

Include only realisations or acquisitions for cash. An asset should be regarded as acquired or realised on the day a contract is made to buy or sell the security. Balances due to you on securities which you have contracted to sell or due from you on securities which you have contracted to buy should be included in current items, items 4.3 and 7.8. Newly-issued securities on which further instalments are payable should be entered at cost, ie, the actual payment during the quarter, excluding any amounts due in respect of future instalments which should be entered only when they are paid in later quarters. Securities and loans reported in this section should be those with an **original** maturity of one year or more; shorter-dated investments are to be treated as current assets (all certificates of deposit, however, should be reported as current assets).

8.1.1 - 8.1.4 British Government Securities
Index-linked securities should be shown separately and other securities should be classified to their **residual** maturity. Those with optional redemption dates should be classified by the final date. Include British Transport and British Gas stocks.

8.2.2 Other UK local authority long-term debt
All local authority mortgages other than those entered under item 7.6.2. Mortgages repayable by a **stress** clause should be included here; mortgages with a **break** clause should be included under item 7.6.2.

E TRANSACTIONS IN OTHER ASSETS

10 Other financial assets

10.1 Loans to Northern Ireland Housing Executive
Loans to the Northern Ireland Department of Finance should also be included.

F MORTGAGES

In the case of instalment advances, only amounts advanced during the quarter should be included.

11.1 Housing Associations
Lending to housing associations under Section 8 of the Housing Act 1964.

12.2 Other lump sum payments
Where it is not possible to distinguish between repayments on redemption from other lump sum repayments, a single figure bracketing items 12.2 and 12.3 is acceptable.

(2846)

PRIVATE AND CONFIDENTIAL **BS3**

BUILDING SOCIETIES

ANNUAL RETURNS OF LIABILITIES AND ASSETS

Return of LIABILITIES and ASSETS as at 31 December 19 ____.

Completed returns should be sent (if possible by the end of January) to:

THE SECRETARY GENERAL, THE BUILDING SOCIETIES ASSOCIATION, 3 SAVILE ROW, LONDON W1X 1AF.

Telephone enquiries may be made to 01-437 0655.

Name of building society ____________________

Key number ____________________ Size group code ____________________

In the event of a query, the BSA may contact: ____________________ Tel no ____________

Notes to the return begin on page 2.

All amounts should be entered to the nearest thousand pounds, omitting 000s. **Please** show the last three figures of each entry to the right of each dividing line.

		Book value	
A	**LIABILITIES**		
1.1	Shares and deposits outstanding		
1.2	Time deposits		
2	**Interest accrued but not credited to accounts**		
3	**Current liabilities**		
3.1	Certificates of deposit		
3.2	Other short-term borrowing		
3.3	Current tax outstanding		
3.4	Other amounts payable (please specify items over £500,000)		
4	**Longer-term borrowing**		
4.1	Advances from central government		
4.2	Negotiable bonds		
4.3	Other (please specify items over £500,000)		
5	**Provisions**		
5.1	Tax equalisation and deferred tax		
5.2	Other		
6	**Other liabilities (please specify items over £500,000)**		
7	**Reserves**		
	TOTAL LIABILITIES (1 to 7)		

December 1983

(3150)

-2-

		Market value		Book value	
B	**ASSETS**				
8	**Current assets**				
8.1	Short-term assets				
8.2	Interest accrued on investments				
8.3	Other amounts receivable				
	TOTAL (8)				
9	**Investments**				
9.1.1	British government securities: index-linked				
9.1.2	: other: up to 5 years				
	: over 5 years and up to 15 years				
	: over 15 years and undated				
9.2	UK local authority listed securities and negotiable bonds				
9.3	Other UK local authority longer term debt				
9.4	Overseas government, etc securities				
9.5	Other investments (please specify items over £500,000)				
	TOTAL (9)				
10	**Fixed assets**				
10.1	Office property				
10.2	Other fixed assets				
	TOTAL (10)				
11	**Mortgages**				
11.1	Annuity				
11.2	Endowment				
12	**Other assets**				
	TOTAL ASSETS (8 to 12)				

NOTES AND DEFINITIONS

Valuation

Liabilities and mortgages should be entered at book values; investments and assets other than mortgages should be at both book and market value. Listed UK securities should be valued at closing middle-market prices, unlisted securities at estimated current values and bills at maturity values. Overseas securities should be valued in accordance with generally accepted practice, usually at last or closing prices. Foreign currency items should be converted into sterling at the middle market exchange rate at the end of year. In valuing newly-issued securities on which further instalments are payable include only the amounts of the instalments already paid.

LIABILITIES

Items 1, 2, 3.1, 3.2, 4.1 and 4.2 will be the same as on the quarterly BS2 return.

1.1 Shares and deposits outstanding

Exclude time deposits on which interest is paid gross.

1.2 Time deposits

Deposits of £50,000 and above on which interest is paid gross.

2 Interest accrued but not credited to accounts

Include the provision for bonus under the Contractual Savings Scheme (SAYE); gross interest accruing on time deposits of £50,000 and over should be included under item 3.4.

(3150)

-3-

3 Current liabilities

Those with an **original** maturity of less than one year.

4 Longer term borrowing

Loans with an **original** maturity of more than twelve months.

5 Provisions

5.2 Other

Provisions for anticipated mortgage losses should be included here.

ASSETS

8 Current assets

Those with an **original** maturity of less than one year except for bank deposits and certificates of deposit, which should be included here irrespective of maturity. Exclude local authority mortgages with a stress clause.

8.1 Short term assets

This item will be the same as on the quarterly BS2 return. For definitions see notes to that return.

8.2 Interest accrued on investments

Interest should be calculated gross of UK tax.

9 Investments

9.1.1 - 9.1.4 British government securities

Index-linked securities should be shown separately and other securities should be classified according to their residual maturity. Those with optional redemption dates should be classified by the final date. Include British European Airways, British Overseas Airways, British Transport, British Gas and North of Scotland Electricity stocks. Other securities of public corporations should be entered in item 9.5.

9.3 Other UK local authority long-term debt

All local authority mortgages other than those entered under item 8.1. Mortgages repayable by a **stress** clause should be included here; mortgages with a **break** clause should be included under item 8.1.

10 Fixed assets

10.1 Office property

Premises occupied wholly or in part by the building society.

11 Mortgages

Figures should be gross of provision of anticipated mortgage losses, which should be included under item 5.2. The allocation of mixed annuity and endowment mortgages should be estimated.

Bank of England

(3150)

APPENDIX XIII - LIST OF BUILDING SOCIETY RETURNS 1985

This note has been prepared for the information of societies participating in the various statistical exercises conducted by the Association. Its main purpose is to set out, in concise form, the returns which are made and the dates by which forms should reach the Association.

During 1984 societies will be grouped as follows -

Grouping of Societies

Group	Societies
A1	Largest 5
A2	6th to 16th largest
B	Other Societies with assets in excess of £225 million at 31 December 1983
C	Societies with assets between £50 million and £225 million as at 31 December 1983
D	Societies with assets below £50 million as at 31 December 1983

Groups A1 and A2 are unchanged from the previous year but the thresholds for Groups B and C have been raised to take account of the growth of societies. This may mean that a few societies will be in a different group for 1984. However, for the most part, societies will remain in the same size group.

Statistical Returns

A full list is given of the current statistical returns together with details of the sample, the frequency of the return, the date by which the return should be received and the purpose of the return.

Form	Societies	Frequency	Date Due	Purpose
BS1	A1, A2, B and some of C and D	Monthly	6th of month following relevant month	Monitoring shares and deposits, lending and liquidity
BS2	A1, A2, B and some of C	Quarterly	2 weeks after end of relevant quarter	Monitoring assets and liabilities

Form	Societies	Frequency	Date Due	Purpose
BS2A	A1, A2, B and some of C	Quarterly	2 weeks after end of relevant quarter	Monitoring SAYE Scheme
BS2B	British based societies with branches in Northern Ireland	Quarterly	2 weeks after end of relevant quarter	Monitoring building society activity in Northern Ireland
BS3	A1, A2, B and some of C	Annual	1 month after end of relevant year	Monitoring assets and liabilities at book value
BS4	A1 and A2	Monthly	15th of month following relevant month	Monitoring house prices and advances
SR1	A1 and A2	Monthly	10th of month following relevant month	Monitoring receipts, withdrawals and internal transfers by type of account
SR2	A1 and some of A2	Monthly	10th of month following relevant month	Monitoring receipts and withdrawals by size band
SR3	A1 and some of A2	Half-yearly	1 month after after end of half year	Monitoring investment balances by size band
SR4	A1 and A2	Weekly	Wednesday morning of week following relevant week (return normally made by telephone)	Monitoring receipts, withdrawals and net new commitments
SR5	Societies operating in Scotland	Annual	1 month after end of relevant year	Monitoring building society activity in Scotland
SR7	A1	Quarterly	1 month after end of relevant quarter	Monitoring new house prices in Northern Ireland
SR8	A1	Quarterly	15th of month following relevent quarter	Monitoring Homeloan Scheme
SR9	Liason of the Support Scheme for local authorities	Monthly	2 weeks after end of relevant month	Monitoring of Support Scheme

SR10	"Council Societies"	One month in three	2 weeks after end of relevant month	Monitoring differential mortgage rates
SR11	A1 and some of A2, B and C	Quarterly	20th of month following relevant quarter	Monitoring lending on pre-1919 houses in Northern Ireland
SR12	A1 and A2	Quarterly	2 weeks after end of relevant quarter	Monitoring receipts and balances outstanding by type of account
SR13	A1 and A2	Half-yearly	1 month after end of relevant period	Monitoring arrears

Notes:

1. With the exception of form BS4 (which is returned to the DoE), and the BS2 (which is returned to Bank of England), all the returns are made to the Association.
2. The list does not include returns made to the Chief Registrar (copies of which come to the Association) or to the Registry of Building Societies in Northern Ireland.
3. The list also excludes a return on management expenses and surpluses which is made by the A1 and A2 societies approximately each six months. A separate form is sent out to the societies for each return.
4. Forms SR3 and SR5 relate to Societies' financial years or half year.
5. Some societies which have changed size groups in the past two years may possibly not be required to complete all the forms indicated ot they may be required to complete more returns than those indicated.

Schedule for Making Returns, 1983

The following schedule shows the dates by which the various returns should reach the Association (DoE in the case of BS4). The schedule does not include the following returns -

(a) SR4 –which is made weekly
(b) SR9 –which does not relate to a particular society's activity

Month	Date	Return	A1	A2	B	C	D
January	10th	BS1	x	x	x	some	some
	12th	SR1	x	x	-	-	-
	15th	SR2	x	some	-	-	-
		BS2	x	x	x	some	-
		SR8	x	-	-	-	-
		SR12	x	x	-	-	-
		BS2A	x	x	x	some	-

Month	Date	Return	A1	A2	B	C	D
		BS2B	Societies with branches in Northern Ireland				
	20th	BS4	x	x	-	-	-
		SR11	x	some	some	some	-
	31st	BS3	x	x	x	some	-
		SR3	x	some	-	-	-
		SR5	Societies with branches in Scotland				
		SR7	x	-	-	-	-
		SR13	x	x	-	-	-
February	7th	BS1	x	x	x	some	some
	10th	SR1	x	x	-	-	-
	15th	SR2	x	some	-	-	-
		SR10	x	some	some	some	some
		BS4	x	x	-	-	-
March	6th	BS1	x	x	x	some	some
	10th	SR1	x	x	-	-	-
	15th	SR2	x	some	-	-	-
		BS4	x	x	-	-	-
April	10th	BS1	x	x	x	some	some
	12th	SR1	x	x	-	-	-
	15th	SR2	x	some	-	-	-
		SR8	x	-	-	-	-
		SR12	x	x	-	-	-
		BS4	x	x	-	-	-
		BS2	x	x	x	some	-
		BS2A	x	x	x	some	-
		BS2B	Societies with branches in Northern Ireland				
	20th	SR11	x	some	some	some	-
	30th	SR7	x	-	-	-	-
May	8th	BS1	x	x	x	some	some
	12th	SR1	x	x	-	-	-
	15th	SR2	x	some	-	-	-
		SR10	x	some	some	some	some
		BS4	x	x	-	-	-
June	6th	BS1	x	x	x	some	some
	10th	SR1	x	x	-	-	-
	15th	SR2	x	some	-	-	-

		BS4	x	x	-	-	-
July	10th	BS1	x	x	x	some	some
	12th	SR1	x	x	-	-	-
	15th	SR2	x	some	-	-	-
		SR8	x	-	-	-	-
		SR12	x	x	-	-	-
		BS4	x	x	-	-	-
		BS2	x	x	x	some	-
		BS2A	x	x	x	some	-
		BS2B	Societies with branches in Northern Ireland				
	20th	SR11	x	some	some	some	-
	31st	SR3	x	some	-	-	-
		SR7	x	-	-	-	-
		SR13	x	x	-	-	-
August	7th	BS1	x	x	x	some	some
	10th	SR1	x	x	-	-	-
	15th	SR2	x	some	-	-	-
		SR10	x	some	some	some	some
		BS4	x	x	-	-	-
September	11th	BS1	x	x	x	some	some
	12th	SR1	x	x	-	-	-
	15th	SR2	x	some	-	-	-
		BS4	x	x	-	-	-
October	9th	BS1	x	x	x	some	some
	12th	SR1	x	x	-	-	-
	15th	SR2	x	some	-	-	-
		SR8	x	-	-	-	-
		SR12	x	x	-	-	-
		BS4	x	x	-	-	-
		BS2A	x	x	x	some	-
		BS2B	Societies with branches in Northern Ireland				
	20th	SR11	x	some	some	some	-
	31st	SR7	x	-	-	-	-
November	6th	BS1	x	x	x	some	some
	10th	SR1	x	x	-	-	-
	15th	SR2	x	some	-	-	-
		SR10	x	some	some	some	some
		BS4	x	x	-	-	-
December	11th	BS1	x	x	x	some	some
	10th	SR1	x	x	-	-	-
	15th	SR2	x	some	-	-	-

Month	Date	Return	A1	A2	B	C	D
		BS4	x	x	-	-	-

Note:

Where due date falls on a Saturday or Sunday, the target date becomes the following working day.

Distribution of Aggregated Statistics

For the most part, the aggregated statistics are distributed directly to societies participating in the various exercises. The major results of some of the exercises are published in the Association's monthly press release and the BSA Bulletin.

USEFUL CONTACT POINTS

Statistics Branch
Department of Economic Development
Netheleigh Massey Avenue
Belfast BT4 2JP
Tel: 0232 (Belfast) 63244 Ext. 489

Policy Planning and Research Unit
Department of Finance and Personnel
Stormont
Belfast BT4 3SW
Tel: 0232 (Belfast) 63210 Ext. 2061

Economics and Statistics Department
The Building Societies Association
3 Savile Row
London W1X 1AF
Tel: 01-4370655

Statistics Division 2
Department of Trade and Industry
Sanctuary Buildings
20 Great Smith Street
London SW1P 3DB
Tel: 01-2156211

Cisi –Wharton
Econometric Forecasting Associates
Edbury Gate
23 Lower Belgrave Street
London SW1W 0NW
Tel: 01-7308171

Statistical Unit
Committee of London and Scottish Bankers
10 Lombard Street
London EC3V 1AP
Tel: 01-2838866

Association for Payment Clearing Services
Mercury House
Triton Court
14 Finsbury Square
London EC2A 1BR

Banking Information Service
10 Lombard Street
London EC3V 9AP
Tel: 01-6268486

TSB Group Central Executive
PO. Box 33
25 Milk Street
London EC2V 8LU
Tel: 01-6067070

Financial Statistics Division
Bank of England
London EC2R 8AH
Tel: 01-6014216

Finance Houses Association
18 Upper Grosvenor Street
London W1X 9PB
Tel: 01-4912783

Trustcard
Head Office
93-94 Queens Road
Brighton BN1 3XE
Tel: 0273-724666 (Marketing Department)

Barclays Bank Plc
54 Lombard Street
London EC3P 2AH
Tel: 016261567

Registry of Friendly Societies
15/17 Great Marboro Street
London W1V 2AX
Tel: 01-4379992

SUBJECT INDEX

38: LIFE ASSURANCE AND PENSION FUNDS

GERALDINE KAYE

Fellow in Actuarial Science

City University, London

REFERENCE DATE OF SOURCES REVIEWED

This review is believed to represent the position as at the Spring of 1986, with amendments and additions being made up to the proof reading stage of November 1986.

LIST OF ABBREVIATIONS

ABI	Association of British Insurers
ABMRC	Association of British Market Research Consultants
ACLI	American Council of Life Assurance
APEX	Association of Professional, Executive Clerical and Computer Staff
ASLO	Association of Scottish Life Offices
ARP	Accrued Rights Premium
AVC's	Additional voluntary Contributions
BIA	British Insurance Association
BSO	Business Statistics Office
CAPS	Combined Actuarial Performance Service
CEP	Contributions Equivalent Premium
CIPFA	Chartered Institute of Public Finance and Accounting
CMI	Continuous Mortality Investigation Bureau
CSO	Central Statistical Office
CTT	Captial Transfer Tax
DE	Department of Employment
DHSS	Department of Health and Social Security
DTI	Department of Trade and Industry
EOC	Equal Opportunities Commission
ESRC	Economic and Social Research Council
FES	Family Expenditure Survey
GAD	Government Actuary's Department
GHS	General Household Survey
GMP	Guaranteed Minimum Pension
GSS	Government Statistical Service
HMSO	Her Majesty's Stationery Office
ICA	Institute of Chartered Accountants in England and Wales
ILOA	Industrial Life Offices Association
IPMS	Investment Performance Mounting Service
IR	Inland Revenue
JIA	Journal of Institute of Actuaries
JSS	Journal of Institute of Actuaries Student Society
LAPR	Life Assurance Premium Relief
LLAG	Linked Life Insurance Group
LOA	Life Offices Association
LRP	Limited Revaluation Premium
MEAL	Media Expenditure by Analysis Limited

MIRAS	Mortgage Interest Relief at Source
MSI	Marketing Strategies for Industry
NAPF	National Association of Pension Funds
NES	New Earnings Survey
NHS	National Health Service
OPB	Occupational Pensions Board
OPCS	Office of Population Censuses and Surveys
PAYE	Pay As You Earn (a form of income tax)
PHI	Permanent Health Insurance
PMI	Pensions Management Institute
PRAG	Pensions Research Accountants Group
PRU	Pay Research Unit
PUT	Property Unit Trusts
QRL	Quick Reference List
QUANGO	Quasi-Autonomous Government Organisation
RPI	Retail Price Index
SCPR	Social and Community Planning Research
SERPS	State Related Pension Scheme
SFO	Superannuation Funds Office
TFA	Transactions of Faculty of Actuaries

ACKNOWLEDGEMENTS

No sooner is the ink dry on the paper than new legislation and/or sources of statistics materialise. The main manuscript of this book was completed in November 1985; since then the Green Paper on the new pensions regime has been overtaken by the Social Security Act 1986. A new tax on pension fund surpluses was introduced in the 1986 budget and, more recently, (November 1986) a Pink Paper, a consultative document entitled Improving The Pensions Choice, has been issued by the Inland Revenue. It would be invidious to select only a few items of the main text for updating and any attempt to update the complete text can be thought to be analogous to painting the Forth Bridge. To overcome this problem, a project has been proposed at The City University to set up an on-line register of sources of statistics of pensions and life insurance. This would permit complete coverage of magazine sources —an area which has had to be glossed over for this hard-copy edition because of space limitations. The sources contained in this volume would form the foundations of the register. If, therefore, any reader discovers errors or omissions in this volume, please could they contact the author.

I have taken extracts from all sources quoted in the book for purposes of discussion and criticism and I wish to thank all the publishers concerned for their co-operation. In particular, I wish to thank the Government Actuary's Department for their kind permission to use the explanations in their survey as a basis for that part of my text, which gives the background to pensions. Similarly, I wish to thank the Association of British Insurers for their permission to make use of those definitions and descriptions in their educational literature which have proved relevant to my chapters giving the background to life insurance.

CONTENTS OF REVIEW 38

CHAPTER 1

OVERVIEW

1.1 General

The financial infrastructure in the United Kingdom is complex. Financial institutions act as intermediaries channelling funds from those persons who have more money than their immediate needs, and hence want to save, to those who have less. In acting as intermediaries, institutions are able to monitor the degree of risk involved in an investment and can also help the investor to put strategies into effect. A small scale investor, for example, may wish to achieve a spread of risk, but not have sufficient funds to purchase directly a portfolio of shares. The small investor can achieve his strategy by investing via the medium of unit trusts or unit-linked life insurance. A life insurance policy also provides a good example of the transformation of an investment's maturity and of its degree of risk, particularly the former. A number of small investors take out insurance policies in which they contract to pay regular, relatively small, premiums. The insurance company can aggregate the incoming premiums of individual policies, many of which will have a range of different dates. By using actuarial techniques to compute the monetary value of a variety of financial outcomes the insurance company can make large loans or purchase investments, whilst its funds are continuing to grow, with maturity dates much longer than many of the specific policies, the premiums of which, contributed to the fund. The policy holder meanwhile benefits from protection against future calamity or even death and, indeed the risks entailed in any investment are greatly reduced.

Since its issue in June 1980 the Wilson Committee report on The Functioning of Financial Institutions (Cmd 7937) [B.75] has rapidly been accepted as, amongst other things, a dictionary of terminology. Financial institutions can be divided into three broad categories according to the nature of their operations:

(i) deposit taking institutions, such as banks and building societies;
(ii) institutions such as the insurance companies and pension funds which collect longer term savings, and
(iii) specialised financing agencies, such as Finance for Industry and the National Enterprise Board.

The second group have now more generally become known as the non-deposit taking financial institutions. According to the Wilson Committee [B.75] they include not only insurance companies and pension funds but also unit trusts and investment trust companies. Their most important characteristic is that the funds placed in them are principally long-term. These funds, which represent the long-term savings of millions of individuals have, because of their size, generated much public interest and concern. The funds are invested principally in the United Kingdom in company stocks and shares, government securities and properties.

The environment in which these funds had prospered was seriously questioned by a series of government enquiries. In particular in December 1983 the Government announced an all-embracing enquiry into occupational pension schemes and required that evidence for the first part of this enquiry was to be submitted by January 31 1984. The unprecedented speed with which the Government proceeded demonstrated the importance that it attached to the issues raised and suggested that any consequent legislation would be given a degree of priority. The theme of the review has been towards putting pension provision back to the individual. There is to be much greater disclosure requirements for funds, as well as improved benefits for those members of schemes who change jobs prior to retirement. The Goverment intends to replace the State Earnings Related Pension Scheme (SERPS) by company pensions and personal pensions in April 1987. Under the proposals applicable from April 1987, company and individual pension operations will be interchangeable. At the time of writing, only a Green Paper [B.72] has so far been published. The majority reaction to it has been adverse and it seems likely that the Government will amend its proposals.

In the 1984 Budget the Government removed tax relief from life insurance premiums, with consequent effects on the levels of this kind of protective saving. Life companies are now competing with other forms of saving without the inbuilt advantage of tax relief. Intermediaries are learning to sell life contracts instead of selling tax reliefs. In the same budget the Chancellor removed from life insurance companies a concession relating to the rate of corporation tax on life funds. The change in tax regime is likely to have a marked effect on the future design of policies. The abolition of Life Assurance Premium Relief (LAPR) has freed the planners from the shackles of conforming to the qualifying rules. Now they can design contracts that incorporate complete flexibility over the amount and frequency of premium payments and in the style of benefits provided. Technically, a life policy still needs to conform to the qualification rules so that the benefits can be paid tax-free. But this only applies to higher rate taxpayers. Proceeds are paid free of tax to basic rate taxpayers. Indeed some life companies are producing two versions of life contracts - a more rigid qualifying form for higher rate tax payers and a flexible non-qualifying version for basic rate taxpayers.

Other changes in the financial services field are also forcing life companies to reorganise their sales operations. The line between unit-linked life insurance and unit trusts is now very blurred. Marketing of life and other investment products is becoming more sophisticated, and the savings market itself has become highly competitive. New financial magazines are being introduced often surveying which products are available. Such magazines, although aimed at the general public should not be overlooked by the serious researcher.

Fears that the Chancellor was about to change the tax structure of pension schemes in the 1985 Budget made pensions a topical talking point. Intense lobbying resulted in the Chancellor effectively pledging that there will be no tax changes for pensions during the lifetime of the present government.

The high profile which has been given to pensions issues has lead to a greater awareness of the paucity of accurate statistics in the field. Organisations have therefore had to conduct surveys to substantiate the evidence that they have submitted to the Government's enquiry; in addition the Government itself has commissioned surveys. These surveys tend to be of a one-off nature rather than continuing as part of a series and so only the more important ones are referred to in the present review.

Strictly, comparisons cannot be made across the surveys of different years or of different organisations: since comparisons should only be within the constraints of sampling fluctuations and other such factors pertinent to particular surveys. Statistics can therefore only indicate likely trends which can then be confirmed for example by secondary enquiries. The caveat regarding comparisons across surveys of different years is particularly pertinent in respect of surveys conducted by the Government Actuary's Department [QRL.70] [B.61], [B.62], [B.80], [B.60], [B.79] since it is not widely appreciated that the samples surveyed have been drawn using different data bases. The survey ,relating to 1983, as yet unpublished, bases its sample on that used for the General Household Survey. The sample for the latest published survey [QRL.70] was mainly drawn from the list of establishments obtained by the Department of Employment in its annual census of employment for 1978. The sample for the 1975 survey [B.61] and also the 1971 survey [B.62] were selected by the DHSS from employees' national insurance records. The sample for the first, second and third surveys [B.80] [B.60] [B.79] were selected from records maintained by the Inland Revenue.

1.2 Definition of Field

General insurance (i.e, non-life) companies are not strictly speaking financial institutions in the sense of financial intermediaries between investors and borrowers. Because of their importance in financial markets, however, and the fact that there are many composite companies which carry on both life and general insurance, the Wilson Committee [B.75] decided they should be included in the classification. They are not however included in this review; nor are unit trusts and investment trusts. They exhibit too many marked differences in nature to the two main types of non-deposit taking financial institutions, viz. pension funds and life insurance companies.

In order to avoid repitition and to clarify cross referencing, the introductory chapters set out definitions and provide background knowledge. These chapters are not designed as a text book and it is not intended that they should be read from cover to cover, rather they should be consulted as a means of explaining terms used, as in the QRL.

1.3 Coverage of Sources

The aim has been to list all modern sources of statistics collected by both official agencies and professional associations. In addition, many important sources of statistics have come from private individuals; but no coverage of this field can claim to be exhaustive.

The volume of private surveys far outweighs the amount of information from official sources. Many of the private surveys appear in magazines, rather than books, but that is not to detract from their importance. Where many private organisations conduct similar surveys there is only sufficient room in this review to cover selected examples. In particular there is not sufficient room to cover all surveys covered by magazines. Magazines should therfore be consulted on all topics irrespective of whether a specific issue is referred to by the QRL.

The frequency with which many surveys are repeated by the same organisation as well as the similarity of information covered in surveys conducted by different organisations reflects the scale of the demand for information about this highly competitive commercial area. Where a reference in the QRL states 'annual' this does not imply that identical analyses of data appear each year, but that the analyses in previous years are so substantially similar as not to warrant a separate entry. Where analyses are indentical each year apart from the occasional inclusion or removal of tables as in the case of the National Association of Pension Funds' (NAPF) Survey [QRL.27] this fact will be mentioned in the text.

Most market research surveys are conducted on a confidential basis for a single client and the information is not therefore available to the public. Occasionally, multi-client studies are conducted for a fixed number of subscribers who receive a comprehensive market report as well as a separate confidential report appropriate to their needs. In such cases the comprehensive market report is often published or otherwise available to those who wish to use it, but obviously not the specific individual answers. Occasionally, a firm will conduct a survey purely for publication in the hope of receiving media publicity or a trade association for the use of its members. A few such surveys have been traced for this volume, but there are others. There are directories of market research, but these tend to be biased towards industry and/or the USA. Relevant directories are discussed in Chapter 7.

The Association of British Market Research (ABMRC) will provide a list of market research organisations.

Historical sources have not been covered except in passing either where modern sources also happen to have historical runs of figures (e.g., MQ5 [QRL.32]) or a modern book contains a full bibliography (e.g., *The British Insurance Business 1547 - 1970* [B.7]) or there is some reason for its inclusion other than on its purely historical merit.

There is substantial literature on the historical background to the occupational pension movement; the Pensions Management Institute (PMI) has published a booklet [B.4] which provides a detailed introduction.

The Institute of Actuaries library is assembling a catalogue of where relevent historical studies can be found.

CHAPTER 2

PENSIONS

2.1 General

The British system of providing income for people during their retirement years has three main elements: State pension, occupational pension and private saving.

Sources of statistics on State pensions are largely covered in Vol.II of the *Reviews of UK Statistical Sources* series [B.26] and on private saving in Vol.IV [B.23] and [B.2].

Just over half of the number of employees in employment are estimated to be members of occupational pension schemes [QRL.70]. As a consequence the study of pension funds and their associated statistics is becoming an increasingly frequent activity of social scientists and others. Most of the statistics available on pensions are the result of regular major surveys, (e.g. those of the National Association of Pension Funds and the Government Actuary's Department) and many of the subject categories within these major surveys overlap. Where no specific reference to sources is contained in this chapter it is likely that relevant statistics will be found in either [QRL.70] or [QRL.27] or both. Financial magazines should also be consulted in all subject areas (see chapter 7).

2.2 Legal Background

In the late 19th Century private pensions were granted on an ex-gratia and personal basis to favoured employees of a company often as a reward for long service. Often there was no formal scheme, only statements of intent or merely expections based on custom. Informal arrangements of this character, without legal protection, offered opportunities for abuse. In particular, preferential treatment of individuals often soured employer - employee relations, since the arbitrary nature of the pension award could tempt an employer to use the threat of witholding a pension as a means of placing pressure on an employee. More formal and legally protected arrangements were clearly advisable and there was soon pressure to introduce them generally. Attempts to do so, by establishing pre-funded schemes, soon met fiscal difficulties, and special fiscal arrangements were required. Section 32 of the Finance Act 1921 set the pattern for pension funds as they are now known.

2.2.1 *Legal Structure*

Trust law provides the legal basis for most pension schemes and there has been some discussion as to whether a new statutory basis akin to that relating to companies should be introduced. Peripheral statutory changes not affecting the basic principals of trust law as applied to pension schemes relate to preservation (see 2.7) contracting out (see 2.5.2.1) and equal access to schemes (see 2.8).

To obtain Inland Revenue Approval pension funds must be established under irrevocable trusts, which means that the assets are legally distinct from the employer's assets and beyond the reach of creditors, thus giving employees a measure of security that the assets supporting their benefits will be there when they retire. The rules of a scheme set out the terms under which it is to be operated. They may be schedules to the trust deed or may be in a separate document. The rules and the trust deed are closely linked together and combined they form the trust instrument. There are no precise criteria as to which details should be contained in the rules and which in the deed. Statistical sources do not normally differentiate but treat deed and rules as one. For most statistical sources the important distinction is whether an award is discretionary or not, e.g., the Government Actuary's survey [QRL.70] contains a table comparing the increases in pension promised in the rules with those actually paid. Normally however, the rules set out the promises and the trust deed empowers the trustees to see that the promises are carried out. Further information on the legal background to pension schemes can be found in *Private Occupational Pension Schemes* [B.70].

2.2.1.1 *Trustees* Various categories of individuals or companies can be made trustees; for example, in certain circumstances the employer may be appointed. Another category is that of member trustees. Such trustees may be elected by the members of the scheme or nominated from amongst the members as their representatives. The Governments Actuary's report [QRL.70] provides details of the numbers of schemes which have member trustees according to their status. [QRL.10] contains information as to when member trustees were first appointed to boards of trustees. A trustee can even be a specially constituted company. Statistics on the numbers of schemes and of members according to type of trustee are also contained in [QRL.70].

Another category of trustees in that of pensioneer trustees. A "Pensioneer trustee" is a trustee who is closely involved with occupational pension schemes and has dealings with the Superannuation Funds office (SFO) (the branch of the Inland Revenue dealing specifically with occupational pension schemes) and who is prepared to give an undertaking to the SFO that he will not consent to any termination of a scheme of which he is the trustee, otherwise than in accordance with the approved terms of the winding-up rule. The undertaking has no hidden implications; a pensioneer trustee is not a "watchdog" for the Inland Revenue in any area other than the improper termination of the scheme. The trustees of a "small scheme" (generally those with less than 12 members) must include at least one of whom is a pensioneer trustee.

It is the duty of the trustees to administer a pension scheme in accordance with the trust deed and rules, and in particular to make investments and to ensure that the fund is fairly used for all persons entitled to benefit. In so doing trustees in many cases place prescribed restrictions upon investment [QRL.64]. Trustees are not required by law to report to their members but many do. The NAPF *Survey*

[QRL.27] contains details. [QRL.10] contains further details on the duties of trustees and places these in order of importance as ranked by the trustees themselves.

[QRL.10] also yields a number of insights into the strength of trustees as a collective body. It considers various fields of activity of company secretaries, such as providing information, investment, rules etc. and analyses perceived key influences. Trustees figure in first or second place for each activity.

2.2.2 *Statutory Requirements*

There are no statutory requirements directly affecting the accounts of pension funds. Any statutory requirements arise from the effect of the Companies Act on the accounts of the sponsoring employer. Schedule 8 of the Companies Act 1948 requires companies to disclose any provisions for pensions. An analysis of the disclosure of pension provision in company balance sheets is made in [QRL.20]. Schedule 8 also requires companies to disclose "any other contributions by the company for the purpose of any pension scheme established for the purpose of providing pensions for persons employed by the company, any sums set aside for that purpose and any amounts paid by the company in respect of pensions without being so set aside". Such outlays on pensions are also analysed in [QRL.20]. The Companies Act also contained detailed disclosure requirements pertaining to directors' pensions. Information regarding the accounting policies adopted by companies in the reports of the pension fund itself are contained in [QRL.13]. Because of the lack of a statutory requirement or guidelines there is considerable variation in practice.

In the conclusion to his chapter in *Financial Reporting 1984-5 - A survey of UK published accounts* [QRL.20], Napier writes "The introduction of new statutory disclosure requirements has led to an increase in the number of companies disclosing pensions-related information. Companies are not, however, limiting their disclosure to the bare minimum". Influences other than the change of company law are the publication of ED32 [B.37] and the general interest currently being shown in pension information by the users of financial reports. Since 1984 the NAPF have included a section in their survey on the disclosure of information [QRL.27].

[QRL.10] contains a chapter headed "Members' views, interests and awareness over pensions". It has classified information provided for members into three categories, (a) Employee-related information: explanatory booklets, individual benefit statements and annual reports, (b) Information related to the schemes administration: detailed rules, trust deeds, and (c) Funding information: Actuary's report, breakdown of investments. It shows the pattern of information distribution reported by pension managers in their schemes for each of the three categories and correlates the availability of information with the presence of employee trustees.

The information given in actuarial reports is not in a standard form in either coverage or manner of presentation and does not therefore lend itself to summary in tabular form except in respect of valuation assumptions. These are analysed by members of the Governments Actuary's Department in an article published in *JIA* [QRL.14]. Information regarding the frequency of actuarial reports and how much information is passed to members is contained in [QRL.13].

2.2.2.1 *Local Government*

Regulation B7 of the Local Government Regulations, 1974 laid under Section 7 of the Superannuation Act 1972 require that every fund should be valued by an actuary as at 1 April 1974 and at 31 March in each following fifth year. Regulation B8 requires the actuary to furnish a certificate specifying the rate of contribution, as a percentage of salary roll in the ensuing 5 year period.

2.3 Retirement Age

The state retirement pension is paid to men at the age of 65 (and to women at the age of 60) and usually not before. For people who draw the pension and go on working after these ages there is a system of reductions in the state benefit corresponding to the amount earned. This is commonly referred to as the "earnings rule". For those who defer the drawing of a pension there is a system of corresponding increases. This combined with the Superannuation Fund Office's insistence on a normal retirement age has encouraged employers to introduce a fixed retirement age into their occupational pension schemes. Any lower retirement age would have led to a jump in the level of retirement income at age 65 (60 women), and any higher retirement age would lead to the operation of the "earnings rule" for several years. Despite this, some occupational schemes do have retirement ages other than 65 (60 women), but even in these schemes the retirement ages tend to be fixed rather than flexible. According to the latest available Government produced survey [QRL.70] the majority of members of occupational pension schemes were in schemes with a normal retirement age which coincided with that of the State scheme.

In the past, pension schemes have been seen as part of a scheme to provide an orderly pattern of retirement and career progression, enabling the employee to enjoy a feeling of certainty about his future. A fixed pension age helped to reduce the pressure on the employer to retain old (and possibly disabled) staff and was used as a means of encouraging continuous service. Trends are developing towards flexible retirement ages.

The Social Services committee of the House of Commons, looking into retirement, published a report [QRL.76] recommending a scheme providing for flexibility in retirement age based on a new notional common pension age of 63. The report emphasised that 63 is not to be regarded as replacing either age 60 or 65 in the present system, but merely to be used as a reference point on which the new concept of a flexible retirement age might be based.

The present administration initiated an inquiry into the whole field of pensions, occupational pensions and social security. It is the most far-reaching inquiry since the Beveridge *Report* [QRL.78]. The full ramifications will not be known for some time, although preliminary results are available (in the form of a green paper [B.72]) at the time of writing.

2.4 Tax Structure

The 1921 Finance Act gave the Inland Revenue the right to "approve" Pensions Funds. Approval was only available to schemes set up providing benefits within defined limits. A scheme could only provide "relevent benefits", that is benefits on retirement in various circumstances and on death. The amount and nature of these benefits was limited by reference to salary and length of service. The legislation was revised in 1947 and again in 1970. A fund which had been granted full Inland Revenue approval enjoyed fiscal neutrality, e.g. the employer could deduct his contributions from his gross income as a business expense before calculating the 'net' income on which his tax bill is calculated. Similarly, the employee's ordinary annual contribution to the scheme could be allowed as expenses against his income; and a Fund's income from investments and deposits were exempted from tax.

The Inland Revenue has been given wide powers of discretion with regard to the requirements which they can impose as a condition for a grant of approval. These requirements, initially simple to operate, have in recent years become increasingly extensive and complex as Inland Revenue procedures have become more sophisticated.

An understanding of the detailed contents of these requirements is largely confined to a small body of specialists. Some observers have noted that not only do the current methods of granting tax relief via Inland Revenue approval dictate the general form of scheme but it tends to reduce flexibility. For example, the present practice of placing a special restriction on the amount of benefits for late entrants to schemes who only have a short period of service to normal retirement age, may discourage mobility of labour especially in the later years of a working lifetime when an employee's experience might be invaluable both to a prospective employer and to the national economy.

The deployment of skilled specialists to unravel the complexities of the Inland Revenue's latest practice notes deprives the community of the best use of their skills. It is the combination of all of the difficulties referred to above which has caused many to question not only the cost of pension fund fiscal neutrality but also whether it should exist at all. A pamphlet on this subject, published by the Inland Revenue entitled *Costs of Tax Reliefs for Pension Schemes. Appropriate Statistical Approach*, [QRL.39] attracted much press comment.

The tax regime which applies in respect of approval schemes can be summarised under these heads:

(i) relief on contributions by employers;
(ii) relief on contributions by employees;
(iii) relief in respect of investment income;
(iv) relief in respect of capital gains;
(v) relief in respect of lump sum benefits;
(vi) treatment of pensions as earned income;
(vii) relief in respect of VAT etc.

Pensions in payment are treated as earned income and taxed under the PAYE system, therefore statistics such as those relating to the average amount of pensions in payment by region can be obtained from the *Inland Revenue Survey of Personal Incomes* [QRL.102]. Many recipients of occupational pensions have a total income that is too small to bring them within the operation of Income Tax and hence they are not included in the Inland Revenue statistics [QRL.102]. The *Family Expenditure Survey* [QRL.45] of the Department of Employment probably provides a coverage which is more complete. Relevent statistics are reproduced in the *Governments Actuary's Survey* [QRL.70].

2.5 State Pensions

2.5.1 *The State Graduated Scheme*

The State Retirement Pension consists of three parts, a basic or full rate pension, an additional pension from State Earnings Related Scheme (see 2.5.2) and a graduated pension from the old graduated pension scheme (see 2.5.1). Full details of these benefits can be obtained from the Department of Health and Social Security (DHSS).

In 1959 the first Government earnings-related pensions scheme - the State Graduated Scheme - was introduced. It provided a flat rate pension, plus an earnings-related addition in return for earnings-related contributions. The Graduated Scheme has now been superseded and the maximum benefits which are likely to have been accrued by any individual are of the order of £3 per week (not inflation-linked).

Provision was therefore made for employees who were members of pension schemes which satisfied certain conditions (providing a minimum equivalent benefit comparable with the supplementary state pension) to be excused from participating in (or contracting out of) the new arrangements which came into force in 1961. The DHSS provided the required supervision.

2.5.2 *The State Earnings Related Scheme (SERPS)*

The Social Security Pensions Act 1975 introduced a new State scheme. A Green Paper [B.72] published in June 1985 proposes its phasing out by April 1987, but at the date of writing this review it is unclear whether these proposals will be implemented. The main features of SERPS are a basic flat rate pension (which represents approximately 20% of the average earnings of adult male manual workers) plus an additional pension (after 20 years' contributions) of 25% of a band of earnings above the level of the flat rate pension, but with a ceiling of about 1.5 times average earnings. When the scheme is mature an individual's total State pension will range from 100% of earnings of those on minimum earnings to about 35% at the ceiling. The Act provides for members of pension schemes which meet an approved standard to be contracted out of part of the new arrangements for additional earnings-related pensions. Such contracted-out employees and their employers are allowed a reduction of contributions on the same band of earnings as that relevant to the computation of the additional pension.

The State earnings-related pension scheme provides a pension of one-eightieth of that part of an employee's full taxable pay which falls between the lower and upper earnings limits, revalued up to age 65 for men and 60 for women according to changes in national earnings and indexed to the cost of living after it becomes payable. Each year of membership of the State earnings- related scheme after April 1978 conveys entitlement to the one-eightieth pension, except that if an employee has more than 20 years of such membership, only the best 20 such years ("the best 20 years" rule) are eventually taken into the calculation of the pension, so that the maximum earnings-related pension will be 25 per cent of the appropriate revalued average annual earnings.

The widow's retirement pension comprises the whole of the retirement pension which the husband received on his own account when he died (or accrued to the date of death if the man died during employment). There are also added, subject to overall limitations, any earnings-related component the widow herself earned. Widow's pensions in payment are revalued in the same way as personal pensions. There are similar provisions for a widower's pension if the wife is an employed person.

2.5.2.1 *Contracting Out* For an employee to be contracted out by virtue of membership of an occupational scheme, the scale of the employee's pension on retirement at State pensionable age (65 for men, 60 for women) must satisfy two tests. The first test is that the pension payable (in which may be included any pension arising in respect of years before 1978) must not be less than the pension that the employee would have accrued by way of earnings-related pension in the State scheme had he not been contracted out for the period for which he was contracted out. This required amount of pension is called the "guaranteed minimum pension" or "GMP".

An employee who is contracted out cannot receive less benefit than one who participates. When a contracted out employee retires, a State earnings-related pension is calculated as if he had never been contracted out and there is then deducted the amount of the GMP provided from the occupational scheme. The total pension from State and occupational scheme together is therefore the same as if the employee had not contracted out.

The second test is sometimes referred to as the "quality test". The OPB (Occupational Pensions Board) has issued guidance on the provisions of the Act, and in particular on the quality test because its broad nature requires much detailed interpretation. For an occupational scheme to serve for contracting out, it must provide, in addition to the scales of personal pension, benefits to the widow of a member who dies in service or after retirement. A variety of statistics relating to widows (and widowers) pensions are contained in [QRL.70], [QRL.33] and [QRL.27].

There is no obligation to provide widower's pensions in the case of women members. The amount of the widow's pension must be at least equal to one-half of the GMP of the member, or to one-half of the accrued prospective GMP of the member if he dies before attaining age 65. In the State scheme the widow inherits the whole of her husband's pension, but this feature is not carried through to contracting out. The State retains responsibility to the widow of a contracted-out member for a pension equal to the excess of the member's full earnings-related pension over one-half of his GMP. The second contracting-out requirement in respect of the widow's pension is similar to the quality test of the member's pension, but at the half rate. The GMP element of a widow's pension must be paid to the widow, but the scheme may, with the approval of the OPB, contain a discretion for benefits comparable to any pension in excess of the GMP to be paid instead, wholly or partly to a dependant or dependants of the member.

There are no reliable statistics on the number of persons contracted out at any given time. The best estimates are those obtained from The National Insurance contribution statistics for the number of persons in respect of whom contributions at the contracted-out rate were paid at some time during the year. Details of people ceasing to be contracted-out are contained in the *Review of Contracting Out Contribution Reduction and Related Issues* produced quinquennially by the DHSS [QRL.94].

2.5.3 *Integrated Schemes*

Schemes integrated with the State scheme, are those where the State benefits are deducted when calculating the benefits provided by the occupational scheme. It is common practice to make a deduction from the salary of all members and then use this reduced salary as a basis for contributions (if any) and pensions. The deduction is often related to either the basic State pension for a single person or the lower earnings limit for national insurance contributions.

Care must always be exercised when interpreting any statistics on integrated schemes. Although in a survey a scheme may reply that it is not integrated, this may be because the rules make no explicit provision for it. But it may easily have been one of the many factors considered at the design stage resulting in a lower benefit formula than would have been agreed upon if consideration had not been taken of the State benefits. Records of such discussions are usually lost in the course of time. Statistics on integrated schemes are contained in [QRL.27].

2.5.3.1 *Pensionable Salary*

Many schemes use a definition of salary for pension purposes which excludes fluctuating payments such as commission, bonuses and overtime, and is thus at a lower level than the actual income of the employee. Where fluctuating payments are not excluded they often receive special treatment, for example they may be averaged over a period of years or months in order to provide a more stable figure for contribution and benefit purposes. An analysis of definitions of salary used for pension contributions is contained in the NAPF [QRL.27] as is a table showing the trend of pay-related contributions in works schemes.

2.6 Occupational Pensions Board

The Social Security Pensions Act 1975 established the Occupational Pensions Board (OPB) giving it detailed statutory powers relating to the supervision of the contracting-out arrangements.

The OPB is an independent statutory body ("quango") and its functions in relation to occupational pension schemes operating in Great Britain derive mainly from the Social Security Act 1973 and the Social Security Pensions Act 1975. These functions include:-

(i) ensuring that occupational pension schemes comply with the requirements for the preservation of benefits for members who leave before normal pension age, by giving advice to scheme administrators, and, where appropriate, determining whether schemes' rules conform with the requirements;

(ii) ordering the modification or winding-up of an occupational pension scheme for specified purposes, if asked to do so;
(iii) reporting to the Secretary of State on proposals for regulations relating to occupational pension schemes;
(iv) advising on matters relating to occupational pension schemes, to which the Secretary of State may, from time to time, refer;
(v) administering the arrangements for occupational pension schemes to be contracted out of the earnings-related part of the state pension scheme by issuing, varying or cancelling contracting-out certificates and supervising financial resources and arrangements of contracted- out schemes; and
(vi) ensuring compliances by occupational pension schemes with the requirements for equal access to membership for men and women, by giving advice to scheme administrators and, when appropriate, determining whether schemes' rules conform to the requirements.

Statistics relating to the activities of the OPB such as the number of applications for contracting-out certificates and how they have been dealt with used to be found in an OPB report [QRL.99] which was discontinued in 1981. Certain of these statistics may still be obtainable directly from the OPB. The Executive Office of the OPB is shared by the Superannuation Funds' Office of the Inland Revenue to ease communication between the two bodies. Where the OPB and Inland Revenue appear to be in conflict over an issue, the legislation relating to the OPB overrides Inland Revenue practice.

2.7 Preservation

The 1973 Social Security Act provided that employees leaving service before normal retirement date and having reached age 26 with at least 5 years' qualifying service, must be given a title to a deferred pension. The Social Security Bill 1984 removed the minimum age criteria. The act contained elaborate provisions relating to preservation - the Occupational Pensions Board has the responsibility to deal with them. Supervision is also provided by the Department of Health and Social Security.

The Social Security Bill 1984 Clause 2 (c) and schedule 1 related to the revaluation of the early leavers benefits. In certain circumstances preserved benefits must be revalued in line with price increases up to a maximum of 5% p.a. The Bill also gave members the right to take a transfer value (see 2.7.2).

Statistics relating to the numbers of members of schemes categorised according to the type of preserved pension provisions contained in the rules of the schemes can be found in the *Government Actuary's Surveys* [QRL.70]. A study of schemes which are analogues of the Civil Service scheme [QRL.33] contains data on the increases granted to deferred pensioners, both in deferment and also once in payment. The exact numbers of schemes on a definitive basis, including contracted-out schemes, examined by the OPB and found to satisfy the preservation requirements were until 1981 contained in an OPB report [QRL.99]. Later figures may be available from the OPB.

2.7.1 *Deferred Pensioners*

The term "Deferred Pensioners" describes those ex-employees who have left service prior to normal retirement age but have a deferred/preserved entitlement to benefits from the scheme. Until such time as deferred benefits have been revalued for some time (see previous paragraph) the value of pensions is likely to be relatively low when people ultimately reach retirement (except in the public sector where deferred pensions have been index-linked for some time). The survey commissioned by the Equal Opportunities Commission (EOC) [QRL.15] contains statistics on the proportions of individuals with frozen pensions (another term for deferred pension).

The NAPF *Survey* [QRL.27] provides ratios of deferred pensioners to ordinary members of pension schemes. It provides data on the percentage of schemes granting increases during the period between the date of a member leaving the scheme and becoming retired as well as data on the actual level of those increases.

2.7.2 *Transfer Values*

Most schemes include provisions for the making of transfer payments, under which the value of an accrued pension is transferred to another fund when a person changes his employment. There are a few schemes which appear to have the power to make transfer payments but not to receive them, or *vice versa*, but usually the powers to pay and to receive occur together. The Social Security Bill 1984 makes it compulsory for schemes to both accept and provide transfer payments. At the date of completing this review full regulations have not yet been published. The percentages of schemes which currently accept transfer payments and/or make them available are contained in the NAPF *Survey* [QRL.27]. [QRL.15] shows that the number of people actually transferring pensions is small. This is because of the difficulties involved for those not in the public sector where a group of employers and pension schemes (mainly confined to the public sector) have agreed to a common basis of transfer payments. Such employers refer to themselves as members of the "Transfer Club".

Statistics on transfer payments are also contained in [QRL.70]. Statistics on the type of benefit granted in respect of a transfer payment received, e.g. additional pensionable service, a fixed pension or a combination of the two are contained in the NAPF *Survey* [QRL.27]. The precise benefits awarded on withdrawal from a pension scheme often depend on the exercise of a choice either by the leaver or his employer or both.

Pension Fund Management [QRL.75] is the most recent of the surveys contained in this review which has a section relating to transfer values. Despite the great publicity given to the early leaver issue by the press, many of the finance directors responsible for pension funds who were interviewed for that survey were unable to provide answers to simple questions relating to it.

2.8 Equal Access and Maternity Leave

Since 1978 there has been a statutory requirement for employers to provide equal access to occupational pension schemes for men and women (e.g. no distinction is permitted between entry ages for men and women). The OPB was given the job of supervising the Equal Access legislation and also some aspects of the law relating to maternity leave as they affect pension rights. At the date of writing, the European Parliament is considering a draft directive on equal treatment for men and women in occupational social security schemes. The outcome of these deliberations would have far reaching effects on the design of private occupational pension schemes.

The exact numbers of schemes on a definitive basis, including contracted- out schemes, examined by the OPB and found to satisfy the equal access requirements were, until 1981, contained in an OPB report [QRL.99]. Later figures may be available from the OPB (see 4.4). Statistics relating to the numbers of members of schemes categorised according to the type of equal access provisions contained in the rules of the schemes can be found in the *Government Actuary's Surveys* [QRL.70].

2.9 Schemes

There is no precise definition of exactly what pension arrangements constitute a scheme. Schemes which in one company might be regarded as separate schemes, for example individuals, small numbers of senior staff or other special groups, might by another company be treated similarly, as separate schemes, or be combined as a larger group. In addition, there are a few centralised schemes, usually for a particular industry, to which several thousand employers may affiliate. Statistics of numbers of schemes must therefore be used with caution. This warning is particularly pertinent to the NAPF *Surveys* [QRL.27] (see 5.1) since the majority of the data is categorised by percentages of schemes.

Pension Fund Management [QRL.75] enquired of finance directors (or their equivalent) how many pension schemes (including executives/directors plans) they operated. Replies varied from 1 to in excess of ten.

2.9.1 *Class of Schemes*

It is still common for employers to have separate schemes with a lower scale of benefits for their works employees (variously described as hourly- paid, weekly-paid, operatives, manual workers, industrials, or just 'other than staff employees'). State pension benefits are larger of course in proportion to pre-retirement earnings for the lower-paid than higher-paid workers. The NAPF *Survey* [QRL.27] categorises all of its tables in this manner as staff/workers (in addition to any other relevant split). The *Government Actuary's Survey* [QRL.70] in contrast, splits only a few of its tables in this manner and prefers the terminology manual/non-manual.

2.10 Sector of Employment

Many aspects of pension funds, ranging from design features to investment practice, differ according to employment sector. Coverage in particular varies between type of occupation as shown in [QRL.15]. Some features exhibit their most marked differences between the public and private sectors and this therefore is a categorisation often used. Examples of this are contained in all the major surveys. A particular example could be that almost all pensions paid by public sector employers are indexed to the cost of living, but although the vast majority of members of schemes can, in future, expect to obtain a pension at retirement that takes into account inflation insofar as it is reflected in their salaries before they retire, few in the private sector can expect full protection against inflation after retirement, [QRL.70] and [QRL.27]. However, the State scheme will provide protection in respect of that part of the occupational pension scheme which corresponds to the additional component of the State pension for those who have been contracted-out (see 2.5.2). The importance of this protection will increase over the twenty years as the scheme reaches maturity. In the past it has been more often the large employers that have been granting increases close to increases in the cost of living. Most employers are going beyond the requirements of the rules but there is, of course, no guarantee that they will continue to do so, [QRL.70] [QRL.27].

Other features differ within the public sector and a more detailed breakdown of what is meant by the public sector is required. MQ5 [QRL.32], for example, sub-divides the public sector into local authorities and other public sector schemes since their investment practices differ so greatly.

2.10.1 *Public Sector Schemes*

Of the 23 million employees in Britain about two million are employed by public corporations. There are over a hundred of these statutory bodies. The nationalised industries include those of coal mining, railways and docks, steel, shipbuilding, electricity, gas, national buses, waterways, air transport, freight and oil. Other public corporations include the Bank of England, the Civil Aviation Authority, the broadcasting authorities, boards serving Northern Ireland, and a number of bodies such as the regional water authorities, the passenger transport executives, the new towns development corporations, the Royal Ordnance Factories and the Trust Ports. As the Government proceeds with its privatisation programme, this list can be expected to diminish.

The remainder of the public sector include not only the employees of central government (i.e. all bodies for whose activities a Minister of the Crown, or other responsible person, is accountable to Parliament), but also of local authorities (i.e. the elected councils for defined areas of the United Kingdom) and HM Armed Forces.

2.10.1.1 *Local Authorities*. There are a number of differences between the pension schemes of local authorities and other public sector schemes. An article in *Pensions World* [B.18] sets them out in detail. Arising out of these differences local authorities have set up their own performance measuring service *Local Authority Superannuation Fund Investment Statistics* [QRL.62].

2.10.2 *Private Sector*

Employees in the private sector are those employed by companies and unincorporated businesses, and by non-profit-making bodies, serving companies and individuals which are not subject to government control. The latter includes bodies of a quasi-public nature such as universities.

The private sector is rarely (if at all) sub-divided other than between employed and self-employed: as the self-employed are not permitted access to occupational pension schemes, it may reasonably be assumed that they are excluded from statistical tables unless specific reference is made to them. The self-employed may purchase pensions from insurance companies (see 3.8.4.2).

2.11 Funded Schemes

In the private sector and in other parts of the nationalised industries funds are set up in advance of the anticipated benefit requirements. The arrangement of the incidence over time of the payments intended to meet the future cost of a given set of benefits is referred to as 'the funding plan' or 'pace of funding'. The determination of a correct funding level is a skilled occupation usually handled by qualified actuaries. It is possible that a company's accounts will make provision for a level of funding differing from the 'funding plan'. Such a difference must be noted in the accounts. An analysis of the differences between accounting and funding is found in Tonkin and Skerrat [QRL.20].

UK National Accounts [QRL.109] categorises income and expenditure of pension funds by funded, unfunded and notionally funded schemes.

2.11.1 *Notionally Funded*

The teachers' superannuation scheme is a well known example of a notionally funded scheme. No investments are held in respect of it and yet in most respects it is treated as a traditionally funded scheme. Teachers' pensions are paid by the Exchequer. Employers' contributions and contributions deducted from teachers' salaries are paid to the Exchequer which then pays the superannuation benefits as they fall due. An account called the Teachers' Superannuation Account is maintained. Contributions from teachers and employers are credited to the Teachers' Superannuation Account and expenditure on basic benefits, but not pensions increases, is debited. Each year's net accretion to the account is deemed to be invested at current market prices in Government Securities and the interest payable on those securities is credited to the account. The total contributions, i.e. teachers' and employers' contributions together, are assessed by the Government Actuary as those required, on normal actuarial principles, to meet the cost of benefits debited under the regulations of the Teachers' Superannuation Account.

2.11.2 *Unfunded Schemes*

An example of an unfunded arrangement would be a promise made by an employer to a group of executives to provide them with benefits which exceed those to which they were entitled under the company's pension scheme. It is unlikely that any reliable statistics would ever be available of such arrangements.

Pensions for civil servants and many other public sector employees are also unfunded, i.e. provided on a pay-as-you-go basis. In these cases there are formal arrangements and contributions to the scheme are fixed each year to match the benefit outgo. In practice the two do not always match up exactly and a nominal amount of investment on the part of these funds takes place. The most common form of unfunded scheme is that of the pension scheme for civil servants. It is documented in *Civil Service Pay Research* [QRL.33] in detail. Another form of unfunded scheme is the internally financed scheme. In some countries, particularly Germany, the practice of many companies is to secure their pension commitments not by transferring assets to an external pension fund but rather by accruing the liability in the company's balance sheet. Where a company has an overseas subsidiary using this method of pension provision there is usually a note to the sponsoring employer's accounts [QRL.20].

2.12 Investment Medium

Traditionally, a pension fund whose assets are invested other than with an insurance company is referred to as "self-administered". (The term "self- administered" is related to the investment, not administration, of the fund). The NAPF *Survey* [QRL.27] prefers the term "privately invested".

A pension fund where the main asset is an insurance policy is called an 'insured scheme'. The variety of arrangements has increased; thus for instance, a self-administered fund may pay money to an insurance company as premiums for life insurance policies providing benefits on death in service or to buy annuities for those on the point of retiring. If no money passes to an insurance company, the scheme is clearly self-administered. It is difficult in other cases to know exactly where to draw the line. Some tables in [B.61] are labelled as insurance, part insurance and privately invested to make the distinction clear. This distinction is not however referred to in the other surveys and in particular [QRL.70].

Normally, there are four types of investment methods available to an organisation:

a) through an outside organisation such as a merchant bank or stockbroker
b) by a salaried investment manager who is an employee of the organisation
c) using an investment committee or
d) through an insured scheme with premiums paid to an insurance company.

It is possible for funds to use more than one method by splitting the management of the fund. The above categorisations are those used in *A Survey of Public Sector and Non-Corporate Pension Funds* [QRL.103].

2.13 Entry Conditions

Few employers include all their employees in pension schemes as a matter of course; frequently temporary employees are excluded, or those working only part-time. Many companies only cover certain categories of staff. In some employments membership is voluntary [QRL.27]; in fact when a new scheme is set up it cannot be made compulsory for existing employees. As a result of these factors pension scheme coverage varies from nil to 100 per cent for different companies [QRL.70].

Before being allowed to join an occupational pension scheme, an employee may have to complete a stated period of service or reach a prescribed minimum age, or both. During this "waiting period" the employee pays no contributions and pension benefits do not accrue, (although death benefits are sometimes provided and, very occasionally, ill-health retirement benefits). A different period of service may be required for the employee to be eligible for an ill-health early retirement pension. Such statistics are contained in [QRL.70] and [QRL.27].

Many pensions schemes still require a minimum period of service to be completed after admission to the scheme before a pension will be available at normal retirement age. This is usually expressed as a maximum entry age, above which new employees will not generally be admitted to the scheme, although there may be separate provisions for them to be covered for death benefits should they die in service.

Nearly all members in private and public sector schemes alike are covered for lump sum death benefits immediately upon entry to the pension scheme. In both sectors, cover for widow's pension usually commences at the same time as cover for lump sum benefits.

The Government Actuary's Survey [QRL.70] provides statistics on the numbers of employees not in pension schemes by the cause of their exclusion. Scheme rules commonly give the scheme managers or trustees power to waive or modify the normal eligibility conditions in special circumstances, in particular, where a new employee brings a transfer value from the scheme of his previous employer.

2.14 Contributions

Individual schemes can vary from those where no contributions are required from the members (except possibly for some optional benefits), to a few schemes which are mainly financed by the members. Contributions from both members and employers form a major component of the income of pension funds [QRL.32]. One of the Inland Revenue's requirements for approval of a scheme is that the employer must contribute to it. The level is not specified. In certain circumstances they may be satisfied with only 5% of the cost of the scheme, but normally the proportion is higher [QRL.70], [QRL.32], [QRL.27].

Employers' contributions can be subdivided into normal contributions, additional special contributions and those required to 'make good' deficiencies found at the valuation of the fund and to pay for back-service improvements [QRL.27]. The Companies Act 1981 contained new disclosure requirements concerning pension contributions. Very few companies disclosed normal and special contributions separately in their reports and accounts [QRL.20]. This may reflect a lack of clear definition of normal and special in the ICA's exposure draft on the subject [B.37].

The scheme rules define the method of computation of the contributions paid by members. Sometimes the contributions are assessed as a uniform percentage which is applied to the salary as defined for scheme purposes, which may exclude certain elements of renumeration. Sometimes an amount might be disregarded to allow for national insurance contributions (see 2.5.3) or bonuses and over-time payments might be omitted. In a few schemes the contribution is of a stated amount for each range of salary; the salary used for this purpose may also exclude certain parts of total pay. A third type of contribution found in schemes covering only manual employees is the flat contribution which does not vary with earnings or age, but may in some cases vary according to job status. Other methods of assessing contributions are now rare.

Members' contributions can be subdivided into ordinary annual and additional voluntary contributions. Statistics on the level of contributions paid by members and the methods used can be found in [QRL.32], [QRL.70] and [QRL.27].

2.14.1 *Additional Voluntary Contributions (AVCs)*

In many schemes members have the opportunity to pay additional voluntary contributions to the scheme, or to a separate scheme established for this purpose, in order to secure additional benefits. *Paying for Equalisation* [QRL.15] shows that very few members take advantage of such facilities. The employer rarely makes any contributions towards the extra benefits provided by AVC's [QRL.32] [QRL.70]. Comparisons between the investment medium of the main scheme and the investment medium of the AVC's are provided in [QRL.27].

2.14.2 *Early Leavers*

There are restrictions on the grading of refunds of contributions for those leaving schemes before normal retirement age (see 2.3.3). A member leaving a scheme before completing five years' qualifying service usually only receives a return of his own contributions (if any). In the case of a contracted-out scheme, this refund is usually reduced by the member's share of the premium which is paid to secure the member's guaranteed minimum pension benefits from the State. Instead of a return of contributions, many schemes allow a withdrawing member to choose a preserved pension limited to that purchsed by his own contributions, although trustees often have the discretionary power to increase the amount of the preserved pension to one based on the member's accrued service. Most of the cases exceeding the statutory qualification requirements make a preserved pension based on accrued service available to all withdrawing members, usually with the option of a contribution refund if a member has less than five years' service. A few schemes make an accrued pension available to all members who have completed one, two or three years' service.

2.15 Benefit Structure

Schemes can be structured so that the benefit is defined or the contribution is defined or a combination of both. The most common form of defined benefit scheme is the final salary scheme (see 2.15.1) and the most common form of defined contribution scheme is the money purchase scheme (see 2.15.3). There are also hybrid schemes. An analysis of the percentage of schemes and members who pertain to each classification is contained in the NAPF *Survey* [QRL.27].

2.15.1 *Final Salary Design*

Pensions are now in the majority of cases calculated on a 'final salary' basis, that is, based on salary at retirement or averaged over the final years or months of service. The usual approach is to calculate the pension as a fraction of final salary multiplied by the length of the member's service. This rate of pension accrual varies from 1/45th to 1/100th of eligible earnings per year of pensionable service. 1/60th is the most popular, leading to a pension of 2/3 of final salary for an employee who completes 40 years of relevant service.

The method of calculation of 'final' salary from a member's 'pensionable' salary (2.5.3) in the period prior to his retirement can vary considerably from scheme to scheme. In periods of high inflation, these variations can result in significant differences in the levels of pension provided by otherwise identical schemes. 'Final' salary may be equal to the actual annual rate of salary at retirement or it can be the average annual salary received over a period prior to retirement, commonly one or three years. Where a longer averaging period is used, the level of benefit will be more sensitive to the rate of inflation, and consequently inflation has caused a tendency towards shorter averaging periods. An analysis of final salary schemes by the type of definition used is contained in the survey of the NAPF [QRL.27].

There are many problems caused by the intrinsic nature of the final salary design of benefits. Further details can be found in *Pensions, the Problems of Today and Tomorrow* [B.6] and also in a paper presented by this author to the Institute of Actuaries Student Society [B.16].

2.15.2 *Average Salary Design*

The 'Average Salary' schemes calculate the pension as a fraction of the total salary earned throughout service. Both these and pensions awarded as a flat sum per year of service have suffered a sharp decline in popularity because of the effects of inflation although some 'average salary' schemes now revalue past salaries in line with increases in the cost of living to overcome this drawback.

2.15.3 *Money Purchase Schemes*

Money purchase schemes calculate the pension as the amount purchased by the contributions made by the member and employer from time to time. 'Money purchase' is a convenient arrangement among highly mobile staff, since the pension liability in respect of a particular period of service is met as it occurs.

2.16 Commutation Options

The majority of private scheme members have the option of exchanging part of their pension benefits for a lump sum payment at retirement. This benefit is referred to as 'the commutation option'. The popularity of the commutation option in the private sector has grown significantly over recent years not only because of the obvious advantages of present liquidity. The lump sum can be used to purchase a lifetime annuity at favourable rates - a strategy which also has certain tax advantages. A few private sector schemes provide a lump sum, compulsorily, rather than by way of option, in addition to the pension. It is more common in the public sector to provide a lump sum in all cases - the commutation option is only available in a few schemes such as that of the police and the armed forces. Statistics on the numbers of members receiving lump sum benefits can be found in the Government Actuary's survey [QRL.70]. Statistics relating to the percentages of schemes are contained in *Annual Survey of Occupational Pension Schemes* [QRL.27].

2.17 Pension Payments

The first pension payment is often paid on a fixed date other than the retirement date and represents a proportionate amount of a full period's benefit. Practice in this field is analysed in *Pension Payment Methods - a Survey* [QRL.78].

2.17.1 *Pensions Guarantee*

In order to remove the discontinuity of benefit which can occur when a pensioner dies soon after retirement, many schemes incorporate some form of pension guarantee. This guarantee usually takes the form of either a specified minimum period of payment or a lump sum payment equal to a multiple of the member's pension less any payments he had already received. [QRL.27] contains the results of an enquiry into the general practice in this field.

2.17.2 *Post Retirement Pension Increases*

Practices regarding pensions differ between sectors of employment (2.10). Schemes which guarantee to increase pensions in line with the Retail Price Index would be unlikely to provide periodic reviews over and above the guaranteed increases. Therefore it is not necessarily the case that guaranteed increases plus periodic reviews are any more generous than guaranteed increases with no reviews.

2.18 Early Retirement

The majority of private sector schemes base the early retirement pension on accrued service to the date of early retirement, and then apply a reduction factor. Usually, the accrued pension without any reduction would be available to the retiring employee as a deferred pension commencing at his normal retirement date - the reduction allows for his pension to commence at an earlier age instead. The amount of the reduction, however, can often be varied at the discretion of the employer, and it is known that in some cases this discretion is used to waive any reduction if early retirement is occuring within a period of, say, two or three years of normal retirement date. In the public sector pensions are often preserved until normal retirement age or early retirement.

Some schemes provide an immediate pension on early retirement based on accrued service and without any reduction, but the conditions under which such pensions are available tend to be more restrictive than in schemes where a reduction is applied, possibly limiting availability to members over the age of 60 or within five years of normal retirement date and possibly requiring a longer minimum period of service. Thus these schemes can in practice be less generous than some schemes that have been regarded as applying a reduction. Some schemes provide an early retirement pension calculated by applying a reduction factor to the pension based on full potential service to normal retirement date. There is little difference between these and schemes based on accrued benefits and reduced, since the former reduction factors are larger.

Many schemes which are integrated (see 2.5.3) from the normal retirement date, do not apply any deduction when calaculating the pension available on early retirement. An even incidence of income during retirement is provided, because the early retirement pension falls when the State pension commences as the deduction is applied at normal retirement date. In a few schemes, a member retiring early is given an option to exchange the usual level pension for a higher rate until State pension age and a lower rate thereafter.

Statistics relating to early retirement are contained in both [QRL.70] and [QRL.27]. In particular the frequency of adoption of various methods used in calculating the early retirement pension is contained in [QRL.27]. It shows the two principal ways in which the early retirement arises, namely upon the initiative:

(i) of the employer, possibly as part of a redundancy programme,
(ii) of the member, though with the employer's consent.

2.18.1 *Ill-Health Retirement*

In nearly all schemes there is provision to pay a pension commencing immediately on premature retirement on grounds of ill-health. In the private sector the most common arrangement is for the pension to be calculated on the basis of the accrued service, i.e. the actual service rendered before ill-health retirement, thus taking no account of service which would subsequently have earned pension had ill-health not intervened. On the other hand many schemes in the private sector are now providing ill-health pensions of the same amount as would have been paid at the normal retirement age, i.e. based on full potential service and without reduction for early payment. Most public sector schemes and many of the private sector schemes pay ill-health pensions which have a basis somewhere between these extremes of full potential service and of service to date of ill-health retirement only. The analysis of methods of calculating ill-health retirement benefits contained in the NAPF *Survey* [QRL.27] extends to 7 (including 'Other Methods').

2.19 Death Benefits

The general pattern of benefits on death in service is for a one-off cash amount to be paid with, in most cases, a widow's or dependant's pension. In order to differentiate the one-off cash payment from the pension, this form is often referred to as a lump sum benefit. In addition to these benefits, there is often a return of the member's own contributions (if any) with or without interest. In a few schemes the level of the lump sum benefit or the availability of a return of contributions depends on whether or not a member leaves a widow or dependant eligible for a pension. A table showing the amount of lump sum payable as a multiple of salary is contained in the NAPF Survey [QRL.27].

Many occupational pension schemes provide not only for payments to be made on the death of the member whilst in service but also when he dies as a pensioner (after normal retirement or ill-health retirement). This benefit takes various forms: the most obvious is a continuing, but usually smaller, pension to the widow. Many pension schemes have a 'guarantee period' where once the pension has commenced payment it is payable for 5 to 10 years regardless of whether the pensioner survives or not; this provides "protection" in the event of early death. Full statistical details are contained in the Government Actuary's survey [QRL.70] and the Survey of the National Association of Pension Funds [QRL.27]. [QRL.70] provides details of the difference in benefits granted to men and women.

The two main methods of distributing lump sum death benefits are via discretionary trusts and automatically to the deceased's legal personal representatives. The former method requires the member to complete an expression of wish form during his lifetime. This is normally adhered to, but it is not a legally binding document. The advantage of the former method is that it usually avoids the payments of CTT. Despite this the NAPF survey [QRL.27] shows that a significant minority of schemes still use the latter method.

Pension Fund Management [QRL.75] provides an analysis of whether death-in-service benefits are provided from the same fund as the main pension scheme or under a seperate scheme. This is further analysed by the investment medium of the pension scheme.

2.19.1 *Widow's Pensions*

The last decade has seen a dramatic increase in the proportion of male members of private sector schemes who have an entitlement to a widow's pension should they die in service; to a large extent this increase may be a result of schemes altering their benefit structure to comply with the contracting-out requirements of the Social Security Pensions Act 1975. Relevant statistics are contained in [QRL.27] and [QRL.70].

Should a widow remarry, it is shown in the Government Actuary's survey [QRL.70] and the NAPF survey [QRL.27] that the normal practice in the public sector is for her pension to be suspended or stopped entirely, except for the guaranteed minimum pension (see 2.5.2). In the private sector, however, many members are in schemes where the payment of a widow's pension is unaffected by her remarriage. For the remaining members, the pension will often continue at a lower level, but usually only at the minimum rate acceptable for contracting-out purposes.

Where commutation (see 2.16) of a member's pension is permitted at retirement, the prospective widow's pension payable on death after retirement is normally based on the member's pension before commutation has taken place.

2.19.2 *Widowers' Pensions*

A large minority of private sector members are in schemes which provide pensions for widowers on the same basis as they provide widows' pensions. In most of these cases a pension is provided to the legal spouse on the death of any member, although a few only pay a spouse's pension if he or she was financially dependant on the member. Other schemes provide for pensions to widowers who were wholly or mainly dependent on their wives under the rules which provide for dependants of deceased members generally. Fuller details are contained in the Government Actuary's survey [QRL.70] and the survey of the NAPF [QRL.27].

CHAPTER 3

LIFE INSURANCE

3.1 Introduction

In modern parlance, the terms insurance and assurance are frequently interchangeable. The use of the word insurance normally implies that a contract of indemnity is involved, hence "term insurance" (see 3.8.2) as no payment is normally made if the policyholder survives, and in the wider context, general insurance. The use of the word assurance normally implies some form of certain return, hence endownment assurance (see 3.8.3) as a payment is normally made whether the policy-holder lives or dies –and in the wider context –life assurance. Historically, in 1978 the LOA/ASLO (6.3) did try to rationalise on the use of the words insurance / assurance but it proved an impossible task and was abandonned.

In 1762 the "Society for Equitable Assurance on Lives and Survivorships" was founded. It was the first institution in the world designed to conduct life insurance on a scientific basis. Today the original fundamental principles remain unchanged.

One of those fundamental principles of insurance is known as "insurable interest". The effect of this legal phrase is that a person can only contract with an insurer provided that, that person or that person's family would suffer some financial loss as a result of the insured event occurring. However, husband and wife are deemed to have an unlimited interest in one another's and their own lives, so legally they may take out personal accident and life policies for up to any amount they wish. In practice the insurance companies themselves impose limits on the size of policy that they will issue on any one life.

A husband earning £10,000 per annum may have to provide considerable justification if he wishes to insure his wife's life for £10 million (using say a 1 year term insurance policy –the cheapest form available).

Life insurance policies are generally arranged as contracts under which the premium is assessed according to the class of insurance, the expected average expenditure over the period and its likely variation (which inherently involves consideration of the insured's circumstances at inception). Since the rate of mortality increases with age the practice necessarily involves the accumulation of funds to meet the claims of the later years and normally a level premium is charged for the increasing risk. At any time the fund is the excess of the premiums over the cost of the risk in the earlier years. (Statistics on the size of total funds in each of the latest five years can be found in *Life Insurance in the UK* [QRL.60]). This fund, together with future premiums, should be sufficient to pay for future risks. Thus in life insurance the concept of averaging is taken in two dimensions:

(i) over the pool of risks, and

(ii) over the duration of the contract.

In setting the premiums the actuary does not deal with one factor at a time in isolation of the others. The calculation of premiums involves the interplay of many factors, at least three predominate: (a) mortality, (b) interest and (c) expenses. Other technical elements must, however, also be considered.

Life insurance policies were originally designed to provide protection for a person's family in the event of an untimely death. With many insurance policies the insured, if he survives to the end of a specified term, receives back a sum of money referred to as the maturity value. Many people do not like to think of the possibility of their own death and because of the availability of the maturity value such people have been encouraged to think of insurance policies as investments for the future. It is often said that such insurance is "sold and not bought"; many policies today are designed as investment vehicles, often in a highly sophisticated fashion. Since the removal of tax relief on life insurance premiums (LAPR) in the 1984 Budget, insurance policies have been even harder to sell. This has led to an even greater emphasis on marketing. There are companies which review the deployment, level and timing of expenditure on advertising, including insurance. An example of such a company is MEAL which maintains a microfiche library of advertisements in the national press, magazines and television and certain specialist publications. Results are available in a wide variety of data formats, *Advertisement Analysis* [QRL.23]. Insurance Companies' investment expertise needs to be considerable and they are now using this experience to diversify into related fields.

3.2 Legislation

The Insurance Companies Act 1982 [B.50] is a consolidating act and forms the basis of life insurance supervision in the United Kingdom. The form of supervision established in the UK is sometimes referred to as 'freedom with publicity'. Insurance business can be conducted only by institutions which are authorised by part 1 of that Act or are specifically exempted. The exemptions are: (i) Lloyds, (ii) Friendly Societies, (iii) Provident or strike benefits of Trade Unions or Employers Associations.

The 1983 Regulations [B.49] govern the form of an insurance company's return to the Department of Trade and Industry for any financial year ending on or after 15 March 1984. Long term insurance companies other than those registered under the various Friendly Society Acts are also subject to the various Companies Acts from 1948 to date which set out various requirements for a balance sheet, a profit and loss account (including a statement of turnover) and a directors' report. There is no requirement for a revenue account, although most companies do provide one. This still leaves great flexibility in the basis on which the figures are compiled. This flexibility means that caution is required in making comparisons between companies. Aggregation of company results is also difficult.

The detail contained in the long-term revenue account differs between companies. Normally, either the revenue account or the statement of movements in life funds contains information on premiums investment income, benefits, expenses and taxation plus a reconcilliation in the life funds at the start and end of the accounting period.

The Directors' report of an insurance company apart from the normal commentary on the accounts must also contain details of employees: the average number, of employees each week, the average yearly salaries. A note to the accounts must show the number of employees other than directors earning more than a given amount –currently £30,000. A large proportion of these individuals will be part of the sales force.

Exemptions are granted to insurance companies from several of the normal Companies Act requirements, but an auditor can still declare the accounts to be "true and fair" even if the insurer has taken advantage of these exemptions.

The "true and fair view" is one which follows the four fundamental accounting concepts, described in SSAP 2 on *Disclosure of Accounting Policies* [B.77].

Where the insurer is a holding company, it must provide a consolidated balance sheet and profit and loss account for the group. In this respect the Companies Act accounts differ from the returns to the DTI who are responsible for the supervision of the Insurance Companies Acts. Each year the Secretary of State for Trade and Industry is required to report to Parliment on the excercise of his powers, [QRL.53]. As well as detailed statistics *Insurance Annual Report* [QRL.53] provides background information such as the conditions attaching to specific authorisations.

Thus a UK life insurance company will need to provide two sets of financial statements each year: accounts for its shareholders [QRL.90] and returns [QRL.93] for the Department of Trade and Industry. Returns must be made within six months of the end of a financial year. Only three of the larger companies have year ends other than 31st December. Unless a company has been granted an extension for supplying its figures financial information should be available at Companies House from August in respect of the previous year. Information on sources of aggregated figures is detailed in section 7.5. *Returns under the Insurance Companies Act* [QRL.93] include the revenue account, balance sheet and profit and loss account (these accounts must be audited because of the requirements of the Companies Act) and any report of the auditors must be attached. Copies of [QRL.90] and [QRL.93] are usually available on request to each individual company.

The traditional United Kingdom freedoms are increasingly coming under scrutiny and, with the advent of Common Market regulations, will have to be modified. The entry of the United Kingdom into the European Economic Community in 1969 meant that the United Kingdom could no longer regulate its institutions without some regard to other Member States, however complete harmony in the field of life assurance regulations is still a long way off.

3.2.1 *Classes of Business*

Valuation of liabilities regulations, which had been under discussion for some years came into operation from 1 October 1982. There are now seven classes of long term business and seventeen classes of general business where previously there were only two classes of long term business, *viz* ordinary long term business, and industrial assurance business, [B.1], (those two categories of insurance business are not now recognised as separate classes by the regulations [B.49]. *Life Insurance in the United Kingdom* [QRL.60] continues to use this breakdown).

3.2.2 *Long Term Business*

The seven new classes of long term business are:

(i) Life and annuity
(ii) Marriage and birth
(iii) Linked long term
(iv) Permanent Health
(v) Tontines
(vi) Capital redemption
(vii) Pension fund management

The classes of business exhibit many different features, mostly of a technical nature. Until 1976 detailed summaries of each company's valuation returns were contained in *Insurance Business Statistics* [QRL.54]. These summaries were presented separately for each class. The DTI hope to resume publication of some such statistics in the 'near' future. The *Business Monitor* MQ [QRL.32] splits its statistics between long term and general; many statistics such as those contained in [QRL.53] do, whilst others such as [QRL.30] do not even separate life insurance from pensions.

3.2.3 *Valuation Returns*

Section 18 of the Act [B.50] requires a periodic actuarial investigation of companies which carry on long term business. An annual requirement was introduced in 1981 [B.51]; previously it was for an investigation once every three years. The investigation has to cover a valuation of the liabilities and the determination of the actuarial surplus, i.e. the excess of the assets held in the fund over the liabilities and at least once every five years a statement of the long term business has to be drawn up, (see 4.2, 5.2.2.1 and 9.5).

The account and balance sheets, including any statements required, other than the actuary's abstract and the five-yearly statement of long term business, must be audited. All accounts, actuarial reports and auditors' statements must be deposited with the Department of Trade and Industry within six months of the financial year end. The deposited documents [QRL.93] are available for public inspection, but each policyholder and shareholder has a right to receive directly a printed copy of the returns submitted. In practice most of the larger companies would make their returns freely available.

The returns require to be analysed and sub-totalled within each type of business in the sequence specified below:-

(i) Life assurance business
(ii) General annuity business
(iii) Pension business
(iv) Permanent health business
(v) Capital redemption business

The information is then to be further analysed and sub-totalled as follows:-

(i) non-linked contracts: with participation in profits
(ii) non-linked contracts: without participation in profits
(iii) linked contracts

Within each of the sub-divisions required above the appropriate types of insurance form the following list and are to be shown separately:-

(i) whole life assurance
(ii) endowment assurance
(iii) pure endowment assurance
(iv) term assurance
(v) other assurance (to be specified)
(vi) deferred annuity
(vii) annuity in payment
(viii) other annuity (to be specified)
(ix) group pension
(x) group life
(xi) other group (to be specified)
(xii) permanent health insurance
(xiii) capital redemption assurance
(xiv) annuity certain

There is little consistency in presentation of valuation returns [QRL.93] and they are difficult to consolidate. *Whitakers Almanack* [QRL.112] attempts to list the valuation assumptions used by the principal life offices but in the majority of cases has to resort to saying "various".

The *British Insurance Industry Statistical Review* [QRL.4] compares company press release figures with their actual valuation returns. Many of the directories reviewed in Chapter 7 contain abridged valuation returns for the companies they list.

Chapter 9 contains several recommendations for improvements to the valuation returns of life offices.

3.2.3.1 *Zillmerisation* The "setting up" costs of a life policy are high and often far exceed the first year's premium. The DTI permit offices to amortise expenses in their valuation returns [QRL.93]. The method most normally used is referred to as Zillmerisation after Dr. Zillmer, its inventor.

3.3 Friendly Societies

Friendly societies were originally formed in the last century to provide mutual protection for members against events such as death, sickness, retirement and unemployment, often on a very local basis, at a time when social security provision was minimal.

Some societies have separately registered branches –commonly called orders. Centralised societies are those whose business is conducted directly by the society, without separately registered branches. Collecting societies are friendly societies conducting industrial assurance business (although some also write ordinary branch business) and friendly societies may also be classified according to the nature of their main business. This is done in the *Report* of the Registrar [QRL.26]. Background information about all the categories of Friendly Societies is set out in *Friendly Societies* [B.12].

3.3.1 *Finance Bill 1984*

Although Friendly Societies began in the Middle Ages, many more recently established societies had until the 1984 Budget been set up solely to enable them to offer savings plans of around £500 a year without tax on the underlying investment funds. The advantages of such schemes took some time to become known to the public, but in the months before the 1984 Budget the idea was spreading fast and in those few months some 300,000 policies were sold. The 1984 Budget contained proposals which were extremely complex and were designed to curtail these new societies.

That Budget ensured that in future societies can offer tax exempt contracts only where the sum assured (the minimum death benefit) does not exceed £750 per person and the basic annuity payments do not exceed £156 per year. Although these new societies were formed solely to make maximum use of tax concessions to Friendly Societies the Government's proposed clampdown threatened the viability of many of the established Friendly Societies.

3.4 Industrial Assurance

Premiums for industrial insurance policies are payable at intervals of less than two months and are collected by agents who call at policyholders' homes. This "home service" method of premium payment is the main difference between industrial and ordinary business. A more technical definition is contained in the *Report* of the Chief Registrar of Friendly Societies [QRL.26] who administers the primary regulations governing industrial assurance contained in the Industrial Assurance Act 1923. There are regulations in that Act which extend the information on companies' industrial business beyond that required by the DTI.

Industrial companies may also carry on other forms of insurance business. Statistical information relating to industrial assurance companies can be found in the *Report* of the Chief Registrar of Friendly Societies [QRL.26].

3.5 Industrial and Provident Societies

A society may qualify for registration under the Industrial and Provident Societies Act 1965 for many diverse reasons. These are set out in [QRL.26]. Some insurance and superannuation societies are so registered. The most notable is the Co-operative Insurance Society.

3.6 Reinsurance Companies

Reinsurance companies are the insurers' insurers. A paper entitled *Developments in Life Reinsurance* by R.W.A. Howe and R.W. Douglas [B.15] provides a detailed introduction to the subject.

3.6.1 *Net Premiums*
The expression 'net premium' has several different meanings in the field of insurance. When used in the context of reinsurance it means that part of the premium left to the ceding insurance office after it has paid a reinsurance premium across to its reinsurer. When used in the context of the insurance company's valuation it has an entirely different and highly technical meaning and the reader is referred to an actuarial textbook: *Actuarial Practice of Life Assurance* [B.10]. The confusion to those not completely familiar with the industry arises because both terms are used in the returns that the life insurance industry make to the Department of Trade and Industry. A further meaning given to the term is the mathematical or pure premium required solely to secure payment of the contractual sum assured i.e. the premium charged to the policyholder less any allowances for expenses etc.

3.7 Taxation

Care must be taken in interpreting any series of statistics on the cost of tax relief on life insurance premiums. The method of granting tax relief on life insurance premiums was changed in 1979 resulting in cash flow differences in certain series of statistics such as those contained in *Inland Revenue Statistics* [QRL.52]. Prior to 1979 the policyholder paid a gross premium to the insurer; he then obtained tax relief through PAYE or direct assessment. From 1979 the policyholder paid the net premium to the insurer; the insurer then claimed tax relief from the Inland Revenue. Data showing the amount of premium relief passing from central Government to the life funds is contained in the "Blue Book" [QRL.109]. In the 1984 Budget speech the Chancellor said: "The main effect of life assurance premium relief today is unduly to favour institutional rather than direct investment. It has also spawned a multiplicity of well-advertised tax management schemes, and no less than 50 pages of legislation attempting to deal with its abuse. I therefore propose to withdraw the relief on all new contracts made after today".

The current position is set out in the *Allied Dunbar Tax Guide* [B.22] an annual publication. Many forms of specialist advisors issue abbreviated guides to any budget changes within 24 hours of the relevent budget as well as more general guides during the year. An example of such a service is *Budget Guide* [B.31]. An historical introduction to life insurance taxation is set out in the Millard Tucker Report of 1954 [B.74].

3.8 Types of Insurance Policy

There are many life insurance companies in Britain offering a range of policies and details of which offices are authorised to conduct business are contained in the *Insurance Annual Report* [QRL.53] as well as other publications. Life insurance comes in two forms: protection and investment. These two basic goals are often mixed in one product and include elements of both of these aims. The total number of types of policies on offer when taking the various options which are available into account may well run into thousands. Many financial magazines (some of which are reviewed in Chapter 7) regularly contain surveys and articles about the various types of life insurance policies. The main basic types of policy are Whole of Life (see 3.8.1), Term Insurance (see 3.8.2), Endowment Assurance (see 3.8.3), Annuities (see 3.8.4) and Permanent Health (see 3.8.5). Most of these basic types of policies can be further categorised by the following three groupings: With Profits (see 3.8.7), Without Profits (see 3.8.6) or Unit Linked (see 3.8.8).

Care must be taken when interpreting the number of policies issued by a company. At one extreme one group policy or master policy may be issued to cover many individuals and at the other extreme a cluster of many policies may be issued to one individual. Such clusters of policies may in certain circumstances prove more tax effective than a single policy.

3.8.1 *Whole Life Insurance*

A whole life insurance policy guarantees to pay an agreed sum of money to a beneficiary when the policyholder dies. The premium payable each year will depend on the amount of money to be assured and on the person's age and health at issue, and in some cases occupation. This premium is paid every year for the remainder of the preson's life. Payments can stop when the person retires, or at some other specified age in which case the policy is referred to as a "limited premium whole life policy" rather than just a "whole life policy". The premium for a limited premium whole life policy is, of course, higher than for an otherwise exactly similar whole life policy.

3.8.1.1 *Single Premiun Bonds*

Technically these are whole life insurance policies purchased by a single amount rather than regular premiums. These are almost exclusively for investment, and the insurance payment in the event of death is usually minimal.

3.8.2 *Term Insurance*

Term (or temporary) insurance is similar to whole life insurance except that the company will only pay the benefit if the policyholder dies during the agreed term or period of time. The policyholder similarly has only to pay his premium for an agreed term or period of time and not for his whole life. This type of policy provides a temporary form of protection. Because the insurance company may not have to pay the benefit, it charges far less for this type of policy than for a whole life policy.

3.8.2.1 *Level Term* Here the sum insured, which the policy-holder chooses at the outset remains fixed throughout the term of the policy. If the policy-holder survives, then he does not receive any payment. Level term insurance is one of the cheapest forms of life insurance.

3.8.2.2 *Convertible Term* With a convertible term policy a policy-holder has the same basic cover as for the level-term insurance, with the additional option of being able to convert it to another kind of policy should he wish to do so. Usually the options can be exercised at any time during the term of the policy. If the policy-holder does convert his policy he would automatically be accepted for insurance, whatever the state of his health at that time. However, the premium for the converted policy would be the normal rate applicable to the policy-holder's age at the time he exercised the option. The extra cost for convertible term compared with level term is relatively small.

3.8.2.3 *Decreasing Term/Mortgage Protection* As the name "decreasing term" implies, the sum insured decreases during the term of the policy. With this type of policy, substantial cover is provided in the first year, reducing each year by a pre-determined amount. Compared with level term insurance, the policy-holder can buy a much larger initial sum insured for any given premium, but at some point the cover will become identical with the level term value and then diminish.

Decreasing term insurance is often used in conjunction with building society loans or mortgages and for this reason is often called "a mortgage protection policy".

3.8.2.4 *Family Income Benefit* Under a family income benefit policy the insurers pay not a lump sum, but a regular fixed tax-free income, starting when the policy-holder dies and continuing to the end of the term of the policy.

3.8.3 *Endowment Assurance*

With endowment assurance, the policy-holder is able to save for the future while insuring his life at the same time. The policy-holder pays premiums for an agreed amount insured, over an agreed period of time. This date in the future, when the agreed period of time has been reached, has been written in the policy. It is called "the maturity date". On the date of maturity the policy-holder recevies his benefit. If the policy-holder dies before the date of maturity is reached no more premiums are paid and the full benefit is paid to the beneficiaries. Of course, endowment insurance is more expensive than most other types of policy. These policies are often used for straightforward investment purposes, although one of the commonest forms is for mortgage repayment. Instead of gradually repaying the capital of the mortgage loan only interest is paid to the building society; the capital is repaid at the end by the pay-out on the separate endowment policy.

In April 1983 mortgage interest relief at source (MIRAS) was introduced. This made mortgage endowment policies an attractive method of mortgage repayment. This fact is reflected in the new business figures of life offices for that period, *Life Insurance in the UK* [QRL.60].

3.8.4 *Annuities*

An annuity differs from the three main types of insurance policy so far mentioned. With each of the other types of policy, an agreed sum of money is paid –either to the policy-holder on an agreed date, or, if he dies, it is paid to the beneficiaries. With an annuity policy, the benefits start to be paid on an agreed date, and then continue to be paid at regular intervals, for the rest of the policy-holder's life. Where the agreed date is more than one year in the future, the annuity is referred to as a deferred annuity. Annuities can be split into "non-pension" and retirement annuities. The purchase price of an annuity is often referred to as the 'consideration'.

3.8.4.1 *"Non-pension" Annuities* With certain exceptions, such as annuities arising under a direction in a will or in trust under a pension scheme or in respect of services as an employee, an annuity normally involves the payment of a capital element under section 230 of the Taxes Act 1970. The Capital element is determined by dividing total purchase money or premiums paid by an expectation of life at the vesting date of the annuity according to prescribed tables. The portion of the annuity designated as the capital element is free of tax, and the remainder is taxed as income. If the annuity does not involve such a capital element then it is wholly taxed as income.

3.8.4.2 *Retirement Annuities*

Retirement annuity contracts are available under the provisions of Section 226 of the Taxes Act 1970 as amended later and must have as their main object the provision for the individual of a life annuity in old age. they are aften referred to as "personal pensions" and details of the amounts sold by life offices can be found in [QRL.60]. The intention of these provisions is to give the self-employed, and those who are employed but are not eligible for membership of an employer's pension scheme, a tax advantage similar to that enjoyed by contributors to occupational pension schemes (see chapter 2). The tax basis is that the interest build-up of the annuity is tax-free while the annuity is taxed as income. Contributions to such policies attract tax relief at an individual's highest marginal rate since they are deducted from the individual's income before income tax is assessed. Statistics relating to the numbers of such policies owned and their distribution by income and family circumstances can be found in the tables relating to "Deductions" in the Inland Revenue's *Survey of Personal Incomes* [QRL.102].

A directory of retirement annuities currently marketed together with their salient features is contained in [QRL.63]. Appendix 3.1 contains a specimen page defining the features.

3.8.5 *Permanent Health Insurance*

Relatively little has been done by the life insurance industry to popularise disability insurance in the form of Permanent Health Insurance (PHI). The word Permanent refers to the fact that policies are non-cancellable by the insurance company; renewal cannot be refused by the office. These policies provide for the payment of income during a period of incapacity due to sickness or accident. The benefit commences payment after an agreed period of incapacity called the "deferred period" which can vary from a few days to up to two years. The aim is to provide an income while the policy-holder is unable to work, rather than a recompense for injury and pain. It is not necessary for the incapacity to be permanent (no likelihood of recovery) and it can be of a very minor or temporary nature provided the policy-holder is genuinely unable to continue employment. There is only a limited amount of statistical data on which to base a rating table (see 6.5.2) [QRL.34], [B.32], [QRL.35], [QRL.36], [QRL.37], [QRL.38], [B.33]. (Sickness statistics produced by the Government agencies do not provide a suitable data base as they do not normally break down absence by duration). National Insurance data break statistics down at the 28 week level, this one duration is not sufficient. Individual PHI in the United Kingdom is almost exclusively written on a non-profit basis (see 3.8.6). This is surprising as future claim levels may be quite different from the current experience and a basis which allows an office to make some adjustment to the policy terms if the experience differs from anticipated would normally be expected.

Group PHI schemes are sometimes written in conjunction with occupational pension schemes providing not only an income to the sick employee but the maintenance of his contributions to the pension scheme during incapacity. Figures on the quantity of both group and individual PHI schemes written by life offices are contained in *Life Insurance in the UK* [QRL.60].

One of the statistics contained in [QRL.60] is for the "maximum benefits insured p.a." PHI lends itself to self-selection against the office –often referred to by technicians as 'moral hazard'. It is, of course, difficult for any physician to say with 100% certainty that specific disabilities will cause inability to work to earn a living e.g. backache and depression. It has been felt by PHI insurers that irrespective of how high the salary earned, there should be a monetary limit on the PHI benefit which should be underwritten.

A magazine supplement entitled *Permanent Health Insurance Review* [QRL.82] is published annually. As well as topical articles it contains explanations of the various jargon terms in use in this particular field. It then sets out the variations in practice of the competing offices e.g. after explaining that in general female lives must be gainfully employed to obtain cover it sets out the various exclusions relating to female lives which can be imposed by companies, listing those which impose them after each specific type of clause. It lists all companies operating in this field together with a "brief" description of the type of policy they offer. It also provides comprehensive rate tables.

3.8.6 *Without Profit Contracts*

Under a without-profits policy, the policy-holder pays a regular premium for a fixed sum insured, agreed when he takes out the policy. Whether a claim is made at death or maturity in one year or in thirty years' time (if appropriate) only this fixed sum assured is payable. Without-profit policies are sometimes called "non-profit" or "non-participating" policies.

3.8.7 *With Profits Policies*

If a policy-holder buys a with-profit policy, he pays a higher premium than he would for an otherwise exactly similar non-profit policy, but any benefit is then made up of two parts: (a) a fixed basic sum insured plus, (b) a share in the overall profits of the insurer. These profits are added in the form of "bonuses", normally reversionary bonuses added to the policy throughout its life and a terminal bonus added when it is cashed in.

Every few years, each insurer values the assets of his fund and estimates the future liabilities of his insurance contracts in force. As a result of this periodic valuation, most of the surplus is distributed to policy-holders in the form of tax-free bonuses, (see 4.2). It must be remembered that although "surplus" is the insurance term for profit, the meanings are, by no means identical. As surplus depends on the overall experience of the insurer, one would theoretically expect bonuses to fluctuate considerably after each valuation. In practice, the life office actuaries in charge of the valuation are careful not to distribute to policy-holders the whole of each year's surplus. They often transfer in (or out if more appropriate) a proportion to (or from) a special equalisation reserve.

3.8.7.1 *Reversionary Bonuses* Reversionary bonuses are not paid out in full as cash sums when they are declared. Instead they are added to the basic sum assured and paid out whenever a claim is made. Most UK bonuses are of this form.

3.8.7.2 *Simple Bonuses and Compound Bonuses* Offices declare reversionary bonuses using either a simple or compound rate where simple and compound have the same meanings as in relation to interest calculations.

3.8.7.3 *Interim Bonuses* When a company declares a reversionary bonus after one of its periodic valuations, this applies only to the policies in force at the valuation date, and even then only for the period between the valuation just made and the one before that. However, if a policy-holder makes a claim, say six months after the valuation date, he is also entitled to a share of the profits which the insurer has earned since the last valuation.

The insurer will not wish to make an additional full-scale valuation of assets and liabilities to determine the appropriate share of the profits for this short period, therefore at each valuation a special rate of interim bonus applicable to all future claims payable until the next valuation may be announced. This interim bonus is usually a conservative estimate of the next reversionary bonus. It is not guaranteed, and in theory the insurer can discontinue it, though this would be most unusual.

3.8.7.4 *Terminal Bonuses* Over the last fifteen years or so, many insurance companies have introduced a bonus designed to reflect the large capital gains which they have made. (In Canada the method was in use in the 1920s). These bonuses, paid in addition to the ordinary reversionary bonuses are allocated only to policies becoming claims by death or maturity. They are liable to fluctuate in line with general investment conditions, and the particular experiance of each insurer. The amount of some terminal bonuses also depends on the time the policy has been in force when the claim is made. Terminal bonuses are usually expressed as either a percentage rate of the declared reversionary bonuses attaching when a claim is made or as a proportion of the basic sum assured plus bonuses.

3.8.7.5 *Low Cost Policies* A "low cost policy" is a combination of a with-profits endowment policy and a reducing term assurance policy. The principle is that the insurance cover provided by the term assurance will decrease at the same rate as reversionary bonuses are added to the with-profits policy.

The low cost policy is usually cheaper than a full with-profits policy because part of the life insurance in the early years is provided by the term assurance.

Low cost policies are often used for endowment mortgages. The reducing term insurance in the early years provides the money to pay on the mortgage in the event of untimely demise.

3.8.8 *Unit Linked Policies*

The term "unit linked" in relation to a policy describes the form of investment medium used for the premiums. A unit linked policy is connected or "linked" directly with particular investments that the insurance company is making. The benefit that the policyholder finally receives will depend on the success of these particular investments at the time the benefit is paid.

The prices achieved by units of these funds are normally reported in the financial press. This is not always the case; some newspapers charge a fee for inclusion whilst others are limited by considerations of space. The frequency with which funds are valued varies from daily to monthly. The policyholder is concerned with the difference between the offer prices at which he is allocated units and the bid price at which they are being cashed. It is not generally appreciated when considering performance that a change in management policy can cause an alteration in unit prices of up to 15% without any movement in the market value of the underlying assets. *Unit Pricing* by T.W. Parry [B.20] contains worked examples.

In 1971 a committee was appointed by the Secretary of State for Trade and Industry to consider certain matters relating to linked life business. The committee reported in 1973 [QRL.17]. Much of the evidence contained in that report is still relevant today.

As with conventional policies, unit linked policies can also be roughly divided into a small number of groupings (see 3.8). For a conventional policy the split between that portion of the premium going to investment and that to expense is completely left to the actuary's discretion. For a unit linked policy the split is stated explicitly in the description of the policy. The benefit under the policy is directly linked to the units in which the policy is invested. The units to which the policy is linked are not legally segregated from the remainder of the life assurance company's assets. This is relevant when the life company is making its own tax calculations and in the rare event that the company is liquidated. Despite the fact that for unit linked policies the expenses theoretically are explicitly stated, there are many complications in the design of the policies which prevent direct comparisons between their own and the products of different companies. There are several different types of unit currently being marketed. Accumulation units are the most common. Any income earned by the fund is "rolled up" or "accumulated" to increase the price of the units. Distribution units, although common for authorised unit trusts, are not so for life funds. Income from the fund is used to buy further units rather than increase the value of existing units (as in the case with accumulation units). Capital units are accumulation units with a high level of management charge.

Companies quoting unit prices in newspapers [QRL.49] sometimes show a series of prices for the same fund. This occurs where the amount of management charge deducted from the fund has had to be increased but the wording of the linked policies did not permit it. A new series of units was therefore formed. The wording of modern policies is more flexible.

Many magazines conduct surveys of aspects of the policy such as levels of explicit expense, investment performance of the units to which the policies are attached as well as aspects of the design of policies. It is important when using these surveys to consider the purpose of the sponsoring organisation in launching the survey, (see also Chapter 8).

Charges differ considerably between companies and also between annual and regular premium contracts. Allocation terms vary even more and further variables are the amount invested and the age of the investor. A regular survey of unit linked contract charges (relating to personal pension plans) and allocation terms is contained in *The Martin Paterson Personal Pensions Survey* [QRL.63].

CHAPTER 4

LIFE AND PENSIONS

4.1 Introduction

The theoretical background of the two subjects life and pensions is very similar. Both require a detailed understanding of actuarial techniques. It is in the practical application that wide differences emerge. Pensions practioners have therefore formed their own institutes (see chapter 6). Nonetheless, even on the practical side there are overlaps caused by life insurance companies selling pension products, indeed, the majority of self-employed pensions are marketed by life insurance companies. (See 3.8.4.2).

Difficulties in interpreting the true size of the pensions movement are caused not by being able to separate, in all cases, that part of the life companies assets attributable to pensions contracts e.g., in many Government and Bank of England statistics produced for national accounting purposes [QRL.48], [QRL.30], [B.48] and [QRL.109] no attempt is made to separate assets attributable to life and pensions contracts.

4.2 Valuations

In order to tell if a life (or pension fund) is likely to meet its obligations, it is not sufficient merely to charge against revenue the normal payments made during a period by way of premiums to insurance companies (or the contributions to a retirement benefit scheme). It is necessary to consider all aspects of contractual obligations. To do this an actuarial valuation is required. Such a valuation makes various assumptions to reflect the anticipated average experience of the fund. It then uses the technique of discounted cash flows to place a value on the fund. Discounted allowance is made not only for interest but also for various other contingencies such as mortality and lapses. The results of an actuarial valuation are highly dependent on the various assumptions chosen. These may well depend on the purpose for which the valuation is being prepared. In the case of a life office it may be to see if the life office is solvent, to value it for a prospective purchaser or to determine the level of bonus which the company can support. In the first use the assumptions must be conservative, in the second (if being performed by the vendor) optimistic and in the third consistent over a period of years. The result of an actuarial valuation without knowledge of the basis and purpose for which it has been prepared is therefore difficult to interpret.

Financial Reporting [QRL.20], by Tonkin and Skerrat, has analysed pension fund valuations disclosed in reports and accounts into those on a discontinuance basis (based on current levels of salary and periods of service) and those on this basis of a going concern basis (based on projected levels of salary). Report and accounts rarely show actuarial assumptions and the caveats mentioned above in relation to life offices apply as strongly to pension funds.

4.2.1 *Surplus*

The twin concepts of valuation and surplus have been developed by the actuarial profession side by side. After a valuation has taken place the excess of the value of the assets over the value of the liabilities is referred to as surplus. Surplus is therefore a function of the valuation basis. In a fund which is open for new business there must be some carry-forward of surplus, whether explicit (or hidden in the valuation assumptions) which will serve to maintain the stability of the fund. Surplus and profit are different. Profit is independent of the valuation basis and cannot be known until the fund is finally closed. To be able to say precisely what is the present value of potential profit, it would be necessary to have precise knowledge of future experience.

In a life office the distribution of surplus is at the discretion of the actuary and normally emerges in the form of bonuses on with profit policies. One of the reasons for the popularity of unit-linked policies was the percieved removal of this element of discretion from the life office.

In an occupational pension fund many more people are involved with the results of the actuarial valuation than is the case for a traditional life office. Because of the wider involvement of non-actuaries the term has acquired many connotations not relevant in the life office context. The Pensions Research Accountants Group (PRAG) has therefore set up a working party on pension fund surplus (see 6.8). One of its terms of reference is to define what are, pensions fund surpluses. It is hoped that the PRAG working party will report in 1987. A survey of *Approaches to Pension Funding* [QRL.3] currently being conducted by the City University Centre for Research in Insurance and Investment, also discusses this question.

4.3 Standard Mortality Tables

The lives insured by a particular life office (or lives who are members of a given scheme) are a selection from the population of the country as a whole. They may well exhibit different features from those of the remainder of the population. If it is practicable, a life office (or pension fund) will construct a mortality table based upon its own experience. This is not usually possible and standard mortality tables are used. In the case of pension funds, a table based on the general population may be most appropriate. Life offices on the other hand are likely to require a table based on the mortality experience of other life offices [QRL.21]. These standard tables are only guides and individual offices may exhibit a markedly different experience.

4.3.1 *Initial Selection*
Different offices have different standards for selecting which lives to accept on standard terms. This often depends upon the type of business that they are transacting. Potential policyholders may be required to undergo a medical examination: the mortality experience of policyholders who take such an examination is investigated separately. As any policyholder who is not "fit" is charged an 'extra premium' and not included in the investigation, it is to be expected that the experience of medically examined policyholders is better than that of those not so examined. This effect, referred to as 'initial selection', wears off. Mortality tables reflect it by having special rates for the first few years of a policy, 'the select period', and higher rates for subsequent years, 'the ultimate period'. [QRL.21].

Other forms of initial selection occur because of self-selection. e.g. mortality for annuitants [QRL.22] is normally higher than for assured lives [QRL.21].

4.3.2 *Sex*
Standard mortality tables are not usually a good guide to female mortality, even where a separate table is published. Until recently fewer policies were issued on female than on male lives [QRL.34-38] and [B.33]. It is likely therefore that those females purchasing policies were a select group exhibiting characteristics differing from their peers. The exception is in the use of annuity tables [QRL.22], where traditionally annuities have been purchased for females.

This is equally true of those pension schemes large enough to generate their own experience data. A large proportion of the female working population do 'part-time' work [QRL.70] and are therefore not eligible for an employer sponsored pension fund.

4.3.3 *High Ages*
There is scanty data available at high ages and that which is available should be treated with caution. Many whole of life policies (see 3.8.1) are sold with a limited premium paying term. One of the reasons for this is to prevent long-lived policyholders complaining that the premiums that they have paid exceed the amount of the sum assured. If a policyholder dies after premiums have ceased and he has not made details of his policies easily available for his executors, then the insurance company will not be notified of his death.

4.3.3.1 *Certificate of Existence* Periodically life offices (and pension funds) will write to aged policyholders (pensioners) to ask them if they are alive. The form that they are thus required to complete is referred to as a Certificate of Existence. The objective in the case of life offices is probably purely for audit purposes. In the case of pension funds the objectives are more manifold. Apart from purely audit purposes and to certify continued existence it may be to identify cases of re-employment, cases of widows who have remarried or cohabited or even to confirm that children were continuing to receive full-time education.

The results of a non-rigorous survey on practices regarding certificates of existence used by pension funds is contained in *Pension Payment Methods* [QRL.78].

4.3.4 *Duplicate policies*
Statistics on duplication among linked policies are contained in *CMI Report No. 6* [QRL.38]. It is common practice for policies with large premiums to be issued as duplicate policies with many small premiums. Such duplicates are fairly easy to eliminate from a mortality investigation. A person who has bought one policy from a life insurance company is likely to consider them favourably (if he has not had any bad dealings with them and most will have had *no* dealings) and if wanting a subsequent policy will choose them once again. A proportion of policyholders will therefore have more than one policy on their lives. Such duplicates are much harder to eliminate from an investigation. If a policyholder with six policies dies, it is recorded as six deaths. At higher ages this can prove significant.

4.3.5 *Lapses*
The term 'lapse', 'withdrawal', 'surrender', and in the case of pensions 'transfer', are often synonymous, although within an organisation specific attributes may be designated to one or other of the terms, e.g., lapse is often used to mean withdrawal in the first two years only. Life and pension plans are essentially designed as long-term contracts. Life policies and those pension plans sold through life insurance offices have heavy setting-up costs leaving little money available to pass back to policyholders who withdraw early. In the 1970's low surrender values attracted adverse publicity by the financial media. High estimates of withdrawal rates were made (with scant statistical foundation) and blamed on the 'hard-sell' techniques of insurance companies. Since then, a 'cooling-off' period has been introduced by the Government permitting a policyholder to change his mind about buying a policy without penalty. This cooling-off period does not apply to Section 22.6 pension policies. The main source of information on withdrawal rates in life insurance companies is in an paper in the *Transactions of the Faculty of Actuaries* vol. 36 [QRL.105], based on Scottish data relating to 1976 and 1977. In this study the term withdrawal was used to denote removing a policy from the live file, due to premature termination of the contract, with or without payment of a surrender value. It does not include the conversion of a policy to a paid-up amount, the reduction of premium and/or sum assured or the surrendering of bonus. For a discussion on methods of improving this paucity of data (see 9.5.8).

The Statutory returns relating to friendly societies which are collated in the annual *Report* of the Registrar of Friendly Societies [QRL.26] contain statistics on lapses.

Transfers between pension schemes exhibit additional problems since there is a social dimension to occupational pension schemes as well as the purely fiscal dimension. The OPB has produced a report "Improved protection for the occupational pension rights and expectations of early leavers" [B.48].

4.4 Investments

4.4.1 *General*
The main categories of investments in which pension funds can be invested are cash and short term deposits, fixed interest, index-linked gilts, equities (including

convertibles), property (excluding property unit trusts), property unit trusts, overseas securities, others. This is the breakdown used by the NAPF survey [QRL.27]. Life office funds are invested in similar media, but in different proportions. (The differences reflect the length of term and nature of the liabilities which require matching). The breakdown of assets used by the ABI survey [QRL.60] is ordinary stocks and shares, British Government and local authority statistics, real property and ground rents, mortgages, debentures, overseas, other.

A far more detailed breakdown is contained in *Business Monitor* MQ5 [QRL.32] which is the main official source of such statistics for both life and pension business.

For life offices one of the forms required for the statutory returns [QRL.93] is a statement of admissible assets and liabilities. This statement is completed for each fund or group of funds for which separate assets are held. The form shows 20 different categories of assets. The assets are valued as required for statute and the method may be either that of market or book value. Care should be taken in interpretation when comparing an individuals figures with those in its report and accounts [QRL.90] or when aggregating results.

Detailed breakdowns of investments of pension funds are contained in many of the "market research" surveys e.g. *Pension Fund Management* [QRL.75]. This also contains information relating to investment policy, administration etc.

4.4.2 *Managed Funds*

Most major life offices in the United Kingdom run managed (sometimes referred to as pooled) funds offering a pooled investment service. A pensions managed fund is effectively a unit trust available to tax-exempt pension funds only, set up by a life office and normally administered by a specially established subsidiary company of that life office. The investments of subscribers are pooled and investment management functions —including reclaim of tax and reinvestment of dividends – are performed by the company offering the managed fund. Other administrative functions may also be performed. There is in practice no insurance element merely a pooling of the investments. The investment management team usually forms part of main investment team of the parent life office.

Subscribers to managed funds buy units which entitle them to share in a fund. At predetermined intervals, usually once a month, the assets of the fund are valued and a buying and selling price determined by the managed fund company for units in the fund. Certain managed funds quote only one price which is normally, the price at which units can be bought, but could occasionally be a selling price depending on the net cash flow into the fund. Usually units in the managed fund can only be purchased or sold on valuation dates.

A directory of managed funds is contained in *Survey of Pooled Pension Funds* [QRL.101]. Typically this gives details such as fund type; fund manager; date the fund commenced; investment policy; minimum investment charges included in price; charges not included in price; bid/offer spread; date units issued; date of income distributions and conditions on which units are surrendered and/or switched.

4.4.3 *Segregated Funds*

The terms managed fund and segregated fund are often used interchangeably by commentators. There is a significant difference. The underlying assets of a managed fund form part of the assets of the life office and managed funds are entered in the normal returns that life companies must make to the Department of Trade and Industry, [QRL.93].

Segregated funds are invested separately from the funds of the parent office and are accounted for separately and are not even held in the name of the life office.

The life office merely offers an investment service in much the same way as would a stockbroker or merchant bank. These funds do not normally appear in a life office's returns to the DTI except to the extent that a fee is charged for the services and these fees appear as an item of income.

4.5 Performance

There are three aspects of investment performance that are pertinent to this review: the performance of (1) funds themselves, either funds managed by a life office (including pension funds) or pension funds managed by some form of investment adviser, (2) life office shares (and the shares of employers sponsoring pension schemes) when quoted, (3) life office products.

PRAG, in its first report, *Financial Reports for Pension Funds* [B.39] expressed the opinion that "interpreted correctly, comparative investment performance measurement offers trustees a useful vehicle for discussing the fund's performance with their investment managers".

Investment performance services tend to provide short term appraisals but performance results are only significant when considered over a period long enough to have statistical validity. It is important therefore that they are "interpreted correctly" and that e.g. "hire and fire" decisions relating to investment managers are not made on the basis of one set of results.

Investment performance monitoring is concerned with comparing, as objectively as possible, the relative skills of investment advisers as well as analysing in depth where such skills have been well deployed and less well deployed, since among other analyses it attempts to show how much of the variation in return comes from policy decisions and how much from the actual selection of stocks and shares. In the United Kingdom, increased interest has been paid to this subject in the last ten years. In 1972 the Society of Investment Analysis published its recommendations for the measurement of portfolio analysis of pension funds [B.57].

4.5.1 *Fund Performance*

A Survey of Public Sector and Non-Corporate Pension Funds [QRL.103] enquired into funds' objectives in evaluating investment performance. Reasons mentioned included maximisation on long-term growth, maximise income, keep up with the best funds, stability of return, minimisation of investment risk, monitor effectiveness of investment managers and maintain the real value of the fund.

It must be stressed that all performance statistics are by definition suspect. The timescale is clearly the overriding factor and since timing is probably the most important single determinant of success or failure the arbritrary choice of any period of time or starting date can produce a totally misleading impression of investment managerial capability. The shorter the timescale, the less impact will fundamental investment criteria on price movements and the greater has to be the reliance on investor psychology. If different organisations are used to measure the performance of a fund a careful check must therefore be made of the dates on which measurements are made.

Performance statistics relate only to organisations or specific funds within them; they can rarely if at all be attributed directly to a particular manager. All performance statistics must be assessed in the light of answeres to questions regarding

a) the background of the organisation concerned: its history, size, management structure, access to origional research
b) freedom given to individual managers
c) administration
d) communication
e) charges

A fuller discussion of the subject is contained in an article in *Pensions World* by Norman Freethy –"Choosing your investment manager" [B.11].

Most of the measurement systems available use either some form of 'time-weighted' return, money-weighted return or an equivalent measurement as a basis of comparison. The 'time-weighted' rate of return is essentially the rate at which the fund would have grown without any new money, but with investments otherwise as for the actual fund. A money-weighted rate of return measures the rate of return which has been earned on the assets of the fund, by assuming that the rate is applied for the whole period of the calculations. The calculation of an accurate time-weighted rate of return is normally complicated and can involve frequent valuations. Time-weighted rates of return are often used in preference to money-weighted rates of return since the former are independent of the cash flow into the fund, a factor that is normally beyond the control of the investment manager; for example, a fund which receives new money just prior to a period when a high rate of return is achieved will show a greater money-weighted rate of return than a fund which does not receive any new money. The time-weighted rates of return will, however, be the same.

Problems associated with performance measurement of insurance and pensions funds include that of determining how the performance of investment managers who are required to adopt a conservative attitude to risk compare with say the FT Index. This problem has been reduced with the advent of index-linked gilts which make it possible to define a "risk-free" return which is relevant to a long term fund. Pension funds and property funds in particular do not lend themselves easily to performance testing. The chief problem in calculating rates of return is the absence of regular valuations. Further information can be found in: *Measurement of Investment Performance for UK Pension Funds*, a PRAG publication [QRL.64], *Measurement of Pension Fund Investment Performance* by D.P. Hager [B.13], *Investment Performance of Pension Funds* by J.P. Holbrook [B.14], *The Property Market, Property Valuations and Property Performance Measurement* by D.P. Hager and D.J. Lord [QRL.7]. Even more difficulties arise when measuring property investment performance as only actual realisation can give a true valuation and until then managers rely on valuers' judgements. A formal property index is being prepared jointly by the Royal Institute of Chartered Surveyors and the City University Centre for Research in Insurance and Investment. Many funds feel it adds credibility to the measurement of their performance to have it conducted by external companies. Most consultants now provide an individual assessment of the performance of a special fund, not only against some neutral yardstick but also against other funds which are thought to be comparable. Details of the available services and of the kind of information they produce are to be found in a booklet produced by the Pensions Research Accounts Group (PRAG) [QRL.64].

Many firms of consultants undertake investment performance measurement. The majority conduct only smallish surveys amongst their own clients or else compare performance against an index. Some of the major firms of consulting actuaries, have grouped together to form Combined Actuarial Performance Service (CAPS), [QRL.74]. This group, together with the other two major measurers of investment performance, Cubie Wood and Wood Mackenzie, [QRL.76] dominate the market in terms of numbers of funds measured. There are other groups with somewhat different approaches who have found specialist positions in the market e.g. Wyatt [QRL.101] and Martin Paterson Associates [QRL.63]. Local Authories conduct their own performance measurement through CIPFA [QRL.62].

Many funds have performance measured by more than one organisation and [QRL.103] contains a study of which type of organisation is employed for measuring performance.

4.5.2 *Shares*

The prices of shares are quoted in many of the daily and Sunday newspapers. [QRL.49]

The earnings of a proprietary life company are not comparable with that of most other commercial enterprises quoted on the Stock Exchange. They are a proportion of the surplus (see 4.2.1) and are directly related to the amount set aside to fund the bonuses on the with profit business and are not an expression of the profitability of the enterprise during that year of operation. To use a life company earnings as a means of comparing the rating and success of a life office share compared to any other share over a short period is misleading.

Life offices prepare many detailed statistics in the form of Department of Trade Returns [QRL.93] but there is little evidence that this detailed DTI material is being used for fundamental analysis to determine the strength of the office and/or its bonus prospects. In general investment analysts are influenced by short term earnings estimates and by the historic dividend record. Until recently when analysing the shares of employers sponsoring pension schemes, scant attention was paid the pension scheme.

Many firms of stockbrokers have research departments which monitor the performance of individual companies in countries throughout the world, as well as political and general economic news that may affect a sector of industry. Many such brokers employ highly sophisticated techniques to produce secondary information relating to pension funds and life insurance companies. Most of the larger brokers analyse as investments all the quoted non-deposit taking institutions and publish statistics on insurance companies. A list of brokers can be obtained from the Stock Exchange Information and Press Department. The most comprehensive collection of broker research reports is held by the Science Reference Library in London.

4.5.3 *Life Office Products*

Life insurance (including those plans designed to provide personal pensions) has for many years been one of the foremost savings media in the UK. The saver has available to him a comprehensive array of contracts marketed by a large number of companies. The saver's choice of contract and of life company is vital to his return. Surrender values and paid up policy values normally offer a poor return on the money thus far invested making it difficult for the saver to change his mind regarding the company and/or contract best suited to his needs. It is difficult to assess the prospects of the various contracts and/or the life company. The rewards for selling life products are high. Professionals are well aware of the uncertainties of predicting the future; many intermediaries rely on comparisons of the past performance of companies. This has led to the growth of magazines providing such comparisons; most also provide projections into the future of past performance. Recently several life office actuaries at their companies' annual general meetings have voiced the fear that "bonuses" are at a historically high level and it may not be possible to maintain that level in the future. It is misleading, therefore, to predict future performance on the basis of current bonuses.

For an intermediary to select a life company on the basis of its past performance is a relatively simple exercise, provided he has comparable maturity values available for all the life offices offering the specific contract considered. These figures are published at least once a year by the various magazines of the insurance press. The tables in the various magazines are produced at different times of the year permitting the adviser to remain up to date. (There are also specialist rate guides publishing such tables far more frequently). The various magazines may use different ages and terms for their specimen policies but the adviser can still make a comprehensive analysis with little loss of accuracy.

The charts show a wide variation between companies. It is not the top company which should be examined more closely by the adviser but the one which in successive years ranks higher and higher. A company which is endeavouring to become more competitive will not be able to feature near the top of the charts for some time.

Past performance tables should be studied closely to examine how terminal bonuses have been dealt with. Their inclusion/exclusion can markedly alter the ranking of a company; terminal bonuses can account for as much as one third of the maturity value for specific companies. A magazine obtains free publicity each time a life office advertises itself as the "winner" of XYZ Magazine's performance table; one magazine group uses different methods of analysing performance for each of its magazines with a view to producing a variety of winners.

When inspecting rate tables for life insurance products the following points must be born in mind:

a) an office's relative position for rates may be different for different amounts ages and durations.
b) offices quoting higher premiums may be giving better surrender values or other benefits
c) the quality of service given to policyholders requirements does not show up in statistical rate tables.

4.6 Administration Costs

A Survey of Public Sector and Non-Corporate Pension Funds [QRL.103] attempts to investigate administrative costs by asking those responsible for non-insured pension funds to *estimate* the *total* administration costs of their fund during the fiscal year to 1980 for (a) internal costs including salaries and other overhead costs which can be calculated, (b) fees paid to managers, advisers and for other outside services excluding brokerage, (c) brokerage commission charges, (d) property purchase, sale and management.

Care must be taken in interpreting any statistics on administrative costs including those of the above-mentioned survey. There are many services which are "free" in one fund but are "costed out" in another, such as the salaries of the investment managers or less directly the relevant costs in the personnel department dealing with those salaries. *Pensions Payment Methods* [QRL.78] asks the question "Who produces the pensioner payroll"? For many organisations the answer was that it was the responsibility of the parent organisation. *De facto* recognition is given to this problem in *Business Monitor* MQ5 [QRL.32] and the Government Actuary's *Survey* [QRL.70] by labelling administrative costs as administrative costs met by the fund. Recognising the problem does not solve it and it is a problem which is likely to get worse with the introduction of dual capacity by the Stock Exchange (see 9.4.2).

Other examples of hidden costs occur when considering indirect investment *via* unit trusts and managed funds where the expenses are allowed for in the price.

One of the tables in the statistical abstracts in the annual *Report* of the Registrar of Friendly Societies [QRL.26] provides ratios of management expense to premium income and also to total income. Such ratios are commonly used as a guide to a company's efficiency. Such ratios should be treated with caution. The level of a company's management expense depends heavily on the type of business it is writing. The expense associated with an endowment policy is far higher than that associated with a mortgage protection policy. Unfavourable comparisons between two companies may be solely due to the mix of business. Similarly a decreasing ratio for a specific company may be due to a switch in the type of business written rather than improving efficiency.

CHAPTER 5

GOVERNMENT STATISTICS

5.1 Introduction

The economy, for national accounting purposes, is divided into sectors; the two sectors relevant to pension funds are the personal sector and the financial companies and institutions sector. Each of these sectors may have up to five sets of related accounts:

(1) income and expenditure (balance:saving)
(2) capital (balance: financial surplus/deficit)
(3) financial transactions
(4) capital and financial transactions receipts and expenditure
(5) holdings of financial assets and liabilities

Figures relating to pension funds are usually combined with those relating to life insurance funds and for practical reasons they are often difficult to separate. In the national accounts, life insurance and pension funds are treated as part of the *personal sector* for the income and expenditure accounts, but as part of the *financial companies and institutions sector* for the capital and financial accounts. Pension fund income from employers' contributions and investment income forms part of personal sector income, as it crosses sector boundaries, whereas pension fund income from employees' contributions does not fit in to this sector as it does *not* cross sector boundaries. Similarly, although pension fund expenditure in the form of administrative expenses forms part of personal sector expenditure crossing sector boundaries, expenditure in the form of pensions and other benefits represents transfers within the sector and so does not form part of personal sector expenditure.

The difference between the funds' income and expenditure represents the net amount which the funds have available for investment. In the personal sector financial account it is recorded as an increase in people's claims on the funds, and in the accounts of the financial companies and institutions as a corresponding liability. Finally, transactions of the funds are recorded in the capital financial accounts of the *financial companies and institutions sectors*. The consequence of all this, and presently the source of much confusion, is that, in balance sheet terms, the funds remain the property of the personal sector so that any increase in them is often referred to as an increase in personal saving, but the assets of the funds which are held by the funds to match this liability to the personal sector are assets of the *financial companies and institutions sector*. An article in the September 1979 issue of *Pension World* [B.24] entitled 'Pension Funds and National Accounting' by Peter Stibbard, then a chief statistician at the CSO provides an excellent introduction to the subject, although parts of it are now dated. More detailed explanations of national accounting are contained in the *Financial Statistics Explanatory Handbooks* [B.40] and *United Kingdom National Accounts;* Sources and Methods *[B.85] published by the CSO*

5.2 Department of Trade and Industry

5.2.1 *Self Administered Pension Funds*

5.2.1.1 *Surveys into Financial Assets* The Department of Trade and Industry conducts two regular sample surveys covering the financial assets of all self-administered pension funds, both private and public sector, (until 1983 the public sector was dealt with by the CSO). The first is a quarterly inquiry into the transaction of assets of the funds; the second is an annual inquiry into the asset holdings of the funds. The information collected is primarily to provide input for the national and financial accounts (see introductory section above), however results are published in *Business Monitor* MQ5 [QRL.32]. This monitor is published quarterly and gives details of net investment by insurance companies and pension funds. Copies of the two sets of questionnaires are included in Appendix 5.1. The quarterly survey was introduced in the early 1960's following the Radcliffe Report on the *Working of the Monetary System* [B.87].

Similar considerations apply to the two surveys and so they are dealt with collectively. Insured schemes are excluded from the inquiries to pension funds as in most cases it is difficult, if not impossible, to separate the value of attributable assets of the pension funds from those of the assets attributable to other insurance contracts written by the insuring office and on an individual fund basis a pension fund manager would certainly not know how to put a value on an insurance policy. PRAG has dealt with the problem in detail in *Valuing Insurance Policies for Accounts Purposes* [B.86]. The assets of insured schemes are covered by inquiries into insurance company assets see (see 4.2.2.2). Transactions in assets and liabilities are reported in 'cash values'; holdings for the calendar year ends are reported at 'market value' and failing that, 'written down book value'.

The surveys are entirely voluntary and the methodology used involves a sample based on the known pension funds being contacted. The problem occurs in the word "known", as there is not, at present, an official list of private self-administered funds, although the Occupational Pensions Board have, on several occasions, recommended that such a register should be compiled. The Social Security Bill, 1984 included the statement that such a registry of schemes is planned. It is to be financed by fees paid for lodging and inspection of documents. At the time of writing this review many detailed requirements have still to be specified by regulations.

The list of private self-administered funds currently in use by the Department was originally drawn up in 1978 and previous statistics have been rebased on information relating to the population of such funds at the end of 1978. These rebased statistics were published in *Business Monitor MQ5* [QRL.32] for the second quarter of 1981, however, in that issue only the most recent figures are on the revised basis. The first consistent set of figures to be published was in 1982. The Department consulted the directory sections of *Pension Funds and their Advisors* [QRL.12] and the *NAPF Yearbook* [B.59]; additionally they wrote to the companies listed in the "Times top 1000" list. Each year a check is made by the Department of all pension schemes listed for the first time in the latest issues of these publications and, where necessary, additions are made to the Department's list. The Department therefore feels confident that they have covered the "larger" schemes. There is doubt as to whether the sample provides adequate average of the smaller schemes. The statistics collected on private, self-administered pension funds are intended for use in the "flow of funds" accounts in *Financial Statistics* [QRL.48] and *Bank of England Quarterly Bulletin* [QRL.30]. As part of statistics on the "flow of funds", estimates are made of the "total money" flowing from pension funds: size of funds is therefore more important than the total number of funds. The existing list may be adequate for the purposes intended, but nonetheless the Department expects to repeat the rebasing exercise in the late 1980s.

At intervals, "known" companies who are not contributing to the survey are contacted and asked if they would like to participate. As the prior agreement of participants has been obtained in this manner before questionnaires are sent out, there is a fairly consistent response although some funds may "drop out" for a year or so. Those funds which do not wish to participate in the survey are asked to submit a schedule of investments and/or the details and reports which they supply to members. Some funds, particularly the smaller ones, contribute figures only once a year. To provide estimates of results for non-participating private funds, these funds are divided into strata by net assets as measured at the end of 1978. The results for participating funds are then approximately grossed up within these strata by value of assets. Returns are received from about 50% of private sector funds by value of assets. The response from local authorities is about 90% by value of assets. The response for public corporations is variable. There are about eight very large funds in the public corporation sector so that non-response by even one of these is significant. It is important to realise that only funded schemes are included. No estimates are made for notionally funded or unfunded schemes in statistics published by the DTI in MQ5 [QRL.32].

The CSO's *Financial Statistics Explanatory Handbook* [B.40] gives a table of "Reliability gradings" for the government produced statistics. It is of interest to note that at the time of writing this review the statistics relating to private sector pension funds are given the lowest grading. This grading is given where either the figures require a substantial amount of estimation or the coverage is known to be significantly incomplete.

5.2.1.2 *Income and Expenditure Survey* This survey was introduced only recently for private sector funds and so no "routine" has yet been established for it. Similar enquiries have been directed to public sector funds for a number of years. The DTI sends inquiry forms to funds in the private sector and to public corporation funds. The same sample used for the enquiries referred to in 5.2.1.1. Similar inquiries to local authority funds are carried out by the Department of the Environment and the Welsh and Scottish Offices. The first set of results were published for all the funds in the 3rd quarter issue of the 1983 *Business Monitor* MQ5 [QRL.32]. It is hoped eventually to be able to publish results in the 2nd quarter editions, but any publication details will first be mentioned in *British Business* [B.30]. The Income and Expenditure Survey supplements the Government Actuary's survey [QRL.70] which in future may be less detailed in this respect.

The breakdown of Income and Expenditure used at present is as follows:

Income	Expenditure (Normal and Additional)
	Payments to members and their dependents: - Refunds of contributions
Contributions of employees	Transfers to other pension schemes
Rents, dividends and interest receivable	Other expenditure - Interest and rent payable - Administrative costs met by the fund - Miscellaneous expenditure
Transfers from other pension schemes	Total expenditure
Other income	
Total income	
Surplus of income over expenditure	

5.2.1.3 *Publication details* Processed survey results are passed to the Central Statistical Office for further use by them. Some results, however, are tabulated directly by the Department of Trade and Industry and published under their auspices as follows:

1) A quarterly article together with summary statistics appears in *British Business* [B.30] about three months after the quarter end to which the quarterly survey statistics relate.
2) A much more detailed breakdown of the results appears in "Insurance Companies and Pension Funds Investments (*Business Monitor* MQ5 [QRL.32]) published about four months after the quarter end to which the statistics relate. Summary statistics are published at about the same time in *Financial Statistics*. [QRL.48]
3) An article with summary statistics of the balance sheet annual survey appears in *British Business* [B.30] usually in September.
4) A more detailed breakdown of the results of the balance sheet annual survey appears in "Insurance Companies and Pension Funds' Investment" *Business Monitor* MQ5 [QRL.32] published in the second quarter issue.
5) The *Annual Abstract of Statistics* [QRL.25] provides a long series of asset holdings statistics.
6) An annual supplementary table in *Financial Statistics* [QRL.48] gives an analysis of the assets and liabilities of pension funds by size of fund.

This table is misleading. The assets and liabilities being analysed are shown at market value for the appropriate year but are categorized by the fund size that they were in 1978 i.e., say that there was one fund which in 1978 was worth £15m and by 1985 was worth £100m. £100m then of its assets would be spread into the different categories of securities and totalled to £100 million but it would be inserted in the category £15-24.9m.

To add to the confusion there is a continuation of this table labelled number of funds by size of funds (1). Note (1) to this table says current size of funds: total assets less liabilities (market values). This table does what it says and analyses by current size of fund - the number of funds. It provides no information on income and expenditure. The explanatory handbook [B.40] is less than helpful.

A further annual supplementary table in *Financial Statistics* [QRL.48] gives a more detailed analysis of income and expenditure than in [QRL.32]. It includes insured, notionally funded and unfunded schemes.

There may be discrepancies between the figures reported in the various places, because of printing timetables which may not allow for the publication of the latest information. The articles appearing in *British Business* [B.30] mentioned in 1 and 3 above are always referenced in the subsequently published MQ5 [QRL.32] which contains the more detailed breakdown. No specific reference to *British Business* [B.30] will, therefore, be given in the QRL of this review. The Department publishes all available material in MQ5 [QRL.32]. (Where an entry is marked N/A this is because the information may be applicable to only one company and would breach its conditions of confidentiality).

5.2.2 *Insurance Companies*

5.2.2.1 *Statutory Returns* The Department of Trade and Industry has a supervisory role in respect of most insurance companies and receives statutory returns from them. Friendly societies are covered by separate legislation and are dealt with by a different department,see (see 4.10). These statutory *Returns* [QRL.93] are designed to give warning of likely problems relating to the solvency of the companies. The regulations regarding the statutory returns are complicated, (see also 3.2.2).

The forms for the statutory returns [QRL.93] have recently been revised to enable the Department to engage in more detailed scrutiny of each company's financial condition. So far only the first 16 forms have been formated by the Department, though not all of these apply to companies transacting only life business. Copies of relevent forms are contained in Appendix 5.4. Companies are required to follow the format of a specimen form in the regulations [B.49] for subsequent forms. There are potentially about 80 forms. A small booklet entitled *Statutory Regulation of Long Term Business* by W.M. Abbot [B.1] explains in a simple fashion the regulations as well as the contents of each form. A more comprehensive booklet is *The Insurance Companies (Accounts and Statements) Regulations 1983. A practical guide and commentary* by J.A. Philpott [B.21].

The valuation returns [QRL.93] contain figures for premium income, but these are on a 'receivable' rather than 'received' basis and exclude single premiums which are common in group schemes as regular whilst others do not. Offices are not consistent in this treatment with regard to press releases and other marketing material.

Attempts to obtain amounts of pensions in payment from [QRL.93] are also fraught since many group schemes are written on a 'deposit administration' basis. Employers concerned only pay the balance of contributions in excess of pensions to the insurance company and so the insurance company will have no statistics on pensions paid. Other difficulties of calculating pensions in payment are that many individuals (for reasons of tax efficiency) take the maximum commutable sum (if there is such an option in a scheme) and use it to buy an individual annuity. There are strong arguments for saying that such annuities are really pensions. Other problems occur where schemes have an open market option permitting a retiring member to use a cash sum to buy a pension from whichever company provides the 'best deal'. Once the cash has been passed it will enter the statistics as an individual pension and be inseparable from statistics on section 226 contracts. The data in the *Company Consolidated Balance Sheet* relates to worldwide business, but may be limited to the main company only, or to the company and selected subsidiaries. In particular, overseas subsidiaries may be omitted. The varying basis of the returns does not make comparisons or aggregations very meaningful and no comprehensive consolidation for recent years is known. *Whitakers Almanack* [QRL.112], the *British Insurance Industry, A Statistical Review* [QRL.4] and *Post Magazine Almanack* [QRL.56] all contain unconsolidated synopses of the accounts. Prior to 1969, consolidated figures were available in *Insurance Business Statistics* [QRL.54]. It must also be noted that whilst figures in a company's balance sheet must give a true and fair picture of the company's business there is some flexibility in accounting policies allowed and results from different companies are not always on the same basis.

The Department's computer system is being programmed to help with the examination of the new returns and it is hoped that this will permit additional analyses to be conducted and made available to the public on request. Because statutory returns are designed for the specific purpose outlined above, they do not fulfil all the statistician's needs, e.g. they do not give all the subdivisions needed for balance of payments purposes, nor consistently between category of asset do they give market value for assets. All statistics derived from the DTI returns must be treated with caution because of lack of consistency between offices and even within the same office between different forms, in the manner used to complete the forms. Some of these problems are discussed in chapter 9: others below. Until 1976 detailed analyses were published in *Insurance Business Statistics* [QRL.54]. This was superceded by *Business Monitor* MA16 [QRL.55]. It is currently four years in arrears. The new computer systems will probably permit more speedy publication of the relevant data. It gives brief details of the net premium income and total assets for each authorised insurer in the UK. Also included are figures for total premiums by main class of business and for total assets. It is fairly common where an insurance company has a subsidiary, transacting managed pension fund business only, for there to be significant transfers of money between the parent and the subsidiary. Such transfers are usually treated as premium income in the recipient's DTI returns. Thus, the aggregate premium income figures in MA16 [QRL.55] will significantly overstate the actual premiums received by the life industry. The premium income figures in *Life Insurance in the United Kingdom* [QRL.60] attempts to eliminate these intra-group transfers as far as possible.

The *Insurance Annual Report* [QRL.53] is a report laid before Parliament summarising the exercise by the Secretary of State for Trade and Industry of his functions relating to Insurance. It lists companies authorised to carry on insurance business in Great Britain and the classes of business they are permitted to transact; new authorisations and authorisations revoked; and provides summary statistics. The report also contains a list of Statutory Instruments which are applicable to insurance companies. Until 1981 the Report also contained a selection of summary statistics relating to assets, premiums and claims. These statistics are now published in MA16 [QRL.55]. Current authorisations and revokations are published in *British Business* [B.30].

5.2.2.2 *Insurance Companies Voluntary Survey* The survey has been fully described in the *Financial Statistics Explanatory Handbook* [B.40] and little needs to be added. A copy of the survey forms are similar to those for pension funds which are contained in appendix 5.1. The survey is voluntary and the British Insurance Association (BIA), now part of IBA, acts as a collecting agency for the completed questionnaires of its members. Amongst both members and non-members of the BIA the response of overseas companies authorised to do business in the UK is not as good as desired. The Department deals directly with those companies which are not members of the ABI. (Prior to 1967 only BIA members were included). A small sample of such companies are sent questionnaires. As the BIA represents 90% of the insurance market when measured by premium income, the small sampling fraction among the non-members is not significant.

At present certain small companies are asked only to complete the transactions form once a year. Although these companies are individually small in terms of total premium income, each usually specialises in one line of business and may be important in its own field. Estimates are made to allow for this, but are not wholly satisfactory. Since 1984 an additional question has been asked in the holdings survey asking offices to attribute their assets to life and pensions. In most cases such a split is not made for the practical day to day functioning of the office and companies will enter a notional figure. This notional figure is normally based on liabilities since that is the notional split generally made for tax purposes. Such statistics must therefore be treated with caution.

5.2.2.3 *Income and Expenditure Survey* It is hoped to publish aggregate figures for the Revenue account details of Insurance Companies for 1984 by early 1986. Figures have been obtained from statutory returns ignoring inconsistences. Results will be published in MQ5 [QRL.32].

5.2.2.4 *Linked Life Assurance Report* Linked Life Assurance Report [QRL.17] was presented to Parliament in April 1973. Despite its age it still provides a valuable insight into the workings of insurance companies offering linked life policies. The paper contains a statistical appendix.

5.2.2.5 *Publication details*

1. Statutory returns made by insurers may be inspected and copies obtained at the appropriate companies' registration office. Which office is appropriate will depend upon the point in the UK in which the insurer is registered.
2. *Business Monitor MA16* Insurance Business Statistics [QRL.55] published annually, provides a summary of premiums and assets of individual insurance companies derived from annual returns.
3. *Insurance Business Annual Report* [QRL.53] contains a concise analysis of insurance business during the year, and a complete list of insurers authorised to carry out business in Great Britain.
4. Aggregate statistics of assets and liabilities, income and expenditure, and profit and loss of UK incorporated insurance companies for years up to 1977 were published in the *Annual Abstract of Statistics* [QRL.25] 1983 edition. Aggregate statistics for the years 1978 to 1981 were not produced, but it is intended to

produce aggregate statistics for later years as part of the computer analysis of statutory returns received.

5. A quarterly article describing the net acquisition figures derived from the voluntary survey is published in *British Business* [B.30] about three months after the relevant quarter. An article describing the annual holdings figures usually appears in September, [B.30]. The articles appearing in [B.30] are always referred to in the subsequently published MQ5 [QRL.32] which contains a more detailed breakdown. No specific references to *British Business* [B.30] will, therefore, be given in the QRL of this review.
6. The quarterly net acquisition figures are usually published in *Financial Statistics* [QRL.48] about four months after the quarter to which they relate. The annual holding figures are normally published about nine months after the year end to which they relate. *Financial Statistics* [QRL.48] provides statistics on insurance companies' quarterly investment transactions and annual asset holdings, for longterm funds and, separately, for general funds. End-year holdings of assets at market valuations are shown for the latest 2 years and transactions data are provided quarterly for the latest 10 quarters and annually for the latest 2 years. Supplementary tables show figures of transactions in securities and also loans for house purchase. Net capital issues of insurance companies also appear in *Financial Statistics* [QRL.48] and used to appear in *Bank of England Quarterly Bulletin* [QRL.30] (until December 1978). The latter publication continues to include an analysis of insurance companies' transactions in British government stocks.
7. A more detailed breakdown of the statistics than is given in [QRL.48] appears in *Business Monitor MQ5* [QRL.32] which is also published about four months after the quarter to which it relates for the quarterly survey and in the second quarterly issue for the annual survey. *Business Monitor MQ5* [QRL.32] gives transactions in assets—purchases, sales and net investment, in British Government securities; UK local authority securities, company securities (UK and overseas), land and property, mortgages and loans. Balances of cash and other short-term assets and borrowings are also given. Separate statistics appear for long-term and for general funds. The edition for the first quarter of 1975 contains an historical run of figures from 1962.

End-year holdings of assets at market values are also given in the second quarter's issue each year. Annual totals of net investment and annual asset holdings are given for the latest 5 years. Quarterly net investment is given for the latest 5 quarters, and purchases and sales for the latest quarter.

5.3 Inland Revenue

A wide ranging but detailed description of statistics produced by the Inland Revenue Statistics division is contained in the sixth volume of this series –"Personal Incomes" by T. Stark [B.23]. The reference date of the sources reviewed is July 1975, but despite this, most of the commentary is still highly relevant.

The public is encouraged to contact the Statistics Division of the Inland Revenue if a particular analysis in which they are interested does not appear to be published, as many other tabulations are available at cost. An example of such a tabulation is occupational pensions in payment split into main pension, subsidiary and wives. At one time it was thought that the IR figures provided a considerable underestimate of occupational pensions since so many of them fall outside the PAYE act. With increasing computerisation many of the larger organisations pass across details of all pensions payments without bothering to seperate out those below the threshold.

5.3.1 *Inland Revenue Statistics*

Since 1970 a series of volumes entitled *Inland Revenue Statistics* [QRL.52] has been compiled annually by the Board of the Inland Revenue. From 1981 onwards certain tables have been omitted. Data omitted relate to earlier years and have therefore appeared in earlier volumes or are being published separately in *The Survey of Personal Incomes* [QRL.102]. Each volume contains a comprehensive general introduction as well as a detailed but more specific introduction to each section. The introductory notes contain information such as limitations on the interpretations which should be placed on certain statistics. The type of information contained is the amount of stamp duty collected on life policies, the PAYE deducted from annuities, occupational pensions in payment as well as the costs of various forms of tax relief and information relating to wealth.

5.3.1.1 *Estimates of marketable Wealth attributable to pension rights* Estimates of marketable wealth attributable to pension rights, which were used in the 1981 edition of *Inland Revenue Statistics* [QRL.52], were originally published in the 5th *Report* of the Royal Commission on the Distribution of Income and Wealth [B.9], in paragraphs 189 and following. The calculations were conducted by the Government Actuary's Department and are based on assumptions which form part of a consistent set of assumptions used for Government Projections, but which, when taken in isolation, could mislead.

Life assurance policies on a deceased's own life are valued in the statistics as the full sum insured and bonus, if any, which is only payable on death or maturity. This is correct when looking at the estate of a deceased person, however in the hands of the living a policy is worth only its surrender or market value, which is usually much less than the sum assured; see Chapter 3 in *Reviews of UK Statistical Sources* by Atkinson and Harrison [B.2].

An article *Distribution of Wealth in the United Kingdom: Effect of including pension rights, and analysis by age-group* [QRL.5] presents recent work on this subject. It contains incidental statistics such as occupational pension rights as a percentage of household wealth.

5.3.2 *Survey of Personal Incomes*

The Inland Revenue *Surveys of Personal Incomes* are conducted yearly and the results are published approximately two years in arrears, in book form [QRL.102]. (Until 1978 the survey was published as part of *Inland Revenue Statistics* [QRL.52]). The introduction to the book is detailed and gives all necessary information regarding background, survey methods and obvious ambiguities appearing in the tables and an appendix to the book contains a copy of the survey form. The survey contains no information on non-taxable income and most incomes below the tax exemption limit. This is relevant for the table showing life assurance premiums and reliefs by family circumstances, as no cases of life insurance sold to persons below the tax thresholds will enter these tables. (This particular table does not appear from 1979-80 onwards as the tax regime changed in 1979). It is also relevant to the table showing the amount of occupational pensions in payment since many individuals for whom this is the only source of income may find that they are below the tax thresholds.

5.3.3 *Cost of Tax Relief*

In September 1983 the Board of the Inland Revenue published a pamphlet entitled *Cost of Tax Reliefs for Pension Schemes: Appropriate Statistical Approach* [QRL.39]. The purpose of the paper was to consider the present methodology for costing the tax reliefs for pension schemes. (There had previously been a table setting out the costs of tax relief on pensions contained in *Inland Revenue Statistics* [QRL.52]). The paper warns the reader not to take figures out of context, warnings which have not always been heeded by the press. The figures for the cost of tax relief may not occur if the tax regime alters as no assumptions have been made as to the number of pension funds which would wind-up if pension fund tax relief were withdrawn. Intergenerational differences have not been referred to as they were outside the terms of reference of the study. Furthermore, many of the results have taken into account Treasury economic forecasts which have not been published and are not available to the public. Care is recommended in the interpretation of the results of the pamphlet.

Care must also be taken to take into account the assumptions underlying the statistics as these are not always given, e.g. a) the pamphlet estimates the cost of taxing employers' contributions (if this were possible) in the employee's hand, but excludes the public sector and only takes into account the private sector funded schemes; or b) it estimates the cost of taxing employers contributions as notionally assessed in employees hands; it treats this as a fringe benefit and not as an addition to salary thereby not assessing tax on anyone earning less than £8,500.

5.4 Occupational Pensions Board

The Occupational Pensions Board is an independent statutory body (quango). Its functions are detailed in 2.6. Until 1980, Section 66(b) of the Social Security Act 1973 required the OPB to produce an *Annual Report* on its activities [QRL.99]. The *Report* contained various statistics, many of which are no longer available. These statistics related to such things as contracting-out, preservation and equal access, standard documents, modifications and windings up and rate changes. The statistics, which are still available, are concerned with management information rather than the contingently useful variety, but the last published report of the OPB (June 1981) gives a guide to the type of information which may still be available e.g. it contains a section on standard documents detailing the number of draft standard documents it received during a year, how many were available for use by the end of the year, how many had been subject to detailed discussion but which had not been brought into use and how many were still under consideration at the year end.

The OPB does not provide a list of "contracted out" schemes. (Files at the OPB are kept manually). Even if provided with additional staff the Board is uncertain that such a list would be available for publication because of confidentiality requirements. It has been pressing for a number of years for a computerised index of schemes, initially in a report on solvency in 1975. Even if the individual pension scheme names could not be issued, this would enable useful incidental statistics to be derived, including the total number of contracted out schemes, and it would make it easier to obtain random samples of schemes for the purpose of the Government Actuary's survey questionnaire. Its most important function, however, would be as a tracing service for "early leavers". When a member leaves a scheme he has no more contact with it until he retires. If, in the meantime, the company has changed its name, been taken over, or merged, he may find it difficult to trace the original scheme. If, he has changed his address the scheme may also be unable to contact him. The Social Security Act 1984 has proposed the setting up of such a register. At the time of writing this review, detailed regulations have not been issued. It appears likely that the register will be handled by private enterprise rather than by the OPB.

5.5 Bank of England

The Bank of England produces statistics showing the changes in financial assets and liabilities relating to insurance companies and pension funds as component parts of the "Flow of Funds" accounts and "Matrix". These statistics are published in the *Quarterly Bulletin* [QRL.30]. The format of the matrix is the same as that published by the CSO in *Financial Statistics* [QRL.48] (see 5.6) but the Bank provides seasonally adjusted statistics. Quarterly data from 1963 are available on application. The United Kingdom Flow of Funds accounts 1963-76 [B.84] published by the Bank in May 1978 describes the objectives and coverage of the financial accounts. It contains a statistical appendix, but all the information relevant to this review is obtainable elsewhere (refer to QRL under individual entries). An earlier publication *An Introduction to Flow of funds Accounting: 1952-1970* [QRL.58] contains very rough estimates of the flow of funds dating back to 1952. An article in the September 1978 issue of the *Quarterly Bulletin* is entitled "Balance Sheets for Insurance Companies" [QRL.29]. It introduces a sector series of integrated balance sheets and flow accounts for insurance companies. Because of the volume of data involved the article includes only a sample table, for 1976, but balance sheets for earlier years, beginning in 1963, are available on request. The 'balance sheet' breakdown is very detailed extending to 40 items. The Bank is again involved in a similar "one-off" exercise to produce data on a quarterly basis from 1975-1985. Statistics published in the *Quarterly Bulletin* [QRL.30] are available in machinable form. The machinable data contains longer runs than the published data. More information can be obtained from the Bank of England.

5.6 Central Statistical Office

Although many statistical publications are attributed to the CSO it mainly employs material produced by other Government Departments. Most tables carry the name of the originating department. Until 1982 the CSO collected information regarding local authority, nationalised industry and other public corporation pension funds. This work is now shared with the Department of Trade and Industry.

Many of the statistics in CSO publications relating to pensions and insurance are grouped together with banking, finance and business services. Where such a wide grouping is employed no reference will be made in the QRL of this review. Nor will reference be made in the QRL to data which can be found in more detail in other publications, e.g. the data on net inflow into life and superannuation funds in the *Monthly Digest of Statistics* [B.58] is contained in far more detail in *Financial Statistics* [QRL.48]. The QRL therefore makes reference only to [QRL.48].

5.6.1 *The CSO Pink Book*

The *United Kingdom Balance of Payments* [B.48] provides data on the overseas net earnings of United Kingdom insurance companies and pension funds for the latest eleven years. An article accompanying the table containing the data describes some of the estimating procedures to derive the data. Prior to 1982 it had been assumed that the income of pension funds was at a similar rate to that of investment trusts. The data for insurance earnings relates mainly to general insurance companies, but no breakdown is available to attribute part of it to life insurance companies.

5.6.2 *The CSO Blue Book*

The *United Kingdom National Accounts* [QRL.109] provides a table of the income and expenditure of life assurance and superannuation schemes. The exact breakdown is as follows:

Funded schemes (including life assurance)

- Contribution of employers
- Contribution of employees
- Individual premiums for policies Regular or Single
- Rent dividends and interest receipts
- Transfers from notionally funded schemes
- Less Pensions and other benefits paid
- Less Administrative costs, etc.
- Net increase in amount available for investment Notionally Funded schemes
- Contribution of employers
- Contribution of employees
- Other income
- Less Pensions and other benefits paid
- Less Transfers of liability to funded schemes
- Surplus Unfunded Schemes
- Contributions of employers
- Contributions of employees

Less Pensions and other benefits paid

A note to the table details the total amount of premium relief from central government to life insurance funds. Another note states that the figure for administrative costs of life insurance funds "includes tax on the investment income of life funds." A similar table appears as a supplementary table in [QRL.48] but does not contain the tax note. It does, however, give additional information relating to local authorities and public corporations.

5.7 Government Actuary's Department

5.7.1 *Government Actuary's Survey*

The first survey of occupational pension schemes conducted under the auspices of the Government Actuary's Department related to the year 1956 [B.79]. Since then surveys have been made at approximately four-yearly intervals. The most recently published survey related to 1979 [QRL.70]. It is proposed that the survey relating to 1983 will be published in September 1986. The next survey will be conducted in 1987 and it is hoped to publish the results in the spring of 1989. Only the 1979 survey will be referenced in the QRL. The tables in earlier surveys are not identical, but it is felt that the information contained in [QRL.70] will provide sufficient guidance as to what is available.

The purpose of the GAD's survey is to examine the extent to which employees in the UK are covered by occupational pension schemes and to describe the nature and amount of benefits which become payable on retirement and on death and the contributions they pay. In addition, it covers such matters as the income and outgoings of pension funds and the number and amounts of pensions being paid.

The survey is the most significant in the pension field, not only because of its coverage of all types of employers and sizes of business throughout the UK, together with members of H.M. Forces, but also because of the comprehensiveness of the subjects covered, such as membership, size of funds and benefits on change in employment. (A copy of the questionnaire is included in an Appendix to each edition of the survey). Employers are requested to return a copy of their printed rules and/or explanatory booklet together with the completed questionnaires. This enables the Government Actuary's Department to analyse topics which are not directly covered by the questionnaire. The commentary accompanying each table in the survey results identifies such information.

Such results may be less reliable than the remainder of the survey as these are based on a smaller sample, (not all respondents sent in sets of the rules). The subject on which questions are asked as well as their precise content can change from survey to survey to reflect matters of topical interest and points raised in critical reviews in the press as well as to incorporate requests from interested parties such as the TUC, CBI and OPB.

The survey is conducted on a voluntary basis and suffers from most of the usual limitations afflicting voluntary surveys. The survey organisers are diligent in their follow-up procedures for cases of non-response. The method of collection and the methodology of processing the survey data is very fully and clearly described in the published book of survey results and requires little comment. The source of the random sample of employers to whom questionnaires are sent varies with each survey and is likely to change again for any future survey, since with time some sources disappear and others emerge or have become more reliable and/or easier to use. Each set of survey results names the source for its sample, but does not highlight the change, possibly as the Department does not think it will significantly affect the comparability of results across the years; e.g. the 1979 Government Actuary's Survey was based on a random sample of employers chosen mainly by the Department of Employment from the list of establishments obtained in its annual Census of Employment at June 1978. The survey questionnaires were therefore sent to the address given to the Government Actuary's Department by the Department of Employment. In general the address was merely 'the employer', although where it was known that the employer was a large company, the addressee was changed to 'the Pensions Manager'. All returned communications were addressed to the Government Actuary.

The 1983 Government Actuary's survey was addressed to the employers of a random sample of employees in the government General Household Survey (GHS) (see 5.8.2) who said that they were or might be members of pension schemes (see appendix 5.2). The 1979 Government Actuary's survey had showed that the GHS assessment of the proportions of employees in pension schemes gave results on accord with the method previously used of asking employers about the proportions of their employees who were members. Not all returned communications in the 1983 survey were addressed to the Government Actuary: in order to protect the anonimity of the respondants some were sent to the Social Survey Division of the Office of Population Censuses and Surveys.

The published survey results for the 1979 survey [QRL.70] extend to over 70 tables. Most tables distinguish between schemes which relate to the public sector and private sector, and some differentiate in the public sector, between public corporations, central government, local authorities and the armed services. Each table is preceded by a paragraph giving background information and analysing the results. It is not possible to obtain tabulations of the survey results other than those published. The published survey results also contain a copy of the relevant questionnaire, commentary and details of the survey procedure.

A press release [QRL.71] was issued in December 1984 giving advance details of the survey for 1983. These figures are not final and are subject to correction when the final survey is published.

5.7.2 *Report by the Government Actuary on the Teachers' Superannuation Scheme for England and Wales from 1971 to 1976*

The teachers' Superannuation Scheme is notionally funded. No investments are held in respect of it and yet in most respects it is treated as a traditionally funded scheme. The Government Actuary produces a valuation *Report* [QRL.92] which includes background information. The *Report* provides statistics on numbers and salaries of teachers by sex, and the numbers of pensioners by type of pension, with a statement of the value of future benefits and contributions, compared with the value of the future interest income and redemption proceeds of the notional securities held, and a consolidated revenue account. Scales of assumed salary progression, probabilities of death, withdrawal or retirement on grounds of age or ill-health are also tabulated.

Similar reports are published for Scotland and Northern Ireland.

5.7.3 *Report by the Government Actuary on the National Health Service Superannuation Scheme 1974-1979*

The NHS Superannuation Scheme is also notionally funded, (See 2.11.1. and 4.7.2) [QRL.91]. During the valuation period 1969-74 clerical records relating to the NHS Superannuation Scheme were transferred to computer. Details of how these computer files are maintained is contained in the earlier report [B.73] as are comments on statistical limitations of the data supplied.

Statistics on numbers of contributors and average salaries (in broad employment categories by sex) are quoted, and numbers and amounts of pension by sex of pensioner. A table is given of the values of future benefits and contributions together with the value of the notional assets of the scheme; there is also a consolidated revenue account.

Scales of assumed salary progression, probabilities of death, withdrawal or retirement on grounds of age or ill-health are tabulated for each of the employment categories. The above report related to England and Wales. The *Report by the Government Actuary on the National Health Service Superannuation Scheme for Scotland 1974-79* [QRL.66] presents similar statistics. Both reports are part of a series issued every 5 years.

5.7.4 *Civil Service Pay Research - The 1980 Review of the Adjustment for Differences in Superannuation Benefits (Report by the Government Actuary).*

A deduction is made to the pay of civil servants to allow for the extent to which superannuation benefits are, on average, more valuable than those in comparable employments. This forms part of the "fair comparisons" process of determining Civil Service pay which is normally referred to as PRU. PRU establishes comparisons between individual jobs inside and outside the Civil Service and collects information of the total remuneration and other conditions of service of the outside analogues including superannuation and other fringe benefits. The PRU reports provide the negotiating parties with the raw data which has to be analysed and adjusted to take account of differences in pension arrangements and other conditions of service. The detailed procedures are set out in the Civil Service Pay Agreement. The Government Actuary advises the two sides on the evaluation of superannuation items.

The *Report* [QRL.33] gives details of the pension and death benefit arrangements of 600 employments (covering 328 separate but anonymous organisations). The various forms each benefit might take are tabulated for all schemes; specimen rates of mortality and of salary progression adopted for the comparison are also given.

5.7.5 *Inquiry into the Value of Pensions (Chairman: Sir Bernard Scott).*

The *Report* [QRL.16] contains tables showing actual expenditure on retirement benefits and expenditures as a percentage of the pay bill in four public service groups, i.e. Civil Service, Local Government, NHS and teachers for the financial years 1970/71 - 1979/80 and estimates for 1980/81.

5.8 The Office of Population Censuses and Surveys (OPCS)

OPCS was formed in 1970 by merging the General Register Office and the Social Survey Department. The Social Survey Division of the OPCS carries out both continuous surveys and *ad hoc* projects. The two most important of its continuous surveys are the Family Expenditure Survey (FES) [QRL.45] for which the Department of Employment (DE) analyses the results and publishes the final report, and The General Household Survey (GHS) [QRL.50]. The objectives and survey methodology of the Social Survey Division of the OPCS is fully described in an article by F.E. Whitehead in Volume 29, no.24 of *The Statistician* (1980) [B.27].

5.8.1 *The 1981 Census*

Persons of Pensionable Age [B.68] is a publication deriving directly from the 1981 Census. It gives statistics of the population who were 60 or over (women) or 65 or over (men) on census night as well as details of the household size and housing conditions in which they live.

Pensioners [QRL.81] shows the distribution of people of pensionable age in Great Britain at the time of the 1981 Census, and changes that have occured this century, including changes in the counties with the highest and lowest proportions of pensioners in the population in 1921 and 1981, the proportions of pensioners who are owner occupiers or who have cars in metropolitan and non-metropolitan areas, changes in the numbers of pensioners during this century, and post-Second World War, increases in numbers of pensioners living alone.

5.8.2 *General Household Survey*

The *General Household Survey* (GHS) [QRL.50] is a multi-purpose survey designed to monitor changes primarily at national level in most of the important variables with which social policy is concerned. There have been several articles published concerning the survey in *Statistical News*, and in particular "Estimating the Characteristics of Non-Respondents in the GHS" by R.Barnes, published in volume 30, page 17. [B.3]

The GHS is a continuous survey based on a voluntary random sample of some 15,000 private households throughout Great Britain. It is carried out by the Social Survey Division of the Office of Population Censuses and Surveys and is sponsored by the Central Statistical Office. The sample used since 1975 involves a two-stage stratified rotating design, described in Chapter 1 of the introduction report. A detailed account of the survey's origins, aims, and methods was given in the Introductory Report. [B.42].

Following the recommendations of the review by Sir Derek Rayner of statistical services throughout the government, a White Paper of April 1981 confirmed that, from January 1982, the cost of the General Household Survey [QRL.50] should be reduced by 28 per cent. From that date the sample size was cut by approximately 15 per cent, and economies made in field and clerical procedures.

In addition to the tables included in the published reports, tabulations for the years since 1971 are held by Social Survey Division and are available on request, subject to resources and reliability, provided that (a) the confidentiality of informants is preserved, (b) any work based on analysis of GHS data is the responsibility of the researcher only, and (c) any report or paper for use at a lecture, conference or seminar, is first submitted to OPCS for clearance. Copies of data tapes are available for specific research projects (subject to certain conditions) from the ESRC Survey Archive at the University of Essex. Many questions in the GHS [QRL.50] differ from year to year.

This survey now gives the most reliable and comprehensive information available on the proportions of employees in pension schemes according to sex, marital status, age, working hours, occupation, economic sector and industry, earnings, preserved pensions etc., and amounts of contributions and pensions. (Unfortunately it does not give numbers rated up from sample to population size, or corrected for any known bias.) Pension scheme membership questions were asked in 1972, 1973, 1975, 1976, 1979, 1982, 1983, 1985 and 1987, but the amounts of individual's contributions paid and pensions received are asked every year. Results start to become available about one year after the end of the calendar year in which the questions are asked.

In the 1983 questionnaire –the results of which will not be known for at least two years –one question asked for the name and address of the occupational pension the person belonged to, the length of membership etc.

Copies of specimen questionnaires can be obtained by writing to Social Survey Division of the Office of Population Censuses and Surveys. Those questions relevant to occupational pension schemes are reproduced in Appendix 5.2

5.9 Department of Employment

5.9.1 *Family Expenditure Survey (FES)*

The FES was introduced in 1957. It is a continuous inquiry into the expenditure and income of domestic households in Great Britain. The main purpose of the inquiry is to provide a source of the weighting pattern of the Index of Retail Prices, but it is also designed to meet other needs. The survey deals with household characteristics : income and employment including data on occupational and other pensions and includes estimates of household expenditure on life insurance and pension contributions for the latest year [QRL.45].

Special quarterly indices for one-person and two-person "pensioner" households are also published. "Pensioner households" are defined and discussed in annual articles in *Employment Gazette* [QRL.44] as well as in each introduction to *FES* [QRL.45]. The survey contains a wealth of demographic and other information about the retired population. Much of this will not be referenced in this review as it cannot be attributed directly to recipients of occupational pension schemes.

Some data is analysed according to the "other retired households". These are households in which more than a quarter of the household's income derives from occupational retirement pensions and/or income from investments, annuities etc. Such analysis will be referenced.

The FES provides considerably more information on the subject of pensions than is given in the annual report. Computer data bases are available for surveys from 1983 which facilitate the production of *ad hoc* analyses.

The analysis by household of FES data obscures 'individual' data. For example, if an analysis was required to show the number of people in receipt of pensions from various sources two people in the same household in receipt of a public sector pension would be counted once only. Conversely a person in receipt of pension income from more than one source (public, private, annuity) is counted as a household in each of the three analyses. A separate survey is carried out for Northern Ireland using identical questionnaires and coding practices so that results may be merged if the user requires.

The responsibility for the running of the Family Expenditure Survey (FES) in Great Britain is divided between the Social Survey Division of the Office of Population Censuses and Surveys (OPCS) and the Department of Employment (DE); while the overall design and content are kept under review by an inter-departmental committee under the chairmanship of the Central Statistical Office (CSO). The main publication in which data from the survey appear is the full report issued in the latter part of each year entitled, for example, *Family Expenditure Survey* 1984 [QRL.45]. Articles on the FES are published in *Employment Gazette* [QRL.44] to give early results for the main series. Subsequently data from the survey appear in various other government publications. The published survey data is preceded by a detailed introduction as well as a liberal commentary.

A detailed handbook listing sampling, fieldwork coding practices and related methodological experiments which extends to nearly 150 pages is published by HMSO, *Family Expenditure Survey Handbook* by Kemsley, W.W.F., Redpath, R.U. and Holmes, M. (1980) [B.17]. The handbook is aimed at the user of FES data as well as the survey specialist. Additionally each year an informative pack [QRL.46] aimed at users of FES computer tape (a suitably anonymised tape of data from the FES survey which is lodged with the ESRC data archive) is published. This gives full details and processing of that year's survey data.

5.9.2 *New Earnings Survey*

The Department of Employment's *New Earnings Survey* (NES) [QRL.67] is an annual survey of the earnings and hours of a random sample (one percent) of employees in employment in Great Britain for one pay-week or longer pay-period in April. Information is obtained in confidence from employers under the Statistics of Trade Act 1947. A similar survey is carried out in Northern Ireland.

The survey covers employees in all grades in all occupations, in all types and sizes of business in all industries and services, except for private domestic servants and the armed forces.

The basic questions remain unchanged from year to year; other questions are included in particular years and in some cases, may be repeated at intervals. The first survey on the present scale was carried out in 1970; in the first few years the form of the questionnaire was more variable.

The Survey results are classified by sex, age-group, sub-region of employment, collective agreement/wages council, industry and occupation. The published results concentrate on full-time adult employees whose pay for the survey pay-period was not affected by absence and part-time women, distinguishing those in manual from those in non-manual occupations. Since the survey returns relate to individuals, the survey provides information not only about averages for identifiable groups of employees but also about the make-up of their total pay. Some tables from 1984 are not strictly comparable with those preceding though the differences are of minor importance. The introduction to that edition of NES sets out the technical differences.

The details of pay in the pension and life insurance movements should be treated with caution. Pension funds are trust funds and not employers of individuals in the same manner as are the other financial institutions. Most individuals working for occupational pension schemes are in fact employed by the sponsoring employers and will therefore figure in the statistics for the industry of the employer and not for pensions. Statistics for life insurance are not broken down from those of general insurance. Analyses available in more detail or in a form not published will be supplied on request provided the results are considered reliable enough for release.

5.9.3 *Triennial Survey of Labour Costs in Great Britian*

This survey [B.82] contains information on voluntary social welfare payments by employers for the benefit of employees, including the *per capita* amounts paid into superannuation and other private funds, group life insurance premiums and pensions paid directly to employees. These items are not separated out and are therefore unlikely to be useful to a pensions or life insurance practitioner. There will therefore be no mention in the QRL. The reference is retained here since the *Guide to Official Sources* [B.47] implies that this is a viable source of pensions data. The latest results appear in *Employment Gazette* [QRL.44].

5.9.4 *Employment Gazette*

Employment Gazette [QRL.44] is the official journal of the Department of Employment and is published once a month by HMSO. Each issue contains the latest available labour market data. Statistics relating to the work and working conditions of people involved in the pension industry are available on a regular basis as are details of sundry "one-off" surveys.

5.10 Registry of Friendly Societies

There are many categories of Friendly Societies and industrial insurance companies, (see 3.7). They are required to make annual returns to the Registry of Friendly Societies in addition to any annual returns under the Insurance Companies Act.

Each year the Registrar of Friendly Societies produces a *Report* [QRL.26] containing much general background information and statistics relating to Friendly Societies and industrial assurance companies.

The report sets out the Acts of Parliament and provisions under which the registry is required to operate. The report then contains a description of the developments of each of the main groups of societies and comments on the implications of these developments. There is then a statistical record of the Registry's work and statistical abstracts from the annual returns.

5.11 Department of the Environment

5.11.1 *Housing and Construction Statistics*
Housing and Construction Statistics [QRL.51] contains details of insurance companies' house purchase loans. These figures are calculated by a monthly survey of 16 BIA members who between them undertake 65% of all BIA members house purchase loans. The BIA members' survey shows the number of UK houses on which loans have been made and the amounts advanced. The figures are divided into primary and topping up loans and into new and old houses. Also primary loans are analysed by purchase price of house. Aggregated figures of their survey are available from BIA (5.7).

5.11.2 *Local Authority Pension Schemes Survey*
There are a number of differences between the administration of local authority pension schemes and the other public sector funds as well as, of course, public sector funds; these differences are fully described in an article by Roger Morton entitled 'Local Authority Superannuation Funds' published in *Pensions World* [B.18] June 1981.

The Department of the Environment collects details of their pension funds at the same time as its other statistics. It publishes in *Local Authority Financial Statistics* [QRL.61], a table which replicates on a national scale the form used on an individual basis. The Department itself has no specific use for these figures except to pass them across to other user departments and therefore suggest that any queries be directed to the Department of Trade and Industry.

5.12 Department of Health and Social Security (DHSS)

The DHSS, although primarily concerned with Social Security maintains an overview of private pension provision in order to observe how the private and public sector provisions supplement each other. From time to time this may require the commissioning of individual surveys.

5.12.1 *Attitudes of members of occupational pension schemes to portable Pensions*
When the Inquiry into Provision of Retirement (see 1.1) was instituted the concept of personal portable pensions was new and the likely demand unknown. Gallup was commissioned by the DHSS to carry out surveys, [QRL.42], [QRL.43]. The surveys were conducted in February and March 1984. For reasons not disclosed the DHSS gave the results a low profile when they became available. The survey results are more detailed than those highlighted by the Department in its published commentary [B.69].

In the main the tables reproduced in the commentaries represent the answers to qualitative questions. Little indication of the mass of quantitative information contained in the full survey results is provided. The commentary contains the caveat that "as with any market research the replies of the people interviewed are only a general guide to pension preferences. The surveys give an indication of possible interest in personal pensions, not a precise forecast of the number who would opt for them if free to do so".

The survey reports are printed out in four volumes: men in private sector/ men in national or public service/ total women/ total. Each volume contains about 100 pages. The questions are reproduced as part of the report as are various definitions and some information pertaining to the methodology. The enquiry was entitled "Attitudes of Members of Occupational Pension Schemes to Portable Pensions" but many of the questions went wider including e.g. a query on the length of time that members have spent with each employer.

The sample was a quota sample. 10% of the sample are automatically back-checked either by phone or by post as are any questionnaires where there appear to be inconsistent replies. Few respondents refuse to supply names and addresses once shown identification by the interviewer. In those cases where a refusal is made it is dependent on the interviewer's standing with Gallup as to whether the interview is accepted or rejected. A second survey took place of attitudes of non-members of occupational pension schemes to portable pensions [QRL.43]. In this case only the totals were published. Rather than reference each item in these surveys, the QRL will contain general references such as "attitudes to pensions" and the full questionnaires are reproduced in Appendix 5.3. The questionaire for non-members is similar and two pages shorter.

5.12.2 *Population, Pension Costs and Pensioners' Incomes [QRL.85]*

The Secretary of State for Social Services established an Inquiry into Provision for Retirement in November 1982. A paper was published in June 1984 providing an informed background to the discussions which were part of that inquiry. Part one is a note by the Government Actuary's Department providing estimates of the future costs of pensions. The estimates relating to occupational schemes are taken from a paper published in the *Journal of the Institute of Actuaries* [QRL.6] Part two ofthe paper, produced by the DHSS Economic Advisers' Office, compares the spending power of people over pension age with that of people below. Only data relating to occupational schemes will be referenced.

The approach used in the paper is to compare pensioners with the rest of the population; though individual pensioners may not perceive their own living standards in this fashion. Newly-retired people in particular may compare their current position with their working income immediately before retirement, when both husband and wife may have been earning and children were no longer financially dependent. Such comparisons may be important to the individual at the time and to a person's pre-retirement planning. They do not, however, take account of the costs of raising children. Older pensioners, who have been retired longer, may be more interested in comparing themselves with the current population below pension age then in their own income when last at work. Details about the methods and assumptions used are published in an Annex to the paper. The paper is also concerned with i) the progress of pensioners' incomes since 1951 - ii) information about pensioners' incomes today - iii) projections of pensioners' incomes up to 2025/6 and iv) the outlook for home ownership by pensioners.

5.12.3 *Review of Contracting-out Contribution Reduction and Related Issues*

Every five years the Secretary of State for Social Services is required to review:

(a) the reductions in primary and secondary Class 1 contribution rates for employees who are contracted-out under Part III of the Social Security Pensions Act 1975; and

(b) the actuarial tables prescribed in regulations for the purpose of calculating accrued rights premiums, pensioners' rights premiums and limited revaluation premiums; and

(c) the percentage, prescribed in regulations, for fixed (pre-award) revaluation of accrued rights to guaranteed minimum pensions for early leavers (at present 8.5% p.a.); and

(d) the percentage, available under the Pensions Act, for revaluation of accrued rights to guaranteed minimum pensions for the 5 years preceding a cessation of contracted-out status (at present 12% p.a.).

Most of the statistics in [QRL.94] therefore relate to the state-scheme and would appear to fall outside the scope of this review. The statistics can however be used to derive information relating to occupational schemes e.g., the figures shown for ARPs are referenced since they are payable only when an occupational scheme ceases to be contracted out. The numbers paying CEP's and LRP's indicate the number of individual members ceasing to be contracted out, the scheme itself remaining contracted out. Section 28 of the Social Security Pensions Act 1975 require the Government Actuary to take into account when making his calculations any change in the factors affecting the cost to occupational pension schemes of providing GMP's.

Relevant statistics contained in the report include mortality ratios derived from population data but adjusted for information provided by CMI and a large number of occupational schemes in the public sector. Although attention must be paid to a loading for expenses little information has been provided concerning its derivation.

CHAPTER 6

PROFESSIONAL AND TRADE ASSOCIATIONS

6.1 National Association of Pension Funds

The principal trade association in the pensions movement is the National Association of Pension Funds (NAPF). It was founded in 1923 as a non-profit organisation whose main aim is to promote interest in all matters relating to pensions and retirement. The Association represents the interest of all types of occupational pension arrangements, whether in the public or private sector and whether they are insured or privately invested and is recognised by the Inland Revenue, DHSS, other government and various official bodies as the representative body for employers with Pension Funds in the U.K. There are two classes of membership (a) ordinary member (schemes) and (b) associate member (consultants etc.). Associate members are usually advisers from ancillary services such as consulting actuaries, stockbrokers etc., who wish to be kept aware of the latest developments in the pensions world. The two classes of membership are not mutually exclusive and, for example, a firm of consulting actuaries who have their own self administered pension scheme would belong to both classes of membership.

While the NAPF is recognised by Government Department, etc., as representative of the pensions industry, in practice it is likely to be a representative only of the "better" schemes, since to join the NAPF a member must have been concerned and interested in his pension schemes. Just under 50% of employees who are members of pensions schemes are represented by the NAPF –the schemes to which they belong being a member of the Association; this despite the fact that only 3% of employees with pension schemes are members of the NAPF. Pension schemes which are members of NAPF are generally larger schemes. (There is a significant number of one and two person schemes and the Government Actuary's Department Survey [QRL.70] estimates that there are about 60,000 such schemes in existence).

The NAPF maintains a small library of literature and documents relating to pension matters, including pension fund reports and accounts for the use of its members. The Association also makes annual presentations, called the Golden Pen Awards, to stimulate improved presentation of pension fund reports and accounts. A condition of entry for this award is that a copy of the document will be placed in the NAPF library to be available for inspection without restriction, [QRL.90]

A year book is produced with simple, *unsummarised*, statistical information and names of advisers, [B.59] The information is provided from results of an annual questionnaire sent to all ordinary members of NAPF. Where the NAPF receives no reply, a basic entry showing name and address only is published. A fuller directory is contained in *Pension Funds and their Advisers* [QRL.12]. The NAPF also publishes occasional booklets on matters of interest to the pensions industry which include *A guide to good practice –Member participation in pension schemes* [B.46], *Trusteeship* [B.83], *Valuing Insurance Policies for Accounts purposes* [B.86], *Accounting for Overseas Investments by United Kingdom Pension Funds* [B.29], *Financial Reports of Pension Funds* [B.39] and *Code of Practice, Information to Members of Pension Schemes* [B.35]. Many of these are itemised in the general bibliography. The Association cooperates in the production of *Pensions World* [B.67], a monthly journal devoted to authoritative articles on pensions and related subjects.

6.1.1 *NAPF Annual Survey*

A common question posed to pension consultants by employers is "What is the usual practice?" and it is this question that the NAPF sought to answer with its surveys [QRL.27]. The NAPF previously conducted "mini surveys" of about 200 schemes whenever requested by a member who wanted the "market view" on a particular topic. The member was asked to bear the costs of the exercise and the results were made available to the requesting member and participants. From 1974-1980 the service was provided in parallel with the main survey (see below). As the "main" survey improved and most queries were covered by it, the "mini survey" service was discontinued. In the event that a company wishes to determine a common practice, the NAPF consider that correspondence amongst companies of a similar size could prove more beneficial than a "mini survey" conducted by the NAPF among anonymous and possibly dissimilar companies.

The NAPF "main" survey produced annually, is now in its tenth year, and is comprehensive. It covers topics under such broad headings as: (i) Income and Expenditure of Funds (ii) Nature of Schemes (iii) Benefits Provided and (iv) Matters relating to the Social Security Pensions Act 1975. The survey was at one time changed every year, but this was found to be confusing to the reader and time consuming to the compilers who needed to update their computer programs to allow for the revised questions and groupings.

The survey questionnaire is submitted to all ordinary members of the NAPF. The results are published in booklet form. The booklet contains a copy of the questionnaire and all tables are cross referenced to the appropriate question. The results are analysed and discussed. The commentary gives an explanation of changes in statistics from year to year where the reason is not immediately obvious.

The questionnaire covers 11 closely typed pages, the questionnaire is produced annually as an Appendix to the survey report. To eliminate ambiguity or misinterpretation of the meaning of the questions, a glossary and guidelines are attached to the questionnaire when sent to members. Both are reproduced in full in the published survey. Whenever a defined term is used in the questionnaire it is printed in block capitals. When completing the questionnaire, members are instructed to use information at the latest date for which all questions can be answered conveniently and the approximate answers should be given whenever accurate figures are not available. There is no provision for the questionnaire to distinguish such approximations from accurate replies. Other instructions include the fact that employees permanently outside the UK and all matters relating to them and their pensions should be excluded whenever possible; staff and works schemes are separately classified.

The response rate to the survey fluctuates and details are contained in the introduction to each report. It is mainly in respect of smaller schemes that forms are not returned. In terms of number of employees the response seems sound. Statistically, though it is clear that the larger schemes dominate.

Whilst it is absurd to give equal weight to, say, the ICI scheme and a one person scheme, in practice the 1000 schemes with average membership of 1000 members each may be more likely to influence the thinking of employers than that a single scheme with say, one million employees would influence its peers. Employers are interested in the policies of firms of comparable size and tend to take no more than a passing interest in that of industrial giants.

The questionnaire is rendered anonymous at the NAPF Headquarters by detaching the top sheet containing the member's name. The forms are then numbered. Only the NAPF head office is aware of the relationship between this coding and the company names, so that the information is in practice rendered confidential.

The same coding is used each year so that a check can be made then the results are anaylsed as to whether the same companies are responding. Although roughly the same number of companies respond each year e.g. in 1981 and 1982, only 75% of the 1982 respondents had responded in 1981. Figures from year to year are not totally comparable, and it may be difficult to determine from the published results whether a change is due to an underlying trend or a change in the mix of respondents.

The questionnaires are analysed by a firm of consulting actuaries. The answers are manually vetted and inconsistencies of a numerical nature (usually obvious from cross referencing etc.) are eliminated. If a question is poorly answered (which happens infrequently), it is possible to refer to the originator via the NAPF head office (see previous paragraph).

The published survey results contain nearly 100 tables, but if other tabulations are required they are available on request from the NAPF. Since any annual differences are too slight to be significant, the possibility of publishing the survey biennially rather then annually, with a brief survey in the alternate year, is being actively considered by the NAPF.

6.2 Association of British Insurers

The ABI was founded in July 1985 as a structure to replace the Accident Offices Association, the British Insurance Association, the Fire Offices Committee, the Industrial Life Offices Association, the Life Offices Association and the existing insurance bodies with one trade association under a chief executive who amongst his other activities would also act as a spokesman for the industry. The changeover has been low key with little publicity. It is likely that some members of the public may refer to the previously existing trade associations for some time after the completion of this review. For this reason they have been treated separately rather than under the gambit of the umbrella organisation. The ABI is now the principal trade association for the insurance company market.

It should be borne in mind that since the absorption of the LOA into the new ABI (together with the old BIA which mainly looked after general insurance) there may be changes in the format of publications in the future, though it is unlikely that continuity will be perilously disturbed.

6.3 Life Offices' Association

The Life Offices' Association (LOA) has recently been brought within the umberella of the Association of British Insurers (ABI). It was the principal trade association for life offices in England and Wales. Its objects were the advancement and the protection of the interests of ordinary long term insurance business and cooperation with any other association having similar objects. The Industrial Life Offices Association (ILOA), dealing exclusively with industrial insurance.

Quarterly *New Life Insurance figures for the quarter* [QRL.69] and annual *New Life Insurance Business* [QRL.68] figures of new business are prepared for press release by the LOA (and now the ABI). In these circumstances time is of the essence and offices are instructed to provide estimates where actual figures are not yet avaliable.

The quarterly new business figures [QRL.69] relate to individual life business only. They are not comparable with the annual figures [QRL.68] which include occupational pension and life insurance schemes. Figures for occupational and self-employed pensions when shown separately should be treated with caution as many companies find difficulty in separating them.

6.3.1 *Life Insurance in the United Kingdom*

Each year the LOA, ASLO, ILOA and LLAG jointly publish a booklet *Life Insurance in the United Kingdom* [QRL.60] of summary statistics related to the life insurance industry. Figures are given for the current year as well as the previous four. The booklet contains an appendix listing the contributing offices. For the years 1951/1971 figures related to member offices only; from 1972 these encompass the majority of the industry, not merely member offices. It is difficult to quantify non-response but the LOA estimate is that this is insignificant, being limited to the smallest of non-member companies and may amount to no more than 1%.

The annual return of statistics is submitted to contributing offices in February of each year, to be returned to the LOA or ASLO if appropriate, by the end of March. Many figures can be extracted from the companies' DoT returns. Each company completes the returns according to its own year end, but the majority of year ends fall on 31 December. No correction is made for those which do not. For the purposes of these returns "UK Contracts" is interpreted in a consistent manner with the DoT returns, but where a company no longer writes business overseas (even where a small amount of such business remains in force) it may be amalgamated with the UK business. Returns from individual offices are treated in confidence and only aggregate figures are released.

6.3.2 *EEC Statistics*
Since the accession of the United Kingdom to the EEC, statistics on the source of premium income, sums assured in force at end of year and the total size of the ordinary long term business fund have been collected as part of the Annual Return of Statistics in respect of the business of UK insurers and their subsidiaries in the life insurance markets in other member states *EEC Statistics* [QRL.40]. This series of statistics is proving useful in assessing the growing interest of UK life insurers in the Common Market. Returns are made by LOA and ASLO members in August of each year.

6.3.3 *UK Life Insurance: Sources of New Business*
The Intermediaries Committee of the LOA decided that following the enactment of the Insurance Brokers (Registration) Act 1977 it was appropriate to establish a system whereby statistics relating to sources of new premium income are collected from life offices annually *Sources of New Business* [QRL.100]. Occasional surveys had been conducted in 1974 and 1976. The first regular annual return was made in respect of the year 1982, that being the first year in which the category of registered broker was meaningful.

Compared with the form used in a survey conducted in 1976 as part of the Association's response to the Department of Trade's enquiry on insurance intermediaries, the main changes introduced are that registered insurance brokers are now shown as a separate category of intermediary and that the categories of business have been brought into line with the quarterly returns of new business supplied to the Associations, with the addition of a column for sponsored pension scheme business.

Results are not confidential, but have not been made generally available.

6.4 British Insurance Association (BIA)

The BIA was founded in 1917 with the objects of protection, promotion and advancement of the common interests of all classes of insurance business. Membership is open to all insurance companies authorised by the Department of Trade to transact business in the United Kingdom. It represents over 320 insurance companies. The BIA is mainly concerned with general insurance; however there is close co-operation with the LOA (and both are now merged as part of the BIA). The BIA is in the process of producing a source document for Insurance Statistics [B.34]. Some chapters are available in skeleton format (See 7.6.1).

6.4.1 *Insurance Facts and Figures*
In November each year the BIA publishes a booklet entitled *Insurance Facts and Figures* [B.52]. It contains many tables in a graphic form and information based on direct surveys of its membership, fuller details of which are contained in *BIA Member Statistics*. Other figures are extracted from Government sources and these sources are listed in an appendix.

6.4.2 *BIA Members Statistics*
This document contains a collation of the figures provided by BIA members. All of whom are required to complete five survey forms each year. The figures in *BIA members statistics* [QRL.31] differ slightly to those in the published statistics card (a brief summary of BIA statistics) and press releases since these earlier figures were provisional and may have been subject to revision in the light of late returns.

The booklet [QRL.31] contains brief notes which include details of where estimates have been made and definitions to accompany the tables. The majority of the figures relate to general insurance.

The surveys containing information relevant to this review are those relating to premiums and investments.

Each year the BIA conducts a survey of its membership regarding investment holdings and income in respect of worldwide business. Figures are given separately for long term and general business. Prior to 1972 information on investment holdings is at book value only. Prior to 1957 information is limited and not split into long term and general insurance. From 1972 to 1976 offices were requested to supply market values if possible but from 1977 market values were mandatory.

6.4.3 *UK Market Statistics*
The object of the study *United Kingdom Market Statistics* [QRL.108] is to estimate the total UK insurance business written, whether by companies, friendly societies or Lloyds. It aims to overcome many of the deficiencies in the official statistics on premium income.

It sets out the basis it uses to calculate net written premiums in the UK for long term business broken down into ordinary long term and industrial branch business.

6.4.4 *Insurance Premiums in the UK*
Premium income is one of the most basic measures for the insurance industry, and yet at times it can prove extremely difficult to find precisely the figures which are needed, particularly if they are wanted for a long run of years. One of the reasons for this is that premiums can be defined in a variety of ways and it is simply not feasible either for companies or for a trade association such as the BIA to produce premuim statistics by every possible definition. These differences in definition can also make it difficult to compare one published series with another. Therefore the purpose of *Insurance Premiums in the United Kingdom* [QRL.57] is to bring together under a single cover some of the main premium income series which are available, to clearly define them, and wherever possible to present them to cover the run of years from 1960 to date. Each table has detailed accompanying notes subdivided into the following headings: Source, Basis, Coverage.

Figures published by the Department of Trade and Industry will cover all companies authorised to write insurance business in the UK but will not include Lloyds or bodies such as Friendly Societies. No figures from this source are included in [QRL.57] either, due both to difficulties in definition and to the tardiness with which they are published.

6.5 Institute and Faculty of Actuaries

There are two main professional bodies of actuaries in the United Kingdom: The Institute of Actuaries in London and the Faculty of Actuaries in Edinburgh. The Institute was formed in 1848 and received its Royal Charter in 1884. The corresponding dates for the Faculty are 1856 and 1868. Though the Institute and Faculty are closely allied by a common interest and have similar entry standards, each body functions independently and holds its own examinations as well as publishing its own learned journals. To become an actuary in the United Kingdom it is necessary to qualify as a Fellow of one of the bodies.

Other professional bodies of Actuaries include the Association of Consulting Actuaries which was founded in 1952. It draws its membership from among those independent professionals engaged in private practice.

Since its origins in the eighteenth century, the actuarial profession has been responsible for a succession of investigations into human mortality and morbibity, and for the construction of standard tables. In the course of research, actuaries have employed data derived from a wide variety of sources. Apart from the census and death records of the general population, use has been made of statistics relating to groups of lives such as government annuities and pensioners, the membership of friendly societies and superannuation funds, and the policy-holders and annuitants of life assurance companies.

6.5.1 *Professional Journals*

Both the Institute and the Faculty of Actuaries house extensive libraries covering actuarial and kindred subjects and hold regular sessional meetings to discuss matters of professional interest. The papers, together with a record of the full discussion, are published in the *Journal of the Institute of Actuaries* [B.54] and *Transactions of the Faculty of Actuaries* [B.81] respectively. Examples of papers follow:-

Actuarial Reports on Pension Fund Valuations by D.F. Renn and C.M. Stewart [QRL.14] In carrying out his sixth survey of *Occupational pension schemes* (see 4.7.1) [QRL.70], the Government Actuary requested employers with schemes having more than 100 members to submit their latest actuarial report. A wide selection was received. Since they were not fully representative, it was thought more appropriate to give a description of their content for the benefit of the profession rather than to attempt to produce a definitive statistical report of the survey [QRL.70]. Various valuation assumptions are discussed and in particular, the 'net' interest rate up to retirement (interest less the general increase in the level of earnings) and after retirement (interest less the annual increases of pensions in payment) are classified according to usage by funds.

An Investigation into the withdrawal experience of Ordinary Life Business by J.G.R Grombie et al. [QRL.105]

This paper contains an investigation into the withdrawal rates among the policy holders of seven Scottish life insurance companies and covers the years 1972-76 with an appendix giving the results for 1977. The number of policyholders under investigation were in excess of 0.75 million. The rates of withdrawal were analysed by class of policy and duration since inception. Further investigations were carried out, mainly on the 1976 data, examining the rates by age at entry, sex, size of sum assured, frequency of premium payment, length of premium paying term, type of agent introducing the business. Comparisons were made of the level of withdrawal rates among the various companies and also the variations from year to year separately. A graduation of the combined data for 1975 and 1976 for each of the main classes of business was carried out. The paper was discussed at the Faculty of Actuaries and the full discussion is recorded with the paper. Much of the discussion concerned the methodology of the investigation. Since that data has been made available to the City University Actuarial Science Department, who have taken advantage of the G.L.I.M. statistical package in carrying out modelling based upon it. No results have yet been published, although seminars have been held and it is anticipated that a paper will appear in JIA in 1987.

Projections of the Costs of Occupational and State Pensions, by J.L. Field [QRL.6] Projections of occupational pension scheme membership and expenditure were made for the Wilson committee [B.75], this paper revises and extends those projections. The paper itself comments on the paucity of reliable statistics on which to base the projections. In order to study the build-up of the pension paid on retirement a model consisting of 200 representative working (or non-working) lives was constructed for 100 men and 100 women showing their employment and scheme membership status in each six-month period from their sixteenth to their seventeenth birthdays. The representative careers were a combination of three sets of data each relating to 200 careers, but from different sources.

The Growth of Pension Rights and their impact on the National Economy by B. Benjamin, F.W. Bacon, N.D.W. Elphinstone [QRL.2] - 1954 this paper is of historical importance. It predates even the earliest of the Government Actuary's Survey's. As part of its investigation it "ascertained, as far as possible, the present situation with regard to the volume of current pensions, pension rights, and numbers of members covered by existing pension schemes, and hence to estimate the volume of future emerging pensions".

6.5.2 *Continuous Mortality Investigation Bureau (CMI)*

Until the Continuous Mortality Investigation Bureau was established in 1923, standard tables of mortality for insured lives and annuitants were prepared by *ad hoc* committees established from time to time as required. Since the Bureau, with effect from 1 January 1924, started to collect data annually from individual life offices, it has been responsible for the preparation and publication of standard tables. The latest table for insured lives is the A 1967/70, *Tables for assured lives* [QRL.21], based on the experience of the four years 1967/70. For annuitants the latest table is the A(90) *Tables for annuitants* [QRL.22]. It is based on annuitants' experience for the same four years, but mortality rates are projected to 1990 so that the tables are appropriate for use during the 1980s. A similar table, the PA(90) *Tables for Pensioners* [QRL.73] based on the same principles, has been prepared in relation to pensioners. *Considerations Affecting the Preparation of Standard Tables of Mortality* [B.36] sets out the methodology and the difficulties faced by the CMI.

Currently, investigations are carried out into the mortality of male and female lives under whole life and endowment insurances, into the mortality of male lives under similar insurances issued in the Republic of Ireland and into the experience under certain classes of temporary insurance and linked life insurance, the male and female mortality experiences of immediate annuitants, pensioners under life office pension schemes, and those holding retirement annuity policies issued under the provisions of the Finance Act, 1956, and subsequent amending or consolidating legislations. As from 1972 the Bureau extended its activities to the sickness data experience under permanent health insurance policies, with data under individual policies and group policies investigated separately.

Investigations are also conducted into the causes of death among male insured lives, female insured lives, annuitants and pensioners.

In 1982 a new investigation was undertaken into the mortality of insured lives suffering from certain health impairments at the time of completing a proposal for insurance; their mortality will also be analysed according to cause of death. From the same year 1982, all the insured lives investigations which did not already cover females have been extended to include them. From 1983 an investigation was started into the mortality under joint life first death policies effected on the lives of one male and one female. The Bureau normally supplies contributing offices with summaries for each investigation of its own mortality experience and of the mortality experience of all offices combined, for the latest year for which analysis has been completed.

Up to and including the investigations for the years 1963/66, reports summarizing and commenting on the results of investigations were published in the *Journal of the Institute of Actuaries* [B.54] and the *Transactions of the Faculty of Actuaries* [B.81]. From 1973 separate volumes of reports entitled *Continuous Mortality Investigation Reports* [QRL.34] - [B.33] are published and these include the results of the investigations from 1967 onwards. The first volume [QRL.34] contains an introductory chapter on the history and development of standard insurance tables. This history is brought 'up to date' in the introductory chapter. The second report [B.32] examines the history and development of sickness statistics.

All the volumes in the series contain full details of the methodology used and make reference to any potential difficulties in interpretation.

6.6 Institute of Chartered Accountants

The Institute of Chartered Accountants in England and Wales was incorperated by Royal Charter in 1880. The objects of the Charter are to elevate the accountancy profession as a whole by, amongst other things, establishing a high standard of professional practice and general education and advancing the theory and practice of accountancy in all its aspects.

6.6.1 *Professional Journals*

The official journal of the ICA is *Accountancy* [B.28]. Views published in *Accountancy* [B.28] are not necessarily shared by the Council of the Institute. The journal is however often used as a vehicle to publish exposure drafts on accounting standards e.g., [B.38].

The January 1981 edition of *Accountancy* [B.28] contains a survey of reporting practice of some of the largest occupational pension schemes in the country: *Looking into Pension Fund Accounts* [QRL.13] by C.J. Platt. The article shows the results of an examination of the annual reports of 26 of the largest occupational pension funds themselves (not the reports of the sponsoring employer). The survey is not rigorous but many of the aspects covered are not dealt with elsewhere. The aim of the survey has been to deal with (a) the types and range of information included in the reports, (b) the method of presentation, (c) accounting policies adopted, (d) policy as to provision of reports to members, (e) policy as to actuarial valuation, (f) form of report given by the auditor.

6.6.2 *Financial Reporting. A Survey of UK Published Accounts.*

The primary purpose of the survey is to give a factual report of financial disclosure practices of the companies in the sample, supported by detailed background articles *Agricultural Performance Analysis* [QRL.95]. From 1983-84 the survey report also comments on the statistical significance of the tables presented in the analysis sections. The objective is to distinguish between differences in the results which have occurred by chance and those which reflect underlying differences between the reporting practices of companies. The analysis and sample size has increased over the years and the surveys *Financial Reporting* [QRL.20] contain details of sampling methodology.

Since 1980 information relating to pension funds in the private sector has been provided separately. The chapter in the 1984/85 survey is headed Pension Costs. It deals with the disclosure in employer's financial statements of information concerning employees' pensions. The research has been conducted by C.J. Napier, a lecturer in accountancy at the London School of Economics.

One of the analyses related to the number of items concerned with pensions which were disclosed in the sponsoring employer's accounts. Disclosure by those companies included items such as detailed notes of funding policy, the results of actuarial valuations etc. All data is analysed into large listed, small listed and large unlisted companies.

6.7 The Chartered Institute of Public Finance and Accountancy

The Chartered Institute of Public Finance and Accountancy (CIPFA) is the major professional accountancy body for the public sector. Its members are mainly Finance Directors, Treasurers and financial officers working for local and public authorities. Under its Royal Charter, the Institute has a wide range of professional functions, including a comprehensive range of financial and statistical services. The institute compiles and publishes a unique set of statistical information covering local authorities and other parts of the public sector.

6.7.1 *Local Authority Superannuation Investment Statistics*
Local authorities began measuring the performance of their superannuation funds in 1962, soon after the passage of the Trustees Investments Act 1961 [QRL.62]. The reorganisation of local government in 1974 (1975 in Scotland) brought about the merger of all local authority funds outside London within a County Council area (or, in Scotland, the Regional Council area) under the administration of the County or Regional Council. This broke the continuity of the previous statistics and the opportunity was taken to institute a new and improved series. It took time for production of the new statistics to settle down and for local authorities themselves to effect the merger in some cases of more than 30 funds together with transfers of investments relating to employers who moved in 1974 to work for the water authorities or the health service.

By 1977, funds had become stable and a reliable base was established from which results could be accumulated. Each year, now, CIPFA published a booklet containing cumulative performance figures since 1977 and also five year moving averages. An introduction to the booklet sets out methodology and any limitations in the statistics. The most important of these is the fact that the statistics do not cover the full fund as direct investment in property and investment in property unit trusts are excluded. It is hoped that these will be included within the next three to four years. There is no mention however, of any constraints on investment placed on the management of the funds by the policy decisions of the local authority for whom they work.

6.8 Pensions Research Accountants Group (PRAG)

In 1976 a small non-profit making research group of accountants was established with the aim of sponsoring reasearch in fields directly of concern to its members and to act as a forum for discussion of current developments. Since then the group has grown and its membership includes not only accountants but also managers of some of the leading UK occupational pension schemes, and practitioners in the actuarial and auditing professions who are interested in the financial administration and reporting of pension schemes. As well as conducting surveys, the group has published several booklets including discussion papers and statements of position *A Glossary for Pension Schemes* [B.43], *Pensions Terminology –A Glossary for Pension Schemes* [B.66], *Pension Funds and Value Added Tax Law, Practice and Reform* [B.65], *Valuing Insurance Policies for Accounts Purposes* [B.86], *Pension Payment Methods, A Survey* [QRL.78], *Measurement of Investment Performance for United Kingdom Pension Funds* [QRL.64], *Accounting for Overseas Investments by United Kingdom Pension Funds* [B.29], *Financial Reports of Pension Funds* [B.39] and *Pension Funds: Information needs of members and pensioners* [QRL.77].

6.8.1 *Measurement of Investment Performance for UK Pension Funds*
From autumn 1979 to early 1980 the group undertook a study of the services offered to pension funds for measuring investment performance. A booklet *Measurement of Investment Performance for UK Pension Funds* [QRL.64] was published in 1981 giving

a detailed account of the survey, its purpose, methods and results including much background commentary. The survey questionnaire is reproduced in the published booklet. Parts of the survey are now dated but a list of survey participants is included in the booklet so that direct enquiries may be made of them.

The main emphasis of the report [QRL.64] is on comparative performance i.e. the achievements of one investment manager measured against others (4.6). Its survey of investment performance services shows that there are differences between the services in techniques, coverage and presentation.

6.8.1.1 *Survey of Investment Constraints* Comparative investment performance measurement needs to recognise any constraints imposed upon the investment manager as a manager can only be held responsible within the scope of his discretionary authority. A separate questionnaire was issued at random to 20% of the ordinary membership of the NAPF and produced a 45% response. The results of this survey are also contained in [QRL.64] and include information regarding restriction on types of investment, level of investment and the frequency of review of such restrictions.

6.8.1.2 *New Survey* Significant advances have been made since the first survey and a new survey has been proposed. The aim of the new survey is twofold: to stimulate measurers to extend their services and frame say 10 key questions that all trustees should ask of those who measure the performance of the funds for which they are responsible. The new questionnaire incorporates the majority of the questions asked in the 1981 publication but it has been expanded to cover risk and additional investment sectors such as venture capital and traded options. Provision is made for the respondents to list all the investment sectors for which their service normally calculates rates of return.

The committee considers that it is important that users are aware whether or not investment expenses are taken into account (see 4.6) and also the effect on borrowings. One section is concerned with the services provided for the investment measurement of pooled funds and property portfolios.

Preliminary papers have been drafted by committee members covering the following subjects:

1. Investment expenses.
2. Risk analysis.
3. Internal measurement services.
4. Communication of results.
5. Managed funds and unit trusts.
6. Relationship with the actuarial valuation.

The committee is expected to present its full report in 1987.

6.8.2 *Survey of Pension Payments Methods*

The survey was conducted during May and June 1980. It surveyed the procedures and payment methods used by a small sample of UK pension funds in the administration of their pension payrolls. The organisations completing the questionnaire are not statistically representative of all UK pension funds; results should not be assumed to indicate general practice. Details of the survey including the method used to select the sample and a reproduction of the questionnaire are contained in *Pension Payment Methods A Survey* [QRL.78].

The aim of the survey was to determine current practice in a variety of organisations giving administrators the opportunity to weigh their own procedures and methods of operation against those of other funds.

The final question of the survey asked "Which future developments or current practices might be considered in order to improve the service offered to both the pensioner and the fund?" As might have been expected the most popular response was the distribution of a newsletter. (It is relatively cheap to produce, can be widely distributed at a modest cost and is almost certain to be well received and read). Other suggestions included, the introduction of reular meetings of pensioners, the distribution of Christmas cards, a Freefone telephone service and food hampers.

The main survey did not cover the subject of certificates of existence. This is an area of concern to payroll administrators. The results of such a (separate smaller) survey (amongst PRAG membership) conducted in October 1979 are also reported in [QRL.78]. The respondents to that questionnaire are not the same as those who replied to the main questionnaire, and the purpose of including the section is to supplement other information in [QRL.78].

The survey covers such matters of practice as objectives, frequency, staffing, methods and value placed upon it.

6.8.3 *Pension Fund Administration Costs*

A working party on pension fund administration costs was formed by the PRAG to examine methods of enabling the administrative costs of pension funds to be compared and thus of assessing their efficiency. The working party decided that pension fund administration expenses divided into two main categories of activity, i.e. administration of benefits etc. and investment management, and to investigate each separately.

To make a comparison of pension fund administrative costs, the study introduced the concept of a standard fund with specified pensions administration responsibilities. The most appropriate standard to use was that of a free standing pensions office and the study assumed the following activities of a UK based scheme.

(i) The setting up and maintenance of membership records.
(ii) The collection and recording of contributions; the recording of pensionable pay.
(iii) Calculation and payment of benefits including all related payroll and computer activities.
(iv) The preparation and issue of benefits statements and other regular information to members.
(v) Scheme supervision (including trustees and management meetings, rule changes etc.).
(vi) Actuarial reporting and supervision.
(vii) All accountancy functions relating to the above (including the preparation of final accounts) but excluding investment accounting costs.

The costs of the following activities were specifically excluded:

(i) Pre-retirement counselling.
(ii) Pensioner welfare activities.
(iii) The work of local divisional personnel staff and/or local management.
(iv) The involvement of trustees (either internal or external) and company directors etc.

The method being used for this comparison of cost and assessment of efficiency is a multiple regression analysis model. Work on this was carried out at Sheffield Polytechnic. Data for 1983 year ends was analysed for 46 schemes selected as having data of a good enough standard. To improve the response rate for a survey relating to 1984 and 1985 data an article describing the progress of the working party will appear in the February 1986 issue of *Pensions World* [B.67].

The work relating to investment expenses is not as advanced as the former and has involved some radical rethinking about the methods of accounting for investment costs. PRAG is hoping that in time it may lead to a new exposure draft.

6.8.4 *Information needs of Members and Pensioners*

Sixty to seventy companies were approached to gauge interest in the survey to pension scheme attitudes. Individual questionnaires were supplied to members and pensioners of 25 companies who had indicated an interest in such a survey and replies were received from 18 of those companies.

The responses have been analysed separately for each employer and a total analysis was carried out for all employers and the results studied by the Working Party. The analysis was subdivided into two age groups (under/over 40 for members in service and under/over 65 for pensioners) and two geographical regions (south of England/remainder).

Each employer participating in the survey also completed an administrator's questionnaire which gave details of the information provided to members/ pensioners by his particular scheme. Attempts were made to correlate the answers to these questionnaires with the individual questionnaires so that any factual inaccuracies in the latter could be determined before results of the analyses were published. This exercise also helped to indicate the extent to which administrators are not aware of what information members receive or members are not aware of what information administrators provide. The correlation was achieved (a) by asking administrators for comments on the responses to their own questionnaires and (b) by individual employer analysis by members of the Working Party.

A fourth sub-group of the Working Party will provide an overall analysis by 6th July 1984 of the results of the 18 administrators' questionnaires with a view to indicating the general level of information provision of those employers analysed. A fifth and final sub-group will prepare a note on the background to the survey with a view to inclusion in the final report.

Many of the results indicated that the sample might be biased; for example there was a very high positive response to the question "Did you read and understand your brochure?" This might imply that the respondants are amongst the more sophisticated membership, that there is greater than expected interest in the brochure, or simply that the respondents did not wish to give the impression that they were simple.

Because of responses such as these, the results have been published with the following comment. "We would emphasise that we have not treated this survey as a major item of statistical research, but merely as an attempt to examine what we believe has not been considered to any significant extent elsewhere –namely to find out what information members and pensioners of schemes actually want in relation to what they already receive" *Pension Funds: Information needs of members and pensioners* [QRL.77].

The report contains a copy of the questionnaire and all results are commented upon.

6.9 Stock Exchange

The Stock Exchange provides a market for the purchase and sale of securities. At present, the members of the Stock Exchange, consist of Brokers (agents for clients) and Jobbers (dealing as principals in specific securities). This division is in a state of flux. Many Stock Brokers do more than merely carry out client's buying and selling orders. They may act as investment analysts, researchers and advisers on a range of financial topics for individual savers, for investing institutions and for companies seeking investment.

The Science Reference Library carries the most comprehensive set available of those Broker Bulletins available to the general public. Most broker information is confidential to clients. *Marketing Surveys Index* [B.56] is a loose leaf register of market research and contains details of research published by some brokers. It is not comprehensive.

6.9.1 *The Stock Exchange Survey of Share Ownership (A supplement to the Stock Exchange fact service)*

The committee of the association decided that, as there had been a great deal of press and other comment on the subject of small, self administered pension schemes without adequate research or information, due partly to the lack of adequate statistics, they would attempt to remedy the situation by conducting a survey of their membership *Analysis of assets of members* [QRL.24].

The survey is produced by the Economics Department of the Stock Exchange and indicates the trend of share ownership until the end of 1981. The survey contains full details of methodology and a commentary on the results. The previous survey was done by the CSO for 1975 *The Ownership of Company Shares: A Survey for 1975, Studies in Official Statistics. No.34* [B.63]. Details of methodology are given greater detail than for [QRL.104]. Earlier sources include a survey for 1963 *The Owners of Quoted ordinary shares –A Survey for 1963* [B.25] and one of 1957-70 *The Pattern of Ordinary share Ownership 1957-70* [B.19]. Additionally Bristow and Dobbins *The Growth and Impact of Institutional Investors: a report to the research committee of the Institute of Chartered Accountants* [B.45] estimated the ownership of 42 companies, into 3 classes from the ICA's 1974/5 survey of published accounts *Financial Reporting* [QRL.20]. It is not possible to establish for any completely individual company the nature of the ownership concealed by a name. With almost half the holdings of pension funds held by nominees [QRL.104] the strength of conclusions drawn from any further analyses must be limited. The Stock Exchange has noted: "This might be the last survey which can be carried out using present methods because of the increasing amount of shares held in nominee names on companies' registers. Anaylsis of these nominees, totalling a little over one-third in the present survey presents a major difficulty. The growth of overseas interest in UK stocks is likely to increase nominee holdings still further".

6.10 Association of Pensioneer Trustees

The association exists to promote high standards of conduct within the profession, to negotiate with the SFO on all rulings affecting small, self-administered funds (usually those with less than 12 members) and to provide outside bodies and the public generally with a better understanding of the pensioneer trustees function. (For an exact definition of 'pensioneer trustee' refer to memorandum No. 58 of the Joint Offices of the SFO and OPB).

6.10.1 *Methodology of Survey*

On 6th January 1983 the survey questionnaire was sent to all members of the association to be answered as at 1st December 1982. Confidentiality of the replies to the survey was ensured by retaining the services of a major firm of chartered accountants with considerable experience of this sort of confidential survey. Information relating to an individual scheme was sent direct to them and individual information was not released by them to any member of the committee or anyone else.

The information was analysed and released to the committee in the form of aggregate data which could not be related back to individual practitioners. Each questionnaire was numbered and also had a tear-off slip bearing both the name of the member and the number. On completion of the questionnaire the tear-off slip was sent to the secretary of the association to provide a means of obtaining further information on poorly answered questions from specific replies without breaking confidentiality. The use of this facility was not required. The results *Analysis of assets of members* [QRL.24] are presented as information without any detailed statistical analysis. It should be noted that the response was poor.

6.11 Pensions Management Institute (PMI)

The Pensions Management Institute does not currently produce any relevant statistics (other than an analysis of its membership by type of employer). The PMI is an educational establishment and was set up to provide tuition and examination facilities leading to a nationally recognised qualification for its members, together with the range of services normally associated with such a body.

6.12 Society of Investment Analysts

The Society was formed in 1955. Its objects are to achieve, foster and maintain high standards of professional ability and practice in investment analysis, portfolio management and related disciplines; to encourage the creation and interchange of ideas and information among those engaged in such activities; to advance public understanding of their functions and techniques and the operation of the security and other investment markets and to support and promote the interests of the investment community. Regular meetings are held in London and Glasgow.

CHAPTER 7

PERIODICAL PUBLICATIONS

7.1 Daily Newspapers

Newspapers rarely prove to be primary sources of financial information. They do, however, report and comment on published survey results e.g. life offices' new business figures which are usually first published in the national press. There is no consistent date for the release of such figures nor is there one specific newspaper that can be guaranteed to publish full results. Some help can be gained from consulting either the financial pages of the London evening press or the *Financial Times* [QRL.49].

Life companies' press releases of new business figures must be treated with caution. The quality of statistical content varies considerably between companies and in many cases bears little relationship to actual reality (as set out by the following year's revised press release). Aggregate figures relating to life insurance offices are released by the IBA. *New Life Insurance Business* [QRL.68] and *New Life Insurance figures for the quarter* [QRL.69]. They also publish figures relating to new business in *Life Insurance in the United Kingdom* [QRL.60]. The figures in [QRL.60] are more accurate than either of [QRL.68] or [QRL.69] since the life offices have had more time to scrutinize any relevant information and provide revised figures to the IBA.

On the exceptional occasion that an original survey is commissioned by a newspaper it is likely to be of a one-off nature in response to a topical news item and thus soon outdated. For this reason no references are made to such occasional surveys in this volume.

The *Financial Times* [QRL.49] provides primary data on a continuing basis and is the source of most pricing information of life insurance unit linked funds and pension unit linked funds.

The *Financial Times* does not guarantee the comprehensiveness of its information. Companies have to pay for inclusion in its lists which can prove expensive; most companies require many entries. The FT does not guarantee the accuracy of any entries, since many are received close to its publishing deadlines, over the phone.

7.2 Periodicals

In the months between the publications of the Government's Green Paper on the Reform of Social Security and the date of writing several new magazines devoted to the subject of pensions have been introduced. It is likely that there will be many more in the future. It is for this reason that no attempt has been made in this volume to list all relevant financial magazines. The Science Referance Library is, however, in the process of completing such a project to provide a listing of magazines of financial interest.

Many magazines serve the field of personal finance. They vary in periodicity and in market objectives; some are aimed at the public, some at professional intermediaries whilst others are aimed directly at those working in the life insurance industry and/or the pensions movement. Almost all regularly reproduce relevant statistics produced by Government and other sources and frequently initiate surveys of their own. Many of these surveys are repeated each year; editorial policy as to retaining outdated information changes frequently.

All subjects are covered by magazines (see 9.1.4), but primary information contained in magazines is normally more likely to relate to specific life insurance products, comparisons and descriptions of features, rates and/or projections for specimen ages and terms. Magazine articles also provide valuable background information. Magazines producing surveys are likely to feature that fact in their year-end index. Full reference to magazine surveys would require a review in itself. Space precludes all but general reference to say that magazines cover all topics. Chapter 9 suggests the introduction of a computer data base for such information.

Those specialist magazines likely to include survey information of a primary nature include *Which?* [QRL.111], *Planned Savings* [QRL.83], *Pensions* [QRL.79], *Money Management* [QRL.65], *Policy Market* [QRL.84], *Pensions Management* [QRL.80]. Many general magazines contain articles of a financial nature.

7.2.1 *Limitations of Magazine Surveys*

Magazines do not have control mechanisms to ensure that the life offices complete survey forms correctly. This is particularly pertinent for several reasons:

(i) Survey questionnaires are often of considerable length, between 3 and 5 pages is not unusual.

(ii) The form is often assigned for completion to a junior member of staff.

(iii) Many questions are concerned with policies which were sold say ten years ago and are no longer marketed. The life office may therefore not wish to spend time on them, especially if details are difficult to find and/or it knows that the results are likely to be bad.

Nor are any sanctions available for non-response, save publication of that fact, together with the survey results.

7.2.2 *Consultancy Service*

Many of the specialist magazines offer a "consultancy service". Some are prepared to reanalyse data in a suitable form if required. In particular [QRL.83] and [QRL.65] maintain data bases on the fund information they publish plus certain additional information. These data bases can be manipulated to produce performance statistics.

External researchers may find that the magazine surveys are highly accurate since they have established contact points within the financial institutions and are likely to attain a high response rate. The limitations implicit in the magazine surveys (7.2.1) apply as forcefully to the survey material returned to an external research worker.

7.3 Rate Guides

Many financial magazines contain rate tables for specimen policies. These provide a guide for financial advisers to the terms currently being offered on specific contracts. There are also, however, publications specialising in rate tables. *Rateguide* [QRL.88] is updated daily on Prestel or weekly in the format of a looseleaf handbook. *7 Day Update* [QRL.89] is also a weekly looseleaf handbook. *Savings Market* [QRL.96] is published quarterly. Its format differs from that of the previous two services. Its appearance is as a normal magazine but a tabular presentation is used throughout. The publication describes its purpose as "providing within one cover as many useful facts and figures about the different types of savings as possible."

7.3.1 *Ordinary Branch Life Assurance Handbook*

The *Ordinary Branch Life Assurance Handbook* [QRL.72] is published in the form of a loose-leaf directory which is regularly updated. The handbook is separated into three sections. The first is a directory of life offices. For each office it provides information relating to executive personnel, branch offices and life subsidiaries. It provides abbreviated financial statements, including the balance sheet, revenue account, new business figures, valuation and investment analysis. Also provided are outline descriptions of the types of policies written by the office. Where appropriate, rate tables are given for level and convertible term, low cost endowment, mortgage protection, family income benefit, whole life with and without profits, limited payment life, endowment with and without profits maturing at 60 and 65 years of age. The second section of the book provides comparative rate tables. A third section provides supplementary information which might prove relevant to a professional adviser e.g. expectation of life tables, specimen cash values, income tax allowances etc.

7.3.2 *Unit Linked Life Assurance Handbook*

United linked life assurance handbook [QRL.106] is a companion volume to [QRL.72] providing corresponding information relevant to unit linked products. In the section relating to individual companies information is provided about the funds to which products can be linked. Such information includes details of advisers, managers etc., frequency of valuations, management charges and a historic record of prices and bid/offer spread.

The section giving supplementary information provides a history and background to the unit linked market. It also describes in detail the various types of contracts which are available. It contains less additional information than [QRL.72] but does include height and weight charts, expectation of life and various compound interest tables.

A third section provides performance tables. These are updated every six months. They show the effect of a £10 per month investment in various funds and take no account of policy charges.

7.4 Directories

Directories and compendia contain abstracts of statistics which are relevant to the subjects of pension and life insurance. Only the most useful and/or well-known are mentioned. This section should be regarded as complementary to the detailed Quick Reference List section. It should also be noted that many of the references in this section, as well as containing more general information, are primary sources in their own right. Many of the volumes reviewed in (7.3) and (7.6) contain directory sections.

7.5 Pension Fund and Insurance Directories

7.5.1 *Pension Funds and their Advisers [QRL.12]*

The major reference containing information relating to individual funds has been the publication *Pension Funds and their Advisers* [QRL.12] which lists nearly all major funds and is widely recognised as being the authoritative directory for this sector. It lists virtually all UK companies or organisations with over 500 employees as well as all major firms of advisers and also contains information on the major North American and European pension funds and their advisers. The book gives in order of size the capital value of the pension funds as shown in their latest set of accounts available at publication date. In addition, for the six largest funds an estimate is made of the value at the end of March prior to publication. Where a group manages several funds for which total values only are given, this is noted. Funds with values below £10 million are omitted from the published list but are available on request.

The questionnaires sent to the various categories of advisers and the funds themselves differ slightly in detail. From 1986 [QRL.12] will contain an analysis of funds by geographical area and size and type of investments.

7.5.1.1 *The NAPF Yearbook* This contains similar information to that in *Pension Funds and their Advisers* [QRL.12]. However *NAPF* [B.59] is limited to the membership of the NAPF whereas [QRL.12] is not.

7.5.2 *Whitakers Almanack - The Year Book*

The *Almanack* [QRL.112] was first published in 1868. The cover refers to it as "the reference book (to) an amazing variety of subjects in one renowned annual volume – all the facts at your fingertips at home or at work". It contains much background information related to the topic of this book (e.g. the latest rates of National Insurance and cash benefits, the addresses of Government and public offices and names of senior staff and taxation details). It contains a directory of all insurance companies giving date of establishment, nature of business and address as well as details of new business and accounts for the principal companies.

7.5.3 *The Insurance Directory and Year Book (Post Magazine Almanack)*
This directory [QRL.56] was first published in 1842. Its title pages refer to it as containing statistics and facts of ordinary life, industrial life etc. but this does little to describe the wealth of information compressed into one volume.

Its directory of insurance companies contains details of capitalisation and senior management as well as head office and branch office addresses. It provides a list of allied companies with dates of establishment and alliance, as well as similar lists for amalgamated companies and also for wound-up companies. It also provides a complete listing with their purposes and addresses of insurance associations and institutes right down to, if that is the correct expression, actuarial dining clubs. For the premier associations it lists the names of members.

It contains sections with synopses of new business written by long term insurers and also synopses of their revenue accounts. The synopses of the revenue accounts break down income into: net premiums and considerations (regular/single), dividends, increase (decrease) in value of assets brought into account (realised/unrealised), and other income and expenditure into: claims paid and outstanding, commission and expenses, other outgoings including tax (but not on profits), increase (decrease) in fund over year, long term fund at year end, other departmental reserves at year end, yields on departmental funds (gross/net), percentage of commission and expenses to premium income.

7.5.4 *British Insurance Industry Statistical Review*
Professor R. Carter of Nottingham University and Arthur Godden have since 1982 produced an annual review of the British insurance industry. The sources that the compilers use are DTI returns, published accounts, and published HMSO and trade association statistics. (Where tables can easily be found in the primary source document no further reference for this publication will be found in the QRL). The statistical techniques they use are, to quote, "hard grind" which, rephrased more formally, can be stated as collation, basic and ratio analysis. Its pension content to date is limited to insured claims. *The British Insurance Industry* [QRL.4] is a unique source of up to date information on both individual companies and their aggregates in that it brings together information on the life and non-life insurance market. Tables and graphs are provided for rapid reference and easy comparison and the compilers provide comment and analysis throughout.

Premium income is the most common unit of measurement to gauge an insurance company's size. The first section ranks British insurance companies in order of their net retained premiums i.e. after reinsurance ceded and including the business written by their insurance subsidiaries.

The next section relevant to this review compares the new business figures provided by life offices in the form of press releases with their net premiums per the DTI returns. [QRL.4] uses the term revenue premiums to mean net premiums shown in the long term business revenue account, including consideration for the granting of an annuity and premiums recoverable from the Inland Revenue.

The table showing long term investments breaks them down into fixed interest (government, other and total), equities, mortgages and loans, land and property, deposits and cash. Percentage distributions are also shown.

7.5.5 *Crawfords Directory of City Connections*

The directory commenced in 1977 [B.8]. It contains details of the financial connections of several thousand UK listed, USM/OTC and unquoted companies, major miscellaneous organistations and most large pension funds in the UK.

The book is divided into ten parts. The first part gives an alphabetical list of listed companies and investment trusts, USM/OTC and unquoted companies, organisations and major pension funds with their advisers. Seven of the other parts are alphabetical listings of advisers in categories such as stockbroker, accountant etc. showing in each case which of the companies in part 1 have specified them as advisers. One part contains an investment research index. This shows the specialisations of most UK stockbroking firms with institutional research and advisory services. The final part contains a section detailing insurance companies with some of their known pension fund clients.

7.5.6 *Pension Fund Indicators*

This booklet [B.64] has primarily been produced for its stockbroker publisher's own pension fund clients. Its aim is to aquaint those involved in the pension fund industry with patterns of pension fund investment over the years and thus to provide a background to discussions of investment policy for particular funds.

Most of its statistics are drawn from Government sources and the NAPF *Annual Survey of Occupational Pension Schemes* [QRL.27] but they are presented in a clear manner with commentary. The booklet contains a short topical bibliography.

7.5.7 *Catalogue of Insurance Statistics*

The IBA (see 6.4) is in the process of producing a catalogue of insurance statistics [B.34]. It is being issued initially in a skeleton format and each section expanded and reissued as time allows.

7.5.8 *The British Insurance Business 1847-1970*

A survey of insurance records, sponsored by the BIA, was conducted during 1972-1975 [B.7]. The first part of the book includes chapters on life insurance and the financial framework of insurance. Both chapters include extensive bibliographies. The second part of the book sets out the results of the survey. The first and largest part of this section is devoted to the history and records of 300 British insurance companies. For each of these companies it describes the origin, scope and location of its archives.

7.5.9 *Permanent Health Insurance Review*

This *Review* [QRL.82] compares all PHI products and their individual features, as well as providing much background information. The main section (35 pages long) compares policy conditions by company. A further section (17 pages long) summarises the approaches taken by the various companies to each policy condition. Sections also deal with tax, reinsurance etc. The statistical section (18 pages for

1985/86 edition) provides tables comparing the companies premium rates for different deferrment periods, entry ages, expiry ages and female loadings.

7.5.10 *Financial Times Publications*

Self-employed Pensions [QRL.97], *Executive Pensions and Benefits* [QRL.41] and *Unit Linked Savings Plans* [QRL.107] all follow a similar format. They contain a comprehensive survey of relevant schemes, analyses are made of the plans in such a manner to put companies on a comparable basis where possible (See to 4.6.3).

7.6 Performance Measurement Services.

Section 4.6 describes briefly some of the various types of measurement sevices available, their background and some of their limitiations (see also 4.5). Performance tables of any description imply that a "winner" exists. This fact is taken advantage of by magazines who publish "league" tables (see 7.2). The winner of each league table may wish to gain advantage by acknowledging the fact in advertising material. The magazine producing the table thereby obtains free publicity. One group of magazines uses different methods (all acceptable on different rationales) to calculate its performance tables to achieve different winners –where possible. Performance tables should be viewed with caution and as well as looking at methodology the *raison d'etre* of any table should be investigated.

Those services marketed by the major firms of consultants are less open to abuse of this sort as each firm normally only markets one survey; the results are also not as publicly available. Some of these privately circulated services are described below.

7.6.1 *Investment Performance Monitoring Service (IPMS)*

The principal aim of the Investment Performance Monitoring Service (IPMS) run by Cubie Wood [QRL.59] is reporting on the performance of pension funds to the appropriate trustees. A general report with suitably non-attributed statistics is prepared as well as the individual reports which are of course confidential to the client concerned.

The service started in 1976 and has grown rapidly so that currently there are nearly 800 portfolios being measured. There are three principal areas of activity, the first being individual performance assessment for each fund, the second being a similar type of assessment but aimed at the investment managers themselves for their own internal purposes, and, finally, a survey of insurance company managed funds. Each of these services works on a quarterly reporting basis, although league tables are currently only produced annually.

The purpose of the insurance company managed fund survey is to display the current performance of each of the various funds; this is done in the form of time-weighted rates of return which are calculated from the offer prices quoted to Cubie Wood by the insurance companies. There are only a few companies who do not provide end of calendar quarter prices. In those cases notional offer prices are calculated by using the offer price quoted at the allocation date nearest to the calendar quarter end, with the assumption that each sector moves in line with their appropriate index. An IPMS standard fund has been constructed with a sector distribution which, for any period, is representative of the "average" United Kingdom private sector pension fund, with investment in each sector being in an index which is representative of that sector. Full details are contained in the report.

The funds have been grouped together according to their investment policies and comprise mixed funds with property, mixed funds without property, equity funds, international funds, property funds and fixed interest funds. The yearly and annualised returns are shown for each fund since its inclusion in the survey within this period. There are also tables giving the ranking performance of the yearly and annualised returns for the last five years. Those rankings do not take into account the varying construction of the different funds.

7.6.2 *Pension Fund Investment Performance*

The funds covered by CAPS range in size from £1 million to £100 million and all of the major institutions which manage pension fund assets are represented in the sample, broadly in proportion to their market impact. Not all funds measured by CAPS are included in their "sample" fund which is deemed to be unbiased and a suitable "fund" against which to measure the performance of actual funds.

The CAPS service employs the "time-weighted" rate of return. Full details of methodology and other associated services are contained in an explanatory booklet. Individual reports are prepared for participants and once a year a general report based on the sample fund is made available to participants and other interested parties *Pension Fund Investment Performance –General Report* [QRL.74]. Much background information is contained in this general report.

7.6.3 *The Martin Paterson Personal Pensions Survey*

The survey report [QRL.63] commences with a directory section detailing all contracts currently marketed as self-employed retirement annuities (3.5.4.2). A sample page of this directory section is contained as Appendix 3.1. It continues with a section which analyses the performance of unitised investment funds to which personal pension plans can be linked (see 3.5.4.2). The tables included in the survey divided into twelve investment categories and give the performance of the accumulation units of these funds by reference to the movement of the buying (offer) price. The report [QRL.63] contains technical details. It also contains sections on unit linked contract charges and allocation terms.

7.6.4 *Pension Fund Service*

[QRL.76] is at the time of writing this review the largest of the measurement services available, largest when measured both by number of funds and total assets measured. Funds are compared against the Wood Mackenzie Pension Fund Index which indicates the performance of the aggregate of pension funds participating in the service.

7.6.5 *Survey of Pooled Pension Funds*

The survey report [QRL.101] defines pooled pension funds as (a) exempt unit trusts, (b) property unit trusts and (c) insurance company managed pension funds. The aim of the survey is to provide full details of the investment performance of all the available pooled pension funds in the UK on a quarterly and up to date basis. A profile plus background information and operating details is provided for each fund. This information is updated annually unless an interim significant change occurs. Section 4.4.2 details typical information contained in this section. Introductory sections to the report contain full explanations of the technical aspects of investment performance analysis in general and as applied specifically in the survey. The performance tables are based on time-weighted rates of return and show the returns achieved over periods of three months to ten years. Funds are divided into ten categories dependent on their investment policy.

7.7 Abstracting Services

Most abstracting services and registers are heavily biased towards the USA, industry or both.

7.7.1 *Government Guides*

The GSS produce two guides [B.44] and [B.47]. [B.44] is free and contains brief details such as frequency and cost about all major goverment publications. It also lists departmental responsibilities and initial contact points. [B.47] contains far more detail including information about *ad hoc* reports and articles.

7.7.2 *Insurance Research Register*

The Insurance Research Register was set up and funded by the IBA at the Centre for Research in Insurance and Investment at the City University to be a computerised database of all academic work either completed or in progress since 1976 in the UK in insurance and related fields. The Register will hold abstracts that can be recalled by the use of key words. Amongst other things the database will be able to give information concerning authors, titles, keywords, etc., which can assist a potential researcher in obtaining information. At the date of writing this review The Register is not operational but it is eventually intended for it to be available, by some means, to all interested researchers in this particular field.

7.7.3 *Marketing Surveys Index*

Is updated monthly in loose-leaf format [B.56]. It is a register of market research and also covers some brokers' reports. At present it is not comprehensive in the areas pertinent to this review.

7.7.4 *International Directory of Published Market Research*
This is currently in its ninth edition (1985) [B.53]. Its first edition was in 1976. Out of over 10,000 entries emanating from nearly 400 market research agencies less than ten refer to UK sources relevant to this review.

7.7.5 *Warwick Statistics Service*
Warwick Statistics Service, although part of Warwick University is run as a commercial information service. Warwick has one of the largest collections of international statistical and marketing data in the UK. In particular it covers all UK Government publications. At present coverage of pensions and life insurance sources is not great, but this is being kept under review. Regular one-day seminars are held on sources of information for business.

7.8 Database Systems

The number of data bases relevent to the study of the social sciences is increasing rapidly. Few at present contain much information directly relevant to the field of life and pensions. (Relevant data bases have been mentioned in context in this review). This is likely to change in the near future as more pensions information becomes available in companies' reports and accounts. Information on which databases are available can be obtained from Warwick Statistics Service.

CHAPTER 8

ACADEMIC AND OTHER MISCELLANEOUS RESEARCH

8.0 Introduction

There is no central register of academic research. Even within a specific university there is not normally a specified individual one can contact to discover what research is currently being or has been undertaken. It is therefore very much a matter of knowing exactly whom in an institution is likely to be supervising a specific line of research if one wishes to obtain details. General letters often tend to go unanswered. This chapter contains a selection of academic research, but cannot claim to be comprehensive.

The Centre for Research in Insurance and Investment at The City University is setting up a register (see also chapter 7) one aim of which is to provide an up-to-date source of recent research relevant to life and general insurance. It may later be expanded to cover allied fields such as investments, and privately administered pension schemes. A base year of 1977 has been set for the register. It is hoped that it will cover all relevant academic research as well as that of other bodies. It is also hoped that the register will be operational by the end of 1986. Another database which is in the process of being set up and which will permit easier gathering of academic research is that of 'British Expertise in Science and Technology'. Each UK academic is to be contacted to supply details of the areas of his expertise and research. These entries will then be comprehensively key-worded and regularly updated.

8.1 Employee Participation in the Management of Pension Schemes

The Centre for Research in Industrial Democracy and Participation at Glasgow University was awarded a grant by the Leverhulme Trust to investigate employee participation in the management of pension funds [QRL.10]. The investigation under the direction of Professor Laurie Hunter was conducted by Jeff Hyman and Tom Schuller (both of whom have now left Glasgow University).

The research originated from two broad trends. First, the growing concern with the prospects for participation, direct or indirect, in decisions which affect the working lives of employees which has been reflected in the steady growth of voluntary arrangements for participation both in relation to work procedures and also in broader areas such as the management of pension funds.

Secondly, the growing awareness of the significance of the behaviour of large institutional investors in relation to the economy and, in the case of pension funds, to the well-being both of employees and of the funds' beneficiaries. The administration of these funds, and their accountability, is clearly a matter of interest and significance.

The following objectives for the research were identified:

(i) a comparison of the ways in which employee participation is implemented in different pension funds.

(ii) an assessment of the efectiveness of this participation in terms of increasing employee involvement in the affairs of the enterprise.

(iii) determination of the ways in which participation in pension fund management influences the administration and performance of the fund, including its accountablity to members and to the public.

(iv) identification of the factors which determine the effectiveness of participation as outlined above.

In order to achieve these objectives a two-stage approach was adopted. The first stage consisted of a postal survey of about 500 funds, chosen on a random basis, to build up a broad picture of the origins and patterns of pension fund participation and the ways in which schemes operate. The survey questionnaires were sent to fund managers, or to their equivalent. Completed questionnaires returned to the Centre were treated in absolute confidence and following transfer of the data onto computer cards, the questionnaires were destroyed.

The second stage comprised a more detailed investigation of 120 funds, to include large and small funds based on asset size, funds from the public and private sectors, and in-house and outside managed funds. This stage was based on interviews with employee trustees, other members of trustee boards or equivalent bodies, fund managers and investment advisers. As is normal in such cases, all information received was treated in confidence and no names of participating organisations or individuals were to be disclosed without the express permission of those involved. The relevant questionnaires extend to 47 pages and are available on application to Mr. Schuller.

Attention was paid to the following issues:

(i) the *criteria* according to which the fund is managed–and in particular whether the introduction of employee representatives has lead to any changes in these criteria;

(ii) the *performance* of the funds in terms either of the rate of return on investments or of such other criteria as may be established;

(iii) the *accountability* of the fund, with particular reference to the quality and availability of information;

(iv) *administrative practices,* particularly in relation to discretionary benefits.

As to the factors which determine the effectiveness of participation, the following potential influences were envisaged; the interpretation of trustee obligations; the quality of information made available to trustees; the training they receive; and the management structure of the funds. One strand of the research was to identify the major determinants of effective participation as revealed by the study and to evaluate their relative importance.

The *Summary Report* [QRL.10] is 64 pages, little of which is tabular. A more factual analysis of the survey results is available from the authors direct. A book is expected to be published in late 1985.

The report contains a section on its research approach and explains some of the limitations imposed by practicalities. One of these limitations is that the survey of employee representatives was distributed solely to union members; the questions dealing with trustees ignored the constraint that they operate within the confines of the trust deed. The section dealing with employee involvement in investment decisions ignored the common situation where the employer underwrites the performance of the fund and there may therefore be less justification for involvement.

8.2 Paying for Equalisation - a survey of pension age preferences and their costs

The House of Commons Social Services Committee published a report in October 1982 [B.76] which recommended equalisation at a notional, retirement age of 63, with the possibility of retiring on an actuarily reduced pension from age 60, or of continuing to work until age 65 and earning an increased pension [QRL.15] (see 2.1.2.3). The Equal Opportunities Commission was concerned that any proposals should take into account the views of the men and women who would be affected by any change. In 1981, the Commission decided to sponsor its own study, and contracted Social and Community Planning Research to carry it out. Social and Community Planning Research (SCPR) is a charitable trust which undertakes research in the social, political and economic sciences. The Commission's study focussed on the possibility that individuals might be willing to pay more, say, in national insurance contributions, in order to equalise the pension age–a possibility which would have a substantial impact on the cost, and hence feasibility, of any proposals for change. Additional information was collected about attitudes towards flexible pension ages and gradual retirement.

Methodologically the study was not straightforward. Firstly, the research required detailed cost estimates to be available of equalising the pension age at different ages. The Department of Health and Social Security provided the Commission with cost estimates which had been prepared for the Select Committee.

Secondly, a way had to be found of translating global costs into costs which individuals, according to their circumstances, might have to bear. Thirdly there was the problem of introducing quite complex cost information to individuals during the course of the survey interview. And fourthly, some means had to be devised whereby individuals could trade-off their pension age preferences against the consequent personal costs. The ways in which these and other methodological problems were tackled are set out fully in the report.

The study was carried out by personal interview among a sample of people aged between 25 and the State retirement age excluding the wholly retired. A response rate of 75% was achieved, providing 4,415 completed interviews for analysis.

To provide some background to views on pension ages, the report documents the financial provision people had made, or anticipated, for their retirement. It considered whether individuals were or were not members of occupational schemes and the relationship with age/sex and income level. Other financial provision whether already made or anticipated was also examined. It is these objective areas which are referenced in the QRL. The detailed responses on attitudes are given only a global reference.

One of the main difficulties faced by the research was the complexity of the subject matter under question. In order to make response choices realistic it was necessary to impart a considerable amount of information to the respondents. This had to be in a form which could be easily understood and could be used in the context of a structured survey. After extensive piloting, a form of sequential questioning was adopted such that the more detailed implications of equalisation were gradually introduced and the consequences of specific options tentatively presented. All details including the questionnaire are included in the survey report.

8.3 An investigation of unquoted holdings of UK Financial Institutions

There has been considerable interest in unquoted investment and in venture capital [QRL.1]. Financial institutions have increased their activities in this area, and much discussion has taken place concerning the desirability of making finance more readily available to small unquoted business. It is to meet this need that a study has been undertaken, sponsored amongst others by the NAPF and the Stock Exchange.

The study was conducted during 1983/84 by Mr Donald Adamson and had as its objectives:

(i) to establish the current position in terms of funds, of a comprehensive range of UK financial institutions, committed to unqoted investment;

(ii) to attempt a proper classification of unqoted holding according to their geographical, industrial and financial characteristics;

(iii) to attempt an assessment of the results achieved so far (bearing in mind the long term nature of the business);

(iv) to examine the principal differences between the UK and the US in this field.

The study has taken the form of a survey followed by interviews. The report sets out the limitations of the survey and comments in detail upon results.

8.4 A survey of Public Sector and Non-Corporate Pension Funds 1980

This Survey [QRL.103] is designed to cover top tier local authority pension schemes as well as those of nationalised industries and other public sector organisations *not* included in central government schemes, universities, trade unions and charities. The survey covers aspects of investment methods, advisers and policy, performance measurement and attitudes to outside management. It also covers basic statistical materials such as numbers of employees, size of fund movements (net flow of funds is defined as contributions plus dividends, interest and other income, less pensions and other benefits) and cost of administration. There is a technical appendix giving methodology. All the results are broken down by fund types, namely:- State corporation, other public corporations, universities, unions, local authorities, metropolitan county, non-metropolitan county, London borough, Scottish region and Welsh county. All participating funds are named in the technical appendix as is a copy of the questionnaire. Some of the results are updated in [QRL.75].

8.5 Pension Fund Management 1984

The survey was designed to explore current pension fund investment and administration policies and methods, changes in investment method and management, criteria for choice of manager and services required, and attitudes to possible future developments in pensions [QRL.75].

There are 1,074 schemes covered in the survey. Interviews were conducted with the senior company executive responsible for recommendations on method of pension fund management, normally the financial director. The published survey results contain a technical appendix on methodology. All tables are accompanied by commentary.

One of the sections of the report concerns staff and fees. It reports on the number of *people involved* in company pensions administration in-house. These figures should be used with caution as no indication is given as the whether they are employed by the sponsoring employer or the trust fund itself. The former is the more normal. (see 4.6).

8.6 Life Insurance and Asset Holding in the United Kingdom

[QRL.18] was the result of a survey undertaken as part of an ESRC financed programme in Quantitive Economics at the London School of Economics.

Many statistics on wealth are derived from the value of people's estates. These figures include a value to life insurance policies of the sum assured plus relevant bonuses etc. which is payable in full on death. If the individual had been alive only the surrender value would have been relevant. The authors of [QRL.18] are suggesting methods to overcome this problem. Using previously unpublished data made available by the Inland Revenue the authors of [QRL.18] have calculated the percentage of wealth, for various ages and estate range, accounted for by life policies.

8.7 Land Ownership by Public and Semi-Public Institutions in the UK

Land ownership by public and semi-public institutions in the UK [QRL.9] by Alan Harrison, R.B. Tranter and R.S. Gibbs was published by the Centre for Agricultural Strategy of Reading University in 1977. It sets out the results, methodology and background of the survey detailed in the title of the report. The survey was conducted by post. One of the categories in the survey was Financial Institutions; this covered three main groups: insurance companies, occupational pension funds and property unit trusts. Most of the final results have not been broken down into the three sub-groups.

8.8 Financial Institutions, their Investments and Agricultural Landownership

Financial Institutions, their Investments and Agricultural Landownership [QRL.19] contains the results of a survey conducted by Anthony Steel when he was a third year student at the Department of Land Management and Development of Reading University. The paper contains detailed information about the survey, including the questionnaire and methodology and comments on the results. The main criticism of the survey is that it asked for investment splits as percentages instead of by absolute amounts. This means that an institution with £100 million of assets is given the same weight as an institution with only £10 million of assets. Countering this criticism is the fact that because the questions were so simple there was a very high response rate. Mr. Steel periodically updates the survey results.

8.9 Agricultural Performance Analysis

Savills and Tyms have collaborated to present an analysis of the growth of institutional investment in farmland and of its performance in terms of rental growth, capital growth, total return and yield. The analysis is currently devoted solely to the area of let land held by the institutions. The method adopted and its value for performance analysis is discussed briefly in the main report [QRL.95]. A description of the methodology and data collection procedures is available in a separate report. For each property the date of purchase, its purchase price, subsequent spending on improvements and annual rent and valuation figures are all recorded, as well as the size of the property, its location, land grade and tenure. This allows an analysis of the investment performance of sectors of the market in terms of their rental growth, capital growth, total return and yield. There has been no subdivision of the results into the constituent bodies of the financial institutions sector, i.e. pension funds, life offices and property unit trusts.

8.10 Inventing Retirement

Professor Leslie Hannah of the London School of Economics and Political Science is conducting research into the history of pension funds, and is shortly to publish a book called Inventing Retirement. [QRL.8]. It contains estimates of the coverage of pension schemes pre 1936 as well as discussing the importance of pension schemes in relation to surveys.

8.11 Equal Treatment in Occupational Pension Schemes

The objectives of this study [QRL.11] were:-

to investigate disparities in the provision of benefits for the men and women members of occupational pension schemes;

to examine rules relating to access to schemes which disadvantage particular groups of employees –specifically part-time workers;

to explore the use made of 'discretion' as excerised by trustees and managers;

to obtain information regerding provisions for and practice regarding pension cover during leave for maternity and child care;
to ascertain pensions managers' views, priorities for improvement, and attitudes towards equalisation of benefits;
to establish the views and involvement of Trade Unions in this area.

The report [QRL.11] sets out in full the methodology used and comments in great detail upon the results. Much of the analysis is qualitative rather than quantative and therefore the entries in the QRL do not give a true indication of the content of this work.

8.12 APEX Pensions Survey 1985

The main objective of this survey was to provide comparators between a number of selected company pension schemes which would then be used in negotiations for the improvement of pension benefits on behalf of the Union's members [QRL.28]. In addition, an overall analysis of current practice was to be made of the company schemes selected. Secondary aims were to assess the amount of money involved in the schemes covered. The survey report is unusual in that it specifies which companies do what. The information collected has been retained to provide a database to allow the APEX Research Department to respond to requests for information. The Survey was conducted in conjunction with the Department of Humanities and Social Science, University of Bath. The Report contains important notes on the limitations of the survey and its methodology. Most results are given without comment but they have been used by APEX to revise their guidelines and these are available as a seperate document.

8.13 Research commissioned by Life Offices

Surveys commissioned by Life Offices are done either with marketing in mind or as a public relations exercise and a support to the sales force. This does not detract from either the value of the quality of the statistics produced. Space precludes a comprehensive library of life insurance companies' surveys but in any case most life offices' surveys are occasional and of ephemeral interest; apart from selected details the results of such surveys are normally of a private and confidential nature but may be made available to genuine researchers. The *Insurance Directory* [QRL.56] will provide a list of Life Offices' head office addresses; their marketing directors and/or librarians may supply current research findings.

Amongst recent surveys was one on attitudes to pension schemes commissioned from Gallup by the Legal and General Assurance Society Ltd. It was the forerunner of the DHSS survey ([QRL.42] and [QRL.43]). Most of the information obtained was incorporated in the later survey and so no reference to the Legal and General survey will appear in the QRL. Another of their surveys commissioned from Gallup on self-employed pensions was presented in a glossy marketing brochure free on application to Legal and General [QRL.98]. Presenting survey results in such formats appears to be a new trend from many life offices. Legal and General conduct many surveys and maintain a very comprehensive library of statistics and other information on a wide range of topics relevant to a large financial organisation.

An example of a survey conducted by a different life office was one by Sun Life to ascertain the public's attitude towards life insurance and life insurance salesmen. Fieldwork was carried out between 21-25 July 1983 in 165 sampling points. A total of 1,880 respondants were interviewed. A quota sample designed to be representative of all adults aged 15+ in Great Britain. Details of the sampling fieldwork and weighting used are shown in a technical appendix to the report [QRL.86]. The report comments on the results and is split into three sections: existing life insurance, life insurance sales techniques and attitudes to life insurance company representatives. The survey was then updated in May 1984 [QRL.87].

The main feature of this later survey was to ascertain the public's attitudes towards life assurance following the removal of tax relief on new policies in the 1984 Budget. Fieldwork was carried out between 24-29 May 1984 in 167 sampling points. A total of 2,000 respondents were interviewed face to face in their own homes. The sample used was a quota sample designed to be representative of all adults aged 15 and over in Great Britain. Results were broken down by age, sex and social class. Due to considerations of space, the QRL will contain only these entries mentioned above.

8.13.1

A research index of work being conducted within life offices is maintained by the Institute of Actuaries. There are currently nearly 80 projects on the list: none involve primary sources of data but many make use of statistical models. Surveys such as those described in 8.13 would not appear in the index.

CHAPTER 9

DESIRABLE IMPROVEMENTS

This chapter gives a brief description of some development both in sources of statistics and in their presentation, which would improve the current availability of information about life offices and pension funds.

9.1 General Problems

9.1.1 *Communications*

One of the problems which is common to emerging movements and industries is that of communication and in particular the use of jargon.

The Pensions Research Accountants Group (section 6.8) recently determined,

(i) to provide an explanation of terms commonly used by one or more sectors of those professionally concerned with occupational pension schemes, for the assistance of all who have to deal with such schemes during the course of their work or studies; and

(ii) to encourage those concerned to communicate more effectively by the use of a common vocabulary.

A first edition of the resultant glossary [B.43] was published in 1980, in 1984 a revised edition [B.66] was published, jointly with the Pensions Management Institute (see 5.10). The widespread adoption of the glossary in its entirety should lead to improved clarity and understanding in the pensions movement.

Many of the statistics in the life insurance field purporting to measure similar items for different companies or even the same item for the same company for different enquiring organisations prove not to be comparable. The reason for this is that different definitions are given to the same item by different people, e.g. does the term "new business" include reinsurance ceded? What is the difference between a "lapse" and a "surrender"? What is meant by a term such as "underwriter"?

9.1.1.1 *Superannuation versus Pension* The PMI/PRAG glossary [B.66] takes meanings of pension and superannuation as being generally understood and therefore defines neither. The Chambers 20th Century Dictionary defines superannuation as "the act or state of superannuating ; A Pension : a regular contribution paid by an employee towards a pension. (L super, above; *annus* year)".

The similarity of meaning between the terms pension and superannuation is acknowledged in Government sources by a reference in each appropriate index instructing readers who look up superannuation to refer also to pensions and *vice versa*. Academic, popular and commercial contexts nearly always use the term "pensions". Government sources however, prefer on many occasions to use the term superannuation. It is difficult to determine a consistent difference in the use of the terms in these Government sources. Greater clarity would be achieved if the term superannuation was allowed to fall into disuse.

9.1.2 *Compatability of Data*

Much of the data collected in the life insurance field is incompatible in matters of "trivial" detail, e.g. some offices when recording details of female lives merely record tham as males with ages reduced by an appropriate number of years (a device used for premium fixing purposes) whilst others use the true age and classify them as females. It should not be difficult to code them so that they can be used for statistical purposes. Some offices record age at death as age nearest birthday, others as age next or last birthday. Again, it should not be too difficult to reach an agreement - on a consistent definition for age at death, thus making it easier for uniformly based statistics to be supplied to, for example, the "Continuous Mortality Investigation" (section 6.5.2).

Another example is contained in the information published annually in *Life Insurance in the United Kingdom* [QRL.60] which is not consistent with the official statistics collected for the transactions of the life funds in financial assets in MQ5 [QRL.32]. The information provided by the ABI, for instance, about the size of life insurance funds includes overseas business, whilst the information provided for MQ5 [QRL.32] purports to exclude overseas business.

It would be desirable if an industry-wide working party could be established to recommend standards for consistency of data. Most companies now have computers for a major part of their data processing and routine administration. If a "standard" were available, it could easily be written into the soft-ware for data assembly from basic policy records.

9.1.3 *Timing*

Nearly all published information would be far more useful if it were published more rapidly after the end of the period to which it relates.

9.1.3.1 *Government Voluntary Surveys.* Many of the large performance measurers have their clients' information passed to them via computer as an event happens e.g. when details of an investment transaction are entered from a contract note to a company's own administration systems the information is simultaneously passed to the performance measurers.

The largest of the performance measurers now claims it has information regarding over half of all pension funds assets. A great deal of this information must be obtained automatically and thus speedily. The information obtained for the DTI voluntary surveys is neither as accurate nor speedy as could be desired. Could they not link up with the commercial measurers so that one of the services the measurers provide is the results to the DTI's enquiries. From an industrial company's point of view it must be cheaper to ask the measurer to provide an additional computer output than to compile it manually (The initial programming charge should not be onerous as it will be spread over so many companies or could even be funded by Government since it would so improve the reliability of its surveys it would presumably cut the compliance and accuracy costs).

9.1.4 *Bibliographical Control of Sources*

Before a source can be used, the potential user must be aware of its existence. The traditional means of finding out sources of information is via bibliographies and indexing and abstracting services. Whereas elaborate services exist for American sources (some of which claim to cover Europe but mention only one or two UK sources) no comparable publications exist in the UK in the field of pensions and life insurance. Chapter 8 covers relevant directories. Particular mention must be made of the *Catalogue of Insurance Statistics* [B.34] currently being compiled by the ABI. Whilst [B.34] will provide extremely useful it will not completely fill the gap. What is required is an interactive computerised abstracting service covering all non-official sources such as trade journals and stockbroking reports. A restricted system has recently been set up by the City University Centre for Research into Insurance and Investment and it is hoped to expand it to meet the above requirement.

9.1.5 *Confidentiality*

Insured pension schemes represent only a small proportion of the total as regards assets. The reverse is the case when one considers performance and other related statistics available to the general public. Many organisations provide performance measurement services for self-administered funds. In general companies are numbered so that the company receiving the information (knowing its own number only) can see how it has performed relative to other companies, but not who they are. This "confidentiality" of the results means that performance information is not available to the membership of a scheme (unless it has a very enlightened set of trustees). Even with the new disclosure regulations such information will not be made available. No apparent reasons exist why members of self-administered schemes should be less well- informed than members of insured schemes, especially now when all members will have the right to "opt out" of their occupational scheme and make their own provision for a personal pension.

9.1.7 *Life Insurance and Pensions Statistics "User Group"*

The Statistics Users Council was set up in 1960. There is a note in the *Journal of the Royal Statistical Society* detailing its history to date [B.5]. Amongst the main aims of the council is a desire to improve the availability and quality of statistics in general as well as the accessibility to official statistics. The council has stated its intention to form sector groups in order to bring together users with a common interest on a particular field of statistical activity. It is to be hoped that such a sector group is formed in the fields of life insurance and pensions statistics.

9.2 Segregation of Data

Life insurance and pensions business is in many cases written within the same operating company. As a result the funds are merged and cannot easily be separated for statistical purposes. Pensions business has become increasingly important for life offices in recent years, and separate figures are desirable for the income and expenditure and the total assets held in respect of pensions business. This would make it possible to obtain estimates of total savings through pension schemes. No reliable figures are at present available. Unfortunately it is difficult and costly for life offices to provide this information.

Life funds must account separately for their pensions business for tax purposes. This is done on a purely notional basis e.g., it may be to a company's advantage to inflate the magnitude of its pension business to as great an extent as is permissable to the relevant authorities and is therefore statistically invalid. In practice, therefore, it is unlikely that reliable separate figures will be available until legislation is introduced to enforce the separation of the assets of pensions and life insurance business.

9.3 Underwriting Statistics

9.3.1 *Mortality Investigations - Sex*

There are currently before the Commission of the European Communities, proposals concerning the principle of equal treatment for men and women in occupational pension schemes. [B.71]

Article 6 of the proposed directive states that it would be contrary to the principle of equal treatment to provide for benefits which differ as between the sexes in levels or amounts or to set contributions at different levels for the same level of benefits, "by taking into account different factors of calculation, actuarial or otherwise, with regard to the phenomena of ill health, mortality or life expectancy." At the date of writing this review, it is still not clear whether or not the Directive would stop continued investigation of mortality rates for the two sexes separately.

A mortality investigation conducted regardless of sex is, arguably , not just useless but also dangerous. The observed mortality rates would depend on the proportions of each sex at each age, and there is no reason in general to suppose that these would be either smooth or uniform. Nor would they be the same from time to time. Thus a comparison between one year and another, or between different populations, would be invalidated by varitations in the proportions of the sexes in the two investigations being compared. A change in mortality rates over time might be genuine or might be because of a change in the proportions of each sex in the sample being investigated. One can never tell whether a mortality table that had been constructed from an investgation that ignored sex would be appropriate to another population in which the proportions of the sexes might differ. It is therefore essential that mortality investigations continue to be carried out paying regard to the sex of those investigated (as indeed of any other important differential medical improvement–since risk assesment is essentially a discrimination process).

There is a danger that, if benefits are to be equal for both sexes, (as is being proposed in the UK for personal pensions) it may seem unecessary to record the sex of the member of a pension scheme (or life insured as appropriate). It must be made clear that the recording of sex is essential, both for a correct assesment of the cost of the benefits, and for a correct investigation of the experience of the scheme. This applies whether one is considering a life policy or a pension scheme that is self-administered or insured with a life office. Even if compelled to over equal contributing and benefit conditions for the two sexes it is prudent for scheme operators to know the amount of cross-subsidy between the sexes.

9.3.2 *Mortality Investigations - Options*

Seminars on the subject of life underwriting data often commence with the statement that there is sparse data available on this subject in the UK compared with that available in the USA This is particulary true of the data on non-smokers discounts and many of the options now being attached to policies either to aid "product differentiation" or because the design of many modern insurance contracts is said to be aimed at the "sophisticated investor". Such contracts tend to have many options attached. Some of these options have a long tradition in the UK, such as waiver of premium option, others such as, a capital disability option, have only been introduced into the UK market recently, although they have for a long time been popular in Australia. No attempt has been made for the purposes of major mortality investigations, to segregate policies to which such options attach from those to which they do not. Such data collection should commence immediately if it is not to be too late to be of value. For example, it may already prove to be too late to collect the data on sex differentiated policies which would be necessary to convince the EEC of the virtue of separate statistics.

9.3.2.1 *Mortality Experience of Pension Funds.* Few actuarial reports of pension funds explicitly state which mortality rates have been used, how that basis compares with the mortality experience of current pensioners and what provisions have been made for future mortality improvement. This is not surprising as the trustees to whom such reports are addressed are entitled to rely on the actuary's judement regarding these matters. It does not mean, however, that no attempt can be made to answer the question often asked (in particular in relation to the social security contracting-out reduction). "What mortality basis is customarily used by the actuaries of accupational pension schemes?" This lack of information can easily be remedied. The NAPF could perhaps include in its Code of Practice [B.35] or the Institute of Actuaries could issue a directive to its members, that actuarial reports should contain a section with such information. Alternatively, the Government Actuary (section 4.7.1) or the NAPF (section 5.1) could include appropriate direct questions in their future surveys.

9.4 Investment

9.4.1 *Financial Media*

The lifting of exchange control regulations in the UK in 1979 has led, naturally, to an expansion of the proportions of the assets of life insurance and pension funds invested overseas.

Contemporaneously, the dollar has strengthened against the pound. Many investment managers, wishing to retain American shares, wish at the same to take a profit in the premium dollar. Consequently 1984 was the first year that currency hedging and trading featured significantly in the investment operations of life insurance companies. There is likely to be an accounting problem on how to report the currency trading and hedging in the statistical returns.

This accounting type problem is likely to recur each time a financial medium emerges. It last exhibited itself with the need to separate index- linked securities from fixed interest. Then the time lag in Government statistics between introduction and separation was four years. The problem is next likely to occur as a result of the growing importance of financial futures.

9.4.2 *Accountancy Standards*

There is a great need for clear and consistent definitions of terms, e.g. there is considerable ambiguity in the use of terms such as management expenses and investment income, (9.1.1) and with how such items are spread across a company and are treated in various returns.

The development of accountancy standards can only serve to improve statistical returns. In addition the harmony of accounts and statistics will help to increase the credibility of both.

9.4.2.1 *Dual Capacity* A fundamental reform of the methods of book-keeping and accounting for investments is required when the Stock Exchange introduces "dual capacity" in order to allow a more consistent measurement of investment performance as between one portfolio and another. Under "dual capacity" brokers will have the option of charging an overt fee combined with prices close to "best" or a smaller (or even no fee) with prices which are at some distance from the market. Any such reform of book-keeping should also permit other "free" services to be monitored, (see 4.7).

9.5 Department of Trade and Industry Returns

The Department of Trade and Industry Returns (when instituted) were intended to provide enough detail for an independent actuary to carry out a valuation on an alternative basis. This ideal has not been realised. There are offices whose data is presented rigorously and adequately. For the majority, however, there is evidence of loose classifications, inadequate segregation of the different classes and vague definitions combined sometimes with errors and inconsistencies.

The following statistical shortcomings of the DTI returns are particularly in need of attention from the relevant authorities.

1. *Treatment of realised and unrealised gains/losses* There is inconsistency between offices as to how they treat realised and unrealised gains and losses on their assets. It is the DTI's intention that where such gains and losses are used to alter the value of the fund they should be shown in the appropriate named boxes of Form 40. Many offices, however, put all realised and unrealised gains or losses in an investment reserve and then transfer amounts from this reserve, as required, to the revenue account. This difference in treatment can be highly confusing to the uninitiated, in particular becausc they will find no item labeled "investment reserve" in Form 14.
2. *Separation of life annuity accounts* The summary of changes in business (Form 43), analysis of new business (Form 41) and details of business in force (Forms 55 and 56) segregate business between life assurances, general annuities, pension business, permanent health and capital redemption business. But, the revenue account details are only partially segregated into these five categories. Therefore, one cannot build up separate revenue accounts for the different categories of contract.
3. *Separation between UK and overseas contracts* The same problem arises here as under 2., *viz.* the revenue account details are only partially separated. Even where this separation is given in the revenue account, it is only shown in terms of total premiums receivable, total expenses and total claims payable.
4. *Separation of group and executive pension business* Companies are required to separate group from other business. There is a difficulty of definition of group. An enthusiastic salesman may sell a scheme for 10 lives hoping to see it increase to 100 whereas in fact it may in subsequent years fall to 2, but still remain classified as group by the insuring company. One company may consider 3 lives a group and another 33. A consistent definition should be introduced based on number of lives in a scheme rather than each company determining its own size definition dependent on under-writing policy. A more sensible destinction than "group" and "other" would, in fact, be occupational pension scheme business and other. This would enable S 226 (self-employed) business to be separated from occupational business in the returns. At present in many returns S 226 and executive pension business cannot easily be separated (if at all). This is most important when estimating e.g. pensions in payment.
5. *Details of group business* Details regarding group pension business are not shown in the summary of changes in business (Form 43). The new business details (Form 44) for group pension business only relate to new schemes and give no details of increments under existing schemes.
6. *Segregated Funds* Funds "managed" by insurance companies may or may not appear in the DTI returns according to who retains ultimate control over investment decisions, even though for all practical purposes these decisions are taken by the investment managers of the insurance companies. In any statistics on market share insurance companies are likely to include the assets of these segregated funds, (see 4.5.1). The companies sponsoring an occupational pension fund which uses this form of investment is also likely to

consider such funds as part of its own assets when completing any statistical returns. [QRL.27] requests fund managers to exclude insurance company managed fund units, but [QRL.70] gives no such guidance, although attempts have been made to isolate them. It is difficult to estimate the extent of double counting of specific occupational pension funds when determining the size of the pensions movement. The DTI returns should require companies to set out details of segregated funds under their management in as much detail as is required for managed funds.

7. *Comparability of Data* Despite the introduction of new forms to facilitate the computerization of the returns (4.2.2), it is extremely difficult to compare data between offices. Further guidelines should be tabled which would enable aggregate data to be more easily produced.
8. *Persistency of business* In Australia detailed returns relating to persistency are required from life offices regarding lapse rates. In the UK some returns relating to persistency are only required from Friendly Societies. If similar returns to those in Australia were required in the UK, it would be easier to judge the quality of the sales force.

9.6 Marketing Information

9.6.1 *General*

There is little statistical information of a "marketing nature" available. Some journals intended for the public are helpful, but are mainly concerned with performance information (i.e., size of maturity values) and very rarely give information concerning bonuses or sizes of funds. Companies collect data specifically for a given exercise and apart from the selected results which the company chooses to publish, the remaining results are not generally available. In addition, there is no standardised way of reporting figures. Thus, if several companies are contacted for information on surrender values, the inquirer may find they are presented in such a variety of ways that he cannot collate them, (see section 9.1.1). In America there is a free publication called the *Life Insurance Fact Book* [B.55]. It is a principal source of statistics about the life insurance business. The *Fact Book* data are derived from annual statements provided by life insurance companies, and through surveys conducted by the American Council of Life Insurance who publish it. It goes into far more detail than its UK equivalent by the ABI [QRL.60] and a similar publication in this country should be welcomed by research workers. The *Fact Book* [B.55] contains over 100 pages of useful tables and includes such information as:

(a) average amounts of life insurance in force per family/per insured family;
(b) average size of policy purchased each year; and
(c) distribution of policies by age, sex, size, income of insured, type and premium mode.

9.6.2 *Premiums*

Greater clarification is required concerning the nature of non-pension life insurance premium payments, e.g. whether they include or exclude reinsurance premiums.

Anyone who has worked in a position which requires the comparison of life insurance new business figures would be able to say how difficult it is to make comparisons, not only between companies, but also for the same company over a period of years because of the arbitrary inclusion and exclusion of single premiums and/or pension business to suit the purposes of the marketing department, (see also 9.1.1 and 9.4.2).

9.6.3 *Persistency*
There is also a need for industry-wide information on the persistency of business, not just by type of policy but according to selling medium, type of intermediary and method of payment of premiums, and category of policyholder (recognising, for example, age, sex and social class as important factors), (see also 9.5)

9.6.4 *Pensions in payment*
Many schemes offer the option of taking a lump sum payment on retirement (see 2.16). In most cases it is advantageous to an individual to avail himself of the option and then reinvest the money in a purchased life annuity if his intention is to maximise his pension. Payments from such annuities will not feature in any statistics on the amount of pensions in payment from occupational pension schemes. This ommission could be remedied by an additional question in say the *General Household Survey* [QRL.50], (see also 9.5 point 4). Additionally there are no satisfactory statistics on lump sum payments on retirement irrespective of the effect just mentioned.

There are few satisfactory statistics from which to estimate the relationship between pensions in payment and household income. In the National Income and Expenditure tables provided by the Government Statistical Services [QRL.109] it is not possible to isolate retirement pensions entirely, since the figures for life insurance and pension payments are grouped together. The cost of supplementary benefit paid to pensioners is also not separated out. Futhermore, there is no way of measuring the income drawn by retired people from savings other than through pensions and life assurance. This is also true for the *General Household Survey* [B.15] and the *Family Expenditure Survey* [B.38] published data.

9.7 Register of Pension Funds

The pensions industry has grown. It is impossible to say to exactly by how much with accuracy since no register exists of all pension funds. The register considered most authoritive is a commercially based one called *Pension Funds and its Advisors* [QRL.12] and it is used as a source even by Government Departments. A register for enquiries to private sector funds was orignally held by the Inland Revenue, but this has not been kept up to date; the manual records were never weeded and to do so now would probably be more time-consuming and costly than to start from scratch again.

A register is required for two main purposes a) for assistance with drawing of statistically reliable samples and in particular to allow that the size of total assets to be estimated and b) to provide a tracing service for early leavers. When a person leaves a scheme he has no more contact with it until he retires. If, in the meantime, the company has changed its name, been taken over, or merged, he will find it very difficult to trace the original scheme. If, in addition, he has changed his address so that when the scheme tries to contact him it cannot, the coming together of the two parties is likely to be a lost cause.

The Government has recently passed enabling legislation for such a register, but its actual information has been delayed indefinetely after meeting opposition from the Trade and Professional Associations on administrative grounds. If such a register were maintained by the Inland Revenue in computer form and were compulsory for all new funds or existing funds on communicating with the Revenue for any reason – much as has been done for the computerisation of records of national savings holders it would appear that any administrative problems can be overcome.

9.8 Pension Projections

Most of the statistical sources listed in this review merely present their results rather than attempting to make any detailed analysis. It is almost as though the science of statistics has not yet reached the pensions practitioners. This is mainly due to the difficulty of obtaining certain data which are vital to statistical projections. One of these pieces of data is the accrued benefits. At present all projections of the future cost of pensions rely on far more approximations than we would desire since no data (other than the recently commissioned Gallup Survey [QRL.42], or [QRL.43]) are publicly available on accrued benefits.

This omission is being rectified by a suitable question inserted into the latest *General Household Survey* [B.41]. The results will not, however, be available for at least 2 years. Let us hope that this will provide a fresh impetus for the introduction of statistical techniques to this field.

QUICK REFERENCE LIST - TABLE OF CONTENTS

QUICK REFERENCE LIST

Type of data	Breakdown	Area	Frequency	QRL Publication	Text Reference
Industrial Assurance					
Analysis of assurances discontinued	company paying various options/ paid up various options	GB	latest year	[QRL.26]	5.10 All subjects are covered by magazines - see 7.2
New business	number of assurance/ annual premiums	GB	latest year and selected year	[QRL.26]	5.10
Income and expenditure	premiums/ interest/ miscellaneous/ claims on death/ claims on maturity/ surrender values/ management expense/ miscellaneous/ shareholders dividends/ funds at year end	GB	latest year and selected years	[QRL.26]	5.10
Analysis of surplus and distribution	net liability at valuation date/ industrial assurance fund/ surplus/ composition of surplus/ distribution of surplus/ companies by name	GB	latest year	[QRL.26]	5.10
Lapses as a % of new business	companies by name	GB	latest years and selected years	[QRL.26]	5.10
Ratio of management expense to premium income	company by name	GB	latest year and selected years	[QRL.26]	5.10, 3.6
Income	Premium/ interest/ mean funds/ yield	GB	latest year	[QRL.26]	5.10
Industrial Assurance	total benefits paid/ number of policies/ total funds	GB	latest two years	[QRL.26]	5.10
Disputes brought to the Industrial Assurance commissioner	brought forward/ awards made/ referred/ disposed/ carried forward	GB	latest year	[QRL.26]	5.10

Industrial Insurance	number of new policies/ number of policies converted to paid up/ new business premiums/ n.b. premiums adjusted for inflation to 1970 prices/ total premiums/ total premiums inflation adjusted/ total funds/ total funds inflation adjusted	GB	latest two years	[QRL.26]	5.10
Administration Expenses					
Expenses of management and other branch outgoings	industrial branch/ ordinary branch/ management expenses/ commissions/ UK taxation/ transfers to shareholders	UK	annual	[QRL.60]	6.3.1 five years data
Analysis of expenses of life offices	commission/ management expenses/ initial/ renewal	UK	annual	[QRL.93]	5.2.2.1
Loading for expenses		GB	1981	[QRL.94]	5.12.3
Expenses of management and other branch outgoings	industrial branch/ ordinary branch/ management expenses/ commissions/ UK taxation/ transfers to shareholders	UK	annual	[QRL.60]	6.3.1 five years data
Staff involved in company pensions administration	number/ investment method/ size of fund/ future change likely	GB	1984	[QRL.75]	7.10
Life office links	charges	GB	monthly	[QRL.106]	7.3.2
Administrative costs met by fund	Sector	UK	Annual since 1982	[QRL.15]	8.2
Unit linked personal pension contract charges and allocation terms	Initial charge, annual fund charge, accumulation units, capital units, period for which units issued, policy charges, allocation terms	GB	Quarterly	[QRL.63]	7.6.3
Estimated cost of fund administration	Type of fund; level; type of administrative cost	GB	1980 1984	[QRL.103] [QRL.75]	8.4, 8.5
Friendly Societies					
Analysis of investments	Type of society/ type of investment	GB	selected and latest year	[QRL.26]	5.10
Income and Expenditure	Type of society/ number on register/ adult members/ juvenile members/ Total income of which premiums and interest/ Total benefits of which death, maturity and surrender values/ Total other expenditure of which fund expenses and management expenses	GB	selected years and latest year	[QRL.26]	5.10

Type of data	Breakdown	Area	Frequency	QRL Publication	Text Reference
Collecting societies	new business/ claims on death/ claims on maturity/ surrender for cash/ surrender for no benefit/ number in force at year end	GB	selected years and latest year	[QRL.26]	5.10
Collecting societies	management expense/ premium income/ total income/ ratios/ industrial/ other insurances	GB	selected years and latest year	[QRL.26]	5.10, 3.7
New taxable business	whole life/ endowment/ mortgage protection/ type of society/ number of pols/ annual premiums/ sums assured	GB	selected years and latest year	[QRL.26]	5.10
Members, benefits, funds	type of society	GB	selected years and latest year	[QRL.26]	5.10
Formal documents	type of society/ partial amendments of rules/ full amendments of rules/ changes of office/ declarations of solvency/ notice of appointment of liquidator/ final winding ups/ charges on assets/ exemptions from accounts/ special dates for annual returns	GB	latest year	[QRL.26]	5.10
Type of Society	collecting societies/ orders/ branches/ others/ number of societies/ membership/ benefits/ total funds	GB	latest two years	[QRL.26]	5.10
Registrations	new/ total/ number of members	GB	latest year	[QRL.26]	5.10
New Business					
Source of premium income	type of intermediary	UK	annual	[QRL.100]	6.3.3
Premiums	insurances and annuities/ personal pensions/ total/ linked/ annual/ single	GB	quarterly	[QRL.69]	6.3
Anaylsis of new business	single /regular /no. of contracts /premiums /sums assured or annuities p.a. / linked /non-linked /par /non-par /types of contract	UK	annual	[QRL.93]	5.2.2.1
New Business	premiums /sum insured /annuities p.a.	GB	annual	[QRL.69] and [QRL.68]	6.3

Individual life and annuity	annual premiums / single premiums (including considerations for annuities) sums insured / annuities p.a. (deferred & immediate)	UK	annual	[QRL.60]	6.3.1 five years data
Industrial life	number of contracts / annual premiums / sums insured	UK	annual	[QRL.60]	6.3.1 five years data
Ordinary individual	Total/ linked/ annual premiums/ single premiums/ sums insured/ number of contracts	UK	annual	[QRL.60]	6.3.1 five years data
Individual annuity	number of contracts/ single premiums/ annual premiums/ immediate annuities p.a./ deferred annuities p.a.	UK	annual	[QRL.60]	6.3.1 five years data
Personal pensions	number/ annual premiums/ single premiums/ deferred annuities p.a./ reversionary annuities p.a.	UK	annual	[QRL.60]	6.3.1 five years data
Permanent health	number of contracts/ estimated number of lives covered/ annual premiums/ single premiums/ maximum benefits insured p.a.	UK	annual	[QRL.60]	6.3.1 five years data
Press release compared to actual	company/ new business; single, regular, revenue premiums/ net premiums per DTI return by class.	GB	annual	[QRL.4]	7.5.3 two years data
Ranking by premium income	company/ general/ long-term total / increase in total percentage over year/ ordinary/ industrial	GB	annual	[QRL.4]	7.5.3 two years data
Synopsis of new business	company/ number of contracts issued/ net sums assured/ net annual premiums/ net single premiums	UK	annual	[QRL.111]	7.5.2
Synopsis of long term business	company/ regular/ single/ number of contracts/ premiums/ sums assured/ linked/ non-linked/ life/ general annuity/ pension; individual, group/ PHI/ ordinary/ industrial	UK	annual	[QRL.56]	7.5.2
Press release	various	GB	annual or quarterly	[QRL.49]	7.1
Individual Premiums	regular/single	UK	annual	[QRL.109]	5.6 eleven years data
Policies	no./ type of policy/ type of linkage	GB	annual 1961-71	[QRL.17]	5.2.2.4

Type of data	Breakdown	Area	Frequency	QRL Publication	Text Reference
Net premiums	no./ type of policy/ type of linkage	GB	annual 1961-71	[QRL.17]	5.2.2.4
Business in Force					
Personal pensions	number/ annual premiums/ deferred annuities p.a./ reversionary annuities/ annuities in payment p.a.	UK	annual	[QRL.60]	6.3.1 five years data
Permanent health	number of contacts/ number of lives covered/ annual premiums/ maximum benefits insured p.a.	UK	annual	[QRL.60]	6.3.1 five years data
Individual life	total/ linked/ number of contracts/ annual premiums/ sums insured plus bonuses	UK	annual	[QRL.60]	6.3.1 five years data
Summary of change in business	life /annuity /pension /PHI /capital redemption /no. of contracts /annual premiums /in force at start /new business /deaths /maturities /surrenders / lapses /other /in force at year end	UK	annual	[QRL.93]	5.2.2.1
Industrial life	number of paying policies / number of free policies / annual premiums / sums insured plus bonuses	UK	annual	[QRL.60]	6.3.1 five years data
Press release compared to actual	company / new business, single, regular, revenue premiums / net premiums per DTI return by class	GB	annual	[QRL.4]	7.5.3 two years data
Individual life and annuity	annual premiums / sums insured plus bonuses / annuities p.a. (deferred and immediate)	UK	annual	[QRL.60]	6.3.1 five years data
Net written premiums - ordinary long-term	UK /EEC (excluding UK) /USA / other overseas	GB	annual	[QRL.31]	6.4.2
Individual annuity	number/ annual premiums/ immediate annuities p.a./ deferred annuities p.a.	UK	annual	[QRL.60]	6.3.1 five years data
Group life and pensions	estimated membership/ premiums/ pensions in payment/ present employees/ members with preserved pensions/ members receiving pensions/ members of group life schemes	UK	annual	[QRL.60]	6.3.1 five years data

Business from EEC	premium income/ sums insured/ size of fund/ country of origin	UK	annual	[QRL.40]	6.3.2
Net written premiums in the UK	ordinary long-term/ industrial	UK	annual	[QRL.108]	6.4.3 data since 1977
Net written premiums	worldwide/ ordinary/ industrial/ ABI members/ ABI by class/ ABI total	UK	annual	[QRL.57]	6.4.4
Policies	no/ type of policy/ type of linkage	GB	annual 1961-71	[QRL.17]	5.2.2.4
Net liabilities at year end	type of policy/ type of linkage	GB	annual 1961-71	[QRL.17]	5.2.2.4
Net premiums worldwide	individual authorised insurer	GB	annual	[QRL.55] [QRL.54]	5.2.2
Income and Expenditure (Life Offices) (may include pensions written by life offices)					
Synopsis of profit and loss account	Company/ items of income and expenditure/ excess (shortfall) of income over expenditure/ profit and loss balance/ shareholders funds	UK	Annual	[QRL.56]	7.5.2
Synopsis of annual accounts	Company/ life and annuity funds/ life premium income/ considerations for annuities/ rate of interest earned/ interest assumed at valuation	UK	Annual	[QRL.111]	7.5.2 Principal companies only
Synopsis of revenue accounts	Company/ class of business/ income by type/ expenditure by type/ ordinary/ industrial	UK	Annual	[QRL.56]	7.5.2
Analysis of claims	life/ general annuity/ pension/ PHI/ capitol redemption/ on death/ maturity/ surrender/ lump sum/ periodic payments	UK	annual	[QRL.93]	5.2.2.1
Analysis of premiums of life offices	life/ general annuity/ pension/ single/ regular/ PHI	UK	annual	[QRL.93]	5.2.2.1
Payments to industrial branch policy holders	death claims/ maturities/ surrenders	UK	annual	[QRL.60]	6.3.1 five years data

Type of data	Breakdown	Area	Frequency	QRL Publication	Text Reference
Payments to ordinary branch policy holders	death claims/ maturities/ annuities/ surrenders/ refunds under occupational pension schemes/ payments under PHI and other long-term contracts/ total to UK policy holders/ total to overseas policy holders	UK	annual	[QRL.60]	6.3.1 five years data
Premium income for ordinary long-term business	annual premiums for life, annuities and pensions/ single premiums for life, annuities, and pensions/ premiums for permanent health and other long-term insurances	UK	annual	[QRL.60]	6.3.1 five years data
Balance sheet and Revenue accounts for linked funds		UK	annual	[QRL.93]	5.2.2.1 see also [B.49]
Revenue account	Premiums /investment income /non linked assets brought into account / linked assets brought into account /claims payable /expenses payable / interest /tax /fund b/f /fund c/f /other	UK	annual	[QRL.93]	5.2.2.1
Revenue account	detailed	UK	annual	[QRL.93]	5.2.2.1
Statement of Income and Expenditure for Life Offices	Transfers to other accounts /investment income receivable before tax / management expenses /interest payable before deduction of tax /taxation / dividends	UK	annual	[QRL.93]	5.2.2.1
Expected income from admissable non-linked assets	type of assets /value /income /yield /redemption period of fixed interest	UK	annual	[QRL.93]	5.2.2.1
Analysis of claims	life /general annuity /pension /PHI /capital redemption /on death /maturity / surrender /lump sum /periodic payments	UK	annual	[QRL.93]	5.2.2.1
Revenue account	detailed	UK	annual	[QRL.93]	5.2
Analysis of premiums of life offices	life /general annuity /pension /single /regular /PHI /	UK	annual	[QRL.93]	5.2.2.1
Reports and accounts	various	UK	annual	[QRL.22]	

Source of overseas premium income	country	UK	annual	[QRL.60]	6.3.1 five years data
Expenses of management and other branch outgoings	industrial branch/ ordinary branch/ management expenses/ commissions/ UK taxation/ transfers to shareholders	UK	annual	[QRL.60]	6.3.1 five years data
Ordinary branch income	premium income; UK, overseas/ investment income/ other	UK	annual	[QRL.60]	6.3.1 five years data
Expenditure on acquiring companies	expenditure/ no. of companies	UK	annual	[QRL.25]	5.2. six years data
Net acquisition cash values	type of asset/ life/ pension	UK	quarterly	[QRL.48]	5.2.1.3 very detailed breakdown five years data
Net investment	type of security/ class of business	UK	quarterly	[QRL.32]	5.2.1 first quarter 1975 contains historical run of figures from 1962
Net earnings by insurers		UK	annual	[QRL.110]	5.6 - eleven years data
Net earnings overseas by UK insurers		UK	annual	[QRL.110]	5.6 - eleven years data
Synopsis of revenue account for longterm insurance	company/ class of business/ income by type/ expenditure by type/ ordinary/ industrial	UK	annual	[QRL.56]	7.5.2
Income and Expenditure (Pension Funds)					
Surplus	funded, unfunded, notionally funded	UK	latest 11 years	[QRL.109] [QRL.48]	5.6 Refer also to preceeding section
Cash flow ratio	description/ number of funds/ range/ % of funds	GB	quarterly	[QRL.74]	7.6.2
Allocation of new money	type of securities	GB	quarterly	[QRL.74]	7.6.2 on Life Offices
Annual expenditure	company	UK	annual	[QRL.12]	7.5.1

Type of data	Breakdown	Area	Frequency	QRL Publication	Text Reference
Net earnings by UK pension funds		UK	annual	[QRL.110]	5.6 eleven year data
Annual contribution income	class of scheme/ type of contribution	GB	annual	[QRL.27]	6.1.1
Reports and accounts	various	UK	annual	[QRL.22]	6.1
Expenditure on retirement benefits in four public sector groups	amounts/ percentages of payroll/ pension increase	GB	1970-81	[QRL.16]	5.7.5
Income and expenditure	annual pension outlay/ total lump sums paid on retirement/ total lump sums paid on death	GB	annual	[QRL.27]	6.1.1
Revenue account	components of public sector/ private sector/ item	UK	1975, 1979	[QRL.70]	5.7.1
Net flow to funds	type of fund/ level of flow	GB	1979-80, 1984	[QRL.103] [QRL.75]	8.4 - 8.5
Net investment	type of security/ acquired/ realised	UK	quarterly	[QRL.32]	5.2.1 detailed breakdown of securities
Net investment	sector/ type of investment	UK	quarterly	[QRL.48]	5.2.1.3
Income and Expenditure (Life and Pensions)					
Net earnings by UK insurers		UK	latest 11 years	[QRL.110]	5.6 This section covers data that are not shown for separate categories
Financial accounts	sector/ type of industry/ personal/ overseas	UK	quarterly	[QRL.48]	5.2.1 - 5.6
Financial accounts	sector / type of asset	UK	annual	[QRL.109]	5.6.4.1
Financial accounts - Central Government	assets and liabilities / sector / type of transaction	UK	annual	[QRL.48]	5.6 four years data
Financial accounts personal sector	type of asset / liability	UK	annual	[QRL.109]	5.6 eleven years data
Annual investment income	Company	UK	Annual	[QRL.12]	7.5.1

Changes in Financial Assets and Liabilities		GB	annual - 1952-1970	[QRL.58]	5.5 - Very rough estimates 1952-63, one line on sector accounts
Net increase in amount available for investment	Contributions on employers/ of employees/ rent etc/ transfers/ pensions and other benefits paid/ administrative costs/ public corporations/ local authorities	UK	Annual	[QRL.48]	5.6 Supplementary table
Change in financial assets	sector	UK	quarterly	[QRL.30]	5.5 - One line in "Flow of funds Matrix"
Income and Expenditure	funded/ notionally funded/ unfunded	UK	annual	[QRL.48] [QRL.109]	5.6 eleven years data
Integrated balance sheet and flow accounts	level flow/ residual adjustment/ revaluation	GB	1976	[QRL.29]	5.5 - data for 1952-76 available on request from the bank, data for 1975-85 is in preparation
Life insurance and superannuation funds financial accounts	type of transaction	UK	annual	[QRL.109]	5.6 eleven years data
Net surplus of life assurance and pension funds		UK	Quarterly	[QRL.48]	5.2 - Financial account of personal sector with a contra entry in the other financial institutions sector. five years data
Financial transactions	personal sector/ financial sector	UK	Quarterly	[QRL.30]	5.5 - 5.2.2. four years data

Type of data	Breakdown	Area	Frequency	QRL Publication	Text Reference
Net inflow into life insurance and pension funds		UK	quarterly	[QRL.48]	5.6 one line in sources and uses of funds of other financial institutions. five years data
Transactions in life assurance and pension schemes	funded/ notionally funded/ unfunded	UK	annual	[QRL.48]	5.6 - supplementary table. ten years data
				[QRL.22]	
Investment (Life Offices)					
Market value of holdings of long-term funds	stocks and shares/ mortgages/ property/ other	GB	latest year	[QRL.31]	5.7.1
Market Value of Insurance Companies Assets	long-term, general, type of asset	UK	annual	[QRL.25]	5.6 - 4.2 eleven years data
Unquoted holdings	direct/ indirect/ number of holdings/ total cost/ total book value/ average cost/average book value/ % of total assets/ length of time held in portfolio/ location/ industrial classification	UK	1984	[QRL.1]	8.3
Holdings in property	insurance - long-term funds, general funds/ pension funds - private sector, local authority, other public sector/ % of m.v. of fund/ % of m.v. net investment	GB	1970 - 1982	[QRL.7]	
Market value of long-term funds of insurance companies assets	type of security	UK	annual	[QRL.48]	5.2. ten years data
Total assets	individual authorised insurer	GB	annual	[QRL.55] [QRL.54]	5.2.2

Assets held at market values	type of security/ class of business	UK	annual	[QRL.32]	5.2.2 - usually 2nd quarter - first quarter of 1975 contains an historical run of figures from 1962. five years data
Analysis of linked assets	fund/ valuation price/ no. of units/ value of units inverted in other internal units	UK	annual	[QRL.93]	5.2.2.1
Balance sheet	detailed	UK	annual	[QRL.93]	5.2.2
Analaysis of admissible assets		UK	annual	[QRL.93]	5.2.2.1 See also [B.49]
Re-allocation of nominee and trustee holdings to beneficial owners	pension funds/ insurance companies/ other specified categories	GB	1981	[QRL.104]	6.9.1
Distribution of market value of shareholdings between categories of registered shareholder	pension funds/ insurance companies/ other specified categories/ survey strategy	GB	1963, 1969, 1975, 1981	[QRL.104]	6.9.1
Distribution of shareholdings between categories of beneficial share holder by market value	insurance companies/ banks/ various other specified groupings	GB	1963, 1969, 1975, 1981	[QRL.104]	6.9.1
Total investment	class of investment	UK	annual	[QRL.60]	6.3.1 two years data
Total life funds	industrial/ ordinary	UK	annual	[QRL.60]	6.3.1 five years data
Long term funds	market value of holdings/ gross income/ gilts/ other government and municipal stocks/ debs. etc./ stocks and shares/ mortgages/ property/ other	GB	annual	[QRL.31]	6.4.2
Quoted share prices	price/ dividend/ yield/ cover/ P.E. ratio	GB	daily	[QRL.49]	7.1
Long term business investments	company/ type of investments	GB	annual	[QRL.4]	7.5.3 two years data
Farming Investment					

Type of data	Breakdown	Area	Frequency	QRL Publication	Text Reference
Distribution of farms by size	size of farm in hectares/ number of NAPF members holding farms	GB	1977	[QRL.47]	8.7
Agricultural investment by acreage	annual acquisitions/ cumulative total from 1965	GB	annual	[QRL.95]	8.10
Holdings of farm & forest land	Freehold/ leasehold/ in hand/ let/ farm/ forest/ countries	GB	April 1976	[QRL.9]	8.8
Regional pattern of agricultural land ownership	land purchased pre 1976/ purchased 1976 to date	GB	pre 1976, 1976 to date	[QRL.95]	8.10
Rent levels of agricultural property	type of property/ land grade/ returns/ growth	GB	annual	[QRL.95]	8.10
Capital values of agricultural property	Type of property/ land grade/ returns/ growth	GB	annual	[QRL.95]	8.10
Form of agricultural land ownership	sale & leaseback/ other FRI tenancies/ traditional let estates/ other traditional tenancies/ size	GB	latest year	[QRL.95]	8.10
Holdings in property	insurance - long-term funds, general funds/ pension funds - private sector, local authority, other public sector/ % of m.v. of fund/ % of m.v. net investment	GB	1970 - 1982	[QRL.7]	
Types of farming on farms owned by ABI members	arable/ dairy/ livestock/ mixed/ milk farms	GB	1977	[QRL.47]	8.7
Growth of agricultural land ownership in acrage	Pensions funds/ life companies	GB	1970-81	[QRL.19]	7.5 Updated figures available
Annual rate of farmland acquisition	area/ cumulative proportion/ insurance companies/ pension funds	GB	1970 - 1978	[QRL.47]	8.7
Geographical pattern of farmland ownership	MAFF region/ insurance companies/ pension funds/ area/ percentages	GB	December 1977	[QRL.47]	8.7

Farmland ownership	area/ proportion of total/ members of BIA/ members of LOA/ life funds/ general insurance funds/ staff pension funds/ managed pension funds/ unit linked funds/ subsidiaries/ pension funds/ property unit trusts	GB	December 1977	[QRL.47]	8.7
Investments (Pension Funds)					
Unquoted holdings	direct/ indirect/ number of holdings/ total cost/ total book value/ average cost/ average book value/ % of total assets/ length of time held in portfolio/ location/ industrial classification	UK	1984	[QRL.1]	8.3
Average fund asset distribution	category of assets	GB	quarterly	[QRL.74]	7.6.2
Average fund strategies	asset distribution/ cash of flow ratios/ new money allocation/ effect of size on strategy	GB	annual	[QRL.74]	8.5.2 - 10.4 - 10.4.1
Distribution of rates of return	quantities/ asset categories	GB	annual	[QRL.74]	8.5.2 - 10.4 - 10.4.1
Analysis of assets by amount	type of assets/no. of schemes under management	UK	December 1982	[QRL.24]	6.10
Re-allocation of nominee and trustee holdings to beneficial owners	pension funds/ insurance companies/ other specified categories	GB	1981	[QRL.104]	6.9.1
Distribution of market value of shareholdings between categories of registered shareholder	pension funds/ insurance companies/ other specified categories/ survey strata	GB	1963, 1969, 1975, 1981	[QRL.104]	6.9.1
Distribution of shareholdings between categories of beneficial share holder by market value	insurance companies/ banks/ various other specified groupings	GB	1963, 1969, 1975, 1981	[QRL.104]	6.9.1
Distribution of investments	investments (detailed breakdown)/ investment method/ size of fund/ future change likely	GB	1984	[QRL.75]	8.5
Investment medium	insured/ managed fund/ self-administered/ size/ coverage of death in service benefits	GB	1984	[QRL.75]	8.5

Type of data	Breakdown	Area	Frequency	QRL Publication	Text Reference
Investment media of funds using more than one method	proportions in each investment method/ size of fund/ future change likely?	GB	1984	[QRL.75]	8.5
Market value of fund assets	type of fund/ level	GB	1980	[QRL.103]	8.4
Reasons for not investing overseas	type of fund/ sufficient opportunities in UK/ unpatriotic/ risk of currency fluctuations/ inappropriate for UK fund/ poor yield/ other reasons	GB	1980	[QRL.103]	8.4
Retrospective analysis	distribution of pension scheme assets/ time weighted rates of return/ consistency of performance/ individual years/ combined periods	GB	1970 to date	[QRL.74]	7.6.2
Change in financial assets	sector	UK	quaterly	[QRL.30]	5.5 - 5.2.2 - One line in "flow of funds matrix" - No breakdown of figures between life and pensions
Balance sheet at market value	type of security/ sector	UK	annual	[QRL.32]	5.2.1 - detailed breakdown - usually 2nd quarter five years data
Market value of pension fund assets	local authorities/ other public sector/ private sector/ type of asset	UK	annual	[QRL.25]	5.6 - 5.2 eleven years data
Distribution of sizes	class of scheme/value	GB	annual	[QRL.27]	6.1.1
Type of property investments	class of scheme/ commercial/ industrial/ shops/ agriculture/ other	GB	annual	[QRL.27]	6.1.1
Comparison between investment medium and number of members	class of scheme/ size of membership/ investment medium/ sector	GB	annual	[QRL.27]	6.1.1

Investment medium	class of scheme/ insured/ privately invested/ insurance managed fund units	GB	annual	[QRL.27]	6.1.1
Equity in insurance and pension funds of the non-bank private sector		UK	Quarterly for 3 years	[QRL.48]	5.6 - one line of financial assets and liabilities table
Investment portfolio distribution	market values/ type of investments/ class of scheme	GB	annual	[QRL.27]	5.1
Distribution of funds invested (other than by insurance companies)	sector/ size of funds (market value)/ number of employers/ number of members/ number of pensioners/ average funds per person	UK	quadrenially	[QRL.70]	5.7
Funds	market value/ net-acquisitions/ insured otherwise/ sector	UK	quadrenially	[QRL.70]	5.7
Annual investment income	company	UK	annual	[QRL.12]	7.5.1
Capital value of investments	company/ UK equities/ fixed interest/ property/ cash & deposits/ others	UK	annual	[QRL.12]	7.5.1
Size	name/ size £m	UK	annual	[QRL.12]	7.5.1
Market value of assets	sector/ type of security	UK	annual latest ten years	[QRL.48]	5.2
Analysis of investments	sector/ size of fund/ type of securities	UK	annual latest 3 years	[QRL.48]	5.2.1.3
Number of Funds	sector/ size of fund	UK	latest five years	[QRL.48]	5.2.1.3
Net increase in amount available for investment	contributions of employers/ of employees/ rent etc, transfers, pensions and other benefits paid, administrative costs, public corporations, local authorities	UK	latest year	[QRL.48]	5.6 - supplementary table
Market value of holdings	sector/ type of investment	UK	annual	[QRL.48]	5.2.1.3
Net investment	sector/ type of investment	UK	annual for latest 6 years quarterly for latest 2 years	[QRL.48]	5.2.1.3
Distribution of Investment portfolio	insurance companies/ pension funds/ equities/ fixed interest/ cash etc./ commercial property/ agricultural property/ agricultural PUT's/ other (commercial) PUT's/ forestry	GB	1981	[QRL.19]	8.9 Updated figures available
					8.7

Type of data	Breakdown	Area	Frequency	QRL Publication	Text Reference
Specific areas of investment	type of fund/ UK property direct/ UK PUT's/ UK ag direct/ UK ag PUT's/ overseas property direct/ overseas exempt unit trusts/ European equities/ North American equities/ Japanese equities/ other foreign equities/ Australian equities/ South African equities/ foreign money market/ currency loans	GB	1980	[QRL.103]	8.4
Distribution of investments	level of investment/ UK equities/ UK fixed interest/ UK PUT's/ UK property direct/ overseas unit trusts/ overseas equities/ direct loans/ kept liquid/ fund type	GB	1980	[QRL.103]	8.4
Performance					
How split funds use performance data	decide how to allocate new money/ decide which managers should manage more volatile funds/ other/ investment method/ size of fund	GB	1984	[QRL.75]	7.10
Linked fund prices	company/ fund/ life/ pension	GB	variable	[QRL.49]	8.1 - some prices change daily, others weekly or monthly
Time weighted returns	asset category/ individual years/ aggregated years	GB	quarterly	[QRL.74]	7.6.2
Fund information for life office links	management/ charges/ valuations/ price history/ fund sizes	GB	monthly	[QRL.106]	7.3.2
Performance services comparison	Information submitted by client/ reporting frequency/ reliability/ details of fellow clients/ details of market experience/ promptness/ type of information/ choice of model	UK	1981	[QRL.64]	6.8.1
Performance tables	Fund name/ investment category/ size of fund/ returns over different periods	UK	N/A	[QRL.101]	7.6.5

Performance of funds to which personal pension plans can be linked	Investment medium/ name of company/ size of fund/ percentage growth over 3 months, 6 months/ cumulative performance over each of last 8 years/ rankings	GB	Quarterly	[QRL.63]	7.6.3
Rates of return on assets	sector/ income/ capital/ currency/ market/ stock	UK	quarterly	[QRL.76]	7.6.4
Performance tables of with profit personal pension plans	N/A	GB	Quarterly	[QRL.63]	7.6.3
Main objective in evaluating performance	Fund type/ objectives	GB	1980 1984	[QRL.103] [QRL.75]	8.4, 8.5
With whom performance comparisons made	Type of fund/ other public sector funds/ from measurement tables/ other public sector funds informally/ FT actuaries or other published index/ other external data/ no comparisons	GB	1980 1984	[QRL.103] [QRL.75]	8.4, 8.5
Do users of external comparisons of performance use modern portfolio analysis or beta analysis	Investment method/ size of fund	GB	1984	[QRL.75]	8.5
Investment performance measurement	Number of portfolios monitored/ average annual and annualised rate of return/ range of annual rates of return/ average portfolio distribution	GB	Selcted years since 1976	[QRL.59]	7.6.1
Investment performance measurement	Time weighted rate of return, rank and portfolio code	GB	Annual - 5 years	[QRL.59]	7.6.1
Property indices	Name/ limitations	GB	N/A	[QRL.7]	10.4.1
Managed fund performance	Company/ type of fund/ annual and annualised returns/ annual and annualsed ranking of returns/ market values and asste distributions (last 2 years)	GB	Quarterly for last year, annual from 1973	[QRL.59]	7.6.1
Miscellaneous					
Temporary absence provisions	maternity leave/ paternity leave/ ill-health/ other reasons/ name of company/ provision	GB	1984	[QRL.28]	8.13
Synopses for life offices	balance sheet/ management structure/ specimen surrender values/ loans	GB	monthly	[QRL.72]	7.3.1
Policy fees	yearly/ half yearly/ quarterly	GB	monthly	[QRL.72]	7.3.1

Type of data	Breakdown	Area	Frequency	QRL Publication	Text Reference
Evidence of health	MAR/ ME	GB	monthly	[QRL.72]	7.3.1
Minimum premiums	yearly/ half yearly/ quarterly	GB	monthly	[QRL.72]	7.3.1
All subjects are covered by magazines				[QRL.110], [QRL.83], [QRL.79], [QRL.65], [QRL.84], [QRL.80]	7.2
Projections of occupational pensions	pensions various/ expenditure detailed/ coverage	GB	1951 - 2041	[QRL.6]	6.5.1.3
Number of schemes satisfying equal access requirements	Total; cumulative total	GB	1981	[QRL.99]	5.4 Data after 1981 may be available on application tp OPB
Valuation result and distribution of surplus	Result /composition of surplus /distribution of surplus	UK	annual	[QRL.93]	5.2.2.1
Accrued service	last employer /any employer /male /female /sector	UK	1984	[QRL.42] [QRL.43]	5.12.1 Refer appendix 5.3
Valuation summary of contracts	very detailed.	UK	annual	[QRL.93]	5.2.2.1 See also [B.49]
Long term liabilites and margins	long term funds /claims admitted but not paid /other liabilites	UK	annual	[QRL.93]	5.2.2.1
Statement of solvency	admissible assets /liabilites /margins /unpaid capital /solvency margin / authorised share capital /paid up share capital /share premium account	UK	annual	[QRL.93]	5.2.2.1
Liabilities (other than long-term)	General business reserves /other insurance liabilites /loans secured / loans unsecured /subordenated loan stock /taxation /recommended dividend	UK	annual	[QRL.93]	5.2.2.1
Years of accrued service	Age; sex; number of years; occupational grouping; level of earnings	GB	1981	[QRL.15]	8.2

Historical					
Pensions	Volume of pensions / pension rights / coverage	GB	1954, 1984	[QRL.2]	6.5.1.4 - 1984 figures are projections
Pensions	coverage and other details	GB	pre 1936	[QRL.8]	8.11
Business revenue accounts	name of authorised insurer / detailed breakdown of income and expenditue	GB	annual	[QRL.54]	5.2.2 series ceased 1976
Changes in financial assets and liabilities		GB	Annual 1952-1970	[QRL.58]	5.5 One line in sector accounts. Rough estimates 1952-63
New business	name of company/ number of policies/ annual premiums/ single premiums	GB	annual until 1976	[QRL.54]	5.2.2
Net premiums worldwide	individual authorised insurer	GB	annual	[QRL.54]	5.2.2
Insurance in force	name of company/ type of policy/ number/ amount of sum insured	GB	annual	[QRL.54]	5.2.2 series ceased 1976
Analysis of premiums	gross premiums/ reassurance ceded/ net premiums	GB	annual	[QRL.54]	5.2.2 series ceased 1976
Personal Attitudes					
Attitudes of self employed	happy in work/ why become self-employed/ financial advisors/ planning for retirement/ voting pattern	GB	1985	[QRL.98]	8.14
Attitudes to retirement	detailed	GB	1981	[QRL.15]	8.2 - comprehensive report
Information provided and attitudes towards it	pensioners /members with over 2 years service /members with under 2 years service /before employment /after joining scheme /on becoming a pensioner	England	1985	[QRL.77]	
Attitudes to pensions	detailed items /men in national service /men in public sector /men in private sector /women /members /non-members	UK	1984	[QRL.42] [QRL.43]	5.13.1. Full questionaire in appendix 5.3
Future developments welcomed	Type of fund / types of development	UK	1980	[QRL.103]	8.4

Type of data	Breakdown	Area	Frequency	QRL Publication	Text Reference
Anticipated changes	Desired / expected / investment method / size of fund / type of of advisor / improvement for early leavers / unitising existing funds / new schemmes to be money purchase / other	GB	1984	[QRL.75]	8.5
Attractiveness of life insurance after 1984 budget	more attractive / less attractive / no difference / don't know / sex / age / class / have insurance / aware of tax relief / change	GB	1984	[QRL.87]	8.14
Attitudes to life salesmen	refer to appendix 5	GB	1983	[QRL.86]	8.14
Awareness of budget change	relief abolished / other / don't know	GB	1984	[QRL.87]	8.14
Rates					
Policy loans	maximum/ proportion of surrender value allowed/ minimum loan/ note of interest on new loans/ is current rate applied to exsisting loans	GB		[QRL.84]	8.2
Policy details	type of plan	GB	monthly	[QRL.106]	7.3.2 Stone & Cox Green
Rates	type of contract	GB	monthly	[QRL.72]	7.3.1
Rates	Specimen ages/ terms/ policies	GB	Annual	[QRL.88] [QRL.89]	7.3
Tabular guide of facts and figures for different types of savings	Rates/ performance/ life insurance/ pensions	GB		[QRL.96]	7.3
Permanent Health Rate tables	Company/ age/ expiry age/ deferrement/ premium frequency/ benefit frequency/ group/ individual/ package	GB	Annual	[QRL.82]	7.5.9 Comprehensive
Unit linked personal pension contract charges and allocation terms	Initial charge, annual fund charge, accumulation units, capital units, period for which units issued, policy charges, allocation terms	GB	Quarterly	[QRL.63]	7.6.3
Self Employed Pensions	Rates/ performance	GB	Annual	[QRL.97]	7.5.10
Executive Pensions	Rates/ performance	GB	Annual	[QRL.41]	7.5.10
Unit linked life policies	Rates/ performance	GB	Annual	[QRL.107]	7.5.10

Wealth					
Accrued liabilities of pension funds	market value of funds/ accrued liabilities discounting at 1.5 %/ accrued liabilities discounting at 0.5 %/ wages and salaries	GB	1951 - 2041	[QRL.6]	6.5.1.3
Occupational pensions % of pensioners total income		GB	1951, 1961, 1971, 1981, 1982, 1984, 1985	[QRL.85]	5.13.2
Proportion of pensioners with occupational pensions	age/ marital status	GB	1982	[QRL.85]	5.13.2
Projected percentages of pensioners total gross income from occupational pension schemes	state benefits price linked/ state benefits earnings linked	GB	decenially 1984-2025	[QRL.85]	5.13.2
Distribution of mortgages	level of purchase price	GB	latest 10 years	[QRL.51]	5.11.1
Earnings	make-up of earnings	UK	latest year	[QRL.67]	5.9.2
Mortgages granted by insurance companies	new dwellings/ other dwellings/ number/ average price/ amount lent	GB	latest year	[QRL.51]	4.11.1
Mortgages from insurance companies	gross/ net	GB	latest ten years	[QRL.51]	4.11.1
Expenditure of "other" retired	level of household income/ commodity e.g. fuel, food, tobacco etc./ breakdown of size of household e.g. one adult, two adults, one man, one woman, children etc.	UK	latest year	[QRL.45]	5.9.1 very detailed breakdown of commodities
Source of income of "other" retired	number of households/ normal weekly disposable income/ gross normal weekly household income/ wages and salaries/ self-employment/ investments/ annuities and or pensions/ social security/ imputed income from owner or rent free property/ other sources	UK	latest year	[QRL.45]	5.9.1

Type of data	Breakdown	Area	Frequency	QRL Publication	Text Reference
Payments for life insurance and contributions to pension funds	levels of gross normal weekly income of household/ number and percentage of all households recording expenditure/ region	UK	latest year	[QRL.45]	5.9.1
Percentage of "other" retired households in each region	regions	UK	latest year	[QRL.45]	5.9.1
Percentage of "other" retired households with certain durable goods	one car or van/ two cars or vans etc./ central heating/ washing machine/ refridgerator/ television/ telephone	UK	latest year	[QRL.45]	5.9.1
Housing of "other retired"	type of tenure/ level of household	UK	latest year	[QRL.45]	5.9.1
Number of "other" retired households	levels of gross normal weekly income	UK	latest year	[QRL.45]	5.9.1
"Other" retired households	percentage of all households/ number/ one adult/ one man, one woman	UK	latest year	[QRL.45]	5.9.1
Distribution of income of "other" retired households	details of total gross normal income of households/ details of total disposable income of households	UK	latest year	[QRL.45]	5.9.1
Income from annuities and occupational pensions	level of household income	UK	latest year	[QRL.45]	5.9.1
Social security benefits to "other" retired households	level of income/ level of social security	UK	latest year	[QRL.45]	5.9.1
Other financial provision for retirement	Respondent/ spouse/ member of scheme/ insurance/ endowment/ additional savings/ investments/ private pensions schemes/ AVC's/ smaller house	GB	1981	[QRL.15]	8.2
Life insurance as percentage of net capital	Net estate range/ age groups/ maturity value of insurance/ equity value of insurance/ sex	GB	1975	[QRL.18]	8.6 - 'equity value' defined in paper
Existing life insurance	Refer to appendix 5	GB	1983	[QRL.86]	8.14

What types of insurance do people have	Term/ endowment/ unit-linked/ have insurance but do not know which/ none/ don't know/ sex/ age/ class	GB	1984	[QRL.87]	8.14
Retirement annuity premiums	Range of income/ number of cases/ amount/ family circumstances	GB	Annual	[QRL.102]	5.3.2
Consumer credit and other personal sector borrowing from insurance companies	Amount outstanding/ net transactions	UK	Annual	[QRL.48]	5.6, 5 years data
Income and expenditure of households	Outgoing on life assurance premiums paid by individuals/ income from pensions and other benefits/ income from life insurance and superannuation schemes/ outgoings on contributions of employees to occupational pension schemes	UK	Annual	[QRL.109]	5.6, 11 years data
Life insurance premiums and reliefs by family circumstances	Range of premium/ family circumstances/ number of policies/ amount of premium/ amount of relief		Annual	[QRL.52]	5.3
Classification of insurance policies	Number of cases/ amount on death/ range of wealth	UK	Annual	[QRL.52]	5.3 Refer to [B.2] for explanation of GINI coefficients
Wealth owned by the most wealthy of adult population	Range of wealth/ marketable wealth including and excluding occupational pension rights	UK	Annual 1971-81	[QRL.52]	5.3.1.1
Value of occupational pension rights	Funded/ unfunded/ notionally funded	UK	Annual from 1971	[QRL.52]	5.3.1.1
Wealth in addition to pensions	detailed list of other media /men /women /sector	UK	1984	[QRL.42] [QRL.43]	5.12.1. Refer appendix 5.3
Distribution of personal wealth (including pension rights)	Percentage of wealth owned	UK	Selected years	[QRL.52]	5.3
Aggregate value of accrued occupational pension rights		UK	Selected years	[QRL.52]	5.3
Wealth of individuals	Life policies/ pension rights	UK	Annual	[QRL.52]	5.3

Type of data	Breakdown	Area	Frequency	QRL Publication	Text Reference
Wealth of households	Life policies/ pension rights	UK	Annual	[QRL.52]	5.3
Sales Techniques					
Analysis of advertising	schedules of insertions and transmissions/ monitor of activity/ details of new banks and campaigns/ relative levels of expenditure by media/ seasonality of expenditure	GB	N/A	[QRL.23]	3.1.1.1
Source of premium income	type of intermediary	UK	annual	[QRL.100]	6.3.3
Advertising		GB		[QRL.23]	3.1
Insurance sponsorship		GB		[QRL.84]	7.2
Life insurance sales techniques	Refer to appendix 5	GB	1983	[QRL.86]	8.14
Tax					
Relationship with Inland Revenue	good?/ company deals with pensioners queries?/ centralization of PAYE records/ staff numbers devoted to IR/ records checked by IR?	UK	1980	[QRL.78]	6.8.2
Relationship with Inland Revenue	Requirement for completion/ objective/ frequency/ distribution/ staffing/ method/ value of process	UK	1979	[QRL.78]	5.4.2
Life insurance premiums and reliefs by family circumstances	Range of premium/ family circumstances/ number of policies/ amount of premium/ amount of relief		Annual	[QRL.52]	5.3
Estimated costs of tax relief	various approaches/ employees contribution; funds investment income; pensions; lump sums	N/A	1983/84	[QRL.39]	5.3.3
Income tax on occupational pensions	Range of total income of recipient/ number of cases/ amount of tax/ county and region	GB	annual	[QRL.102]	5.3.2
Costs of tax relief	pension contributions/ self employed retirement annuity payments/ life premiums	GB	annual	[QRL.52]	5.3
PAYE deducted from occupational pensions	Pay/tax deducted	GB	annual	[QRL.52]	5.3, 3 years data

PAYE deducted from insurance banking and finance	Pay/ tax deducted	GB	annual	[QRL.52]	5.3, 3 years data
Income tax receipts from life companies		GB	annual	[QRL.52]	5.3 - 3.3, 10 years data
Stamp duty on life insurance policies		GB	Annual	[QRL.52]	5.3, 5 years data
Premium relief		UK	Annual	[QRL.109]	5.6, 1979-83
Coverage (Pensions)					
Number of active members of schemes	sector	UK	quadrennially	[QRL.70]	5.7.1
Number of pensioners	sector	UK	quadrennially	[QRL.70]	5.7.1
Pension scheme members	sex/ full-time/ part-time/ contracted out status	UK	1983	[QRL.71]	5.7.1 brief details
Distribution of membership	class of scheme/ sector	GB	annual	[QRL.27]	6.1.1
Employee/ member/ pensioner/ ratios	pensioner/ deferred pensioner	GB	annual	[QRL.27]	6.1.1
Number of schemes	class of scheme/ number of members	GB	annual	[QRL.27]	6.1.1
Members	company/ current/ deferred	UK	annual	[QRL.12]	7.5.1
Pensioners	company/ current/ deferred	UK	annual	[QRL.12]	7.5.1
Employeess of companies sponsoring pension funds	companies	UK	annual	[QRL.12]	7.5.1
Numbers of schemes and members	sector/ schemes/ members/ manual/ non-manual	UK	Quadrennially	[QRL.70]	5.7.1
Percentage of employers	sector/ size/ proportion of employees who are members	UK	Quadrennially	[QRL.70]	5.7.1
Local authorities	Employer/ number of different arrangements/ number of employees/ members of schemes	UK	Quadrennially	[QRL.70]	5.7.1
H.M. forces	Number of persons in HM forces/ number of persons in pensionable engagements	UK	Quadrennially	[QRL.70]	5.7.1
Employees in a scheme - private sector	Number of employees in group/ total number of all employees/ employees whose employer has a scheme/ employees who are members of a scheme/ percentage of all employees who are members	UK	Quadrennially	[QRL.70]	5.7.1

Type of data	Breakdown	Area	Frequency	QRL Publication	Text Reference
Public corporation	Nationalised industries/ other/ number of employees/ members of pension schemes	UK	Quadrennially	[QRL.70]	5.7.1
Central government (civilians)	Employer/ number of different arrangements/ number of employees/ members of schemes	UK	Quadrennially	[QRL.70]	5.7.1
Part-time employees	sex/sector	UK	Quadrennially	[QRL.70]	5.7.1
Employers with schemes - private sector	Number of employees in group/ number of employers/ number with a pension scheme/ percentage of employers with a scheme	UK	Quadrennially	[QRL.70]	5.7.1
Employees in pension schemes	sex/sector	UK	Quadrennially	[QRL.70]	5.7.1 Irregular series from 1936
Coverage	Sex; employees/ members/ sector/ contracted out status	UK	Quadrennially	[QRL.70]	5.7.1
Membership	Projections	GB	1951-2041	[QRL.6]	6.5.1.3
Membership	sex/ full time/ part-time/ member/ not yet/ not a member/ not available	GB	1981	[QRL.15]	8.2
Membership	sex/occupation	GB	1981	[QRL.15]	8.2
Profile of sponsoring employer	Investment method; size of fund; turnover of sponsor; number of employees	GB	1984	[QRL.75]	8.5
Membership	respondent/ spouse/ sex	GB	1981	[QRL.15]	8.2
Number of schemes in a company	Number of schemes/ investment method/ size of fund/ total membership	GB	1984	[QRL.75]	8.5
Proportion of people over state pension age in receipt of pensions	married couples/lone men/lone women	GB	1982	[QRL.85]	5.12.2
Profile of employer and employee	refer appendix 5.3	UK	1984	[QRL.42] [QRL.43]	5.12.1
Coverage	type of fund/ all employees/ members/ manual/ non-manual	GB	1980	[QRL.103]	8.4
Financial Advisors					
Type of fund manager		GB	quarterly	[QRL.74]	7.6.2

Services expected from external investment advisers and fund managers	services/ investment method/ size of fund/ advisers/ fund managers	GB	1984	[QRL.75]	7.10
Employees of firms advising pension funds	Companies	UK	Annual	[QRL.12]	7.5.1
Financial advisers	Type of adviser/ name of advisers/ sundry personnel type information/ value of funds managed or advised/ number of clients	UK	Annual	[QRL.12]	7.5.1
Type of outside manager or adviser used	Merchant bank/ stock broker/ insurance company/ clearing bank/ investment management company/ pensions consultant/ property advisers/ other	GB	1980	[QRL.103]	8.4
Factors considered when choosing investment advisers	Type of fund/ factors	GB	1980 1984	[QRL.103] [QRL.75]	8.4, 8.5
Management changes in last 5 years	Method from, to/ size of fund/ reasons	GB	1984	[QRL.75]	8.5
Criteria for choice of managers	Criteria/ investment method/ size of fund/ advisers	GB	1984	[QRL.75]	8.5
Advantages and disadvantages of outside investment management	Type of fund/ reasons	GB	1980	[QRL.103]	8.4
Fees paid to outside organisations	Administration/ other services/ amount/ investment method/ size of fund/ future change likely?	GB	1984	[QRL.75]	8.5
Information Provision					
Reports and accounts	various	UK	annual	[QRL.22]	6.1
Source for answering queries	Personnel dept./ pension dept./ employee representative/ type of query	UK	1982	[QRL.10]	8.1
Key influences on company	activity/ identified key influences	UK	1982	[QRL.10]	8.1
Knowledge of pension schemes by members	level of knowledge/ own pension entitlement/ administration/ investment policies	UK	1982	[QRL.10]	8.1

Type of data	Breakdown	Area	Frequency	QRL Publication	Text Reference
Information provided and attitudes towards it	pensioners/members with over 2 years service/members with under 2 years service/before employment/after joining scheme/on becoming a pensioner	England	1985	[QRL.77]	6.8.4
Pensions information	refer appendix 5.3	UK	1984	[QRL.42] [QRL.43]	5.12.1
Interest in receiving information by members	own pension entitlement/ administration/ investment policies/ level of interest	UK	1982	[QRL.10]	8.1
Satisfaction with information received	own pension entitlement/ administration/ investment policies/ level of satisfaction	UK	1982	[QRL.10]	8.1
Availability of information	employee related / administration related / funding related/ item of information/ % of organisations distributing the information automatically who have employee trustees/ who don't have employee trustees	UK	1982	[QRL.10]	8.1
Patterns of information provision	employee related/ administration related/ funding related/ item of information/ automatic/ on request/ not available	UK	1982	[QRL.10]	8.1
Reports available to members	scheme/ members/ class of scheme/ frequency/ trustee report/ audited pension fund accounts/ investments/ investment performance/ actuarial statement	GB	annual	[QRL.27]	6.1.1
Benefit statement available to members	Members/ class of scheme/ frequency	GB	annual	[QRL.27]	6.1.1
Disclosure of pension "provision"	unfunded/ difference between accounting and funding/ both/ unspecified	UK	annual	[QRL.20]	6.6.2 - 2.2.2
Disclosures concerning actuarial involvement	frequency of valuation/ date and result of most recent valuation	UK	annual	[QRL.20]	6.6.2 - 2.2.2
Results of actuarial valuations	surplus/ deficit/ not clearly stated	UK	annual	[QRL.20]	6.6.2 - 2.2.2
Disclosure of basis of actuarial valuation	discontinuance basis/ going concern basis/ both/ basis not given	UK	annual	[QRL.20]	6.6.2 - 2.2.2

Disclosure of accounting policies	benefit structure/ funded / policy on costs/ funding policy/ use of an actuary	UK	annual	[QRL.20]	6.6.2 - 2.2.2
Disclosure of pensions costs	normal and special costs disclosed separately/ total cost only disclosed/ special cost only disclosed/ no cost disclosed	UK	annual	[QRL.20]	6.6.2 - 2.2.2
Number of items disclosed	number of items disclosed/ mean number	UK	annual	[QRL.20]	6.6.2 - 2.2.2
Actuarial reports	frequency/ quantity of information provided to members/ interim reports	UK	1980	[QRL.13]	6.6.1.1
Accounts - Transactions statement	income and expenditure account/ fund account/ transactions on fund	UK	1980	[QRL.13]	6.6.1.1
Accounts - Net assets statement	Balance sheet/ fund account/ statement of assets and liabilities	UK	1980	[QRL.13]	6.6.1.1
Accounting policies	investments/ income recognition/ historical costs/ audited	UK	1980	[QRL.13]	6.6.1.1
Policy regarding circulation	full report/ abbreviated report/ automatic/ on request	UK	1980	[QRL.13]	6.6.1.1
Trustees					
Contents of trustees report	changes in trustees/ changes in rules/ outline features of scheme/ increase in pension rates/ benefit statements/ investment statistics/ investment policy/ administration expenses/ actuarial reports	UK	1980	[QRL.13]	6.6.6.1
Employee trustees as % of all trustees		UK	1982	[QRL.10]	8.1
Areas in which training requested	finance/ investment/ legal/ other/ 'all areas'	UK	1982	[QRL.10]	8.1
Contribution of employee trustees	trustee activities/ reported level of contributions/ high, medium, low, none	UK	1982	[QRL.10]	8.1
Employee trustees	date of introduction/ number of schemes	UK	1982	[QRL.10]	8.1
Duties of trustees	duties ranked by importance	UK	1982	[QRL.10]	8.1
Frequency of negotiations	member representatives/ pension managers/ frequency	UK	1982	[QRL.10]	8.1
Topics for negotiation	topic/ frequency	UK	1982	[QRL.10]	8.1

Type of data	Breakdown	Area	Frequency	QRL Publication	Text Reference
Number of schemes and members of schemes which have member trustees	sector/ schemes/ members/ status of representative	UK	quadrennially	[QRL.70]	5.7
Numbers of members and schemes	schemes/ members/ sector/ type of trustee	UK	quadrennially	[QRL.70]	5.7
How is scheme governed	type of trustee/ schemes/ class of scheme	GB	1978 and annual from 1983	[QRL.27]	2.2.1 - 6.1.1
Selection of trustees	method/ schemes/ class of scheme	GB	1978 and annual from 1983	[QRL.27]	2.2.1 - 6.1.1
How is chairman nominated ?	employer/ board of trustees/ schemes/ class of schemes	GB	1978 and annual from 1983	[QRL.27]	2.2.1 - 6.1.1
Does chairman have a casting vote?	Yes/ No/ class of schemes	UK	1978 and annual from 1983	[QRL.27]	2.2.1 - 6.1.1
Number of meetings of trustees with investment managers	number of meetings/ number of funds	UK	1981	[QRL.64]	6.8.1.1
Trustee approval for investment	approval in all cases/ certain cases/ not required	UK	1981	[QRL.64]	6.8.1.1
Is management committee involved with investment policy	yes/ no/ schemes/ class of schemes	GB	1978 and annual from 1983	[QRL.27]	6.1.1
Are there member representatives on management committee?	yes/ no/ schemes/ class of schemes	GB	1978 and annual from 1983	[QRL.27]	6.1.1
Benefit Structure (Pension Funds)					
Pension fractions	contracted out status	UK	1983	[QRL.71]	5.7.1

Definitions of pensionable salary	class of scheme/ definitions	GB	annual	[QRL.27]	6.1.1
Schemes for senior executives	no special arrangement/ topping up schemes/ separate schemes/ different benefit scale in combined scheme	GB	annual	[QRL.27]	6.1.1
Benefit structure	% of schemes/ % of membership/ class of scheme/ final salary/ salary grade/ flat rate/ career average/ other	GB	annual	[QRL.27]	6.1.1
Integration	class of scheme/ method/ size of membership/ sector/ investment medium	GB	annual	[QRL.27]	6.1.1
Benefits	before retirement/after retirement/men/women/sector	UK	1984	[QRL.42] [QRL.43]	5.12.1. Refer appendix 5.3
Final salary definition	definitions/ class of schemes	GB	annual	[QRL.27]	6.1.1
Money purchase schemes	% of schemes/ % of membership/ class of scheme	GB	annual	[QRL.27]	6.1.1
Pension payable to members with stated hypothetical salary histories	class of scheme/ 10 years service/ 20 years service/ four combinations of salary over the last five years/ contracted out status	GB	annual	[QRL.27]	6.1.1
Rate of pension accrual	fraction/ % of schemes	GB	1980	[QRL.33]	5.7.4
Rate of pension accrual	class of scheme/ level of accrual/ % of membership/ % of schemes/ sector/ integrated status/ contracted out status	GB	annual	[QRL.27]	6.1.1
Modification on account of contracting out	type of modification/ % of schemes	GB	1979, 1980	[QRL.33]	5.7.4
Method of calculating benefit at normal retirement	% of schemes/ method	GB	1980	[QRL.33]	5.7.4
Integration	type of modification/ % of schemes	GB	1979, 1980	[QRL.33]	5.7.4
Difference in benefits between senior management and staff schemes	benefit	UK	quadrennially	[QRL.70]	5.7.1
Numbers of members with final salary pensions	Method of definition of final salary/ contracted out status/ sector	UK	quadrennially	[QRL.70]	5.7.1
Number of members	contracted out status/ pension formula	UK	quadrennially	[QRL.70]	5.7.1
Entry conditions					

Type of data	Breakdown	Area	Frequency	QRL Publication	Text Reference
Eligibility	compulsory membership/ age limits/ part-timers defined by numbers of hours worked	GB	1984	[QRL.28]	8.13
Entry ages	age/ male/ female/ staff/ works	UK	1983	[QRL.11]	8.12
Employees not in pension schemes	cause for exclusion/ sector/ sex/ manual/ non-manual	UK	quadrennially	[QRL.70]	5.7.1
Number of members	waiting period for lump sum death benefit/ sector	UK	quadrennially	[QRL.70]	5.7.1
Number of members	waiting period for ill health pension/ sector	UK	annual	[QRL.70]	5.7.1
Number of members	sector/ age/ minimum entry age	UK	quadrennially	[QRL.70]	5.7.1
Number of members	minimum service for normal retirement pension/ sector	UK	quadrennially	[QRL.70]	5.7.1
Number of members	sector/ length of service before entry	UK	quadrennially	[QRL.70]	5.7.1
Conditions	% of schemes/ types of condition	GB	1979, 1980	[QRL.33]	5.7.4
Age	minimum/ maximum	GB	annual	[QRL.27]	6.1.1
Waiting periods	class of scheme/ length of waiting period	GB	annual	[QRL.27]	6.1.1
Membership	voluntary/ compulsory/ by invitation/ class of scheme	GB	annual	[QRL.27]	6.1.1
Death in Service Benefits (Pension Funds)					
Lump sum benefit paid by local authorities	death/ retirement	England and Wales		[QRL.61]	5.11.2
Dependants pension	name of company/ method	GB	1984	[QRL.28]	8.13
Lump sum benefit	name of company/ multiple of.salary	GB	1984	[QRL.28]	8.13
Equal opportunities	name of company/ widowers of right/ on proven dependancy/ widowers benfit specified	GB	1984	[QRL.28]	8.13
Death in service benefits	type of benefit/ male/ female	UK	1983	[QRL.11]	8.12
Benefits provided	combination of benefits/ class of scheme/ sector/ contracted status	GB	annual	[QRL.27]	6.1.1
Number of members	circumstances of payment/ sector	UK	quadrennially	[QRL.70]	5.7.1
Number of members	sector/ method of calculating widows pension/ whether remarriage affects benefit	UK	quadrennially	[QRL.70]	5.7.1

Death benefit	sector	UK	annual	[QRL.32]	5.2.1.2 - 3rd quarter issue
Male members	sector/ method of calculating lump sum/ number of members	UK	quadrennially	[QRL.70]	5.7.1
Differences between men and women	sector/ type of difference on lump sum death benefit	UK	quadrennially	[QRL.70]	5.7.1
Conditions for provision of children's benefits	class of scheme/ no benefit/ automatic benefits in addition to any other dependents benefit/ discretionary benefits in addition to any other dependents benefits/ some other basis/ investment medium	GB	annual	[QRL.27]	6.1.1
Widowers benefit on death in service	class of scheme/ no benefit/ as of right/ discretionary/ dependent widower/ independent widower/ investment medium	GB	annual	[QRL.27]	6.1.1
Method of distribution of lump sum benefits	class of scheme/ discretionary trust/ legal personal representatives/ other	GB	annual	[QRL.27]	6.1.1
Amount of lump sum payable	class of scheme/ lump sum as a multiple of salary/ marital status/ sex	GB	annual	[QRL.27]	6.1.1
Method of calculating widows pension	class of scheme/ members/ schemes/ method/ sector	GB	annual	[QRL.27]	6.1.1
Period of payment of widows pension	class of scheme/ period of payment	GB	annual	[QRL.27]	6.1.1
Level of widows benefit	fraction/ class of scheme/ sector/ schemes/ members	GB	annual	[QRL.27]	6.1.1
Lump sum benefits	type	GB	1979, 1980	[QRL.33]	5.7.4
Widows benefits	type	GB	1979, 1980	[QRL.33]	5.7.4
Death after Retirement Benefits					
Dependants pension	name of company/ provision as before any contribution	GB	1984	[QRL.28]	8.13
Lump sum benefit	name of company/ benefit	GB	1984	[QRL.28]	8.13
Childs benefit	name of company/ basis	GB	1984	[QRL.28]	8.13
Dependants benefits other than spouse or child	Name of company/ basis	GB	1984	[QRL.28]	8.13
Spouses benefit reduction for age difference	name of company/ age difference/ reduction	GB	1984	[QRL.28]	8.13

Type of data	Breakdown	Area	Frequency	QRL Publication	Text Reference
Widows benefit ceasing on remarriage	name of company/ actual condition	GB	1984	[QRL.28]	8.13
Equal opportunities	name of company/ widowers of right/ on proven dependancy/ no widowers benefit specified	GB	1984	[QRL.28]	8.13
Level of widows benefits	fraction/ class of scheme/ sector/ members/ schemes	GB	annual	[QRL.27]	6.1.1
Bases of calculating widows pension	class of scheme/ schemes/ before commutation/ after commutation	GB	annual	[QRL.27]	6.1.1
Pensions guarantee rule	conditions when guarantee rule applies/ schemes/ class of scheme	GB	annual	[QRL.27]	6.1.1
Benefits	widows benefit fraction/ type of childs pension	GB	1979, 1980	[QRL.33]	5.7.4
Payment of pension guarantee	class of schemes/ schemes/ lump sum/ pension continues until end of guarantee period/ other method	GB	annual	[QRL.27]	6.1.1
Widowers pension correlated to investment medium	schemes/ investment medium/ dependent widower/ independent widower	GB	annual	[QRL.27]	6.1.1
Widowers benefits	class of scheme/ sector/ schemes/ members/ dependent widower/ independent widower/ no benefit/ as of right/ on a discretionary basis	GB	annual	[QRL.27]	6.1.1
Widows benefit	class of scheme/ members/ schemes/ as of right/ by surrender/ none/ sector	GB	annual	[QRL.27]	6.1.1
Benefits	widows pension fraction/ type of child's pension	GB	1979, 1980	[QRL.33]	5.7.4
Number of members	sector/ type of benefit/ availability	UK	quadrennially	[QRL.70]	5.7.1
Contributions (Pension Funds)					
Contribution rates	accrual rate/ name of company/ employers contribution rate/ members contribution rate/ integrated	GB	1984	[QRL.28]	APEX pensions survey

Annual contributions	company	UK	annual	[QRL.12]	7.5.1
Members contributions	class of scheme/ contributory status/ method of contribution	GB	Annual	[QRL.27]	6.1.1
Average employees annual cont.	class of scheme/ amount/ % of pensionable salary	GB	Annual	[QRL.27]	6.1.1
Contributions of employees	Funded; unfunded; notionally funded	UK	annual	[QRL.109] [QRL.48]	5.6 Data for 11 years
Increases by employer of ordinary contributions	class of scheme/ reason	GB	annual	[QRL.27]	6.1.1
Special payments by employer	class of scheme/ reason	GB	annual	[QRL.27]	6.1.1
Employers average annual costs	class of scheme/ amount/ % of pensionable salary/ contributary status	GB	annual	[QRL.27]	6.1.1
Members contributions	rate	GB	1979, 1980	[QRL.33]	5.7.4
Method of investment of AVC's	schemes/ sector/ class of schemes/ privately invested/ building society/ insurance company/ other/ investment medium	GB	annual	[QRL.27]	6.1.1
Average annual contribution per member	schemes/ members/ contracted out status	UK	quadrennially	[QRL.70]	5.7.1
Numbers of members	levels of contributions/ sector	UK	quadrennially	[QRL.70]	5.7.1
Number of members	sector/ contracted out status/ method of calculating contributions	UK	quadrennially	[QRL.70]	5.7.1
Members paying contributions	percentage of salary/ sector/ contracted out status/ number of members	UK	quadrennially	[QRL.70]	5.7.1
Employers pension costs as % of staff costs	%'s/ not disclosed/ mean ratio	UK	annual	[QRL.20]	
Members making AVC's	sex	GB	1981	[QRL.15]	8.2
Total contributions	type of fund/ level of contribution/ size of fund	GB	1980, 1983	[QRL.103] [QRL.75]	8.4 - 8.5
Refunds	normal; additional; sector	UK	annual (since 1982)	[QRL.32]	5.2.1.2
Employers	sector	UK	annual (since 1982)	[QRL.32]	5.2.1.2 - 3rd quarter issue
Employees	sector	UK	annual (since 1982)	[QRL.32]	5.2.1.2 - 3rd quarter issue
Transfer values	In/ out/ sector	UK	annual (since 1982)	[QRL.32]	5.2.1.2 - 3rd quarter issue

Type of data	Breakdown	Area	Frequency	QRL Publication	Text Reference
Pensions	sector	UK	annual (since 1982)	[QRL.32]	5.2.1.2 - 3rd quarter issue
Contracting out					
Effect of GMP on willingness to accept transfer values	Schemes/ sector/ class of scheme	GB	Annual	[QRL.27]	6.1.1
Numbers ceasing to be contracted out	CEP's/LRP's/ARP's/GMP's preserved/numbers/amounts	GB	quinquenially	[QRL.94]	5.12.3. three years data
Integration of scheme	yes/no/don't know/men/women/sector	UK	1984	[QRL.42] [QRL.43]	5.13.1. Refer appendix 5.3
Ceasing to be contracted out	individuals the scheme remaining contracted out /schemes ceasing to be contracted out /ARP's /CEP's /LRP's /numbers /amounts	UK	annual	[QRL.94]	5.12.3 three years data
Numbers of private sector members	contracted out status/ adjustment to pension for national insurance	UK	quadrennially	[QRL.70]	5.7.1
Numbers of pension schemes	sector/ size of membership/ contracted out status	GB	Quadrennially	[QRL.70]	5.7.1
Method of GMP revaluation	sector/ schemes/ members/ class of schemes/ full/ limited/ fixed/ investment medium	GB	annual	[QRL.27]	6.1.1
Contracting out permitted	schemes/ members/ contracting out/ participating	GB	annual	[QRL.27]	6.1.1
Consents to rule changes	applications for certificates withdrawn, varied, surrendered	GB		[QRL.99]	5.4 - Data after 1981 may be available from OPB
Certificates	issued; refused; cancelled; surrendered	GB	Annual and cumulative total	[QRL.99]	5.4 Data after 1981 may be available from OPB
Number of applications made	consultation required, not required	GB	latest year and cumulative total	[QRL.99]	5.4 - Data after 1981 may be available from OPB

Standard documents processed by OPB	type of processing/ for contracting out purposes/ equal access purposes	GB	1981	[QRL.99]	5.4 - Data after 1981 may be available on application to OPB
Applications for modification and winding of orders	purpose for which modification required, No. of applications received, No of orders made	GB	1981	[QRL.99]	5.4 - Data after 1981 may be available from OPB
Conditions	waiting periods/minimum age/men/women/sector	UK	1984	[QRL.42] [QRL.43]	5.13.1. Refer appendix 5.3
Normal Retirement (Pension funds)					
Normal retirement benefits					
Lump sums	class of scheme/ yes/ no/ schemes	GB	annual	[QRL.27]	6.1.1
Commutation of trivial pensions	class of scheme/ yes/ no/ schemes	GB	annual	[QRL.27]	6.1.1
Lump sums	sector/ lump sum but no pension/ lump sum as well as pension in all cases/ commutation option/ none of previous/ number of members	UK	quadrennially	[QRL.70]	5.7.1
Normal retirement age	company name/ age/ men/ women	GB	1984	[QRL.28]	8.13
Normal retirement age	age/ male/ female	UK	1983	[QRL.11]	8.12
Normal retirement age	Sex/ manual/ non-manual/ retirement age	GB	1981	[QRL.15]	8.2
Normal retirement age	sex/ % of schemes/ age	GB	1979, 1980	[QRL.33]	5.7.4
Number of members	sex/ age/ sector/ normal retirement age	UK	quadrennially	[QRL.70]	5.7.1
Normal retirement age	sex/ class of scheme/ sector	GB	annual	[QRL.27]	6.1.1
Normal Retirement age	men/women/sector	UK	1984	[QRL.42] [QRL.43]	5.13.1. Refer appendix 5.3
Early Retirement					
Qualifying period for ill-health retirement	name of company	GB	1984	[QRL.28]	8.13
Benefit calculation for ill-health retirement	name of company	GB	1984	[QRL.28]	8.13
Notional service for ill-health retirement	name of company	GB	1984	[QRL.28]	8.13

Type of data	Breakdown	Area	Frequency	QRL Publication	Text Reference
Early retirement at members request	name of company/ basis	GB	1984	[QRL.28]	8.13
Minimum eligibility age for early retirement	age/ men/ women	UK	1983	[QRL.11]	8.12
Number of members	sector/ provision for early retirement other than ill-health	UK	latest year	[QRL.70]	5.7.1
Number of members	Basis of pension/ sector on ill health	UK	1979	[QRL.70]	5.7.1
Calculation of ill-health pensions	class of scheme/ method/ schemes/ members/ investment medium	GB	annual	[QRL.27]	6.1.1
Methods used in normal health	sector/ method/ retirement on initiative of employee/ retirement on initiative of employer	GB	annual	[QRL.27]	6.1.1
Type of pension on ill-health retirement		GB	1979, 1980	[QRL.33]	5.7.4
Late Retirement					
Benefits on deferred retirement	type of benefit/ schemes	GB	1979, 1980	[QRL.33]	5.7.4
Pensions in Payment					
Pensions in payment by LAs	members /dependants	E and W		[QRL.61]	5.11.2
Size of new occupational pension		UK	1983	[QRL.71]	5.7.1
Annual rate of increase	sector	UK	1983	[QRL.71]	5.7.1
Number	former employees/ widows & dependents/ sector	UK	Quadrennially	[QRL.70]	5.7.1 irregular series of data from 1936
Average size	sex/ sector	UK	quadrennially	[QRL.70]	5.7.1
Number of pensioners	rate of pension increase/ sector/ whether increase specified in the rules	UK	quadrennially	[QRL.70]	5.7.1
Pensioners Income	occupational pensions/N.I. pension/other social security benefits/ earnings/investment income/income tax	GB	1951, 1961, 1971, 1981, 1984	[QRL.85]	5.12.2

Projection of pensioners income	state/ occupational/ income/ income tax/ benefits price linked/benefits earnings linked	GB	decenially 1984-2025	[QRL.85]	5.12.2
Increases	size of increase in pension promised in rules compared with actual increase	UK	quadrennially	[QRL.70]	5.7.1
Increases on pensions in payment	frequency/ extent/ method of implementation/ integrated	UK	1980	[QRL.78]	6.8.2
Actual increases compared with guaranteed	schemes/ members/ class of scheme/ actual greater than guaranteed/ actual equals guaranteed/ not applicable	GB	annual	[QRL.27]	6.1.1
Post-retirement increases	method of investment/ guaranteed under scheme rules/ not guaranteed but revewed at various frequencies/ not increased/ schemes	GB	annual	[QRL.27]	6.1.1
Guaranteed increases	levels/ sector/ schemes/ members/ class of scheme	GB	annual	[QRL.27]	6.1.1
Average increases	schemes/ class of schemes/ sector	GB	annual	[QRL.27]	6.1.1 - three years figures
Increases in deferred pensions	sector/ class of scheme/ schemes/ members/ none/ at fixed level/ at same level as for pensions in payment/ at some other rate/ level of increase	GB	annual	[QRL.27]	6.1.1
Types of provision for increases	type of increase/ number of schemes/ level of increase/ fixed/ discretionary	N/A	1979, 1980	[QRL.33]	5.7.4
Pensions and other benefits paid	funded, unfunded, notionally funded	UK	latest 11 years	[QRL.109] [QRL.48]	5.6
Occupational pensions in payment as part of total income	Number of cases/ amount/ marital status	GB	Annual	[QRL.102]	5.3.2
Pensions - Lump sums	sector	UK	annual (since 1982)	[QRL.32]	4.2.1.2 - 2.2.2 - 2.5.5 - 3rd quarter issue
NHS Pension Fund					
Changes in membership	sex/ entrants and transfers/ exits by type	England & Wales	1979	[QRL.91]	5.7.3
Rates of decrement used for the valuation	sex/ mortality/ morbidity/ duration of employment/ withdrawal	England & Wales	1979	[QRL.91]	5.7.3
Rates of decrement used for the valuation	sex/ mortality/ morbidity/ duration of employment/ withdrawal	Scotland		[QRL.66]	5.7.3

Type of data	Breakdown	Area	Frequency	QRL Publication	Text Reference
Consolidated revenue account	stock/ amount/ annual interest	England & Wales	1979	[QRL.91]	5.7.3
Consolidated revenue account	stock/ amount/ annual interest	Scotland		[QRL.66]	5.7.3
Notional fund investment		England & Wales	1979	[QRL.91]	5.7.3
Notional fund investment		Scotland		[QRL.66]	5.7.3
Valuation statements		England & Wales	1979	[QRL.91]	5.7.3
Valuation statements		Scotland		[QRL.66]	5.7.3
Pensions in payment	Type of retiree/ number/ amount	England & Wales	1979	[QRL.91]	5.7.3
Pensions in payment		Scotland		[QRL.66]	5.7.3
Contributors	sex/ type of employee/ number/ average annual salary	England & Wales	1979	[QRL.91]	5.7.3
Contributors	sex/ type of employee/ number/ average annual salary	Scotland		[QRL.66]	5.7.3
Teachers' Pension Fund					
Rate of mortality of teacher pensioners	sex/ normal retirees/ ill-health retirees	England & Wales	1981	[QRL.92]	5.7.2
Amount of notional securities		England & Wales	1981	[QRL.92]	5.7.2
Valuation statement		England & Wales	1981	[QRL.92]	5.7.2
Consolidated account of receipts and payments		England & Wales	1981	[QRL.92]	5.7.2
Decrements of teachers during service	sex/ length of service/ death/ withdrawal/ retirement	England & Wales	1981	[QRL.92]	5.7.2
Number of teacher pensioners	sex/ normal retirement/ ill-health retirement/ widows	England & Wales	1976, 1981	[QRL.92]	5.7.2
Total amount of teacher pensions	sex/ normal retirement/ ill-health retirement/ widows	England & Wales	1976-81	[QRL.92]	5.7.2

Average annual amount of teachers pension	sex/ normal retirement/ ill-health retirement/ widows	England & Wales	1976-81	[QRL.92]	5.7.2
Demographic and Valuation Data (Life and Pensions)					
Valuation and surplus	name of insurer/ date of valuation/ years since last valuation/ net liability at valuation date/ net transfers/ fund as per balance sheet/ surplus or deficiency/ composition of surplus/ distribution of surplus	GB	annual	[QRL.54]	5.2 Series ceased 1975
Duplicates among linked policies	age/ policies/ lives/ duration/ sex	GB	1976-78	[QRL.38]	6.5.2
Withdrawal rates	entry age/ duration/ class/ premium paying term/ premium paying frequency by type of sales person	Scotland	1976-77	[QRL.105]	6.5.2.1 work in progress on later data
Net valuation interest rate - post retirement	number of times used/ rate	GB	1979	[QRL.14]	6.5.11
Net valuation interest rate - pre-retirement	number of times used/ rate/ pre-retirement/ post retirement	GB	1979	[QRL.14]	6.5.11
Mortality and other assumptions in civil service scheme		GB	1979, 1980	[QRL.33]	5.7.4
Distribution of people of pensionable age	map	GB	1921, 1981	[QRL.81]	5.8.1
Mortality and Morbidity					
Rates of Mortality	male/female/assumed in 1975 and 1981	N/A	1978, 1998, 2018, 2038, 2058	[QRL.94]	5.12.3
Standard mortality functions - insured lives	single life/ joint life/ rates of interest/ age/ select/ ultimate/ duration	N/A	N/A	[QRL.21]	6.5.2
Standard monetary functions - insured lives	single life/ joint life/ rates of interest/ age/ select/ ultimate/ duration	N/A	N/A	[QRL.21]	6.5.2
Morbidity of insured lives - individual policies	Age/ deferred period/ exposed to risk/ weeks of sickness/ claim rate/ sex	GB	1972 and 1973 1974 and 1975	[QRL.82], [QRL.35]	Data is graduated in [QRL.36] 6.5.2

Type of data	Breakdown	Area	Frequency	QRL Publication	Text Reference
Morbidity experience, group policies	Number of lives/ number of claims/ age/sex/deferred period/ sickness period Age/ sex/ differed period/ sickness period	GB	1973-76	[QRL.37]	6.5.2
Morbidity experience, individual policies	number in force/ claims/ sex/ age/ deferred period/ sickness period	UK	1975-78	[QRL.37]	6.5.2
Proposed standard mortality tables	pensioners/ annuitants/ sex/ age	GB	1967-70	[QRL.35]	6.5.2
Mortality of insured lives	age/ duration/ medical/ non-medical/ sex/ whole life and endowment/ temporary insurances/ linked contracts	UK	1975-78	[QRL.36]	6.5.2
Mortality of immediate annuitants	lives/ amounts/ age/ sex	GB	1975-78	[QRL.37]	6.5.2
Mortality of purchasers of deferred annuities (Finance Act 1956)	sex/ age/ lives/ in deferment/ in payment/ medical/ non-medical	GB	1971-74	[QRL.35]	6.5.2
Mortality of immediate annuitants	sex/ age/ duration	GB	1971-74	[QRL.35]	6.5.2
Mortality of pensioners in life office schemes	sex/ age/ lives/ amounts/ works/ non-works	GB	1971-74	[QRL.35]	6.5.2
Mortality of insured lives	age/ medical/ non-medical/ duration/ cause of death	GB	1967-70 1971-74 1975-78	[QRL.34] [QRL.35] [QRL.37]	Investigation limited to whole of life and endowment policies. The female data is graduated in [QRL.38] 6.5.2
Mortality of immediate annuitants	sex/ duration/ age/ lives	GB	1967-70	[QRL.34]	Report on how data was graduated is in [QRL.82] 6.5.2
Mortality of insured lives	age/ duration/ males/ medical/ non-medical/ whole life & endowment	GB	1971-74	[QRL.35]	6.5.2

Mortality of pensioners in life office schemes	sex/ age/ lives/ amounts/ works/ non-works	GB	1967-70	[QRL.34]	6.5.2
Mortality of pensioners in life office schemes	sex/ age/ lives/ amounts/ works/ non-works/ early retirement/ normal & late retirement	GB	1975-78	[QRL.37]	6.5.2
Standard mortality functions	sex/ age/ rates of interest/ pensioner/ annuitant	N/A	N/A	[QRL.73] [QRL.22]	6.5.2
Standard monetary functions	sex/ age/ rates of interest/ pensioner/ annuitant	N/A	N/A	[QRL.73] [QRL.22]	6.5.2
Mortality functions for person born in 1925	age/ pensioner/ annuitant	N/A	N/A	[QRL.73] [QRL.22]	6.5.2
Mortality rates	age/ calender year of birth/ pensioner/ annuitant	N/A	N/A	[QRL.73] [QRL.22]	6.5.2
Preservation (Pension Funds)					
Benefits on withdrawal	type of benefit/ schemes	GB	1979, 1980	[QRL.33]	5.7.4
Number of members	sector/ type of deferred pension	UK	quadrennially	[QRL.70]	5.7.1
Number of members	sector/ statutory/ non-statutory level of preserved benefit	UK	quadrennially	[QRL.70]	5.7.1
Options on transfer	options taken/options offered/men/women/sector	UK	1984	[QRL.42] [QRL.43]	5.12.1. Refer appendix 5.3
GMP's preserved without payment of state scheme premiums	number/amount	UK	annual	[QRL.94]	5.12.3. 3 years data
Number of schemes satisfying preservation requirements	total/cumulative total	GB	1981	[QRL.99]	data after 1981 may be available on application to OPB
Leavers	sector/ length of service/ type of benefit awarded	UK	quadrennially	[QRL.70]	5.7.1
Transfer values	class of schemes/ schemes/ accepted/ offered	GB	annual	[QRL.27]	6.1.1
Benefits granted for transfer values	schemes/ members/ class of schemes/ sector/ type of benefit granted/ investment medium	GB	annual	[QRL.27]	6.1.1
Members who have transferred contributions from previous schemes	sex	GB	1981	[QRL.15]	8.2

Type of data	Breakdown	Area	Frequency	QRL Publication	Text Reference
Effect of GMP on willingness to accept transfer values	Schemes/ sector/ class of scheme	GB	Annual	[QRL.27]	6.1.1
Transfer values	In/out/ sector	UK	Annual since 1982	[QRL.32]	5.2.1.2 3rd quarter issue
Frozen pensions	sex/ currently member?/ frozen pension of varying years duration	GB	1981	[QRL.15]	8.2
Early leaver transfers	investment method/ size of fund/ allowed to a) any insurance co, b) panel of approved companies, c) not sure, d) not allowed, e) only to new scheme/ many specified reasons for previous replies	GB	1984	[QRL.75]	8.5
Authorisations					
Authorized UK insurers	Names/ classes of insurance written/ accounting year/ sundry information	UK	Annual	[QRL.55] [QRL.54]	5.2.2
Additions and removals to the Registry of Friendly Societies	Types of Societies/ b/f/ ons/ offs with reasons/ c/f	GB	latest year	[QRL.26]	5.10
Use of powers of intervention of Secretary of State	power/number of times specific power used	GB	annual	[QRL.53]	5.2.2
Number of companies authorised for each class of business	class of business/ location of head office	GB	annual	[QRL.53]	5.2.2
Unauthorised insurers under investigation	action taken	GB	annual	[QRL.53]	5.2.2
Number of offices issuing linked life assurance	type of linkage	GB	Annual	[QRL.17]	5.2.2.4 Data for 1961-70
Applications for authorizations	Class of business/ bf/ cf/ recieved/ granted/ refused/ previously authorized/ not previously authorized	GB	Annual	[QRL.53]	5.2.2
Procedure and Practice					

Certificate of Existance	requirement for completion/ objective/ frequency/ distribution/ staffing/ method/ value of process	UK	1979	[QRL.78]	6.8.2.1
Future developments to consider	newsletters/ meetings/ Christmas card/ freefone numbers/ hampers/ advice services	UK	1980	[QRL.78]	6.8.2
Pensions payroll records	years payroll records kept	UK	1980	[QRL.78]	6.8.2
Deductions from pensions payroll	national savings/ PAYE/ private medical insurance/ rents/ staff purchases/ other/ with or without written authority	UK	1980	[QRL.78]	6.8.2
Pensions payment methods	cash/ cheque/ credit transfer/ bankers clearing/ Giro/ other	UK	1980	[QRL.78]	6.8.2
Special facilities relating to pension's payments	overpayment recovery/ combination of payment/ arrears/ tax corrections	UK	1980	[QRL.78]	6.8.2
Pension payslips	are they sent/ method of delivery/ message facility	UK	1980	[QRL.78]	6.8.2
How pensions payroll produced	computer/ manually/ visible record/ other	UK	1980	[QRL.78]	6.8.2
Who produces pensions payroll	parent/ self/ computer bureau/ other	UK	1980	[QRL.78]	6.8.2
How many staff in pensions payroll administration	full-time/ those with additional involvement	UK	1980	[QRL.78]	6.8.2
Size of pensioner payroll	number of pensioners/ number of funds/ number of starters/ number of leavers	UK	1980	[QRL.78]	6.8.2
Full or proportionate pension payments		UK	1980	[QRL.78]	6.8.2
Pensions payment dates	fixed/ by reference to commencement date/ frequency/ number	UK	1980	[QRL.78]	6.8.2
Type of computerised systems	self-designed on company mainframe/ purchased software/ self-design software or mini/ outside bureau/ investment method/ size of fund	GB	1984	[QRL.75]	8.5
Pensions administration	in-house/ manually/ computerised/ specified other methods/ investment method/ size of fund	GB	1984	[QRL.75]	8.5
Variations in valuations of two properties	10 valuations by different surveyors	UK	1984	[QRL.7]	10.4.1

Type of data	Breakdown	Area	Frequency	QRL Publication	Text Reference
Method of decision making by committee	Fund type/ individual transactions left to stockbroker/ council decide/ treasurer/ director of finance/ other	GB	1980	[QRL.103]	8.4
Responsibility for measuring performance	Type of fund/ respondent/ fund manager/ consulting actuary/ independent investment analyst/ CIPFA/ other	UK	1980	[QRL.103]	8.4
Fund investment method	Outside managed/self-invested/ investment committee/ insured/ other/ fund type	GB	1980	[QRL.103]	8.4
Freedom allowed manager	Fund type/ total/ guide-lines for amount/ must consult before major changes/ need approval/ other	GB	1980, 1984	[QRL.103] [QRL.75]	8.4 - 8.5
Responsibility for investment guidelines	Fund type/ the authority alone/ fund manager alone/ jointly/ developed over time/ committee/ others	GB	1980, 1984	[QRL.103] [QRL.75]	8.4 - 8.5
Type of fund investment manager	Class of scheme/own in-house fund manager/ mixture/ some other means e.g. insurance contract/ size of fund	GB	Annual	[QRL.27]	6.1.1
Method of property management	In-house/ external in common with other investments/ separate firm of property advisers/ exempt property unit trust/ property managed fund	GB	Annual	[QRL.27]	6.1.1
Type of investment manager	Internal/ merchant bank/ clearing bank/ stock broker/ managed fund/ other	UK	1981	[QRL.64]	6.8.1
Restrictions on level of investment	6 sectors/ 5 classes of share/ no rstriction/ investment prohibited/ specified percentage/ minimum percentage/ range specified/ other	UK	1981	[QRL.64]	6.8.1.1
Sector restrictions	Frequency of review	UK	1981	[QRL.64]	6.8.1.1
Local authorities fund statistics	name of authority/ size/ time-weighted return/ proportions in various investment/ turnover/ activity/ net investments in various investments	GB	annual	[QRL.62]	6.7 - also cumulative 5 years data

QUICK REFERENCE LIST KEY TO PUBLICATIONS

Reference	Author or Organisation	Title	Publisher	Frequency or Date	Remarks
[QRL.1]	Adamson D	*An Investigation of unquoted holdings of United Kingdom Financial Institutions*	Limited circulation	1985	A copy is held by the NAPF library
[QRL.2]	Benjamin B. Bacon F.W. Elphinstone M.D.W.	"The growth of pension rights and their impact in the natural economy." *JIA* 80 p.141-202	Alden Press	1954	
[QRL.3]	Bernstein G	*A survey of Approaches to Pension Funding*	City University	Forthcoming	
[QRL.4]	Carter R.L. and Godden A.H.	*The British Insurance Industry - A Statistical Review*	Kluwer	Annual	
[QRL.5]	Dunn A.T. - Hoffman P.D.R.B.	*Distribution of Wealth in the United Kingdom: Effect of including pension right, and analysis by age-group.* Review of Income and Wealth, 29 No.3	International Association for Research in Income and Wealth	September 1983	
[QRL.6]	Field J.L.	"Projections of the Costs of Occupational and State Pensions" *JIA* vol. 110 No.444 p.243	Alden Press	June 1983	
[QRL.7]	Hager D.P. and Lord D.J.	*The Property Market*, Property Valuations and Property performance Measurement	Paper to Institute of Actuaries publication forthcoming	28 Jan. 1985	
[QRL.8]	Hannah, Prof L.	*Inventing Retirement*	Cambridge University Press	Proposed 1986	
[QRL.9]	Harrison A.,Tranter R.B., Gibbs R.S.	*Landownership by public and semi-public institutions in the UK* CAS Paper 3	College of Estate Management. Reading	December 1977	
[QRL.10]	Hyman J. and Schuller T.	*Employee participation in the management of pension schemes summary report*	University of Glasgow	May 1983	

[QRL.11]	McGoldrick, Ann	*Equal Treatment in Occupational Pension Schemes*	EOC.	December 1984	
[QRL.12]	Philipp, A.	*Pension Funds and their Advisors*	A.P. Information Services Ltd	Annual	
[QRL.13]	Platt, C.J.	"Looking into Pension Fund Accounts", *Accountancy*	ICAEW	1981	
[QRL.14]	Renn, D.F. and Stewart, C.M.	"Actuarial Reports on Pension Fund Valuations", *JIA* vol. 109 part I page 113	Alden Press	June 1983	
[QRL.15]	Ritchie, Jane and Barrowclough, Ron	*Paying for equalisation*. An EOC survey of pension age preferences and their costs	EOC	May 1983	
[QRL.16]	Scott, Sir Bernard	*Inquiry into the Value of Pensions* Cmnd 8147	HMSO	1981	
[QRL.17]	Scott, Sir Hilary	'Linked Life Assurance' *Report of the Committee on Property Bonds and Equity - Linked Life Assurance*. Cmnd 5281	HMSO	1973	Commonly referred to as "Scott Report on Linked Life"
[QRL.18]	Shorrocks, A.F.	"Life Insurance and asset holding in the United Kingdom", in *Microeconomics and Economic Development* edited by D. Currie, D. Peel & W. Peters	Croom Helm	1981	
[QRL.19]	Steel, A.	"Financial Institutions. Their investments and agricultural landownership." Working paper No.1 in *Land Management and Development Management*	University of Reading. Department of Land Management & Development	January 1983	

Reference	Author or Organisation	Title	Publisher	Frequency or Date	Remarks
[QRL.20]	Tonkin D.J. & Skerratt L.C.L	*Financial Reporting: A Survey of United Kingdom published accounts*	I.C.A.	Annual	Until 1980 called *A Survey of Published Accounts - A Reference Guide to Annual Reports and Accounts.*
[QRL.21]	CMI	*A 1967/70 Tables for assured lives*	Institute and Faculty of Actuaries	1975	six volumes
[QRL.22]	CMI	*A(90) Tables for annuitants*	Institute and Faculty of Actuaries	1979	More extensive sets of functions available on microfiche
[QRL.23]	Meal	*Advertisement Analysis*	Private circulation	1974 to date	
[QRL.24]	Association of Pensioneer trustees	*Analysis of assets of members*	Association of Pensioneer trustees	1984	Limited circulation
[QRL.25]	CSO	*Annual Abstract of Statistics*	HMSO	Annual	
[QRL.26]	Registrar of Friendly Societies	*Annual Report*	HMSO	Annual	
[QRL.27]	NAPF	*Annual Survey of Occupational Pension Schemes*	NAPF	Annual	
[QRL.28]	APEX	*APEX Pensions Survey 1985*. A survey of 50 major United Kingdom company schemes	APEX	August 1985	

[QRL.29]	Bank of England	'Balance Sheets for Insurance Companies', *Bank of England Quarterly Review* [QRL.30]	Bank of England	September 1978	Article
[QRL.30]	Economics Division of Bank of England	*Bank of England Quarterly Bulletin*	Bank of England	Quarterly	
[QRL.31]	ABI Statistics Bureau	*ABI Members Statistics*	ABI	Annual	
[QRL.32]	Business Statistics Office	*Business Monitor*, MQ5, Insurance companies and pension funds' investment	HMSO London	Quarterly	
[QRL.33]	Government Actuary	*Civil Service Pay Research - The 1980 Review of the Adjustment for differences in Superannuation Benefits*	HMSO	1980	
[QRL.34]	Executive committee of the CMI	*CMI Reports*, Number 1	Institute and Faculty of Actuaries	1973	
[QRL.35]	Executive committee of the CMI	*CMI Reports*, Number 3	Institute and Faculty of Actuaries	1978	
[QRL.36]	Executive committee of the CMI	*CMI Reports*, Number 4	Institute and Faculty of Actuaries	1979	
[QRL.37]	Executive committee of the CMI	*CMI Reports*, Number 5	Institute and Faculty of Actuaries	1981	
[QRL.38]	Executive committee of the CMI	*CMI Reports*, Number 6	Institute and Faculty of Actuaries	1983	
[QRL.39]	Board of Inland Revenue	*Cost of Tax Relief for Pension Schemes: Appropriate Approach*	HMSO	September 1983	
[QRL.40]	LOA	*EEC Statistics*	Limited circulation	Annual	
[QRL.41]	Financial Times	*Executive Pensions and Benefits*	Financial Times Publishing Ltd	Annual	
[QRL.42]	Gallup	*DHSS inquiry into attitudes of members of occupational pension schemes to portable pensions*	Social Surveys (Gallup Poll) Ltd	March 13th 1984	4 volumes

Reference	Author or Organisation	Title	Publisher	Frequency or Date	Remarks
[QRL.43]	Gallup	*DHSS inquiry into attitudes of non-members of occupational pension schemes to portable pension schemes*	Social surveys (Gallup Poll) Ltd	March 13th 1984	
[QRL.44]	Department of Employment	*Employment Gazette*	HMSO	Monthly	
[QRL.45]	Department of Employment	*Family Expenditure Survey*	GSS	Annual	
[QRL.46]	Department of Employment	*Family Expenditure Survey. Information Pack*	Department of Employment	Annual	
[QRL.47]	Northfield Committee	*The Financial Institutions: their interests in farmland.* Appendix v of the *Report of the Committee of Inquiry into the acquisition and occupancy of agricultural land.* Cmnd 7599	HMSO	1979	
[QRL.48]	CSO	*Financial Statistics*	HMSO	Annual	
[QRL.49]	Financial Times Ltd	*Financial Times*	Financial Times Ltd	Daily	
[QRL.50]	OPCS	*General Houeshold Survey*	HMSO	Annual	
[QRL.51]	Department of Environment	*Housing and Construction Statistics*	HMSO	Annual	
[QRL.52]	Board of Inland Revenue	*Inland Revenue Statistics*	HMSO	Annual	
[QRL.53]	Department of Trade and Industry	*Insurance Annual Report*	HMSO	Annual	Formerly . Insurance Business Annual Report
[QRL.54]	Department of Trade and Industry	*Insurance Business Statistics*	HMSO	Annual	Ceased publication 1975
[QRL.55]	Department of Trade and Industry	*Insurance Business Statistics* MA16	HMSO	Annual	
[QRL.56]	Post Magazine	*The Insurance Directory and Yearbook - Post Magazine Almanack*	Buckley Press Ltd	Annual	
[QRL.57]	ABI	*Insurance Premiums in the United Kingdom*	ABI	Annual	

[QRL.58]	Bank of England	*An Introduction to Flow of Funds Accountancy: 1952-70*	Bank of England	August 1972	Reprinted in December 1972 with corrections
[QRL.59]	Cubie Wood & Co Ltd	*Investment Performance Monetary Service*	Private circulation	Quarterly	
[QRL.60]	ABI	*Life Insurance in the United Kingdom*	ABI	Annual	(with 5 years figures)
[QRL.61]	Department of Environment - Welsh Office	*Local Authority Financial Statistics England and Wales*	HMSO	Annual	
[QRL.62]	CIPFA	*Local Authority Superannuation Fund Investment Statistics*	Society of County Treasurers and CIPFA	Annual	
[QRL.63]	Martin Paterson Associates Ltd	*The Martin Paterson Personal Pension's Survey*	Martin Paterson Associates Ltd	Quarterly	
[QRL.64]	PRAG	*Measurement of Investment Performance for United Kingdom Pension Funds*	Carl Communications	1981	
[QRL.65]	Financial Times, Business Information	*Money Management and Unit holder*	Financial Times Business Publishing Ltd	Monthly	
[QRL.66]	Government Actuary - Scottish Home and Health Department	*National Health Service Superannuation Scheme for Scotland.* 1974-79	HMSO Edinburgh	1985	
[QRL.67]	Department of Employment	*New Earnings Survey*	Press Release	Annual	
[QRL.68]	ABI	*New Life Insurance Business*	Press Release	Annual	
[QRL.69]	ABI	*New Life Insurance figures for the Quarter*	Press Release	Quarterly	
[QRL.70]	Government Actuary's Department	*Occupational Pension Schemes* 1979: Sixth Survey by the Goverment Actuary	HMSO	1981	
[QRL.71]	GAD	*Occupational Pension Scheme Survey* 1983. Press Release	GAD	December 1984	
[QRL.72]	Stone & Cox	*Ordinary Branch Life Assurance Handbook*	Stone & Cox Publications Ltd	Monthly	Looseleaf updates

Reference	Author or Organisation	Title	Publisher	Frequency or Date	Remarks
[QRL.73]	CMI	*PA(90) Tables for pensioners*	Institute and Faculty of Actuaries	1979	More extensive sets of functions available on microfiche
[QRL.74]	Combined Actuarial Performance Services Ltd	*Pension Fund Investment Performance - General Report*	Combined Actuarial Performance Services Ltd	Annual	
[QRL.75]	City Research Associates	*Pension Fund Management* 1984	City Research Associates Ltd	1984	
[QRL.76]	Wood, Mackenzie & Co	*Pension Fund Service*	Limited circulation	Annual	
[QRL.77]	PRAG	*Pension Funds: Information needs of members and pensioners*	PRAG	1985	
[QRL.78]	PRAG	*Pension Payment Methods - A Survey*	PRAG	1982	
[QRL.79]	Wootten Publications	*Pensions*. The monthly journal of employee benefits and retirement planning	Wootten Publications Ltd	Monthly	
[QRL.80]	Financial Times, Business Information	*Pensions Management*	Financial Times Business Publishing Ltd	Monthly	
[QRL.81]	OPCS	*People in Britain: 2 - Pensioners*	OPCS	1981	Set of large maps
[QRL.82]	Insurance Week	*Permanent Health Insurance*	Kluwer	Annual	
[QRL.83]	Wootten Publications	*Planned Savings*. A review of personal finance and savings	Wootten Publications Ltd	Monthly	
[QRL.84]	Stone & Cox	*Policy Market*	Stone & Cox	Weekly	
[QRL.85]	DHSS	*Population, Pension Costs and Pensioners' Incomes*. A background Paper for the Inquiry into provision for retirement	HMSO	June 1984	

[QRL.86]	Sun Life Assurance of Canada	*Public's attitude towards life insurance salesmen*. Research Study conducted by MORI for Sun Life Assurance Company of Canada	Limited circulation	July 1983	
[QRL.87]	Sun Life of Canada	*The public's attitude towards life assurance* - Port Bridget - May 1984. Research study conducted by MORI for Sun Life assurance company of Canada	Limited circulation	May 1984	
[QRL.88]	Planned Savings Magazine	*Rate guide*	Planned Savings Magazine	Daily and Weekly	Daily - Prestel
[QRL.89]	Money Management Magazine	*Rate Update (7 day)*	Financial Times Business Information	Weekly	
[QRL.90]	Individual Companies	*Report and Accounts*	Individual Companies	Annual	
[QRL.91]	Goverment Actuary	*Report by the Goverment Actuary on the NHS Superannuation Scheme* 1974-1979	HMSO	1985	
[QRL.92]	Goverment Actuary	*Report by the Goverment Actuary on the Teachers Superannuation Scheme* (England and Wales) 1976-1981	HMSO	Quinquennially	
[QRL.93]	Each Authorised Insurer	*Returns under the Insurance Companies Act 1982*	Each Authorised Insurer	Annual	
[QRL.94]	DHSS	*Review of Contracting Out Contribution, Reduction and Related Issues*	Insurance Division of DHSS	Quinquennial	
[QRL.95]	Savills - RTP	*Savills - RTP Agricultural Performance Analysis*	Roger Tym and Partners	Annual	
[QRL.96]	Wootten Publications Ltd	*The Savings' Market*	Wootten Publications Ltd	Quarterly	
[QRL.97]	Financial Times	*Self-employed Pensions*	Financial Times Business Publishing Ltd	Annual	
[QRL.98]	Legal and General	*The Self-employed Report*	Legal and General	1985	
[QRL.99]	OPB	*Seventh Annual Report of OPB* Cmnd 338	HMSO	1981	Annual until 1981

Reference	Author or Organisation	Title	Publisher	Frequency or Date	Remarks
[QRL.100]	ABI	*Sources of New Business*	Limited circulation	1974, 1977 then Annual from 1982	
[QRL.101]	The Wyatt Company	*Survey of Pooled Pension Funds*	The Wyatt Company (UK) Ltd	Quarterly	
[QRL.102]	Board of Inland Revenue	*Survey of Personal Incomes*	HMSO	Annual	Until 1978 published as part of [QRL.52]
[QRL.103]	City Research Associates	*A Survey of Public Sector and non-corporate Pension Funds* 1980	City Research Associates Ltd	1980	
[QRL.104]	The Stock Exchange	*The Stock Exchange Survey of Share Ownership*. A supplement to the *Stock Exchange Fast Service*	The Stock Exchange	1984	
[QRL.105]	Faculty of Actuaries Withdrawal Research Group	"An investigation into the withdrawal experience of ordinary life business", in *TFA* vol 36, p. 262	Faculty of Actuaries	November 1978	
[QRL.106]	Stone and Cox	*Unit Linked Life Assurance Handbook*	BIA	Annual	
[QRL.107]	Financial Times	*Unit Linked Savings Plans*	Financial Times Publishing Ltd.	Annual	
[QRL.108]	ABI Statistics Bureau	*United Kingdom Market Statistics*	ABI	Annual	
[QRL.109]	CSO	*United Kingdom Annual Accounts*	HMSO	Annual	Known as *Blue Book*
[QRL.110]	CSO	*United Kingdom Balance of Payments*	HMSO	Annual	Known as *Pink Book*
[QRL.111]	Consumers Association	*Which?*	Consumers Association	Monthly	
[QRL.112]	J. Whitaker & Sons Ltd	*Whitaker's Almanack*	J. Whitaker & Sons Ltd	Annual	

BIBLIOGRAPHY

[B.1] Abbot W.M. *Statutory Regulation of Long Term Business.* Institute of Actuaries, 1984, (Published as part of the Joint Institute and Faculty of Actuaries Tuition Service Material)

[B.2] Atkinson A.B. and Harrison A.J. *Wealth - Vol VI of Reviews of United Kingdom Statistical Sources.* Maunder (Ed), Pergamon Press, 1978

[B.3] Barnes R. and Birch F. "Estimating the characteristics of non-respondents in the General Household Survey". *Statistical News.*, Vol 30, p.17 (This article is an abridged version of a more detailed paper which is available on request from the authors at the Social Survey Division of OPCS)

[B.4] Bates D.M., Blanch W.J., Hager D.P. *The Effect of UK Legislation on the Development of Occupational Pension Schemes.* PMI, 1978

[B.5] Benjamin B. "The Statistics Users Council - A Note." *Journal of Royal Statistical Society* A (1984) 147 part 4 Royal Statistical Society, 1984

[B.6] Benjamin, Haberman, Helowitz, Kaye, Wilkie, *Pensions, the problems of today and tomorrow.* George Allen and Unwin, Forthcoming

[B.7] Cockerall H.A.L. and Green E. *The British Insurance Business 1547-1970. An introduction and guide to Historical Records in the United Kingdom.* Heinemann, 1976

[B.8] Crawford J. and Dignan J. *Crawford's Directory of City Connections.* Crawford Publications Ltd., Annual, (25 St James Street, London, SW1 A1HG, tel: 839-7000

[B.9] Lord Diamond *The 5th Report of the Royal Commission on the Distribution of Income and Wealth.* Cmnd 6999, HMSO

[B.10] Fisher H.F. and Young J. *Actuarial Practice of Life Assurance* Cambridge University Press, 1971

[B.11] Freethy N. "Choosing your Investment Manager," *Pensions World.* Vol 14. No. 11, Carl Communications Ltd., November 1985

[B.12] Geddes P. and Holbrook J. *Friendly Societies.* Cambridge Press, 1963

[B.13] Hager D.P. "Measurement of Pension Fund Investment Performance." *JSS* Vol 24, Alden Press, 1980

[B.14] Holbrook J.P. "Investment Performance of Pension Funds." *JIA* Vol 104 Alden Press, 1977

[B.15] Howe R.W.A. and Douglas R.W. "Developments in Life Reinsurance." *JIASS* Vol 28 Alden Press, March 1983

[B.16] Kaye G.D. "Topical Pension Problems (A Personal Overview)" *JSS.* Vol.28, March 1985, Alden Press

[B.17] Kemsley W.W.F., Redpath R.U., Holmes M. *Family Expenditure Survey Handbook* HMSO, 1980

[B.18] Roger Morton "Local Authority Superannuation Funds". *Pensions World,* p.353. June 1981, Kluwer.

[B.19] John Moyle *The Pattern of Ordinary share Ownership 1957-70* Cambridge University Press, 1971

[B.20] Parry T.W. "Unit Pricing". *JSS.* Vol 26, Alden Press, 1983

[B.21] Philpott J.A. *The Insurance Companies (Accounts and Statements) Regulations 1983. A practical guide and commentary.* Ernst and Whinney, 1985, (Becket House, 1 Lambeth Palace Road, London SE1 7EV. tel: 928 2000)

[B.22] Sinclair W.I. *The Allied-Dunbar Tax Guide* Oyez Longman, Annual, (Formerly Hambro Tax Guide)

[B.23] T. Stark *Personal Incomes. Vol VI of Reviews of United Kingdom Statistical Sources.* Maunder (Ed). Pergamon Press, 1978

[B.24] Peter Stibbard "Pension Funds and National Accounting". *Pensions World.* Carl Communications, September 1979

[B.25] Stone R., Revell J. and Moyle J.P. *The Owners of Quoted ordinary shares - A survey for 1963.* Chapman and Hall, 1966

[B.26] Whitehead F. *Social Security Statistics. Vol II of Reviews of United Kingdom Statistical Sources.* Maunder (Ed). Heinemann Educational Books, 1973

[B.27] Whitehead F.E. "The Work of the Social Survey Division of OPCS" - *The Statistician.* Vol 29. No.4. Institute of Statisticians, 1980

[B.28] *Accountancy* ICAEW, Monthly

[B.29] *Accounting for Overseas Investments by United Kingdom Pension Funds.* PRAG/NAPF, 1983

[B.30] *British Business.* Department of Trade and Industry, HMSO, Weekly, (4.2 - Formerly Trade and Industry)

[B.31] *Budget Guide.* Leigh Carr and Partners, Annual

[B.32] *CMI Reports - Number 2.* Executive committee of the CMI, Institute and Faculty of Actuaries, 1976

[B.33] *CMI Reports - Number 7.* Executive committee of the CMI, Institute and Faculty of Actuaries, 1984

[B.34] *Catalogue of Insurance Statistics.* BIA, Updated regularly

[B.35] *Code of Practice, Information to Members of Pension Schemes.* NAPF, May 1980

[B.36] *Considerations Affecting the preparation of Standard Tables of Mortality. 51A 101 and TFA 34.* Executive committee of the CMI, Institute and Faculty of Actuaries, 1974

[B.37] *ED 32 Disclosure of pension information in company accounts,* Accounting Standard Committee of the Institute of Chartered Accountants in England and Wales, May 1983

[B.38] *ED 34: Exposure Draft of SORP: Pension Scheme Accounts. Accountancy.* p120, Accounting Standard Committee of the Institute of Chartered Accountants in England and Wales, May 1984

[B.39] *Financial Reports of Pension Funds.* PRAG/NAPF, 1978

[B.40] *Financial Statistics, Explanatory Handbook* CSO, HMSO, Annual

[B.41] *General Household Survey for 1984.* OPCS, HMSO, (so far unpublished)

[B.42] *The General Household Survey, Introductory Report.* OPCS, HMSO, 1973
[B.43] *A Glossary for Pension Schemes.* PRAG/PMI, May 1980
[B.44] *Goverment Statistics: A brief guide to sources.* GSS, HMSO, Annual
[B.45] *The Growth and Impact of Institutional Investors: a report to the Research committee of the Institute of Chartered Accountants.* Briston and Dobbins, ICA, 1978
[B.46] *A Guide to Good Practice - Member participation in pension schemes.* NAPF
[B.47] *Guide to Official Statistics.* GSS, HMSO, Irregular
[B.48] *Improved protection for the occupational pension rights and expectations of early leavers.* Cmnd 8271. OPB, HMSO, 1981
[B.49] *Insurance Companies (Accounts and Statements) Regulations 1983 Statutory Instrument no.1811.* DTI., HMSO, December 1983, (Known as *1983 Regulations.*)
[B.50] *Insurance Companies Act 1982.* (chapter 50). HMSO reprinted 1984
[B.51] *The Insurance Companies Regulations 1981 - Statutory Instrument No.1654.* HMSO reprinted 1984
[B.52] *Insurance Facts and Figures.* BIA, Annual
[B.53] *Internationl Directory of Published Market Research.* Ninth edition. British Overseas Trade Board, Arlington Management Publications Ltd., 1985
[B.54] *Journal of Institute of Actuaries (JIA)* Institute of Actuaries, Alden Press, Three times a year
[B.55] *Life Insurance Fact Book.* American Council of Life Insurance, Annual, (1850 K Street, N.W., Washington, D.C. 20006)
[B.56] *Marketing Surveys Index.* Marketing Stratagies for Industry, Monthly, (Looseleaf)
[B.57] *The Measurement of Portfolio Performance for Pension Funds.* Society of Investment Analysts, 1972
[B.58] *Monthly Digest of Statistics.* CSO, HMSO, Monthly
[B.59] *NAPF.* NAPF Year Book, Annual
[B.60] *A New Survey by the Government Actuary.* Government Actuary's Dept. HMSO, 1966
[B.61] *Occupational Pension Schemes; Fifth Survey by the Goverment Actuary.* Government Actuary's Dept., HMSO, 1978
[B.62] *Occupational Pension Schemes 1971: Fourth Survey by the Government Actuary.* Government Actuary's Dept., HMSO, 1972
[B.63] *The Ownership of Company Shares: A Survey for 1975, Studies in Official Statistics.* No. 34. CSO, HMSO, 1979
[B.64] *Pension Fund Indicators! Long-term Perspective on Pension Fund Investment.* Phillips and Drew, Annual
[B.65] *Pension Funds and Value Added Tax Law, Practice and Reform.* PRAG, Carl Communications, 1983, (8 page update in March 1985)
[B.66] *Pensions Terminology - A Glossary for Pension Schemes.* PMI/ PRAG, 1984
[B.67] *Pensions World.* Carl Communications, Monthly, (It covers the 'Information Bulletin' of the NAPF and is distributed to all their members as the Official Journal of the Association)
[B.68] *Persons of Pensionable Age - Census 1981.* OPCS, HMSO, 1983
[B.69] *Press Release on "The Demand for portable pensions".* DHSS, June 1984

[B.70] *Private Occupational Pension Schemes.* Ellinson, Robin Charles, Oyez Longman, 1979, (New Edition in course of preparation)

[B.71] *Proposed Directive on the Implementation of the Principle of Equal Treatment for Men and Women in Occupational Social Security Schemes, Official Journal of the European Communities.* C134, pp.7-9, Commission of the European Communities, 21-5-1983, (available from HMSO, London)

[B.72] *Reform of Social Security.* Cmnd. 9517, 9518, 9519. Secretary of State of Social Services, DHSS, June 1985, (3 Volumes)

[B.73] *Report by the Government Actuary on the NHS Superannuation Scheme - 1969-74.* Government Actuary, HMSO, 1976

[B.74] *Report of the Committee of Taxation Treatment of Provisions for Retirement.* Cmnd. 9063 (The Millard Tucker Report) Millard Tucker Committee, HMSO, 1954

[B.75] *Report of the Committee to Review the Functioning of Financial Institutions.* Cmnd. 7937. 'Wilson Committee', June 1980

[B.76] *The Report of the House of Commons Social Services Committee on Age of Retirement.* House of Commons Paper. House of Commons Social Services Committee, HMSO, 24th November 1982

[B.77] *SSAP2 on 'Disclosure of Accounting Practices'.*

[B.78] *Social Insurance and Allied Services* (Beveridge Report). Cmnd. 6404, 1942, Beveridge Committee, 1942

[B.79] *A Survey by the Government Actuary.* Government Actuary's Dept., HMSO, 1958

[B.80] *Third Survey by the Government Actuary.* Government Actuary's Dept., HMSO, 1968

[B.81] *Transactions of the Faculty of Actuaries* (TFA), Faculty of Actuaries, Twice a year

[B.82] *Triennial Survey of Labour Costs.* Department of Employment, HMSO, Triennially

[B.83] *Trusteeship.* NAPF, (seven part series of book)

[B.84] *United Kingdom Flow of Funds Accounts: 1963-70.* Bank of England, May 1978

[B.85] *United Kingdom National Accounts Sources and Methods. Studies in Official Statistics.* No 37. CSO, GSS, HMSO, 1985

[B.86] *Valuing Insurance Policies for Accounts Purposes.* PRAG/NAPF, 1981

[B.87] *Working of the Monetary System.* Cmnd 827, 1959, Lord Radcliffe Committee, HMSO, 1959

LIST OF APPENDICES

APPENDIX 3.1

SAMPLE PAGE

PENSION CONTRACT DETAILS

Address:

Types of contract available: Unit-Linked, With-Profits (Category 1, 2, 3 or 4)

With-Profits: Plan Name. **Latest Version Issued:** Date current pension contract first offered.

Unit-Linked: Plan Name. **Latest Version Issued:** Date current pension contract first offered.

Choice of Funds: M, E, P, FI, IL, D, Int, NA, FE, EU, C, IC. (See Glossary on 3rd page of Section). **Valuation Frequency:** Daily, Weekly or or Monthly

		WITH-PROFITS	UNIT LINKED
Premiums:			
Minimum:	Regular e.g.	£500 per annum (p.a.) £50 per month (p.m.)	£250 per annum (p.a.) £25 per month (p.m.)
	Single e.g.	£1,000	£500
Permitted Increases:		Details of when and by how much premiums can be increased.	Sometimes, a lower minimum applies if the single premium is additional to an existing contract
Permitted Reductions:		Details of when and to what level premiums can be reduced.	
Policy Charges:		A fixed monetary addition to regular or single premiums, and/or an extra percentage loading for monthly premiums.	Generally lesser unit allocation for monthly premiums. See Section 5 for all unit-linked charges and allocation terms.

Paid-up policies: Details of the treatment of the policy if premium payments are discontinued and whether, and on what terms, value is retained and future growth in value and benefits are calculated.

Death before retirement: On what terms, if any, the accumulated pension fund is paid to the deceased's estate or beneficiary.

Retirement Age: By statute between 60-75. However some contracts are written to specified ages, and there is sometimes a charge or reduction of capital units on earlier retirement.

Switching Options: Switching or redirecting, part or all of existing investments or future premiums from one fund to another. Details of minimum amount, frequencies allowed and charges. Normally on a "bid to bid" basis.

Waiver of Premiums: Terms on which notional premiums continue to be credited, if the policyholder is incapacitated by accident or sickness.

Special features: Any additional features, for example relating to disability provisions or variations in pension options.

Loanback Terms: Terms of loans or mortgages available in connection with the pension fund. Amount of loan and scale of interest rates.

(12/85)

MARTIN PATERSON
ASSOCIATES LIMITED

APPENDIX 5.1

A voluntary inquiry conducted by the Government Statistical Service

IN CONFIDENCE

For official use					

SUPERANNUATION AND PRIVATE PENSION FUNDS

BALANCE SHEET AS AT 31 DECEMBER 1981

Please correct any errors shown in the name and address

Department of Trade
Statistics Division 2C
Room 330, Sanctuary Buildings
16-20 Great Smith Street
London, SW1P 3DB
Telephone 01-215 5843

31 March 1982

Dear Sir,

This is the form relating to assets and liabilities at 31 December 1981. I should be grateful if you would complete and return it to the above address not later than 30 June 1982. A reply paid, addressed label is enclosed to cover your reply.

The return should cover assets and liabilities held by funds whose investment policy is managed from within the United Kingdom including, if possible, funds of subsidiary companies in your group. Should it be more convenient to make a separate return in respect of funds of subsidiary companies, additional forms will be sent on application.

Your return should relate to your balance sheet at 31 December; if this is not possible, please give figures for the nearest date and indicate on page 3 what the date is.

Yours faithfully

PG Walker

P G WALKER (MRS)
Statistician

GENERAL NOTES *(Please refer also to the detailed notes on page 4)*

Assets and liabilities should be reported at their market value on the date to which this return relates (normally 31 December). The market value of listed securities should be based on the closing middle market price. Where the market price indistinguishably includes interest (as with longer dated British Government securities), such interest should form part of the valuation. In the case of unlisted securities, the market value as estimated by the fund managers should be given, however approximate this may be. Where it is impossible to provide a market valuation for some items the written down book value may be substituted. Similarly investments in land, buildings etc should be shown at current market values as far as these can be estimated by the fund managers.

The value of foreign currency assets should be converted to sterling at the closing middle market spot rate on the date to which this return relates.

The Republic of Ireland is regarded as an overseas country.

SPF 5/81

C3322

IN CONFIDENCE

BALANCE SHEET AS AT 31 DECEMBER 1981

ASSETS Please refer to the notes and definitions on page 4	CODE	Balances at market values, £ thousand
1 Current Assets		
1.1 Cash and short-term assets (items 1 to 3 on quarterly form) (A)	09	
1.2 Amounts receivable from stockbrokers	10	
1.3 Income accrued on investments and rents (B)	11	
1.4 Amounts receivable from Inland Revenue	12	
1.5 Other debtors, UK and overseas (please specify)	13	
2 Public Sector Securities (C)		
2.1 British government and government guaranteed securities by maturity: (D) (E)		
2.1.1 Up to 5 years	14	
2.1.2 Over 5 years and up to 15 years	15	
2.1.3 Over 15 years and undated	16	
2.1.4 Index-linked Treasury stock	61	
2.2 United Kingdom local authority listed securities and negotiable bonds (F)	17	
2.3 United Kingdom local authority unlisted securities, loans and mortgages (F)	18	
2.4 Overseas government, provincial and municipal securities (G)	19	
3 Company Securities (C) (H)		
3.1 Debentures (including unsecured loan stocks and Eurodollar bonds):		
3.1.1 Companies registered in the United Kingdom:		
3.1.1.1 listed	20	
3.1.1.2 unlisted	21	
3.1.2 Companies registered overseas (I)	22	
3.1.3 Convertible United Kingdom debentures (J)	23	
3.2 Preference stocks:		
3.2.1 Companies registered in the United Kingdom:		
3.2.1.1 listed	24	
3.2.1.2 unlisted	25	
3.2.2 Companies registered overseas (I)	26	
3.3 Ordinary stocks: (K)		
3.3.1 Companies registered in the United Kingdom:		
3.3.1.1 listed	27	
3.3.1.2 unlisted	28	
3.3.2 Companies registered overseas (I)	29	
3.4 Authorised unit trust units (L)	30	
4 Loans and Mortgages		
4.1 United Kingdom (including sterling assets for back-to-back loans):		
4.1.1 to parent organisation	31	
4.1.2 for house purchase	32	
4.1.3 to financial institutions (M)	33	
4.1.4 to companies other than financial institutions (N)	34	
4.1.5 other (please specify)	35	
4.2 Overseas (T)	36	

SPF 5/81

IN CONFIDENCE

BALANCE SHEET AS AT 31 DECEMBER 1981

ASSETS (continued) Please refer to the notes and definitions on page 4	CODE	Balances at market values, £ thousand
5 Property unit trust units (O)	37	....
6 Fixed Assets		
6.1 Land and buildings, property and ground rents (P)	40	....
6.2 Other (ie vehicles, office machinery, furniture and fittings, computer equipment, etc)	42	....
7 Other investments (Q) (please specify)		
....	43	....
TOTAL ASSETS		

LIABILITIES Please refer to the notes and definitions on page 4	CODE	Balances at market values, £ thousand
8 Current Liabilities		
8.1 United Kingdom bank overdrafts and other short-term UK bank borrowing (R)	45	....
8.2 Loans from parent organisation (S)	46	....
8.3 Other short-term borrowing: (S) (please specify)		
8.3.1 United Kingdom	47	....
8.3.2 Overseas	48	....
8.4 Amounts payable to stockbrokers	49	....
8.5 Pensions due but not paid	50	....
8.6 Other creditors, UK and overseas (please specify)		
....	51	....
9 Long-term debt (including foreign currency liabilities on back-to-back loans):	57	....
10 Reserves and provisions	59	....
11 Market value of the pension fund (= net assets of fund)	60	....
TOTAL LIABILITIES (= TOTAL ASSETS)		

Date to which return relates if other than 31.12.81 ....

Signature .... *Date* ....

Name .... *Telephone number* ....

SPF 5/81

NOTES AND DEFINITIONS

A Short-term assets are those maturing within one year of their originating date including loans repayable at lender's option within one year of the date of issue. Include, however, any term deposits at UK banks even if for 12 months or over. Include money at call and short notice and other short-term loans, including longer term mortgages other than local authority mortgages, which are repayable by invoking a break clause within the first year. The short-term assets entered under item 1.1 should be of the same type as those entered under items 1 to 3 on the quarterly form.

B Accrued income from investments will normally be included with the value of those investments. If, however, such income is accrued separately it should be shown under item 1.3. Income due but not yet received on investments and rents should be shown under item 1.1 (see note F of quarterly form).

C All investment items should be dealt with by reference to the date of contract rather than the date of payment or receipt of funds. In cases where payment has not been made or received, a contra item must be entered under items 1.2 or 8.4, representing balances due from or to stockbrokers. For listed securities, the market value should be the closing middle market price. For unlisted investments, the fund managers' valuation should be given. However, if you have acquired securities on which further instalments are payable, (or "rights" to subscribe to a forthcoming issue), please enter the total payments made so far (or the cost of the "rights"). Exclude any amounts due in respect of future instalments, (or of future subscription to the new issue) as these will appear in future returns.

D Excluding Treasury bills which should be entered under item 1.1.

E Securities should be classified according to their residual maturity. Securities with optional redemption dates should be classified by their final date.

F Exclude local authority bills, which should be included under item 1.1. Shares of water companies should be included under item 3. Local authorities do not include passenger transport executives, statutory port authorities, regional water authorities in England and Wales or new town development corporations, investment in which should be shown under item 7.

G Overseas government, provincial and municipal securities (other than bills) including those listed in the Stock Exchange Official List (or Yearbook) under "Commonwealth Government and Provincial Securities; Commonwealth Corporation Stocks; Foreign Stocks, Bonds, etc; Corporation Stocks – Foreign; International Bank for Reconstruction and Development".

H Including securities of investment trusts.

I Securities issued by companies registered outside the United Kingdom (including securities of overseas registered companies which are listed on a United Kingdom Stock Exchange).

J Including convertible debentures and loan stocks where rights of conversion into equity are still outstanding.

K Including shareholdings in unit trust management companies.

L A list of authorised unit trusts is enclosed. Shareholdings in unit trust management companies should be shown under item 3.3. Units of unauthorised unit trusts (eg Equity Capital for Industry Ltd) should be included under item 7. Unit trust units should be valued at the bid price.

M Financial institutions (other than UK banks and discount houses on the enclosed pink list) are savings banks, finance houses, insurance companies, building societies, listed investment trusts, authorised unit trusts, superannuation and pension funds, property unit trusts and certain special finance agencies engaged in medium and long term financing of industry in the UK and Commonwealth, eg Finance for Industry Ltd, Equity Capital for Industry Ltd. A list of authorised unit trusts is enclosed.

N Non-financial companies: UK registered public and private companies (including UK registered subsidiaries of overseas registered companies) and UK branches of overseas registered companies, but excluding banks, discount houses and financial institutions (as defined in note M). Include UK co-operative societies.

O Exclude investments in overseas property unit trusts, which should be included under item 7.

P Exclude investment in property overseas, which should be shown under item 7. The market value of land should be as valued during the last three years.

Q Include commodities, gold coins, works of art, insurance policies, annuities etc, and units of unauthorised unit trusts (eg Equity Capital for Industry Ltd). Include investments in overseas property unit trusts and in property overseas.

R Overdrafts and borrowing of less than 12 months, from the banks and discount market institutions shown on the enclosed pink list.

S Loans with an original maturity of 12 months or more should be included under item 9.

T Exclude loans covered by ECGD specific bank guarantees or ECGD buyer credit guarantees, which should be included under item 7.

SPF 5/81

A voluntary inquiry conducted by the Government Statistical Service

IN CONFIDENCE

For official use				

SUPERANNUATION AND PRIVATE PENSION FUNDS
TRANSACTIONS IN ASSETS DURING THE QUARTER
ENDED 31 MARCH 1982

Please correct any errors shown in the name and address

Department of Trade
Statistics Division 2C
Room 330, Sanctuary Buildings
16 - 20 Great Smith Street
London, SW1P 3DB

Telephone: 01 - 215 5843

31 March 1982

Dear Contributor

I should be grateful if you would complete this inquiry form for the first quarter of 1982 and return it to the above address not later than 30 April 1982. A reply paid, addressed label is enclosed to cover your reply.

Would you please refer to the enclosed **white** list of UK banks and other monetary sector institutions when completing questions 1 to 6 of this form.

Yours faithfully

P G WALKER (MRS)
Statistician

NOTES AND DEFINITIONS

This return should cover financial assets held by funds whose investment policy is managed from within the United Kingdom including, if possible, funds of subsidiary companies in your group. Should it be more convenient to make a separate return in respect of funds of subsidiary companies, additional forms will be sent on application.

A Cash book balances including UK coin, note issues of the Bank of England and Scottish and Northern Ireland banks; balances on current and deposit accounts including any term deposit, even if for 12 months or more, held at the Bank of England, National Girobank, Trustee Savings Bank or with offices located in the UK of deposit banks, whether registered in the UK or not (including accepting houses, discount houses and those Channel Islands and Isle of Man institutions in the UK monetary sector, but not savings banks, or municipal banks, deposits with which should be included under item 2.4). All foreign currency balances held in the UK should be included. Bank overdrafts should be shown under item 5.1.
A list of banks and other UK monetary sector institutions is enclosed.

B Short-term assets are those maturing within one year of their originating date, including loans repayable at lender's option within one year of the date of issue, and longer term mortgages which are repayable by invoking a break clause within the first year. Include money at call and short notice except with UK banks and other monetary sector institutions (entered under item 1).

C The value of foreign currency **balances** should be converted to sterling at the closing middle market investment currency rate ruling at the end of each quarter (including 100 percent of the premium); while for **transactions** the rate ruling at the time of the transaction should be used.

D Local authority bills, and unsecured money lent to local authorities, with an original maturity of less than 12 months. Local authority securities, bonds and mortgages should be entered under items 7.2 and 7.3 even if they mature in 12 months or less. Local authorities do not include passenger transport executives, statutory port authorities, regional water authorities in England and Wales or new town development corporations, investment in which should be shown under item 12.

E Financial institutions (other than UK banks and other monetary sector institutions on the enclosed list) are savings banks, finance houses other than those on the enclosed list, insurance companies, building societies, listed investment trusts, authorised unit trusts, superannuation and pension funds, property unit trusts and certain special finance agencies engaged in medium and long term financing of industry in the UK and Commonwealth, eg Finance for Industry Ltd, Equity Capital for Industry Ltd. A list of authorised unit trusts is enclosed.

SPF 1/82

(Continued on page 4)

C3324

IN CONFIDENCE

TRANSACTIONS IN ASSETS DURING THE QUARTER ENDED 31 MARCH 1982

Please refer to the notes and definitions on pages 1 and 4	CODE	£ thousand	
		Balances at end of previous quarter	Balances at end of current quarter
1 Cash in hand and balances with UK banks and other UK monetary sector institutions (A)	01	....	....
2 Short-term assets in the United Kingdom (B)			
2.1 Certificates of deposit issued by UK banks and other UK monetary sector institutions:			
2.1.1 Sterling	02	....	....
2.1.2 Other currencies (C)	03	....	....
2.2 United Kingdom Treasury bills	04	....	....
2.3 United Kingdom local authority bills and temporary money (D)	05	....	....
2.4 Short-term assets with United Kingdom financial institutions (other than banks and other monetary sector institutions) (E)	06	....	....
2.5 Other short-term assets (F) (please specify)	07	....	....
3 Short-term assets overseas (C) (G) (H) (please specify)	08	....	....
Total of Items 1 to 3		....	....
4 Net balances with stockbrokers (I)	44	....	....
5 Short-term borrowing (J)			
5.1 UK bank overdrafts and other short-term borrowing from UK banks and other UK monetary sector institutions (K)	45	....	....
5.2 Other short-term borrowing:			
5.2.1 United Kingdom (please specify)	52	....	....
5.2.2 Overseas (C) (H) (please specify)	53	....	....
		Gross borrowing in current quarter	Repayments in current quarter
6 Long-term borrowing			
6.1 Borrowing from UK banks and other UK monetary sector institutions (including foreign currency)	54	....	....
6.2 Other long-term borrowing (including foreign currency liabilities on back-to-back loans):			
6.2.1 United Kingdom (please specify)	55	....	....
6.2.2 Overseas (C) (H) (please specify)	56	....	....
		£ thousand	
		Assets realised during current quarter - proceeds	Assets acquired during current quarter - at cost
7 Public Sector Investments (L) (M)			
7.1 British Government and Government guaranteed securities:			
7.1.1 with maturity up to 5 years	14	....	....
7.1.2 with maturity over 5 years and up to 15 years	15	....	....
7.1.3 with maturity over 15 years and undated	16	....	....
7.1.4 Index-linked Treasury stock	61	....	....
7.2 United Kingdom local authority listed securities and negotiable bonds (N)	17	....	....
7.3 United Kingdom local authority unlisted securities, loans and mortgages (N)	18	....	....
7.4 Overseas government, provincial and municipal securities (C) (H) (O)	19	....	....

IN CONFIDENCE

TRANSACTIONS IN ASSETS DURING THE QUARTER ENDED 31 MARCH 1982

Please refer to the notes and definitions on pages 1 and 4	CODE	£ thousand	
		Assets realised during current quarter - proceeds *(continued)*	Assets acquired during current quarter - at cost *(continued)*
8 Company Securities (L) (P)			
8.1 Debentures (including unsecured loan stocks and Eurodollar bonds):			
8.1.1 Companies registered in the United Kingdom:			
8.1.1.1 listed	20	....	....
8.1.1.2 unlisted	21	....	....
8.1.2 Companies registered overseas (C) (H) (R)	22	....	....
8.1.3 Convertible United Kingdom debentures (Q)	23	....	....
8.2 Preference stocks:			
8.2.1 Companies registered in the United Kingdom:			
8.2.1.1 listed	24	....	....
8.2.1.2 unlisted	25	....	....
8.2.2 Companies registered overseas (C) (H) (R)	26	....	....
8.3 Ordinary stocks (S)			
8.3.1 Companies registered in the United Kingdom:			
8.3.1.1 listed	27	....	....
8.3.1.2 unlisted	28	....	....
8.3.2 Companies registered overseas (C) (H) (R)	29	....	....
8.4 Authorised unit trust units (T)	30	....	....
9 Loans and mortgages			
9.1 United Kingdom (including sterling assets for back-to-back loans):			
9.1.1 to parent organisation	31	....	....
9.1.2 for house purchase	32	....	....
9.1.3 to financial institutions (E)	33	....	....
9.1.4 to companies other than financial institutions (U)	34	....	....
9.1.5 other (please specify)			
....	35	....	....
9.2 Overseas (C) (H) (V)	36	....	....
10 Property unit trust units (W)	37	....	....
11 Investment in fixed assets (X)			
11.1 Land, existing buildings, property and ground rents	38	....	....
11.2 New buildings (Y)	39	....	....
11.3 Other (ie vehicles, office machinery, furniture and fittings, computer equipment, etc)	42	....	....
12 Other Investments (Z) (please specify)			
....	43	....	....
Total of items 7 to 12	99	....	....

Signature .... *Date* ....

Name .... *Telephone number* ....

SPF 1/82

TRANSACTIONS IN ASSETS OF SUPERANNUATION AND PENSION FUNDS

NOTES AND DEFINITIONS *(continued)*

F Include assets held in the form of bank bills and any short-term assets held with the Crown Agents. Include income due but not yet received on investments, rents and pension contributions. Sums due from Inland Revenue should be excluded from this return but should be included in the annual return. If income from investments and rents is accrued separately this should also be excluded from this return but included in the annual return.

G Include certificates of deposit issued by overseas banks.

H The Republic of Ireland is regarded as an overseas country.

I Net balances due from stockbrokers including amounts due on securities sold for future settlement. Net balances owed to stockbrokers should be included as a negative item.

J Loans with an original maturity of 12 months or more should be included under item 6. Include loans from parent company. Sums due to Inland Revenue and pensions due but not paid should be excluded.

K Overdrafts and borrowing of less than 12 months (including any in foreign currency), from banks and other monetary sector institutions on the enclosed list.

L All investment items should be dealt with by reference to the date of contract rather than the date of payment or receipt of funds. In cases where payment has not been made or received, a contra item must be entered under item 4, representing balances due to or from stockbrokers. However, if you have acquired securities on which further instalments are payable, (or "rights" to subscribe to a forthcoming issue), please enter the actual payment made during the quarter (or the cost of the "rights"). Exclude any amounts due in respect of future instalments (or of future subscription to the new issue) as these will appear in future returns.

M Securities and bonds should be classified by their expectation of life on the last day of the quarter to which the return relates. Securities with optional redemption dates should be classified by their final redemption date. Exclude Treasury bills, which should be entered under item 2.2.

N Exclude local authority bills, which should be included under item 2.3 and shares of water companies which should be shown under item 8.

O Overseas government, provincial and municipal securities (other than bills) including those listed in Stock Exchange Official List (or Yearbook) under "Commonwealth Government and Provincial Securities; Commonwealth Corporation Stocks; Foreign Stocks, Bonds etc; Corporation Stocks – Foreign; International Bank for Reconstruction and Development."

P Include securities of investment trusts.

Q Including convertible debentures and loan stocks where rights of conversion into equity are still outstanding.

R Securities issued by companies registered outside the United Kingdom (including securities of overseas registered companies which are listed on a United Kingdom Stock Exchange).

S Include shareholdings in unit trust management companies.

T A list of authorised unit trusts is enclosed. Shareholdings in unit trust management companies should be shown under item 8. Units of unauthorised unit trusts (eg Equity Capital for Industry Ltd) should be included under item 12.

U Non-financial companies: UK registered public and private companies (including UK registered subsidiaries of overseas registered companies) and UK branches of overseas registered companies, but excluding banks, discount houses and other financial institutions (as defined in note E). Include UK co-operative societies.

V Exclude loans covered by ECGD specific bank guarantees or ECGD buyer credit guarantees, which should be included under item 12.

W Exclude investments in overseas property unit trusts, which should be included under item 12.

X Include any items which appear in your capital account, or rank as capital items for taxation purposes. Exclude overseas investments, which should be shown under item 12.

Y Include any buildings purchased or sold before completion, and expenditure on the improvement of old buildings.

Z Include commodities, gold coins, works of art, insurance policies, annuities etc, and units of unauthorised unit trusts (eg Equity Capital for Industry Ltd). Include investments in overseas property unit trusts and in property overseas. Include loans covered by ECGD specific bank guarantees or ECGD buyer credit guarantees.

SPF 1/82

APPENDIX 5.2

		Code	Route
34. Some people (will) receive a pension from their employer when they retire, as well as the state pension.			*COMPLETE PENSIONS FOLLOW-UP SHEET LATER
Does your present employer run a pension scheme or superannuation scheme for any employees?	Yes	1	Q 35
CODE 2 IF LUMP SUM PAYMENT ONLY	No	2	Q 38
INCLUDE CONTRIBUTORY AND NON-CONTRIBUTORY SCHEMES	DK X		(a)
(a) So do you think it's possible that you belong to a pension scheme run by your employer, or do you definitely not belong to one?	Possibly belongs ..	3 *	Q 38
	Definitely not	4	Q 38
35. Do you belong to your employer's pension scheme?	Yes	1 *	Q 36
	No	2	(a)
(a) Why are you not in the scheme?			
CODE ALL THAT APPLY	Not **allowed** to be in scheme:		
	Job not eligible	4	Q 38
	Not old enough to be eligible	1	Q 38
	Not been with firm long enough to be eligible	2	Q 38
	Too old to be eligible	3	Q 38
	Not interested	5	Q 38
	Other reasons	6	Q 38
36. Did you: RUNNING PROMPT	join your scheme straightaway when you started with your present employer	1	Q 37
	join later	2	Q 37
	or were you already a member of the scheme? .	3	Q 37
	DON'T KNOW	4	Q 37
37. So how long have you belonged to the scheme?	Less than 12 months	01	Q 38
USE CARD E AND PROMPT AS NECESSARY	12 months but less than 5 years ...	02	Q 38
	5 years but less than 10 years	03	Q 38
	10 years but less than 15 years ...	04	Q 38
	15 years but less than 20 years ...	05	Q 38
EXCLUDE ANY EXTRA YEARS EITHER ADDED OR BOUGHT	20 years but less than 25 years ...	06	Q 38
	25 years but less than 30 years ...	07	Q 38
	30 years but less than 35 years ...	08	Q 38
	35 years but less than 40 years ...	09	Q 38
	40 years or more	10	Q 38

38. Have you ever belonged to a pension scheme or superannuation scheme run by any previous employer?

CODE 2 IF LUMP SUM PAYMENT ONLY OR IF ONLY STATE GRADUATED PENSION SCHEME

Yes	1	SEE Q 39
No (inc. if no previous employer)	2	SEE Q 71 PAGE 26
DK	3	Q 40

TO EMPLOYEES WHO BELONG TO PRESENT EMPLOYER'S SCHEME (CODED 1 AT Q 35)

DNA, OTHERS .... X ---- Q 40

39. Did you transfer any pension rights from your previous employer's scheme to your present employer's scheme?

Yes	1	Q 40
No	2	Q 40

40. Have you kept the right to a pension with any previous employer which you are **either** drawing now **or** will be able to draw in the future?

Yes	1	(a)
No	2	SEE Q 71 PAGE 26
DK	3	SEE Q 71 PAGE 26

(a) Is that a pension from just one pension scheme or more than one?

One only	1	(b)
IF MORE, WRITE IN NO. →	......	(b)

(b) (INTRODUCE IF MORE THAN ONE: Thinking about the pension from the scheme you belonged to MOST RECENTLY, BEFORE THAT ONE)

Are you drawing that pension now or not?

	THE ONLY ONE OR THE MOST RECENT	SECOND MOST RECENT	THIRD MOST RECENT	
Yes	1	1	1	(i)
No	2	2	2	SEE Q 71 PAGE 26

(i) At what age did you first draw the pension?

WRITE IN AGE (YEARS) →	....|....	...|..	...|..	SEE Q 71 PAGE 26

OCCUPATIONAL PENSIONS

19. **Are** you at present receiving any pensions from former employers (or husband's employers)?

INCLUDE REGULAR PAYMENTS FROM EMPLOYER FOR EARLY RETIREMENT

CODE 2 IF LUMP SUM PAYMENT ONLY

	Code	Route
Yes	1	(a)
No	2	Q 22

(a) Is that one pension .... 1 — SEE Q 20

or more than one? IF MORE, ENTER TOTAL NUMBER → ...... — SEE Q 20

TO EVER MARRIED WOMEN

DNA, MEN AND SINGLE WOMEN ..... X - - - - Q 21(a)-(c)

20. Is the pension (are the pensions) from your own employer(s) or from your husband's former employer(s)?

	Code	Route
Own employer(s) only	1	Q 21(a)-(c)
Husband's employer(s) only	2	Q 21(d)-(f)
Both own and husband's	3	Q 21(a)-(f)

PENSION(S) FROM **OWN** EMPLOYER(S)

		THE MOST RECENT EMPLOYER	2nd MOST RECENT EMPLOYER	
21. (a) How much was your last payment, **after** any deduction of tax at source? **NET** →		£ p	£ p	
21. (b) What period did this cover?	A week	1	1	
	Calendar month	5	5	
	Other (SPECIFY)	3	3	
21. (c) May I just check, **was** any tax deducted at source?	Yes ...	1	1	(i)
	No	2	2	
	DK	3	3	
(i) So how much was your pension **before** tax was deducted? **GROSS** →		£ p	£ p	
		OFF.USE F6	**OFF.USE F7**	

PENSION(S) FROM **HUSBAND'S** EMPLOYER(S)

		THE MOST RECENT EMPLOYER	2nd MOST RECENT EMPLOYER	
21. (d) How much was your last payment, **after** any deduction of tax at source?	**NET** →	£	p	£	p	
21. (e) What period did this cover?	A week	1	1	
	Calendar month	5	5	
	Other (SPECIFY)	3	3	
	....			
21. (f) May I just check, **was** any tax deducted at source?	Yes	1	1	(i)
	No	2	2	Q 22
	DK	3	3	Q 22
(i) So how much was your pension **before** tax was deducted?	**GROSS** →	£	p	£	p	Q 22

22. Are you at present receiving any rent from property or subletting?	Yes	1	SEE (a)
	No	2	SEE CHECK G
TO LOCAL AUTHORITY TENANTS	DNA	X	Q 23
(a) Is any of this rent for subletting part of **this** accommodation?	Yes	1	Q 23
	No	2	Q 23

23. How much rent did you receive last time, after deducting all allowable expenses?	→	£	p	(a)
(a) What period did this cover?	A week	1	SEE CHECK G
	Calendar month	5	SEE CHECK G
	Other (SPECIFY)	3	SEE CHECK G
	....		

APPENDIX 5.3

Private and Confidential

PENSIONS SURVEY
S 2409 February 1984

Interviewer No	Con No

Good morning/afternoon. I am from Gallup and we are conducting a survey for an important national enquiry into people's pensions. Your views will be most helpful.

1a) Are you currently in paid employment?

1 Yes
2 No *(Close interview)*

b) Are you an employee or self employed?

1 Employee
2 Self employed *(Close interview)*

2 Are you currently employed in the private sector, nationalised
111 industries or in the public services?

1 Private sector) *Skip to Q4*
2 Nationalised industries)
3 Public

3 If public services, ask:
112

SHOWCARD A

Please indicate which of these public services you are employed in:

1 Local government/New Town Authority - *continue interview*
2 Education)
3 Central government) *Close interview*
4 National Health Service)
5 Police/Fire/Armed Forces/Prison Officers)
6 Other public sector *(Write in and continue interview)*

____

4 Irrespective of whether you belong to it, does your employer
113 have a pension scheme? By pension scheme I mean a scheme in which you will receive a pension from your employer, in addition to the pension you will receive from the State.

1 Yes, my employer does have a pension scheme
2 No, my employer doesn't have a separate scheme) *Close*
V Don't know) *interview*

5 Do you belong to your employer's pension scheme?
114

1 Yes
2 No *(Close interview)*

6 Are you between the ages of 21 and 55?
115

1 Yes
2 No) *Close interview*
3 Refuse)

7 Do you know about the State's earnings related pension scheme?
116 This is a pension from the State based on your previous earnings which you receive in addition to the basic State pension, which is the same for everyone.

1 Yes, I know about this
2 Yes, I think I have heard about it
3 No, I have never heard of it.

8 Do you know whether your employer has 'contracted in' to the
117 State earnings related pension scheme, or has your employer 'contracted out' of the State scheme?

1 Yes, contracted in
2 No, contracted out
V Don't know

If don't know:
118

Most employer's pension schmes provide a sizeable pension in addition to the basic state pension. These schemes are usually 'contracted out'. Some schemes provide only a small pension in addition to the State earnings related pension and the basic state pension. These schemes are usually 'contracted in'. Which do you think applies to your employer's scheme?

1 Contracted in
2 Contracted out
V Don't know

9a) How much thought would you say you have given to your
119 pension arrangements generally? *(Read out and code below)*

b) And how much thought would you say you have given to the pension arrangements with your employer's scheme? *(Read out and code below)*

	9a) generally	9b) employer's scheme
A great deal	1	1
Quite a lot	2	2
Not very much	3	3
None at all	4	4
Don't know	V	V

10a) I'd like you now to consider your employer's scheme, in general how satisfied are you with this scheme overall?
121 Are you - *(Read out)*

1 Very satisfied
2 Quite satisfied
3 Not very satisfied
4 Not at all satisfied
V Don't know

b) And how satisfied are you with the retirement pension and
122 the other benefits which the scheme will provide for you and your family? *(Read out)*

1 Very satisfied
2 Quite satisfied
3 Not very satisfied
4 Not at all satisfied
V Don't know

11a) On joining your employer's scheme, what sort of information
123 were you given about the scheme?

1 Booklet
2 Pamphlet
3 Discussion/Verbal
4 Letter
5 Other, write in

X None
V Don't know

124 b) And how well did you understand the scheme then?

1 Very well
2 Quite well
3 Not very well
4 Not at all well
V Don't know

c) In the last two years what additional information have you
125 received from your employer to keep you up to date about the pension fund?

1 Booklet
2 Pamphlet
3 Discussion/Verbal
4 Letter
5 Other (write in)

X None
V Don't know

d) How well would you say you understand your employer's scheme
126 now?

1 Very well
2 Quite well
3 Not very well
4 Not at all well
V Don't know

12 How do you personally view your employer's pension? I mean
127 do you see your eventual pension as - *(Read out and code one or more)*

1 A means for your employer to retain staff
2 Method of compulsory saving
3 Reward for loyalty
4 Gift from your employer
5 Deferred pay
6 A means for your employer to recruit staff
7 Other (write in)

V Don't know

13
128 *SHOWCARD B*

a) Which of the following do you have savings in? *(Code below)*

b) Into which of these do you make regular savings payments? *(Code below)*

c) Apart from the pension arrangements with your employer, do you save in any other way/s for your retirement? *(Write in all responses and code where possible)*

	a)	b)	c)
The Post Office	1	1	1
National Savings Certificates	2	2	2
Premium Bonds	3	3	3
Index linked National Savings certificates	4	4	4
National Giro/Girobank Account	5	5	5
Government SAYE scheme	6	6	6
Bank savings - current account	7	7	7
Bank savings - deposit account	8	8	8
TSB investment/ordinary account	9	9	9
Building Society - ordinary share account	0	0	0
Building Society - extra interest, term share, Easy Access account	1	1	1
Endowment or Life Assurance Policy attached to your mortgage	2	2	2
Endowment or Life Assurance Policy separate from your mortgage	3	3	3
Other insurance policy connected with savings	4	4	4
Purchase of a retirement annuity	5	5	5
Government stock/securities	6	6	6
Unit Trust	7	7	7
Equities	8	8	8
Other (write in)	9	9	9

None	X	X	X
Don't know	V	V	V

134

14 Apart from your employer's pension scheme, have you any
134 other pension arrangments, other than the basic state pension?

1 Yes, have other pension arrangements
2 No, have no other pension arrangements
V Don't know

135

15 If yes:

135 What other arrangements have you made? (Write in)

----

16 Setting aside jobs that you have had lasting less than one
137 year, how many employers including your present employer have you had since you started work? (Write in)

V Don't know

17 What is the longest time you have spent with a single emp-
139 loyer? *(If one job only write in length of employment for that job, then code this for Q18a) and skip to 21a)* (Write in)

------ ---------------- years

V Don't know

18a) How long have you worked for your present employer? *(Code below)*
141

b) How long did you work for your last employer? *(Code below)*

	Present employer	Last employer
Less than 2 years	1	1
2 to 5 years	2	2
6 to 10 years	3	3
11 to 15 years	4	4
16 to 20 years	5	5
21 to 30 years	6	6
31 years or more	7	7
Don't know	V	V

19 *ASK ALL THOSE WHO HAVE HAD MORE THAN ONE JOB:*

143 Was there a pension scheme in your last employment and if so did you belong to it?

1 Yes, I belonged to it - *(Ask 20a)*
2 Yes, but I did not belong to it -)
3 No, there was no pension scheme -) *Skip to 20b)*
4 Don't know)

20 *SHOW CARD C*

144 a) When people leave an employer for a new job, several things can happen to their pension rights. Which of the following happened to you on your last job change: *(Code below)*

IF LAST JOB NOT PENSIONABLE ASK 20b, otherwise ask 20c)

b) Thinking back to your last job, if any, where you were in your employer's pension scheme, which of the following happened to your pension rights when you left that job? *(Code below)*

c) Thinking back to the longest job you have had with an employer in the past, which of the following happened to your pension rights when you left that job? *(Code below)*

SHOW CARD C

	a)	b)	c)
All my old pension rights were transferred to my new job	1	1	1
Some but not all of my pension rights were transferred to my new job	2	2	2
My pension was left with my previous employer to be paid when I retire	3	3	3
Some of my pension rights were left with my previous employer to be paid when I retire	4	4	4
Some of my pension rights were transferred to my new employer or left with my previous employer, the rest was given to me in cash	5	5	5
All my contributions were refunded to me in cash	6	6	6
I got nothing	7	7	7
Other (write in)	8	8	8

Can't remember	9	9	9
Job not pensionable	0	0	0
Don't know	V	V	V

-3-

d) Thinking back to your last job where you were a member of
147 your employer's pension scheme, what other options, if any, were you offered in terms of your pension rights? (Write in)

X No other options offered
V Don't know

e) Why did you choose the option you did? (Write in)
149

X No other options
V Don't know

21a) Have you ever wanted to change your present job but decided
151 against it because you felt that you would lose too much pension if you moved to another employer?

1 Yes
2 No
V Don't know

b) Thinking back to all your previous jobs, did you ever
152 want to change your job but decide against it because you would have lost too much pension if you had moved to another employer

1 Yes
2 No
3 Only had one job
V Don't know

c) Have you ever turned down an actual offer of employment
153 because you would have lost too much pension?

1 Yes
2 No
V Don't know

22 How many times have you had a pension from previous employment
154 *(Read out)*

1 Converted to cash (write in) ---

155 2 Left frozen in previous employment (write in)

---

156 3 Transferred to a new employer (write in)

---

23 Could you now tell me how long you have been a member of your
158 current employer's pension scheme? (Write in)

--- years

24 Was there a waiting period or minimum age required before you
160 could become a member of your employer's scheme? If so - *160*

1 Yes - up to 6 months
2 Yes - more than 6 months - one year
3 Yes - more than one year - 18 months
4 Yes - more than 18 months - 2 years
5 Yes - more than 2 years. (Write in)

---

6 Yes, I became a member at the beginning of my employer's financial year/the next calendar year, following the date I joined the company
7 No, there was no waiting period
8 Minimum age (write in)

---

9 Other (write in)

V Don't know

25 Everybody has to contribute to the State pension scheme
161 for the basic pension but does your employer also make a deduction from your wages or salary for the employer's pension scheme or does your employer pay all of the contribution and make no deduction?

1 Employer makes a deduction from my earnings
2 Employer pays all/makes no deduction from my earnings
V Don't know *162*

26 What is the normal age of retirement in your scheme? (Write
162 in)

V Don't know

27a) *SHOW CARD D*
164 Please could you look at this card and indicate the benefits you expect to get from your employer's pension scheme? *(Please ring one code only for codes 1-4; and thereafter as many as are applicable)*

(1 A pension that does not increase after retirement
(2 A pension that may increase after retirement but not necessarily every year
(3 A pension that increases year by year but not necessarily in line with price increases
(4 An inflation proof pension

5 A guaranteed tax free cash lump sum on retirement
6 A choice of taking some of your pension as a tax free cash lump sum
7 Guaranteed pension if forced to retire early due to an accident or sickness
8 Guaranteed tax free payment if you die before retirement age
V Don't know

27b) *SHOWCARD E*
165 Here is a list of benefits that pension schemes can offer. Taking into account your own circumstances and bearing in mind the cost to you of increasing these benefits, which of these benefits would you like to see increased, remain the same or to be decreased:

	increase	decrease	the same
1 Benefits to your family if you die before you retire	1	1	1
2 Disability pension if you cannot work from ill health before the age of retirement	2	2	2
3 Level of widow's pension if you die after you have retired	3	3	3
4 Level of widower's pension if you die after you have retired	4	4	4
5 The level of your pension when you retire	5	5	5
6 The proportion of pension you can take in a tax free cash lump sum when you retire	6	6	6
7 The amount of protection against inflation of your pension after you retire	7	7	7
8 The option of retiring early with a reduced pension	8	8	8
9 Don't know	9	9	9

28 Nowadays most pensions that people receive when they retire
166 are based on their earnings in the last year or last few years of their working life as well as the length of time they have worked for their employer.

If you had worked for your current employer for all your working life, that is, from the time you left school or college until you retired, do you know what proportion or percentage of your final earnings you would receive as a pension? *(Write in percentage or proportion)*

V Don't know

-4-

207
29a) Now taking into account how long you have worked for your
208 current employer, what proportion or percentage of your final earnings would you expect if you stayed until retirement? *(DO NOT PROMPT - Write in percentage or proportion)*

____

V Don't know *(Ask 29b)*

210 If don't know: *(Prompt)*

b) Could you please try to give an approximate answer, such as 10, 20, 30, 40, 50 per cent or more? *(Write in percentage or. proportion)*

____

V Don't know

30 Did you have the choice of joining your employer's pension
212 scheme, or not?

1 Yes
2 No
V Don't know

31 Many employers make membership of their pension scheme
213 compulsory. Do you regard this as fair or unfair?

1 Fair
2 Unfair
V Don't know

32 If you are to receive a pension related to your final
214 salary then for financial reasons it is necessary for your employer to contribute a lot more towards your pension when you are older than when you are younger. Did you know this?

1 Yes, I knew about this
2 Yes, I think I've heard about this
3 No, I've never heard of this
V Don't know

In fact this arrangement is necessary if an employer is to offer a pension related to your final salary. The alternative is that if employers pay equal contributions for everyone irrespective of their age the pension received cannot be related to your final salary but would depend upon the value of the contributions and the interest received on this up to your retirement. Which do you think is fairer? *(Read out)*

215 1 Everyone is guaranteed a pension related to their final salary but the employer pays more for older people than younger people.

2 The employer pays equal contributions for everyone but the pension received is not based on final salary but will depend on the value of your contributions and the interest received

V Don't know

33 If people were able to make their own pension arrangements and not be obliged to join their employer's scheme, do you
216 think this choice should apply only to people starting a new job or should it be given to existing employees as well?

1 Only to new employees
2 To new and existing employees
V Don't know

34a) How likely is it that you will change employers within the
217 next five years? *(Code below)*

b) And how likely is it that you will change employers before you retire? *(Code below)*

	a) Change next 5 years	b) Change before retire
Very likely	1	1
Quite likely	2	2
Unlikely	3	3
Very unlikely	4	4
Don't know	V	V

35 Do you think that your pension rights would be affected if
219 you chose to leave your employer?

1 Yes
2 No
3 It depends on my new employer
V Don't know

SHOW CARD F

36a) Taking into account your own experience in changing jobs
220 which of the following would you prefer to do with your pension rights on changing jobs? *SHOW CARD*

1 Leave them behind with your old employer to be collected on retirement with its value increasing each year in line with inflation. However, your pension from this source would be related to your old salary.

2 Transfer the value of your old pension rights to purchase new pension rights in your new employer's scheme. However, the final pension from this source would be related to the salary you receive from your new employer, shortly before you retire.

3 On joining your new employer you become responsible for managing your own pension arrangements rather than you joining his scheme and you put into that the value of your pension rights from your previous employer. You can take this pension with you at its full value if you were to change jobs again. If you were to stay with your new employer until you retire the eventual pension you receive from your own arrangements would not be related to your salary and would be higher or lower than your employers pension depending on how well your savings have been managed and the general financial situation.

221 b) Why do you prefer this?

____

____

223 c) *If code 3 at 36a), ask:*

Would you still choose to arrange your own pension rather than join your employer's pension scheme even if your employer made no contribution towards your pension arrangement?

1 Yes
2 No
V Don't know

37a) Currently when people leave a job many of them find that
224 they cannot transfer their pension rights to a new employer's scheme, so they leave their pension rights behind with the old employer.. In other cases they don't transfer their pension to the new employer because they would lose too much pension if they did. Often the pension left behind is 'frozen', by this I mean it does not increase with inflation.

The Government has recently announced plans to help protect against inflation, the pensions that people leave behind - do you think this will solve the pension problems of those people changing jobs, or do you think that something more will be required?

1 Yes, will solve most pension problems when changing jobs
2 Yes, will solve some pension problems when changing jobs
3 No, will solve none of the pension promblems when changing jobs
V Don't know 225

b) What more is needed, if anything, to solve pension problems
225 when changing jobs? (Write in)

____

____

____

____

____

-5-

38 When changing jobs do you think that everyone should have
227 the choice of taking the value of their pension rights to their new employer? *(Code and write in any other comments made)*

1 Yes
2 No
V Don't know

39 Thinking back generally over the job changes you have made
228 in the past where you were a member of the employer's pension scheme how fairly do you think you have been treated with regard to your pension rights?

1 Treated very well
2 Fairly well
3 Unfairly treated
4 I felt cheated out of my rights
V Don't know
6 Not applicable

40 Apart from the normal payments to your employer's pension
229 scheme, people can 'top up' their pension by additional voluntary payments which will buy them extra pension.

a) Have you heard about this?

1 Yes
2 No
V Don't know

b) Do you know whether this is available in your employer's
230 scheme?

1 Yes, it is available *(Ask 40c)*
2 No, it is not available } *Skip to 40d*
V Don't know }

c) If yes:

231 Have you taken advantage of this?

1 Yes)
2 No) *Skip to 41a*
V Don't know)

d) If no or don't know at 40b

232 Would this be of interest to you?

1 Yes
2 No
V Don't know

41a) Thinking generally would you like to have a choice of
233 arranging your pension either with your current employer or on similar terms but with an independent company of your own choosing, such as a building society, a bank, an insurance company or similar financial institution?

1 I would prefer to look after my own pension
2 I would prefer the company to organise my pension
V Don't know

b) Why do you say this?

234

c) Irrespective of whether or not you expect to change jobs,
236 if you were given the choice of your employer continuing to organise your pension or making your own pension arrangements, which would you choose?

1 I would prefer to look after my own pension
2 I would prefer the company to organise my pension
V Don't know

d) And would you want to look after your own pension if your
237 employer made no contribution to your pension but increased your salary to compensate?

1 Yes
2 No)
V Don't know) *Skip to Q41f)*

e) Would you still want to make your own pension arrangements
238 if your employer contributed nothing towards your pension?

1 Yes
2 No
V Don't know

f) Assuming that you were to organise this pension and not
239 your employer, do you think your retirement pension would be as good as, better than, or not as good as your employer's retirement pension?

1 Better than my employer's retirement pension
2 As good as my employer's retirement pension
3 Not as good as my employer's retirement pension
V Don't know

g) Assuming you were to make your own pension arrangements, and
240 not your employer, do you think that the benefits to your family, if you could not work from ill health, or if you were to die before retirement would be:

1 Better than the employer's benefits
2 As good as the employer's benefits
3 Not as good as the employer's benefits
V Don't know

h) Assuming you were to organise your own pension would you
241 prefer to leave the management of your pension arrangements to a professional organisation of your choice, such as an insurance company etc. or would you prefer to choose the investment yourself?

1 ~~Choose a professional organisation to manage my~~ pension
2 Choose the investments myself
V Don't know

42 At present most people pay a fixed proportion of their
242 earnings into their employer's pension scheme each year. How interested would you be in paying less in some years and more in others depending on your age, your family commitments and your financial circumstances with the aim of receiving the same pension?

1 Very interested
2 Quite interested
3 Not very interested
4 Not at all interested
V Don't know

43a) The more you pay into your pension, the larger the pension
243 you can expect to receive when you retire. If you could alter the amount paid in towards your pension subject of course to a minimum, would you contribute?

1 The same - *Skip to Q44*
2 More than - *Ask 43b*
3 Less than - *Ask 43c*
4 Don't know - *Skip to Q44*

b) If more;
244
Do you think this would reduce your other forms of savings, or would it make no difference?

1 Reduce other savings)
2 Make no difference) *Skip to Q44*
3 Don't know)

c) <u>If less:</u>

245 Do you think this would increase your other forms of savings or would it make no difference?

1 Increase other savings
2 Makes no difference
V Don't know

44a) If the choice was available to you would you
246 pay more in contributions to your pension so that you could retire earlier with the same pension as at the normal retirement age?

1 Yes
2 No
V Don't know

b) If the choice was available to you would you
247 less in contributions to your pension so that you could retire later with the same pension as at the normal retirement age?

1 Yes
2 No
V Don't Know

-7-

45 ASK ALL:

260 How many employees, in total, are there in your organisation? (Write in - if exact number is not known ask for an approximate figure)

-------------------- employees

V Don't know

ASK ALL:

46 a) Do you, or your family, own your own home or do you rent it?
261
1 Own: paid for
2 " buying mortgage
3 Rent from council
4 " privately
5 Hostel, lodging etc.
V Refusal/Don't know

262 b) At what age did you complete your full time education?
1 Up to 15
2 16 to 19
3 20 or over
V Refusal/Don't know

ASK ALL:

47 a) How many people are there in your household? ______TOTAL
263
V Refusal/Don't know

264 b) How many dependent children in your household (i.e. under 16 or in full time education) ----- TOTAL

V Refusal/Don't know

48 . Are you employed now?
265 If Yes: About how many hours a week?
Mark an answer in 1st col below

Contact	CWE	Has paid job:
1	1	Full-time (30 hours a week or more)
2	2	Part-time (less than 30 hours a week)
V	V	Refusal/Don't know

49 a) In which profession or industry do you/did you work? *Write in below*
267
b) What is/was your job there? *Write in below and ring code in 1st col below*
c) If manual job: Is/was this skilled, semi-skilled or unskilled?

Contact:

Profession/industry:____________________________

Job:____________________________

Chief wage earner:

Profession/industry:____________________________

Job:____________________________

Contact	CWE	Manual:
1	1	Skilled
2	2	Semi-skilled
3	3	Unskilled
		Non-manual:
4	4	Professional - lawyer, accountant etc.
5	5	Director, manager in business or industry
6	6	Administrator in business/industry/ social services, e.g. department/junior manager -
7	7	Office worker, salesman
8	8	Other non-manual
V	V	Don't know

50 Are you head of the household or the chief wage earner in the household?
269
1 Neither) *Ask Q48-49 again for*
2 Yes - HOH) *Chief Wage Earner (CWE)*
3 Yes - CWE - *Go to Q.51*
V Don't know/refuse

Code both 2 and 3 if applicable

ASK ALL:

51 Do you (or your husband/wife) belong to a trade union?
270
1 Yes, self
2 " husband/wife
3 No

271 Will you tell me your date of birth please? *(Write in and code)*
1 21 to 29
2 30 to 44
3 45 to 55
V Refusal

----

272 52.a) Sex:
1 Man
2 Woman

273 b) Are you:
1 Married
2 Single
3 Widowed
4 Divorced
5 Separated 6 Refusal

c) Socio-economic group:
Non manual:
7 A
8 B
9 C1
Manual:
0 C2
X D

SHOW CARD G

53 a) Here is a scale of incomes. Could you tell me the number alongside the group of incomes which represents your personal income
274

1 2 3 4 5 6 7 8 9

V Refuse/Don't know

b) Now could you indicate the number alongside the group which represents your household's income counting all wages, salaries, pensions and any other income that comes in.

275 Just give me the number of the gourp your household falls into before tax and other deductions.

1 2 3 4 5 6 7 8 9

V Refuse/Don't know

54 a) Please may I have your name, initials and address? (PRINT full details)

Mr/Mrs/Miss:____________________________

Address:____________________________

Town:____________________________

County:____________________________

276 b) Are you on the 'phone? If Yes: May I have the number please (inc. the STD code)?
1 No 'phone
2 Yes (write in no.)
STD:_________:___________

c) Place of interview:
3 Home
4 Street
5 Elsewhere

d) Day of interview:
6 Sunday
7 Monday
8 Tuesday
9 Wednesday
0 Thursday
X Friday
V Saturday

I hereby attest that this is a true record of an interview made strictly in accordance with your requirements with a person who is a stranger to me, and that this form was completed entirely at the time of interview:

Signed: ____________________________

*Date:*__________________1984

APPENDIX 5.4

A Voluntary Inquiry conducted by the Government Statistical Service

IN CONFIDENCE

INSURANCE COMPANIES

TRANSACTIONS IN FINANCIAL ASSETS DURING THE QUARTER ENDED 31 MARCH 1982

Department of Trade
Statistics Division 2C
Room 330, Sanctuary Buildings
20 Great Smith Street
London SW1P 3DB

Telephone 01 - 215 5322

Please correct any errors in the name and address

31 March 1982

Dear Contributor

I should be grateful if you would complete this inquiry form for the first quarter of 1982 and return it to the above address by 30 April 1982. A reply paid, addressed label is enclosed to cover your reply. Please list on page 3 the subsidiaries included in this return.

Separate returns should be made in respect of long-term funds and general funds. Extra forms are available from the address given above. Please indicate overleaf whether this return refers to long-term or general business.

You are asked to note that the definition of UK banks has been widened to include all institutions on the enclosed Statistical Lists.

Yours faithfully

P G WALKER (MRS)
Statistician

NOTES AND DEFINITIONS

Coverage

(i) This return should only be completed by offices in the United Kingdom. Transactions in financial assets should include (a) transactions of UK subsidiary insurance companies and branches in the United Kingdom and (b) transactions in respect of money remitted from overseas insurance agencies, branches and subsidiaries which is invested on head office account. The return should exclude direct investment by a United Kingdom company in its overseas agencies, branches or subsidiaries, and should also **exclude transactions in financial assets by or on behalf of overseas agencies, branches and subsidiaries, even if carried out in the UK. United Kingdom branches of overseas companies should include only those assets held in respect of their UK insurance business.**

(ii) Your own staff and widows pension funds should **not** be included.

A Cash book balances including UK coin, note issues of the Bank of England and Scottish and Northern Ireland banks; balances on current and deposit accounts including any term deposit, even if for 12 months or more, held at the Bank of England, National Girobank, Trustee Savings Bank or with offices located in the UK of deposit banks, whether registered in the UK or not (including accepting houses, discount houses and those Channel Islands and Isle of Man institutions in the UK monetary sector, but not savings banks or municipal banks, deposits with which should be included under item 2.4). All foreign currency balances held in the UK should be included. Bank overdrafts should be shown under item 4.2. A list of banks and other UK monetary sector institutions is enclosed.

B Short-term assets are those maturing within one year of their originating date, including loans repayable at lender's option within one year of the date of issue, and longer term mortgages (other than local authority mortgages) which are repayable by invoking a break clause within the first year. Include money at call and short notice except with UK banks and other monetary sector institutions (entered under item 1).

C The value of foreign currency **balances** should be converted to sterling at the closing middle market spot rate on the date to which the return relates; while for **transactions** the rate ruling at the time of the transaction should be used.

D Local authority bills, and unsecured money lent to local authorities, with an original maturity of less than 12 months. Local authority securities, bonds and mortgages should be entered under items 5.2 and 5.3 even if they mature in 12 months or less. Local authorities do not include passenger transport executives, statutory port authorities, regional water authorities in England and Wales or new town development corporations, investment in which should be shown under item 9.

(continued on page 4)

TRANSACTIONS IN ASSETS DURING THE QUARTER ENDED 31 MARCH 1982

Please refer to the notes and definitions on pages 1 and 4	CODE	£ thousand	
		Balances at end of previous quarter	Balances at end of current quarter
1 Cash in hand and balances with UK banks and other UK monetary sector institutions (A)	01		
2 Short-term assets in the United Kingdom (B)			
2.1 Certificates of deposit issued by UK banks and other UK monetary sector institutions:			
2.1.1 Sterling	02		
2.1.2 Other currencies (C)	03		
2.2 United Kingdom Treasury bills	04		
2.3 United Kingdom local authority bills and temporary money (D)	05		
2.4 Short-term assets with United Kingdom financial institutions (other than banks and other monetary sector institutions) (E)	06		
2.5 Other short-term assets (F) (please specify)	07		
3 Short-term assets overseas (C) (G) (H) (please specify)	08		
Total of items 1 to 3			
4 Borrowing			
4.1 Net amounts due to stockbrokers (J)	44		
4.2 Borrowing from UK banks and other UK monetary sector institutions (K)	45		
4.3 Other borrowing (L)			
4.3.1 UK	46		
4.3.2 Overseas (C) (H)	47		
Total of item 4			
		£ thousand	
5 Public sector investments (M) (N)		Assets acquired during current quarter — at cost	Assets realised during current quarter — proceeds
5.1 British government and government guaranteed securities:			
5.1.1 With maturity up to 5 years	14		
5.1.2 With maturity over 5 years and up to 15 years	15		
5.1.3 With maturity over 15 years and undated	16		
5.1.4 Index-linked Treasury stock	48		
5.2 United Kingdom local authority listed securities and negotiable bonds (O)	17		
5.3 United Kingdom local authority unlisted securities, loans and mortgages (O)	18		
5.4 Overseas government, provincial and municipal securities (C) (H) (P)	19		

TRANSACTIONS IN ASSETS DURING THE QUARTER ENDED 31 MARCH 1982

Please refer to the notes and definitions on pages 1 and 4	CODE	£ thousand	
		Assets acquired during current quarter – at cost *(continued)*	Assets realised during current quarter – proceeds *(continued)*
6 Company securities (M) (Q)			
6.1 Debentures (including unsecured loan stocks and Eurodollar bonds):			
6.1.1 Companies registered in the United Kingdom:			
6.1.1.1 listed	20		
6.1.1.2 unlisted	21		
6.1.2 Companies registered overseas (C) (H) (S)	22		
6.1.3 Convertible United Kingdom debentures (R)	23		
6.2 Preference stocks:			
6.2.1 Companies registered in the United Kingdom:			
6.2.1.1 listed	24		
6.2.1.2 unlisted	25		
6.2.2 Companies registered overseas (C) (H) (S)	26		
6.3 Ordinary stocks (T):			
6.3.1 Companies registered in the United Kingdom:			
6.3.1.1 listed	27		
6.3.1.2 unlisted	28		
6.3.2 Companies registered overseas (C) (H) (S)	29		
6.4 Authorised unit trust units (U)	30		
7 Loans and mortgages			
7.1 United Kingdom (including sterling assets for back-to-back loans):			
7.1.1 House purchase loans	31		
7.1.2 Loans on company policies	32		
7.1.3 Loans to companies	33		
7.1.4 Other (please specify)	34		
7.2 Overseas (C) (H) (V)	35		
8 Investment in fixed assets (W)			
8.1.1 Land, existing buildings, property and ground rents (X)	36		
8.1.2 New buildings (Y)	37		
8.1.3 Other (ie vehicles, office machinery, furniture and fittings, computer equipment, etc)	38		
9 Other investments (Z) (please specify)	39		
Total of items 5 to 9	**99**		

Subsidiaries included:

(a) ....

(b) ....

(c) ....

(d) ....

(e) ....

(f) ....

This return is for LONG-TERM/GENERAL BUSINESS*

****Please delete as appropriate***

Signature ....

Name ....

Enquiries regarding this return should be addressed to:-

Name ....

Date .... *Tel. No* ....

E Financial institutions (other than UK banks and other monetary sector institutions shown on the enclosed list) are insurance companies, finance houses other than those on the enclosed list, savings banks, building societies, listed investment trusts, authorised unit trusts, superannuation and pension funds, property unit trusts and certain special finance agencies engaged in medium and long-term financing of industry in the UK and Commonwealth, eg Finance for Industry Ltd.

F Include assets held in the form of bank bills and any short-term assets held with the Crown Agents. Exclude balances due to/from stockbrokers which should be shown under item 4.

G Include certificates of deposit issued by overseas banks.

H The Republic of Ireland is regarded as an overseas country.

J Net balances due to stockbrokers including amounts due on securities sold for future settlement. Net balances owed by stockbrokers should be included as a negative item.

K Overdrafts and borrowing (including any in foreign currency), from UK banks and other monetary sector institutions on the enclosed list.

L Include foreign currency liabilities on back-to-back loans.

M All investment items should be dealt with by reference to the date of contract rather than the date of payment or receipt of funds. In cases where payment has not been made or received, a contra item must be entered under item 4.1, representing balances due to or from stockbrokers. However, if you have acquired securities on which further instalments are payable (or "rights" to subscribe to a forthcoming issue), please enter the actual payment made during the quarter (or the cost of the "rights"). Exclude any amounts due in respect of future instalments (or of future subscription to the new issue) as these will appear in future returns.

N Securities and bonds should be classified by their expectation of life on the last day of the quarter to which the return relates. Securities with optional redemption dates should be classified by their final redemption date. Exclude Treasury bills, which should be entered under item 2.2.

O Exclude local authority bills, which should be included under item 2.3 and shares of water companies which should be shown under item 6.

P Overseas government, provincial and municipal securities (other than bills) including those listed in the Stock Exchange Official List (or Yearbook) under "Commonwealth Government and Provincial Securities; Commonwealth Corporation Stocks; Foreign Stocks, Bonds etc; Corporation Stocks — Foreign; International Bank for Reconstruction and Development". Investments in the US Marine Trust and similar trust funds, set up in support of head office business, should be included under the appropriate headings.

Q Include securities of investment trust companies.

R Including convertible debentures and loan stocks where rights of conversion into equity are still outstanding.

S Securities issued by companies registered outside the United Kingdom (including securities of overseas registered companies which are listed on a United Kingdom Stock Exchange).

T Include shareholdings in unit trust management companies.

U Shareholdings in unit trust management companies should be shown under item 6. Units of unauthorised unit trusts should be included under item 9.

V Exclude loans covered by ECGD specific bank guarantees or ECGD buyer credit guarantees, which should be entered under item 9.

W Include any items which appear in your capital account, or rank as capital items for taxation purposes. Exclude overseas investments, which should be shown under item 9.

X Include actual expenditure during the quarter on land or existing buildings, the capital cost of freeholds and the capital cost or premium paid for leaseholds acquired during the quarter. Include architects' and surveyors' fees, legal fees, stamp duties, agents' commission etc.

Y Include expenditure during the quarter on the purchase of newly constructed buildings and the construction of new buildings which you have commissioned, the extension or improvement of existing buildings (including the incorporation or replacement of fixtures eg lifts and ventilating systems), site preparation and other civil engineering work, architects', surveyors' and legal fees, stamp duties, agents' commissions etc. The buildings covered include those for leasing out as well as those for your own occupation.

Z Include only financial assets similar to those specified in other items of the return, but which do not fit under those headings. Please give the amount and brief details in respect of each item. Include items such as units of unauthorised unit trusts, investment in property overseas and certificates of tax deposit, but exclude agents' balances and outstanding premiums, income tax refunds, life interest and reversions and sundry debtors, interest accrued and outstanding interest, dividends and rents, and reinsurance balances. Include loans covered by ECGD specific bank guarantees or ECGD buyer credit guarantees.

INS 1/82

A Voluntary Inquiry conducted by the Government Statistical Service
IN CONFIDENCE

For official use				

INSURANCE COMPANIES

FINANCIAL ASSETS HELD AT 31 DECEMBER 1981

Please correct any errors in the name and address

Department of Trade
Statistics Division 2C
Room 330 Sanctuary Buildings
20 Great Smith Street London SW1P 3DB
Telephone 01 - 215 5322

31 December 1981

Dear Sir

I should be grateful if you would complete this inquiry form and return it to the above address not later than 30 June 1982. A reply paid, addressed label is enclosed to cover your reply. Please list on page 3 the subsidiaries included in this return.

Separate returns should be made in respect of assets of long-term funds and general funds. Extra forms are available from the above address. Please indicate on page 3 whether this return refers to long-term or general business.

Your return should relate to your holdings at 31 December; if this is not possible, please give figures for the nearest date and indicate on page 3 what the date is.

Yours faithfully

P G Walker

P G WALKER (MRS)
Statistician

GENERAL NOTES *(Please refer also to the detailed notes on page 4 of this form)*

1. **Coverage**

This return should only be completed by insurance offices in the United Kingdom. Holdings of financial assets should include (a) assets of subsidiary insurance companies and branches in the United Kingdom and (b) assets held in respect of money remitted from overseas agencies, branches and subsidiaries which is invested on head office account. The return should **exclude direct investment by a United Kingdom company in its overseas agencies, branches or subsidiaries** and should also exclude financial assets held by or on behalf of overseas agencies, branches and subsidiaries, even if held in the UK. UK branches of overseas companies should include only those assets held in respect of their UK insurance business.

Your own staff and widows pension funds should **not** be included.

2. **Valuation**

Assets should be reported at their market value at 31 December (or on the date to which this return relates). The market value of listed securities should be based on the closing middle market price. Where the market price indistinguishably includes interest (as with longer dated British government securities), such interest may form part of the valuation, if it is the accounting practice of the office to do so. In the case of unlisted securities, the market value as estimated by the company should be given, however approximate this may be. Where it is impossible to provide a market valuation for some items the written down book value may be substituted. Similarly investments in land, buildings, etc should be shown at current market values as far as these can be estimated by the company.

The value of foreign currency assets should be converted to sterling at the closing middle market spot rate on the date to which this return relates.

The Republic of Ireland is regarded as an overseas country.

INS 5/81

C3342

IN CONFIDENCE

FINANCIAL ASSETS HELD AT 31 DECEMBER 1981

Please refer to the notes and definitions on page 4	CODE	Balances at book values, £ thousand
1. Current Assets		
1.1 Cash and short-term assets (items 1 to 3 on quarterly form) (A)......	09	....
1.2 Net amounts receivable from stockbrokers (B)	10	....
1.3 Amounts receivable from Inland Revenue	11	....
1.4 Other debtors:		
1.4.1 UK (please specify)	12	....
1.4.2 Overseas (please specify) (C)	13	....
2. Public Sector Securities (D)		**Balances at market values, £ thousand**
2.1 British government and government guaranteed securities by maturity: (E) (F)		
2.1.1 Up to 5 years	14	....
2.1.2 Over 5 years and up to 15 years	15	....
2.1.3 Over 15 years and undated	16	....
2.1.4 Index-linked Treasury stock	48	....
2.2 United Kingdom local authority listed securities and negotiable bonds (G)	17	....
2.3 United Kingdom local authority unlisted securities, loans and mortgages (G)	18	....
2.4 Overseas government, provincial and municipal securities (H)	19	....
3. Company Securities (D) (J)		
3.1 Debentures (including unsecured loan stocks and Eurodollar bonds):		
3.1.1 Companies registered in the United Kingdom:		
3.1.1.1 listed	20	....
3.1.1.2 unlisted	21	....
3.1.2 Companies registered overseas (K)	22	....
3.1.3 Convertible United Kingdom debentures (L)	23	....
3.2 Preference stocks:		
3.2.1 Companies registered in the United Kingdom:		
3.2.1.1 listed	24	....
3.2.1.2 unlisted	25	....
3.2.2 Companies registered overseas (K)	26	....
3.3. Ordinary stocks: (M)		
3.3.1 Companies registered in the United Kingdom:		
3.3.1.1 listed	27	....
3.3.1.2 unlisted	28	....
3.3.2 Companies registered overseas (K)	29	....
3.4 Authorised unit trust units (N)	30	....
4. Fixed Assets		
4.1 Land and buildings, property and ground rents (P)	40	....
4.2 Other (ie vehicles, office machinery, furniture and fittings, computer equipment, etc)	38	....

INS 5/81

IN CONFIDENCE

FINANCIAL ASSETS HELD AT 31 DECEMBER 1981

Please refer to the notes and definitions on page 4	CODE	Balances at book values, £ thousand
5. Loans and Mortgages		
5.1 United Kingdom (including sterling assets for back-to-back loans):		
5.1.1 House purchase loans	31	....
5.1.2 Loans on company policies	32	....
5.1.3 Loans to companies	33	....
5.1.4 Other (please specify)		
....	34	....
5.2 Overseas (O) (Q)	35	....
6. Agents' balances, etc (R)		
6.1 Agents' balances and outstanding premiums in respect of direct insurance and facultative reinsurance contracts	41	....
6.2 Reinsurance balances	42	....
6.3 Outstanding interest, dividends and rents	43	....
7. Other Investments at market value (please specify)(S)		
....	39	....
TOTAL ASSETS		

Date to which return relates if other than 31.12.81 ....

This return is for LONG-TERM/GENERAL BUSINESS *

MEMORANDUM ITEM

Capital expenditure on UK land, property, etc contracted for, but not provided for in your accounts — £ thousand ....

Note: Only one figure, covering commitments associated with your combined long-term and general business, is required here. If your company submits two or more returns to this inquiry please show this capital expenditure commitment on one form only — ie do not repeat the same figure on different forms.

Subsidiaries included:-

(a)........

(b)........ *Signature* ....

(c)........

(d)........ *Name* ....

(e)........

(f)........ *Enquiries regarding this return should be addressed to:-*

Name ....

* *Please delete as appropriate*

Date .... *Tel. No.* ....

INS 5/81

NOTES AND DEFINITIONS

A Short-term assets are those maturing within one year of their originating date including loans repayable at lender's option within one year of the date of issue. Include, however, any term deposits at UK banks even if for 12 months or over. Include money at call and short notice and other short-term loans, including longer term mortgages other than local authority mortgages, which are repayable by invoking a break clause within the first year. The short-term assets entered under item 1.1 should be of the same type as those entered under items 1 to 3 on the quarterly form. Exclude overdrafts and other borrowing, balances due to or from stockbrokers and balances due on securities bought and sold for future settlement.

B Include amounts due on securities bought and sold for future settlement. Net balances due to stockbrokers should be shown as a negative item.

C Direct investment in your overseas agencies, branches and subsidiaries should be excluded. The Republic of Ireland is regarded as an overseas country.

D All investment items should be dealt with by reference to the date of contract rather than the date of payment or receipt of funds. In cases where payment has not been made or received, a contra item must be entered under item 1.2 representing balances due from or to stockbrokers. For listed securities, the market value should be the closing middle market price. For unlisted investments, the directors' valuation should be given. However, if you have acquired securities on which further instalments are payable, (or "rights" to subscribe to a forthcoming issue), please enter the total payments made so far (or the cost of the "rights"). Exclude any amounts due in respect of future instalments (or of future subscriptions to the new issue), as these will appear in future returns.

E Excluding Treasury bills which should be entered under item 1.1.

F Securities should be classified according to their residual maturity. Securities with optional redemption dates should be classified by their final date.

G Exclude local authority bills, which should be included under item 1.1. Shares of water companies should be included under item 3. Local authorities do not include passenger transport executives, statutory port authorities, regional water authorities in England and Wales or new town development corporations which should be shown under item 7.

H Overseas government, provincial and municipal securities (other than bills) including those listed in the Stock Exchange Official List (or Yearbook) under "Commonwealth Government and Provincial Securities; Commonwealth Corporation Stocks; Foreign Stocks, Bonds, etc; Corporation Stocks – Foreign; International Bank for Reconstruction and Development". Investments in the US Marine Trust and other similar trust funds, set up in support of head office business, should be included under the appropriate headings. The Republic of Ireland is regarded as an overseas country.

J Including securities of investment trusts.

K Securities issued by companies registered outside the United Kingdom (including securities of overseas registered companies which are listed on a United Kingdom Stock Exchange). The Republic of Ireland is regarded as an overseas country.

L Including convertible debentures and loan stocks where rights of conversion into equity are still outstanding.

M Including shareholdings in unit trust management companies.

N A list of authorised unit trusts is enclosed. Shareholdings in unit trust management companies should be shown under item 3.3. Units of unauthorised unit trusts should be included under item 7. Unit trust units should be valued at the bid price.

O. Exclude loans covered by ECGD specific bank guarantees or ECGD buyer credit guarantees, which should be entered under item 7.

P. Exclude investment in property overseas, which should be shown under item 7. The market value of land should be as valued during the last three years. Include the value of own premises.

Q. The Republic of Ireland is regarded as an overseas country.

R. Include inward treaty balances (including marine) and amounts due from reinsurers both as to amounts due by overseas companies and in the UK, but exclude all amounts due from overseas agents. Make no deduction for amounts due to reinsurance companies, outstanding claims and sundry creditors from the amount of agents' balances, etc.

S. Include only financial assets similar to those specified in other items of the return but which do not fit under those headings. Please give the amount and brief details in respect of each item. Include items such as units of unauthorised unit trusts, investment in property overseas, certificates of tax deposit, insurance policies and annuities. Exclude prepayments and debtors. Include loans covered by ECGD specific bank guarantees or ECGD buyer credit guarantees.

Returns under Insurance Companies Legislation

Form 10

Statement of solvency

Name of Company

Global business/UK branch business

Financial year ended

	Company registration number	Global/ UK	Period ended day	month	year	Units	For official use
F10					19	£000	

		As at the end of the financial year 1	As at the end of the previous year 2	Source Form / Line / Column
Long Term business-admissible assets	11			13 . 93
Long Term business-liabilities and margins	12			14 . 59
Other than Long Term business – admissible assets	21			13 . 93
Other than Long Term business – liabilities (See note 1)	22			15 . 59
Net admissible assets (21–22)	29			
Required solvency margin	31			See note 2
Excess of net admissible assets over required solvency margin (29–31)	39			See note 2
Authorised share capital	41			
Paid up share capital	51			
Share premium account	52			
Uncalled amounts (including share premium) on partly paid shares within the limits allowed by the valuation regulations	53			
Amounts representing the balance of net admissible assets	54			
Total (51 to 54) and equal to line 29 above	59			

Notes

1 The liabilities at line 22 do not include any amounts shown at lines 51 to 54.

2 Lines 31 and 39 are only relevant to a company carrying on general business.

Returns under Insurance Companies Legislation

Form 13
(Sheet 1)

Analysis of admissible assets

Global business/UK branch business

Name of Company

Business: Long Term/Other than Long Term

Financial year ended

Category of Assets

	Company registration number	Global/ UK	Period ended: day	month	year	Units	Category of assets	For official use
F13					19	£000		

Admissible assets				As at the end of the financial year 1	As at the end of the previous year 2
Land			11		
Fixed interest securities	Issued by, or guaranteed by, any government or public authority		12		
	Other fixed interest securities except those in dependents which must be included in lines 31 to 34 and any to be included in lines 61 or 62	quoted	13		
		unquoted debentures	14		
		other unquoted	15		
Variable interest securities except those included at lines 21 to 34	Issued by, or guaranteed by, any government or public authority		16		
	Other		17		
Other variable interest investments	Equity shares except those in dependents which must be included in lines 31 or 33.	quoted	21		
		unquoted	22		
	Holdings in authorised unit trust schemes		23		
Investments in dependents	Insurance companies	Value of any shares held	31		
		Debts, other than amounts which must be included in lines 41 or 51 to 54	32		
	Non-insurance companies	Value of any shares held	33		
		Debts, other than amounts which must be included in lines 41 or 51 to 54	34		
Share options and debenture options			35		
Total (11 to 35)			39		

Returns under Insurance Companies Legislation

Form 13
(Sheet 2)

Analysis of admissible assets

Name of Company

Financial year ended

Category of Assets

Global business/~~UK branch business~~

Business: ~~Long Term/~~Other than Long Term

	Company registration number	Global/ UK	Period ended day	month	year	Units	Category of assets		For official use
F13					19	£000			

Admissible assets				As at the end of the financial year 1	As at the end of the previous year 2
Loans secured by policies of insurance issued by the company			41		
Tax recoveries due from taxation authorities			42		
Deposit and current accounts with approved financial institutions, and deposits with local authorities and Building Societies	Current accounts and amounts on deposit for a fixed term of, or on deposit and withdrawable after giving notice of, 12 months or less after the end of the financial year, and certificates of deposit maturing during that period		43		
	Other		44		
Insurance debts including those due from dependents and individuals	Premium income in respect of direct insurance and facultative reinsurance contracts accepted not yet paid to the company less commission payable thereon		51		
	Amounts due from ceding insurers and intermediaries under reinsurance treaties accepted		52		
	Amounts due from reinsurers and intermediaries under reinsurance contracts ceded		53		
	Recoveries due by way of salvage or from other insurers in respect of claims paid other than recoveries under reinsurance contracts ceded		54		
Debts fully secured on land except quoted debentures (which must be included in line 13), debts due from dependents (which must be included in lines 32 or 34), and debts due from individuals (which must be included in lines 64 or 66)		due more than 12 months after the end of the financial year	61		
		due in 12 months or less after the end of the financial year, or which would become due if the company exercised any right to require repayment within that period	62		
Debts except those which must be included in other lines	due more than 12 months after the end of the financial year	due from companies and unincorporated bodies of persons	63		
		due from individuals	64		
	due in 12 months or less after the end of the financial year, or which would become due if the company exercised any right to require repayment within that period	due from companies and unincorporated bodies of persons	65		
		due from individuals	66		
Total (41 to 66)			69		

Returns under Insurance Companies Legislation

Form 13
(Sheet 3)

Analysis of admissible assets

Name of Company

Financial year ended

Category of Assets

Global business/UK branch business/Community branch business

Business: Long Term/Other than Long Term

	Company registration number	Global/ UK/CM	Period ended day	month	year	Units	Category of assets	For official use
F13					19	£000		

Admissible assets			As at the end of the financial year 1	As at the end of the previous year 2
Shares in Building Societies and Industrial and Provident Societies		71		
Cash		72		
Computer equipment		81		
Other office machinery, furniture, motor vehicles and other equipment		82		
Life interests, reversionary interests and similar interests in property		83		
Linked assets	linked assets in internal linked funds (as shown in line 12 on Form 47)	85		
	other linked assets	86		
		87		
Total of Sheet 1 (13.39)		91		
Total of Sheet 2 (13.69)		92		
Gross Total of admissible assets (71 to 92)		93		
Total of assets valued in accordance with valuation regulations which would have been included in one of the headings above but for the admissibility limits applied by which certain assets are required to be taken into account only to a specified extent		94		
Amount included in line 93 attributable to debts due from related companies, other than those under contracts of insurance or reinsurance		95		

Returns under Insurance Companies Legislation

Form 14

Long Term business liabilities and margins

Name of Company

Global business

Financial year ended

	Company registration number		Period ended day	month	year	Units	For official use
F14		GL			19	£000	

			As at the end of the financial year 1	As at the end of the previous year 2	Source (Form / Line / Column)
Long Term business funds	Ordinary	11			40.16 (all funds)
	Industrial	12			
	Valuation deficiencies	13			
Claims admitted but not paid	Ordinary	14			
	Industrial	15			
Other insurance liabilities	Amounts due in respect of direct insurance and facultative reinsurance contracts accepted except amounts which must be included in lines 14 and 15	31			
	Amounts due to ceding insurers and intermediaries under reinsurance treaties accepted except amounts which must be included in lines 14 and 15	32			
	Amounts due to reinsurers and intermediaries under reinsurance contracts ceded	33			
Other liabilities	Loans secured	41			
	Loans unsecured	42			
	Taxation	44			
	Other creditors	47			
Excess of the value of admissible assets representing the long term business funds over the amount of those funds		51			See Note below
Total (11 to 51)		59			

Amount included in line 59 attributable to liabilities to related companies, other than those under contracts of insurance or reinsurance	61			
Amount included in line 59 attributable to liabilities in respect of property linked benefits	62			

Note
The value of admissible assets representing the long term business funds is determined by deducting from the total value of the admissible assets an amount equal to the liabilities itemised in lines 14 to 47 of Form 14.

Returns under Insurance Companies Legislation

Form 15

Liabilities (other than Long Term business)

Name of Company

Global business/UK branch business

Financial year ended

	Company registration number	Global/ UK	Period ended day	month	year	Units	For official use
F15					19	£000	

				As at the end of the financial year 1	As at the end of the previous year 2	Source Form / Line / Column
General business technical reserves	Unearned premiums		21			See Note below
	Additional amount for unexpired risks		22			
	Claims outstanding (less amounts recoverable from reinsurers)	Reported claims	23			
		Claims incurred but not reported	24			
	Expenses for settling claims outstanding		25			
	Funds		26			
	Claims equalisation		27			
	Other		28			
	Total (21 to 28)		29			
Other insurance liabilities	Amounts due in respect of direct insurance and facultative reinsurance contracts accepted except amounts which must be included in line 29		31			
	Amounts due to ceding insurers and intermediaries under reinsurance treaties accepted except amounts which must be included in line 29		32			
	Amounts due to reinsurers and intermediaries under reinsurance contracts ceded		33			
Other liabilities	Loans secured		41			
	Loans unsecured		42			
	Subordinated loan stock		43			
	Taxation		44			
	Recommended dividend		45			
	Cumulative preference share dividend accrued		46			
	Other creditors		47			
Total (29 to 47)			59			

Amounts included in line 59 attributable to liabilities to related companies, other than those under contracts of insurance or reinsurance	61			

Note The sources are as follows:

Line 21 All forms 21.29.6 + 21.31.6 —(2?.23.3 + 22.24.3 — 22.25.3)
Line 22 Summary form 20.23
Line 23 All forms 22.31.3 + 22.41.3
Line 24 All forms 22.32.3 + 22.42.3
Line 25 All forms 22.21.3 + 22.22.3
Line 26 All forms 24.42.5 + 27.46.3

Returns under Insurance Companies Legislation

Form 16

Statement of other income and expenditure

Name of Company

Global business/UK branch business

Financial year ended

	Company registration number	Global/UK	Period ended: day	month	year	Units	For official use
F16					19	£000	

		The financial year 1	Previous year 2	Source Form / Line / Column
Transfer from (to) Long Term Business Revenue Account	11			
Transfer from (to) General Business Revenue Account Summary	12			20 . 79
Investment income receivable, before deduction of tax	13			See Note below
Other income	14			See Note below
Total (11 to 14)	19			
Management expenses	21			See Note below
Interest payable, before deduction of tax	22			
Taxation, other than that applicable to long term business	23			
Dividends paid and/or recommended	24			
Other expenditure	25			See Note below
Total (21 to 25)	29			
Excess of income over expenditure (19-29)	39			

Note
The amounts at lines 13, 14, 21 and 25 exclude any amounts included elsewhere in the returns.

Returns under Insurance Companies Legislation **Form 40**

Long Term business: Revenue account

Name of Company:

Global business

Financial year ended:

Fund:

Figures are shown net of reinsurance ceded		*The financial year* 1 (£000's)	*Previous financial year* 2 (£000's)
Premiums receivable (less rebates and refunds)	**1**		
Investment income receivable before deduction of tax	**2**		
Increase (decrease) in the value of non-linked assets brought into account	**3**		
Increase (decrease) in the value of linked assets	**4**		
Other income	**5**		
Total income (1 to 5)	**6**		
Claims payable	**7**		
Expenses payable	**8**		
Interest payable before deduction of tax	**9**		
Taxation	**10**		
Other expenditure	**11**		
Transfer to (from) statement of other income and expenditure	**12**		
Total expenditure (7 to 12)	**13**		
Increase (decrease) in fund in financial year (6 – 13)	**14**		
Fund brought forward	**15**		
Fund carried forward (14 + 15)	**16**		

Returns under Insurance Companies Legislation **Form 41**

Long Term business: Analysis of premiums and expenses

Name of Company:

Global business

Financial year ended:

Fund:

				Gross 1 (£000's)	*Payable to or recoverable from reinsurers* 2 (£000's)	*Net of reinsurance (1 – 2)* 3 (£000's)
Premiums receivable (less rebates and refunds) in the financial year	life assurance contracts	single premium	**1**			
		regular premiums	**2**			
	general annuity contracts	single premium	**3**			
		regular premiums	**4**			
	pension business contracts	single premium	**5**			
		regular premiums	**6**			
	permanent health contracts		**7**			
	capital redemption contracts		**8**			
	total premiums (1 to 8)		**9**			
	total premiums at line 9 attributable to	UK contracts	**10**			
		overseas contracts	**11**			
Expenses payable in the financial year	commission payable in connection with acquisition of business		**12**			
	other commission payable		**13**			
	management expenses in connection with acquisition of business		**14**			
	other management expenses		**15**			
	total expenses (12 to 15)		**16**			
	total expenses at line 16 attributable to	UK contracts	**17**			
		overseas contracts	**18**			

Form 55

Amount of Annual Premiums		Proportion of Office Premiums reserved for Expenses and Profits	Value of Sums Assured or Annuities per annum including Vested Reversionary Bonuses	Value of Annual Premiums		Amount of Net Liability
Office Premiums	Net Premiums			Office Premiums	Net Premiums	
6	7	8	9	10	11	12

Form 56

Amount of Annual Premiums				*Non-Unit Liabilities*		
Office Premiums	*Net Premiums*	*Category of Unit Link*	*Unit Liability*	*Mortality and Expenses*	*Options and Guarantees*	*Amount of Net Liability*
8	**9**	**10**	**11**	**12**	**13**	**14**

Returns under Insurance Companies Legislation **Form 57**

Analysis of Unit Liabilities

Name of Unit Link	*Valuation Price per unit* (pence)	*Number of Units Deemed Allocated to Contracts*	*Unit Liability* (£)
1	**2**	**3**	**4**

Returns under Insurance Companies Legislation

Form 42

Long Term business: Analysis of claims

Name of Company:

Global business

Financial year ended:

Fund:

Claims payable in the financial year			*Gross* 1 (£000's)	*Recoverable from reinsurers* 2 (£000's)	*Net of reinsurance (1 – 2)* 3 (£000's)
Life assurance contracts	on death	1			
	on maturity	2			
	on surrender or partial surrender	3			
	total life assurance claims (1 to 3)	4			
General annuity contracts	on death	5			
	by way of lump sums on maturity	6			
	by way of periodical payments	7			
	on surrender or partial surrender	8			
	total general annuity claims (5 to 8)	9			
Pension business	on death	10			
	by way of lump sums on maturity	11			
	by way of periodical payments	12			
	on surrender or partial surrender	13			
	total pension business claims (10 to 13)	14			
Permanent health contracts	by way of lump sums	15			
	by way of periodical payments	16			
	total permanent health claims (15 + 16)	17			
Capital redemption contracts	by way of lump sums	18			
	by way of periodical payments	19			
	total capital redemption claims (18 + 19)	20			
Total claims (4 + 9 + 14 + 17 + 20)		21			
Total claims at line 21 attributable to	UK contracts	22			
	overseas contracts	23			

Returns under Insurance Companies Legislation **Form 43**

Long Term business: Summary of Changes in Business

Name of Company:

Global business

Financial year ended:

		Life Assurance		*General Annuity*		*Pension Business*		*Permanent Health*		*Capital Redemption*	
		No. of contracts	*Annual premiums (£000's)*	*No. of contracts*	*Annual premiums (£000's)*	*No. of contracts*	*Annual premiums (£000's)*	*No. of contracts*	*Annual premiums (£000's)*	*No. of contracts*	*Annual premiums (£000's)*
		1	**2**	**3**	**4**	**5**	**6**	**7**	**8**	**9**	**10**
In force at beginning of year	**1**										
New business	**2**										
Net transfers and other alterations 'on'	**3**										
Total 'on' (2 + 3)	**4**										
Deaths	**5**										
Maturities	**6**										
Surrenders	**7**										
Forfeitures	**8**										
Conversions to paid-up policies for reduced benefits	**9**										
Net transfers, expiries and other alterations 'off'	**10**										
Total 'off' (5 to 10)	**11**										
In force at end of year (1 + 4 − 11)	**12**										

Returns under Insurance Companies Legislation **Form 44**

Long Term business: Analysis of New Business

Name of Company:

Global business

Financial year ended:

Type of Insurance	*Single premium contracts*			*Regular premium contracts*		
	No. of Contracts	*Premiums* (£000's)	*Sums Assured or annuities per annum* (£000's)	*No. of Contracts*	*Annual premiums* (£000's)	*Sums Assured or annuities per annum* (£000's)
1	**2**	**3**	**4**	**5**	**6**	**7**

Returns under Insurance Companies Legislation **Form 45**

Long Term business: Expected income from admissible non-linked assets

Name of Company:

Global business

Financial year ended:

Fund:

Type of asset			*Value of admissible assets as shown on Form 13* 1 (£000's)	*Expected income from admissible assets* 2 (£000's)	*Yield %* 3
Land		1			
Fixed interest securities	issued by or guaranteed by any government or public authority	2			
	other	3			
Variable interest securities excluding equity shares	issued by or guaranteed by any government or public authority	4			
	other	5			
Equity shares		6			
Debts fully secured on land	due more than 12 months after the end of the financial year	7			
	due in 12 months or less after the end of the financial year	8			
All other assets	producing income	9			
	not producing income	10			
Total		11			

Returns under Insurance Companies Legislation

Form 46

Long Term business: Analysis of admissible non-linked fixed interest securities

Name of Company:

Global business

Financial year ended:

Fund:

	Redemption period in years		*Value of admissible assets as shown on Form 13* 1 (£000's)	*Expected income from admissible assets* 2 (£000's)	*Amount payable on redemption* 3 (£000's)	*Gross redemption yield %* 4
Issued or guaranteed by any government or public authority	one year or less	1				
	more than one year but not more than five years	2				
	more than five years but not more than ten years	3				
	more than ten years but not more than fifteen years	4				
	more than fifteen years but not more than twenty years	5				
	more than twenty years but not more than twenty five years	6				
	more than twenty five years	7				
	irredeemable	8				
	total (1 to 8)	9				
Other	one year or less	10				
	more than one year but not more than five years	11				
	more than five years but not more than ten years	12				
	more than ten years but not more than fifteen years	13				
	more than fifteen years but not more than twenty years	14				
	more than twenty years but not more than twenty five years	15				
	more than twenty five years	16				
	irredeemable	17				
	total (10 to 17)	18				

Note: Where for a particular redemption period a number of securities with different gross redemption yields are held the yield in column 4 is the average yield weighted in accordance with the value of the asset.

Returns under Insurance Companies Legislation **Form 47**

Long Term business: Analysis of holdings in authorised unit trusts directly matching liabilities in respect of property linked benefits

Name of Company:

Global business

Financial year ended:

Name of unit trust 1	*Number of units held* 2	*Valuation price per unit* 3	*Value of units held* 4 (£000's)
TOTAL			

Note: For the purpose of these returns the assets have been valued using the bid value of the appropriate units at the valuation date.

Returns under Insurance Companies Legislation **Form 49**

Long Term business: Balance sheet for internal linked funds

Name of Company:

Global business

Financial year ended:

Type of Asset			*Names of funds*				
			(£000's)	(£000's)	(£000's)	(£000's)	(£000's)
Land		**1**					
Fixed interest securities	Government or public authority	**2**					
	Other	**3**					
Variable interest securities		**4**					
Unit Trusts		**5**					
Mortgages on land		**6**					
Building Society shares and deposits		**7**					
Deposits and loans		**8**					
Income due or accrued		**9**					
Cash		**10**					
Other assets		**11**					
Total (1 to 11)		**12**					
Total investment in other internal linked funds of the company		**13**					
Total assets (12 + 13)		**14**					
Amount set aside for tax on capital gains not yet realised		**15**					
Secured loans		**16**					
Unsecured loans		**17**					
Other liabilities		**18**					
Total liabilities (15 to 18)		**19**					
Net asset value (14 – 19)		**20**					

Total amount of unrealised capital gain					

Notes:

Returns under Insurance Companies Legislation **Form 50**

Long Term business: Analysis of units in internal linked funds

Name of Company:

Global business

Financial year ended:

Name of internal linked fund in which invested	Name of unit link	Valuation price per unit	Total number of units in force	Value of total units in force	Value of units held by each internal linked fund in each unit link of other internal linked funds		Value of units in force excluding those held by other internal linked funds (5 – 7)
						Total	
1	2	3	4	5	6	7	8
				(£000's)	(£000's)	(£000's)	(£000's)

Returns under Insurance Companies Legislation

Form 51

Long Term business: Revenue account for internal linked funds

Name of Company:

Global business

Financial year ended:

Names of Funds		(£000's)	(£000's)	(£000's)	(£000's)	(£000's)
Value of net creation of units	1					
Investment income attributable to the fund before deduction of tax	2					
Increase (decrease) in the value of investments in financial year	3					
Other income	4					
Total income (1 to 4)	5					
Value of net cancellation of units	6					
Charges for management	7					
Charges in respect of tax on investment income	8					
Taxation on realised capital gains	9					
Increase (decrease) in amount set aside for tax on capital gains not yet realised	10					
Other expenditure	11					
Total expenditure (6 to 11)	12					
Increase (decrease) in fund in the financial year (5 – 12)	13					
Internal linked fund brought forward	14					
Internal linked fund carried forward	15					

Returns under Insurance Companies Leĝislation **Form 58**

Valuation result and distribution of surplus

Global business: Long Term Business Fund

Valuation result	Fund carried forward		1	
	Bonus payments made to policyholders in anticipation of a surplus		2	
	Transfers out of Fund/Part of Fund	Net transfer to (from) statement of other income and expenditure	3	
		Net transfer to (from) other Funds/Part of Funds	4	
	Net transfer out of Fund/Part of Fund (3 + 4)		5	
	Total (1 + 2 + 5)		6	
	Net liability for non-linked contracts		7	
	Net liability for linked contracts		8	
	Total (7 + 8)		9	
	Surplus (Deficiency) (6 – 9)		10	
Composition of surplus	Balance of surplus brought forward unappropriated from last valuation		11	
	Transfer into Fund/Part of Fund	Net transfer from (to) statement of other income and expenditure	12	
		Net transfer from (to) other Funds/Parts of Funds	13	
	Net transfer into Fund/Part of Fund (12 + 13)		14	
	Surplus arising since the last valuation		15	
	Total (11 + 14 + 15) (= 10)		16	
Distribution of surplus	Bonus payments made to policyholders in anticipation of a surplus		17	
	Allocated to policyholders by way of	cash bonuses	18	
		reversionary bonuses	19	
		premium reductions	20	
	Total allocation to policyholders (17 to 20)		21	
	Net transfer out of Fund/Part of Fund (= 5)		22	
	Total distributed surplus (21 + 22)		23	
	Balance of surplus carried forward unappropriated		23	
	Total (23 + 24) (= 10)		25	
Percentage of distributed surplus allocated to policyholders of Fund/Part of Fund			26	
Corresponding percentage at three immediately previous valuations	latest (date of valuation)		27	
	earlier (date of valuation)		28	
	earliest (date of valuation)		29	

Returns under Insurance Companies Legislation

Valuation Summary of Non-Linked Contracts

Global business: Long Term Business Fund

	Valuation Basis			
Type of Insurance	*Rate of Interest*	*Mortality Table*	*Number of Contracts*	*Amount of Sums Assured or Annuities per annum including Vested Reversionary Bonuses*
1	**2**	**3**	**4**	**5**

Returns under Insurance Companies Legislation

Valuation Summary of Linked Contracts

Global business: Long Term Business Fund

Type of Insurance	*Valuation Basis*		*Number of Contracts*	*Amount of Sums Assured, Annuities per annum, or other measure of benefit, including vested reversionary bonuses*		
	Rate of Interest	*Mortality Table*		*Guaranteed on Death*	*Current on Death*	*Guaranteed on Maturity*
1	**2**	**3**	**4**	**5**	**6**	**7**

USEFUL ADDRESSES

Association of British Insurers (ABI)
Aldermary House
Queen Street
London EC4N 1TT
01 248 4477 (Elizabeth Harris)

ABMRC
Chairman Gerald De Groot
Banderway House
156-162 Kilburn High Road
London NW6
01 328 2218

AP Information Service Ltd
33 Ashbourne Avenue
London NW11 007
01 458 1607 (Alan Phillip)

APEX
22 Worpole Road
Wimbledon
London SW19
01 947 3131/9

British Expertise in Science and Technology (BEST)
Longman-Cartermill Ltd
Technology Centre
St Andrews
Fife KY16 9EA
0334 77660

BIA refer to ABI

CAPS
11 Albion Street
Leeds LS1 5ES
0532 460 416

CARL Communications Ltd
60 Thames Street
Sunbury on Thames
Middlesex TW1 66AF
Sunbury 82627

CIPFA
1 Buckingham Place
London SW1E 6HS
01 828 7661

CSO
Great George Street
London SW1 3AQ
01 233 6193/5

DE (re FES)
Caxton House
Tothill Street
London SW1 9NF
01 213 6909 (Mr Janes)

DE
Statistics A2
Orphanage Road
Watford
Herts WD1 1PJ
0923 28500 Extn 492 or 500

DHSS
(1) Leaflets Department
PO Box 21
Stanmore
Middlesex HA7 1AY
(2) Alexander Fleming House
Elephant & Castle
London SE1 6BY
01 703 6380 (Lee Johnson, Norman Glass or Jon Stern re [QRL.137])
(3) Benefits Division
(For information on National Insurance)
Newcastle Central Office
0632 857111

DTI
Division 2C
Sanctuary Buildings
20 Great Smith Street
London SW1P 3DP
(Alexander Fletcher re Statutory returns)
01 215 5843 (re voluntary surveys Jill Marson 01 215 3162 room 351)

ESRC Survey Archive
160 Great Portland Street
London W1N 6DT
01 6371499

ICA
Chartered Accountants Hall
Morgate Place
London EC2P 2BJ
01 628 7060

ILOA refer to ABI

LOA refer to ABI

Media Expenditure Analysis Ltd (MEAL)
Media Expenditure Analysis Ltd
63 St Martins Lane
London WC2N 4JT
01 240 1903/6

NAPF
12/18 Grosvenor Gardens
London SW1W 0DH
01 730 0585/0734

OPCS Census Customer Services
Titchfield
Fareham
Hants PO15 5RR
0329 42511 Extn 231/296

OPCS Social Survey Division
St Catherines House
10 Kingsway
London WC2 6JP
01 242 0262

Pensions Management Institute (PMI)
PMI House
124 Middlesex Street
London E1 7HY

PRAG
C/o MPA, Metropolitan House
Northgate
Chichester
West Sussex PO19 1BE
0243 785151

SFO, OPB Joint Office
Lynwood Road
Thames Dutton
Surrey KT7 0DP
01 398 4242

Accountancy
56-66 Goswell Road
London EC1M 7AB
01 628 7060

American Council of Life Assurance (ACLA)
1850 K Street
NW Washington
D C 20006

Arlington Management Publications Ltd
87 Jermyn Street
London SW1Y 6JD
01 930 3638

Association of Consulting Actuaries
Rolls House
7 Rolls Building
London EC4A 1NH
01 831 7130

Association of Pensioneer Trustees
417 Midsummer Boulevard
Saxon Gate West
Central Milton Keynes
Buckinghamshire MK9 3BN
(Brian Tatch 01 408 1600 re survey of membership)

Bank of England
Bulletin Group, Economics Division
Bank of England
London EC2R 8AH
01 601 4030 (01 601 4371 Mr Crossley)

British Overseas Trade Board
British Overseas Trade Board C/o DTI
1 Victoria Street
London SW1H 0ET
(Chief Executive –Christopher Roberts)

Buckley Press Ltd
The Butts
Half Acre
Brentford
Middlesex TW8 8BN
01 568 8448

City Research Associates Ltd
Lector Court
151-153 Farringdon Road
London EC1R 3AD
01 833 1681

The City University
10 Northampton Square
London EC1V 0HB
01 253 4399 (Extn 4127)
(Professor S Haberman)

College of Estate Management
CAS
University of Reading
Early Gate
Reading
RGT 2AT

Companies Registration Offices –England
London Search Room
Companies House
55-71 City Road
London EC1Y 1BB

Companies Registration Offices –Northern Ireland
43-47 Chichester Street
Belfast BT1 4RJ

Companies Registration Offices –Scotland
Exchequer Chambers
102 George Street
Edinburgh EH2 3DJ

Companies Registration Offices –Wales
Companies House
Crown Way
Maindy
Cardiff CF4 3UZ

Crawfords Directory
The Economist Newspaper Ltd
25 St James Street
London SW1A 1HG

Faculty of Actuaries in Scotland
23 St Andrew Square
Edinburgh
EH12 1AQ
031 556 6791

Financial Times Business Information
FT Editorial Offices
Greystoke Place
Fetter Lane
London EC4A 1ND
01 405 6969 (Statistical editor Peter Fuller)

Social Surveys (Gallup Poll) Ltd
202 Finchley Road
London NW3 6BL
01 794 0461
(Gordon Heald or Elizabeth Stodel re [QRL.137])

Government Actuary's Department (GAD)
22 Kingsway
London WC2B 6LE
01 242 6828 (John Field)

Inland Revenue (IR)
Statistics Division
Somerset House
London WC2R 1LB
01 438 7381 (Dr Keenay 01 438 7390) (room T8 West Wing)

Institute of Actuaries
Staple Inn Hall
High Holborn
London WC1V 7QJ
01 242 0106

Kluwer Publishing Ltd
1 Harlequin Avenue
Brentford
Middlesex TW8 9EW

Legal and General Assurance Society Ltd
Library
Kingswood House
Kingswood
Tadworth
Surrey
07373 53456

Leigh Carr & Partners
Chartered Accountants
27-31 Blandford Street
London W1H 3AD

Marketing Strategies for Industry (UK) Ltd
32 Mill Green Road
Mitcham
Surrey CR4 4HY
01 640 6621

Martin Paterson Associates Ltd
10 Buckingham Place
London SW1E 6HT
01 828 7243
(James Charlton)

Occupational Pensions Advisory Service
Room 327 Aviation House
129 Kingsway
London WC2B 6NN
01 405 6922

Registry of Friendly Societies
a) 17 Great Marlborough Street
London 2AZ
b) 43-47 Chichester Street
Belfast BT1 4RJ

Science Reference Library
Business Information Section
Southampton Buildings
Chancery Lane
Holborn

Society of Investment Analysts
211/213 High Street
Bromley
Kent BR1 1NY

The Society of Pension Fund Consultants
Ludgate House
Ludgate Circus
London EC4A 2AB
01 353 1688

Stock Exchange
Information and Press Department
London EC2N 1HP
01 588 2355 (Micheal Woodrock re Share ownership Survey)

Stone and Cox (Publications Ltd)
44 Fleet Street
London EC4Y 1BS
01 353 1622/3
(Statistical editor Bill Pearce)

Transfer Club
Superannuation Division
HM Treasury
Alencon Link
Basingstoke
Hants
025629222

Warwick Statistics Service
University of Warwick Library
Coventry CV4 7AL
0203 418938 David Mort

Which?
Consumers Association
14 Buckingham Street
London WC2N 6DS
01 839 1222 Jenny Fieldgrass

J Whitaker and Son Ltd
12 Dycott Street
WC1A 1DF
01 836 8911

Wood Mackenzie & Co
Computer Services Division
Erskine House
68-73 Queen Street
Edinburgh EH2 4NS
031 226 4141 (Kenneth Miller)

Wooten Publications Ltd
150-154 Caledonian Road
London N1 9RD
01 278 7951

The Wyatt Co (UK) Ltd
32 Queen Anne's Gate
London SW1H 9AB
01 222 8033

SUBJECT INDEX